Object-Oriented Software Design in C++

RONALD MAK

M A N N I N G
SHELTER ISLAND

Manning Publications Co.
20 Baldwin Road
PO Box 761
Shelter Island, NY 11964

Development editor:	Marina Michaels
Technical development editor:	Arthur Zubarev
Review editor:	Aleksandar Dragosavljević
Production editor:	Andy Marinkovich
Copy editor:	Lana Todorovic-Arndt
Proofreader:	Jason Everett
Technical editor:	Juan Rufes
Typesetter:	Tamara Švelić Sabljić
Cover designer:	Marija Tudor

ISBN 9781633439504
Printed in the United States of America

contents

preface

The goal of this book is to make you a better programmer.

I wrote the book to pass on what I've learned from decades of professional software development and teaching. I've studied, lived, worked, and taught in Silicon Valley my entire adult life. I've held senior engineering positions at established computer companies and at several startups. I've developed advanced software at IBM Research and at the Lawrence Livermore National Laboratory, and I was a senior scientist at NASA and JPL. I've taught software development at both the undergraduate and graduate levels at several universities, including San Jose State University, which supplies Silicon Valley with more engineers than any other school.

Working with students and junior programmers has taught me that it's important to practice good software design before bad habits set in. As students, we inadvertently learn run and done: as soon as an assigned program runs successfully, it's done! After we turn it in, we may never have to see it again, so good design concepts, such as maintainability, are immaterial. We must unlearn that mentality to have a successful career as software developers.

I am well aware of the pressures to get an application done on time and under budget. Therefore, in this book, I also teach an iterative, incremental approach to software development. If we can't reach the last iteration and complete the product due to an upcoming deadline, we want the results of the next-to-last iteration (or the next-to-the-next-to-the-last iteration) to produce an MVP (minimum viable product). Hopefully, there will be the next release of the product to clean up design problems and add more features.

Experience is the best teacher

In addition to studying the examples in this book, what is the key to becoming a top-tier programmer? It's practice, practice, practice! I hope the saying "Experience is the best teacher" applies both to you as a software developer and to me as the teacher and writer.

acknowledgments

This is such a hard section to write! How can I acknowledge all my teachers from so many years ago who set me off onto the right path, and all the people I've worked with who taught me so much about software development?

Therefore, I'll limit myself only to thanking those who helped me write this book. First are my university students, who unknowingly showed me the best way to present and teach this material. My agent Carole Jelen at Waterside Productions, Inc. got me started on this book. Several reviewers read my scribblings and tested my example programs—it took several rewrites, but I hope the final version justifies their diligence. The reviewers were mostly anonymous at the time, but three of them were colleagues at San Jose State University, so I can thank Cay Horstmann, Robert Nicholson, and Robert Bruce by name. Technical reviewers provided by the publisher included Arthur Zubarev, Juan Rufes, and Frédéric Flayol.

I am extremely impressed by the dedication, care, and effort the publisher Manning put into me and the writing of this book. Senior Development Editor (and fellow multi-cat parent) Marina Michaels and I spent many hours chatting online to improve my writing and keep me encouraged through several revisions. I want Marina to be the editor for my next book and to continue exchanging cute pictures of our cats with her. I had several conversations with Associate Publisher Michael Stephens, who gave me some key tips.

I would also like to thank all the reviewers who took the time to review the manuscript and offer their valuable feedback: Aarif Shaikh, Adhir Ramjiawan, Alan Niederauer, Andy Pasztirak, Anthony Gatlin, Ashwin Perti, Brent Faust, Clifford Thurber, Daut Morina, David Racey, Edward Ribeiro, Eros Pedrini, Federico Kircheis, Frans Oilinki, Gary Pollice, Geoff Barto, Georgios Doumas, Giuseppe Denora, Imaculate Resto Mosha, Johannes Lochmann, John Donoghue, John Montgomery, Jose San Leandro, Joseph Perenia, Katia Patkin, Kent Spillner, Krzysztof Hrynczenko, Mattia Di Gangi, Michael Wall, Nathan B Crocker, Patrick Regan, Paul Silisteanu, Rich Yonts, Richard Siegal, Shankar Swamy, Sriram Macharla, Steven Edwards, Stipe Cuvalo, Thomas M.

Doylend, Timo Salomäki, Tom Jenice, and Walt Stoneburner. Your suggestions helped make this a better book.

Several books greatly inspired me and showed me how to explain software design concepts better. Two of the books innovatively presented their material and were delightfully engaging to read, *Head First Object-Oriented Analysis & Design* by Brett D. McLaughlin, Gary Pollice, and David West (O'Reilly, 2006), and *Head First Design Patterns* by Eric Freeman and Elisabeth Freeman (O'Reilly, 2004). I taught software design classes using Cay Horstmann's *Object-Oriented Design & Patterns* (Wiley, 2005). Cay kindly let me adapt his date and programming-by-contract examples. The book *Design Patterns: Elements of Reusable Object-Oriented Software* by the "gang of four," Erich Gamma, Richard Helm, Ralph Johnson, and John Vlissides (Addison-Wesley, 1995) introduced software design patterns to developers everywhere.

What a career I'm having, working and teaching in Silicon Valley! I cannot give enough thanks for that.

about this book

I sincerely hope software developers will benefit from this book. Developing an application involves gathering and analyzing requirements, applying good design principles, and, wherever it's appropriate, modeling the code after design patterns. The organization of the book follows that progression.

Who should read this book?

This book is for you if you want to become a top-tier programmer who can develop well-designed applications that meet their requirements and are more reliable, flexible, and maintainable. Well-designed applications are more bug free, and they can cost less to produce and perform better at run time. We'll tackle the enemies of good software design: change and complexity. You'll be proud of the applications you design and develop. You will get most out of this book if you are at least a beginning C++ programmer and understand the basics of object-oriented programming.

How this book is organized: A roadmap

The book has 16 chapters organized into five parts. Part 1, "Introduction," introduces software design and a development methodology:

- Chapter 1 discusses what software design is and includes several design examples.
- Chapter 2 shows iterative development to achieve good design.

Part 2, "Design the right application," discusses requirements and good class design:

- Chapter 3 explains how to analyze requirements, and it introduces UML diagrams.
- Chapter 4 is about good class design.

Part 3, "Design the application right," contains examples of good design principles such as encapsulation, loose coupling, coding to the interface, and hiding implementations:

- Chapter 5 explains why it's important to hide the implementations of classes.
- Chapter 6 explains why we shouldn't write code that surprises its users.
- Chapter 7 is about how to design subclasses right.

Part 4, "Design patterns solve application architecture problems," shows how to apply industry-proven design patterns:

- Chapter 8 is about the Template Method and Strategy Design Patterns.
- Chapter 9 is about the Factory Method and Abstract Factory Design Patterns.
- Chapter 10 is about the Adapter and Façade Design Patterns.
- Chapter 11 is about the Iterator and Visitor Design Patterns.
- Chapter 12 is about the Observer Design Pattern.
- Chapter 13 is about the State Design Pattern.
- Chapter 14 is about the Singleton, Composite, and Decorator Design Patterns.

Part 5, "Additional design techniques," examines recursion, backtracking, and multithreading:

- Chapter 15 is about designing solutions with recursion and backtracking.
- Chapter 16 is about multithreaded programs.

I designed the book to be read in order, especially parts 1 through 4. Specifically, chapters in part 4 refer to material covered by chapters in parts 2 and 3. Good software design is not simply using some prescribed coding techniques here or there, but rather, the design principles and patterns build upon and cooperate with each other.

A few chapter sections are marked as optional. I included them for completeness and because their topics are interesting. However, those sections are not required to understand the rest of the book.

About the code

Students (and readers) learn best with lots of examples. Therefore, I've included many examples of poorly designed programs with explanations of why they're bad and how to transform them to well-designed programs.

The example programs in this book use the 2017 version of C++, although you can compile and run nearly all of them with earlier versions of the language. Each chapter, except chapter 3, has example programs. The programs employ a limited set of C++ features so that the design concepts are clear and allow you to apply the concepts to other object-oriented languages.

C++ is a very popular but complex programming language. It was derived from the C language, commonly used for low-level systems programming, but it is also used for high-level application development. The language retains many somewhat fussy

features, designed to help the compiler generate more optimized code and to keep programmers on the straight and narrow. I didn't want to go overboard with such features. An example is the keyword `const` whose usage is very overloaded and can be quite confusing. In my examples, I tried to use `const` and other language features in a straightforward and consistent manner.

This book contains source code both in numbered listings and in line with normal text. In both cases, source code is formatted in a `fixed-width font like this` to separate it from ordinary text. Sometimes, code is also in **bold** to highlight code that has changed from previous steps in the chapter, such as when a new feature adds to an existing line of code.

In many cases, the original source code has been reformatted: added line breaks and reworked indentation accommodate the available page space in the book. In rare cases, even this was not enough, and listings include line-continuation markers (➡). Additionally, comments in the source code have often been removed from the listings when the code is described in the text. Code annotations accompany many of the listings, highlighting important concepts.

You can get executable snippets of code from the liveBook (online) version of this book at https://livebook.manning.com/book/object-oriented-software-design-in-c-plus-plus. The complete code for the examples in the book is available for download from the Manning website at www.manning.com, and from GitHub at https://github.com/RonMakBooks/SoftwareDesignCpp. There you'll find instructions on how to compile and run the programs on the Linux, macOS, and Microsoft Windows platforms. As a bonus, you'll also find slide decks for presenting lectures based on the book's chapters.

liveBook discussion forum

Purchase of *Object-Oriented Software Design in C++* includes free access to liveBook, Manning's online reading platform. Using liveBook's exclusive discussion features, you can attach comments to the book globally or to specific sections or paragraphs. It's a snap to make notes for yourself, ask and answer technical questions, and receive help from the author and other users. To access the forum, go to https://livebook.manning.com/book/object-oriented-software-design-in-c-plus-plus/discussion. You can also learn more about Manning's forums and the rules of conduct at https://livebook.manning.com/discussion.

Manning's commitment to our readers is to provide a venue where a meaningful dialogue between individual readers and between readers and the author can take place. It is not a commitment to any specific amount of participation on the part of the author, whose contribution to the forum remains voluntary (and unpaid). We suggest you try asking the author some challenging questions lest their interest stray! The forum and the archives of previous discussions will be accessible from the publisher's website for as long as the book is in print.

about the author

RONALD MAK is a highly rated instructor of object-oriented analysis and design in C++, Java, and Python at San Jose State University in Silicon Valley. As a senior computer scientist at NASA and JPL, he developed software for major space missions, including the Mars rovers, the International Space Station, cubesats, and the Orion spacecraft. He was a research staff member at IBM Research, where he helped develop systems software for a supercomputer and software for an advanced data science project. He was the enterprise software strategist for the National Ignition Facility (NIF) at the Lawrence Livermore National Laboratory, which is making important breakthroughs in fusion energy. Earlier in his career, he was a software developer and engineering manager at various Silcon Valley companies, including Hewlett-Packard, Sun Microsystems, Apple, and several startups. He has degrees in the mathematical sciences and in computer science from Stanford University. He is an inventor on seven software patents. He has written books on compiler writing, software engineering, and numerical computation, which have been translated into several languages. Despite having done work on the relative motions of planets and calculations that involved Einstein's theory of relativity, Ron is still amazed that the sun comes up each morning and that bicycles don't tip over.

ABOUT THE TECHNICAL EDITOR

JUAN RUFES has been writing code for more than 30 years now. Starting with an 8-bit MSX home computer, he moved on to work on antivirus and encryption, and for the last 12 years in finance, developing low-latency trading system in mostly C++, with some C from time to time. Juan enjoys low-level and system-level programming, and especially C++ code optimization. In his spare time, he enjoys a good book and a nice cup of tea or two.

about the cover illustration

The figure on the cover of *Object-Oriented Software Design in C++* is "Czohadar-aga, ou chef des valets de chambre du G. S.," or "Czohadar-aga, or chief of the valets of the G. S.," published in 1808 (approximately) and is taken from the George Arents Collection, The New York Public Library Digital Collection.

In those days, it was easy to identify where people lived and what their trade or station in life was just by their dress. Manning celebrates the inventiveness and initiative of the computer business with book covers based on the rich diversity of regional culture centuries ago, brought back to life by pictures from collections such as this one.

Part 1

Introduction

A well-designed sustainable application should be the goal of every software development project. Passionate programmers want to use their object-oriented skills and apply good software design principles and industry-proven design patterns to build applications that are flexible, reliable, and maintainable. Well-designed software can be developed faster and pass their tests sooner. Let's escape from the run-and-done mentality! We all want to be proud of the applications we've built.

The development journey to a well-designed application is rarely straightforward. A proven way to achieve success is with a journey of design–code–test iterations. Along the way, we may have to backtrack due to erroneous design decision and redo some iterations. The journey becomes easier as we gain experience by encountering coding situations that good design principles can improve and recognizing software architecture problems that design patterns can solve.

The path to well-designed software

This chapter covers

- The basics of software design
- The benefits of good software design
- How to analyze an application's requirements to design the *right application*
- How to apply good design techniques to develop the *application right*

Well-designed programs do what they're supposed to do. They are more reliable, flexible, and maintainable. Furthermore, they are more easily tested and are often completed sooner than poorly designed programs. Well-designed programs are simply better in many ways.

To improve your software design skills, this book will teach you the principles and patterns that will enable you to develop well-designed sustainable applications. A sustainable application is an application that has a long life, and therefore, we want it to be reliable, flexible, and maintainable. Top-tier design skills are highly sought after by employers in today's competitive job market. Your career requires that you know and apply good software design techniques.

3

Manning Comix

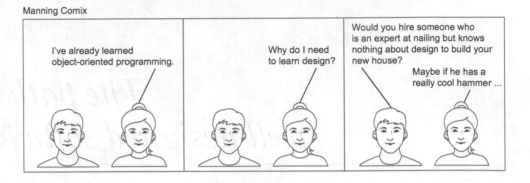

This book will improve your software design skills by teaching object-oriented *design principles* and *design patterns*. Design principles help to improve the design of a few lines of code, a function, an entire class, or a set of classes that work together. Design patterns provide models for solving common software architecture problems. These are built on design principles.

Achieving well-designed software is usually not a straightforward path. We first need to get the application's requirements. Multiple development iterations are often necessary to achieve good design, possibly with some backtracking to recover from bad design decisions. A well-designed application evolves from hard work.

To get the most out of this book, you should be at least a beginning to intermediate C++ programmer. You should be familiar with basic data structures and their algorithms, and you should understand object-oriented programming (OOP). Furthermore, you should be able to program well enough to write applications composed of multiple header (.h or .hpp) and implementation (.cpp) source files and be able to edit, compile, debug, and run them.

Because the techniques in this book for good design build on OOP concepts, we'll review the concepts briefly at the end of this chapter.

1.1   *What is software design?*

Design is a disciplined engineering approach to creating a solution to a problem. For software developers, the solution is a successful application that meets its requirements. We practice disciplined software engineering by applying the design techniques covered in this book to find the best solution path from the requirements to a well-designed, sustainable application. These techniques include design principles that improve our code and design patterns that help solve common software architecture problems.

 Software design is an abstract concept! It won't be like learning how to create something concrete—a website, for example.

 We learn by looking at examples of poorly and well-designed code.

Good design principles can help eliminate bad surprises where code doesn't behave as expected or has poor performance. The principles help make our code more flexible and able to handle changes such as new requirements. Design patterns operate at a higher level of design and are built from the design principles. The patterns are industry-proven models for creating custom solutions to common software architecture problems.

1.2   What you will learn from this book

This book is for beginner to intermediate software developers who want to learn good software design skills. By using many before-good-design and after-good-design program examples, this book will teach you how to

- Apply design principles to improve your code
- Employ design patterns that are industry-proven models for solving common software architecture problems
- Gather, validate, and analyze the requirements for an application to ensure that you write the right application and design it well
- Develop a well-designed application iteratively and backtrack to recover from bad design decisions

> **Learn by example**
>
> We learn best by example. It's not always very effective if someone simply tells us to use a certain design principle or design pattern. We want to see *how* and *why* the principle or pattern makes a program better. We'll try to justify each one with example applications. "Before" and "after" programs will highlight the design improvements.

This book's program examples are in C++, a very popular language for developing applications. C++ is a very complex language with many features. So that we can concentrate on the design principles and design patterns, the program examples will use only basic features of the language.

NOTE   The example programs in this book use the 2017 version of C++.

Will I be able to understand the program examples in this book?

The program examples use only basic C++ features. The design techniques that this book teaches are language independent, and you'll be able to port them to other object-oriented languages.

1.3   *The benefits of good software design*

A sustainable application has a lifespan during which it is deployed, successfully used by its customers, and continually maintained. New releases fix bugs and add new features as the application's requirements evolve. Good software design reliably creates sustainable applications.

> **NOTE** Although an application may require multiple individual programs working cooperatively, each example application in this book is relatively short and simple to make it easy to see the techniques that it exemplifies. Therefore, we'll often use the words *application* and *program* (referring to the program that implements the application) interchangeably.

We want to go beyond quick hacks and the just-get-it-done-on-time-no-matter-what style of programming. Of course, there is nothing wrong with doing a quick hack whenever it's appropriate. Sometimes, you need your computer to do something, and if a line or two of code or a short script will get it done, go for it!

No one can argue against finishing an application on time. By designing an application well, we can often complete it faster. A well-designed application evolves in a systematic manner. It attains the minimum viable product (MVP) status sooner, where it passes tests and meets the minimum set of requirements. If necessary, an MVP can be deployed as the application's first release. A well-designed application is easier to test, and it's more flexible when you need to add features or make other changes.

Our goal is to create well-designed applications that meet their requirements, are completed on time, and are maintainable. Well-designed software

- *Meets its requirements*—It does what it's supposed to do.
- *Is reliable*—It passes its tests and has fewer bugs.
- *Does what its users expect*—When we call a function or create an object, we should not be surprised by its result.
- *Is efficient*—Does not have hidden runtime performance problems.
- *Is flexible and scalable*—When requirements change, it is easy to add new features without increasing the complexity of the software.
- *Enables collaboration*—Developers can work together better and recover quicker from bad design decisions.
- *Is maintainable*—Well-designed code is more understandable by future developers.
- *Uses good design techniques*—Good design techniques can improve the software by, for example, simplifying code and removing repeated code.
- *Employs appropriate design patterns*—Appropriate design patterns are industry-proven models for solving common software architecture problems.
- *Saves time and costs overall*—Good design results in fewer mistakes and major do-overs during development. Any extra time spent upfront to do good design for a

sustainable application will be compensated by decreased maintenance time and costs after deployment and potentially a longer lifespan.

- *Is better code*—You can be proud to develop good code.

OK, I'm convinced that we should write well-designed programs. But how do I know that these are the right design principles and patterns that are worth learning?

The design principles and patterns that this book teaches have been used in industry by many programmers over many years. They are known to improve the design of applications.

1.4 A few design examples

Software design deals with many issues to improve our code. Here are a few illustrative examples. This book covers many more design problems.

1.4.1 Leaking changes

The bane of all programmers is making changes to one part of a program that then requires making changes to other parts. The changes may cascade to rewriting most, if not all, of the program. The following listing is an example `Car` class exhibiting this problem.

Listing 1.1 (Program 1.1 Changes): `Car.h` (poorly designed)

```
class Car
{
public:
    void step_on_brake();
    void insert_key();
    void turn_key();
    void step_on_accelerator();
};
```

In listing 1.2, class `Driver` uses class `Car`.

Listing 1.2 (Program 1.1 Changes): `Driver.h` (poorly designed)

```
#include "Car.h"

class Driver
{
public:
    Driver(Car& c) : car(c) {}

    void start_car()
    {
        car.step_on_brake();
        car.insert_key();
        car.turn_key();
        car.step_on_accelerator();
    }
```

```
private:
    Car car;
};
```

If we aim later for more modern cars, we replace

```
void insert_key();
void turn_key();
```

with

```
void press_start_button()
```

In class `Car`, we would be forced to make changes to class `Driver`. The changes we make in class `Car` leaked into class `Driver`. As we'll see in examples throughout this book, good software design helps to prevent such leaks by reducing dependencies among classes.

1.4.2 *Code that's too complex*

Class `Automobile` is complex because it tries to do too much.

Listing 1.3   (Program 1.2 Changes): `Automobile.h` (poorly designed)

```
class AutomobileApp
{
public:
    void accelerate();
    void adjust_headlights();
    void apply_brakes();
    void change_oil();
    void change_tires();
    void check_brakes();
    void check_tires();
    void rotate_tires();
    void shut_off_engine();
    void start_engine();
    void tuneup_engine();
    void turn_left();
    void turn_right();
    void vacuum_car();
    void wash_car();
    void wax_car();

private:
    Brake brakes[4];
    Engine engine;
    Oil engine_oil;
    Direction heading;
    Headlight headlights[4];
    int speed;
    Soap soap;
    Tire tires[4];
    Vacuum vacuum_cleaner;
    CarWax wax;
};
```

The examples throughout this book show ways to avoid this very common problem by designing each class to have only one major responsibility.

Proliferation of classes is another way programs become too complex. Figure 1.1 illustrates how this can easily get out of hand.

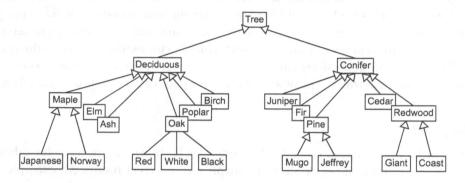

Figure 1.1 A hierarchy of classes and subclasses. Does it have to be so complex? Good design techniques can simplify this data.

Do we really need all those classes? Good design can help to eliminate unnecessary classes from a program. However, sometimes applying good design techniques means adding classes to make a program more flexible. We'll see examples of both.

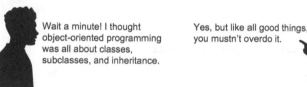

1.4.3 Inflexible code

Suppose we have an application that has class `Pet` with two subclasses `Cat` and `Dog`.

> **Listing 1.4 (Program 1.3 Inflexible):** `Pet.h`

```
class Pet
{
    // ...
};

class Cat : public Pet
{
    // ...
};

class Dog : public Pet
{
    // ...
};
```

Further, let's suppose that in another part of the application, we have the statement

```
Cat *pet = new Cat();
```

This statement is inflexible. What if later we need the variable `pet` to point to a pet `Dog` object? Or what if we added `Hamster` and `Goldfish` subclasses, and we wanted to refer to those types of pets? We would have to modify the source code containing the previous statement because we decided that we would only refer to a cat when we wrote the statement. This is known as *hardcoding*—we froze decisions when we wrote the code.

We'll see how good design techniques encourage us to write flexible code where decisions (such as which type of `Pet` object to refer to) can be made dynamically during run time.

1.4.4   *Surprise!*

If we write poorly designed code, that code may harbor nasty surprises for other programmers who use it, especially if the surprise is incorrect results. An example is the following `Date` class.

Listing 1.5   (Program 1.4 Surprise): `Date.h` (poorly designed)

```cpp
#include <string>

using namespace std;

class Date
{
public:
    Date(int y, int m, int d) : year(y), month(m), day(d) {}

    string date_string() const
    {
        return MONTH_NAMES[month] + " "  + to_string(day)
                            + ", " + to_string(year);
    }

private:
    const string MONTH_NAMES[12] =
    {
        "JAN", "FEB", "MAR", "APR", "MAY", "JUN",
        "JUL", "AUG", "SEP", "OCT", "NOV", "DEC"
    };

    int year, month, day;
};
```

A test program creates and prints a date string in the following listing.

Listing 1.6   (Program 1.4 Surprise): `tester.cpp`

```cpp
#include <iostream>
#include "Date.h"
```

```
using namespace std;

int main()
{
    Date date(2023, 9, 2);   // SEP 2, 2023
    cout << date.date_string() << endl;

    return 0;
}
```

What date string does the program print?

That's an easy one! It's a straightforward class. The program prints SEP 2, 2023, just like the comment says.

You're going to get a nasty surprise!

As many of our example programs demonstrate in this book, a well-designed program does what it's supposed to do and doesn't have surprises.

1.4.5 Common architecture problems

Programmers often encounter software architecture problems that are actually quite common. Design patterns provide models for developing custom solutions to many of these problems. For example, the publisher–subscriber problem involves an application component, known as the publisher, that produces data. Other application components, known as the subscribers, consume the data (figure 1.2). We'll see later in the book how the Observer Design Pattern provides a model for us to develop a solution for this architecture problem.

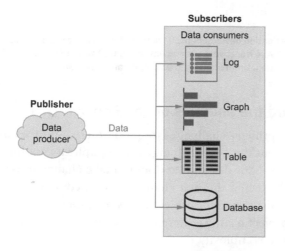

Figure 1.2 Publisher–subscriber is a common software architecture problem. One application component produces data that other application components consume. The Observer Design Pattern provides a model to solve this problem.

1.5   Make sure we're going to build the right application; then, build it right

The critical start to designing an application is to acquire and analyze its requirements to ensure that we're developing the right application. An application, no matter how well designed, is not successful if it doesn't do what it's supposed to. Getting good requirements is the important topic in chapter 3. From the requirements, we can determine the initial set of classes. We then apply good design techniques to build the application right.

1.6   Good design doesn't come easily

It takes practice and experience to consistently develop well-designed software. Developing an application most often requires multiple design–code–test iterations. We must make design tradeoffs, and we may need to backtrack from poor design decisions. It's a rocky path to achieving good design. If instead of developing the software iteratively we tried to complete it in one prolonged coding marathon, we should not expect a successfully working application to simply appear by magic at the end. This Big Bang almost never occurs (figure 1.3).

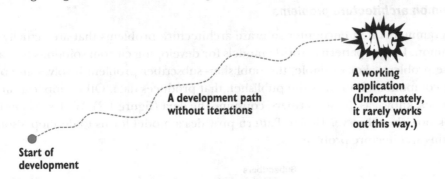

Figure 1.3   The Big Bang theory of application development. If we write lots of code in a prolonged marathon instead of developing the software iteratively, we can only hope that the Big Bang at the end will magically produce a working application. Unfortunately, that magic rarely happens.

1.7   Change and complexity are the enemies of good design

Change and complexity are the primary challenges to good design, and they are the two themes that appear throughout this book. Change and complexity are inevitable facts of life for software developers. Any design that does not take change into consideration will soon run into trouble when the first change request come in. Code can become messy and complex as a development project wears on, especially if there are multiple programmers on the project team. Design principles and design patterns are tools used to deal with change and complexity.

Change can occur during development. As we're writing the code, the application requirements can change. Or we might change our mind about the design and want to rewrite some of our code. After we've completed and deployed the application, we may get requests to add or modify features. Good design enables us to modify one part of our code without needing to modify other parts. Good design promotes the flexibility necessary to handle changes.

However, if we're not careful, trying to make an application flexible enough to handle many changes can increase its complexity. Our programs can become so complex that we won't be able to manage them. Good design also helps to keep our applications from getting out of hand. A good software designer must make tradeoffs often.

1.8 Design with object-oriented programming concepts

This book is about software design for the widely used OOP paradigm of application development. OOP concepts are the foundation of all the good design principles and design patterns covered in this book. Therefore, a quick review of the concepts will help ensure that we're all on the same page.

OOP is based on the following four main concepts:

- Encapsulation
- Abstraction
- Inheritance
- Polymorphism

Encapsulation is about using classes. A C++ class generally contains member variables and member functions. At run time, an application *instantiates* (creates) objects from a class. During run time, an object undergoes state changes. Each state of the object is characterized by a unique set of values of its member variables. An object makes a transition from one state to another whenever its member variables change values. The member functions of an object can operate on the member variables. These functions determine how an object *behaves* during run time.

A class's public members constitute its *interface* and can be accessed by any code, whereas its private members are accessible only by member functions of that class. Protected members of a class are accessible only by member functions of subclasses of that class.

In this book, we'll go beyond the strictly OOP meaning of encapsulation and use it to contain and isolate changes in an application. *Encapsulate What Varies* is a design principle we will use many times. Chapter 5 covers making members of a class private and protected to encapsulate changes to its implementation.

 Are we talking about those leaking changes again?

 Yes! Encapsulating parts of your code that can change is a primary way to prevent a change from forcing you to make changes in other parts.

Abstraction involves ignoring irrelevant details and paying attention only to what's important relative to the application we're developing. Properly using abstraction is an important way to reduce complexity.

Inheritance allows us to create subclasses (child classes) from a superclass (parent or base class). A parent class passes down state information (in the form of member variables) and behavior (in the form of member functions) to its subclasses. Each subclass can add its own additional state and behavior, or it can override (replace) any inherited state or behavior.

At run time, if you have a pointer to an object instantiated from one of the subclasses of a common superclass, *polymorphism* determines how the object behaves (i.e., which member functions execute) based on which subclass instantiated the object. Polymorphism helps to simplify an application's design. Throughout this book, we will see that OOP concepts are the foundation for the design principles and design patterns that the book covers.

Summary

- Design is a disciplined engineering approach to creating a solution to a problem. In software engineering, the problem is to create working software, and the solution is a well-designed, sustainable application.

- Well-designed software is better in many ways, such as being more reliable, flexible, and maintainable. Good design helps ensure that applications are completed on time and do what their clients expect.

- It is possible to become a better programmer by using good software design techniques that include good design principles and design patterns.

- Good design principles help make our code more flexible and able to handle changes such as new requirements. Design patterns are industry-proven models for creating solutions to common software architecture problems.

- Software design starts by acquiring and analyzing an application's requirements to ensure that we're developing the right application. The application must do what it's supposed to do.

- Developing a well-designed sustainable application nearly always requires multiple iterations with backtracking over bad design decisions. It's hard work. Don't rely on a magical Big Bang at the end of a marathon coding session.

- Good software design must deal with the major challenges of change and complexity.

- The design principles and design patterns in this book are based on the object-oriented programming concepts of abstraction, encapsulation, inheritance, and polymorphism.

- Encapsulation also means isolating the parts of a program that can change. Then, when changes do occur, they won't leak out and cause changes to other parts of the program.

Iterate to achieve good design

2

This chapter covers

- An iterative development strategy to achieve a well-designed application
- Backtracking to recover from bad design decisions
- Design principles to improve code

The development path to a well-designed application is almost never straight and narrow. As described in chapter 1, we should not have marathon coding sessions and then count on a magical Big Bang finish.

A much more rewarding development strategy takes an iterative approach. Each iteration builds on the accomplishments of the previous one. Such a strategy is more likely to result in a successful well-designed application.

Manning Comix

The example application in this chapter demonstrates the iterative development strategy, and it includes backtracking over a bad design decision. In addition, the chapter also deals with change and complexity, the major challenges to good design. It introduces several key design principles, which will appear repeatedly in subsequent chapters that will introduce additional design principles.

2.1 Good application design requires an iterative process

By some accounts, Wolfgang Amadeus Mozart was such a musical genius that he could compose an entire symphony in his head and then write it down with few, if any, edits. Hardly any of us is a programming Mozart who can develop well-designed applications in our heads and then write the code perfectly all at once.

> **NOTE** I am not a programming Mozart. Even though the program examples in this book are all relatively short, each is the final version of several hidden iterations I made until I was satisfied.

Indeed, as represented by the informal design decision tree in figure 2.1, the road to a well-designed application is often a bumpy one, with wrong turns and dead ends that require backtracking and rewriting. Each branch of the tree is a development path that either leads to a successful application (the pot of gold) or a dead end (lumps of coal). If we took a dead-end branch, we must back up to the previous decision node and take another branch. After exhausting all possible branches at a node, we must back up again to the next higher node. We hope eventually to find a path to a successfully completed application.

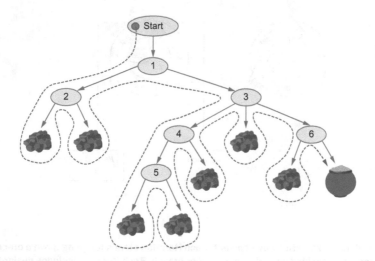

Figure 2.1   A design decision tree and the application development path shown as the dotted line. Each tree node denotes a juncture during development when we must decide to choose a path (i.e., branch) on which to continue. While designing and coding, if we head down a branch that leads to a dead-end (the lumps of coal), we must backtrack to the previous decision node and try another branch. After trying all the branches at a node, we must backtrack to the next higher node and try the next branch from there. We hope to find the path to a successfully completed application (the pot of gold).

The design decision tree in the figure is somewhat misleading because it shows the entire tree with all the branches representing development paths. We rarely know in advance all the decisions we'll need to make while coding. Instead, we construct the decision tree node by node during program development. At each node, we decide the next path to take and create a branch. Of course, we should take the path that appears to be correct and that will result in a good design. However, if that branch turns out to be a decision and coding path leading to a dead end, either because some application requirements changed or because we simply made a bad design decision, we must go back to the node and create a new branch. Once we've run out of branches for a node, we must go back up to the parent node and create a new branch there. We hope to eventually find the path to a successfully completed application. In the worst case, we may have to backtrack to the topmost node and start over from there.

How does this work in practice? Modern agile software development practice advocates that development should progress in a series of iterations. An iteration can represent a trip down a branch of the decision tree. As shown in figure 2.2, each iteration consists of three phases: design, code, and test to incrementally improve or add more features to the application. Only after all of an iteration's tests have passed should we start the next iteration. An iteration can last as little as a few hours to around two weeks. If an iteration lasts longer than that, we're likely trying to do too much during the iteration.

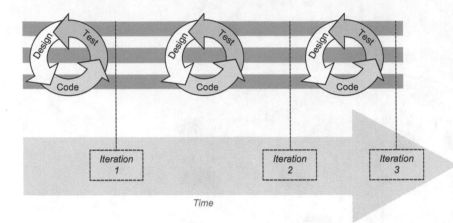

Figure 2.2   Iterations during application development. Each iteration stands for going down a branch in the decision tree, including backing up and trying another branch. Each iteration includes designing, coding, and testing to incrementally improve or add more features to the application. The iterations can take different amounts of time, as short as a few hours or up to around two weeks.

Test-driven development

During each iteration, the intuitive order of activities is design–code–test. However, test-driven development (TDD) is a development process that uses the order test–design–code.

Using TDD, at the start of each iteration, we write the test programs for the features that we want to implement during the iteration. Of course, all the tests will initially fail because we haven't written the code yet that implements the features. The goal of each iteration is to design and write the code that will make all tests for that iteration pass.

As we saw with the decision tree, the series of iterations doesn't imply continuous forward progress. Some iterations are the result of backtracking and taking an alternate path. But don't despair! As you become a more experienced programmer, the decision tree becomes smaller, and you will need fewer iterations to complete your application. However, achieving good design remains a continuous-improvement process.

 All those iterations and backtracking look too tedious! Is it really that much trouble to write well-designed software?

 You'll need fewer iterations and less backtracking after you've gained more experience.

2.2   *Don't let changes leak out*

Woe to the programmer who discovers that making changes to one part of an application requires changes to other parts! In the worst-case scenario, major portions of the application, if not the entire application, will require rewriting.

Chapter 1 mentioned that one of the primary design challenges is to accommodate change. If we write a significant application, we should anticipate what parts will change. There are numerous causes for code changes. Some of the common ones are the following:

- The requirements change. The requirements state what our application must do, or allow its users to do, and they may change both during development and after the application is finished.
- We change our mind about design during development.
- We add new features (or remove the ones that are not needed) from a completed application.

2.3   *Iterate to achieve good design*

For the example application in this section, we will eventually arrive at a good design that encapsulates changes and has other benefits, but only after several iterations of designing, coding, and testing. The example will also demonstrate how it's sometimes necessary to backtrack from a poor design decision that seemed right when we made it.

In the example, we want to develop a book catalogue application that stores a list of books and allows a user to search for books that match the user's target attributes. Here are the application's initial requirements.

- A user must be able to add fiction books and their attributes to the catalogue.
- The attributes for each book shall be the book title and the author's last and first names.
- A user must be able to search for books that match the user's target attribute values.
- Searches for books will depend on matching any number of target attributes.
- String matches of the book titles and authors' first and last names must be case-insensitive.
- A user must be able to specify any number of don't-care (wildcard) target attributes.
- Each don't-care attribute must by default match the corresponding attribute in all books in the catalogue. The remaining target attributes must match exactly.

The purpose of this example is to demonstrate development iterations. We want each iteration to improve the design of the application.

But beware! Possible bad design decisions ahead!
Even though the code after each iteration may look fine, we may discover that we made bad design decisions. Then, we must backtrack and rewrite code to make improvements.

2.3.1   *Iteration 1: Initial cohesive classes*

Looking at the requirements, we can readily design two classes: `Book` and `Catalogue`. At run time, the catalogue will store `Book` objects (listing 2.1). `Book` member variables are a book's attributes: the book's title and author's first and last names. The constructor is passed the attribute values and initializes these member variables.

A note about the examples' coding style

To keep the example programs short and simple, we'll leave out descriptive and explanatory comments that applications normally should have in the source code. Instead, the printed examples will use code annotations.

Having `using namespace std` at the start of a C++ file is often considered a risky practice because it brings many additional names into the scope, which potentially causes name conflicts. But we'll do so in this book to keep the examples short.

Listing 2.1   (Program 2.1 Books-1): `Book.h`

```cpp
#include <iostream>
#include <string>

using namespace std;

class Book
{
public:
    Book(const string ttl, const string lst, const string fst)
        : title(ttl), last(lst), first(fst) {}

    string get_title() const { return title; }
    string get_last()  const { return last; }
    string get_first() const { return first; }

private:
    string title;
    string last;
    string first;
};

inline ostream& operator <<(ostream& ostr, const Book& book)
{
```

The constructor initializes the book attributes.

The book attributes

```
    ostr << "{TITLE: '"   << book.get_title()
         << "', LAST: '"  << book.get_last()
         << "', FIRST: '" << book.get_first() << "'}";

    return ostr;
}
```

The overloaded output operator << for a Book object writes a book's attributes to an output stream (typically cout) surrounded by braces, with a label for each attribute value. Example output would be

```
{TITLE: 'To Kill a Mockingbird', LAST: 'Lee', FIRST: 'Harper'}
```

Compiling, linking, and running the example programs

All the example programs in this book use the 2017 version of C++. The following two commands specify the 2017 standard and will compile, link, and run program 2.1 in a Linux terminal window using the GNU C++ compiler or in a MacOS terminal window using the Apple Clang C++ compiler:

```
g++ -std=c++17 *.cpp -o books
./books
```

The equivalent commands in a Microsoft Windows "Developer Command Prompt for VS" window using the Visual Studio C++ compiler:

```
cl /EHs /std:c++17 *.cpp /link /out:books.exe
books
```

Similar commands will compile, link, and run the other example programs.

In class Catalogue (listing 2.2), private member variable booklist is a vector of pointers to the Book objects stored in the catalogue. Public member function add() creates a new Book object from a title and the author's last and first names and adds the object to the vector. Public member function find() searches the vector for a matching book.

Private static member function equal_ignore_case() performs a case-insensitive comparison of two strings, str_1 and str_2, character by character by comparing the lowercase version of each letter. An empty target string represents a don't-care attribute, in which case the comparison always returns true.

Listing 2.2   (Program 2.1 Books-1): `Catalogue.h`

```
#include <string>
#include <vector>
#include "Book.h"

using namespace std;

class Catalogue
{
public:
```

```
      void add(const string title,
              const string last,
              const string first)
      {
          booklist.push_back(new Book(title, last, first));
      }

      vector<Book *> find(const Book& target) const;

private:
      vector<Book *> booklist;                          ◄─┐ Vector of pointers
                                                           │ to Book objects

      static bool equal_ignore_case(const string string1,
                                    const string string2)
      {
          for (int i = 0; i < string1.length(); i++)
          {
              if (tolower(string1[i]) != tolower(string2[i]))    ◄──┐
              {                                                     │
                  return false;                            Compare the lowercase
              }                                            version of each letter.
          }

          return true;
      }
};
```

Public member function find() is passed a reference to a Book object containing the
target attributes (listing 2.3). It iterates over the books in the booklist vector and calls
equal_ignore_case() to compare the target title, last name, and first name to the
corresponding attributes of each book in the booklist. Shifting all the characters of the
attribute strings to lowercase for the comparison allows us to do case-insensitive string
matching. The function returns a vector of books that matched the target attributes or
an empty vector if no books matched.

Listing 2.3 (Program 2.1 Books-1): `Catalogue.cpp`

```
#include "Book.h"
#include "Catalogue.h"

vector<Book *>Catalogue::find(const Book& target) const
{
    vector<Book *> matches;

    string target_title = target.get_title();
    string target_last  = target.get_last();
    string target_first = target.get_first();

    for (Book *book : booklist)
    {
        if (   equal_ignore_case(target_title, book->get_title())    All
            && equal_ignore_case(target_last,  book->get_last())     attributes
            && equal_ignore_case(target_first, book->get_first()))   must
        {                                                            match.
```

```
            matches.push_back(book);
        }
    }

    return matches;
}
```

We want to define classes that are *cohesive*, each with only a single primary responsibility. The `Book` class is responsible for storing a book's attributes. The `Catalogue` class is responsible for maintaining the list of `Book` objects, which includes adding new books to the list and finding book matches in the list.

The Single Responsibility Principle

A well-designed class is *cohesive*, meaning that it has only a single primary responsibility. A poorly designed class has too many responsibilities. A cohesive class with a clear responsibility is easy to use—there should be no doubt what its purpose is. A cohesive class is easy to maintain—all its member functions and member variables serve a single primary purpose.

In the test program (listing 2.4), function `fill()` loads the catalogue with some fiction books. Function `test()` performs test searches with some target books, and it calls function `search()` to do each search. Some of the target attributes are empty strings that represent don't-cares.

Listing 2.4   (Program 2.1 Books-1): `tester.cpp`

```cpp
#include <iostream>
#include <vector>
#include <string>

#include "Book.h"
#include «Catalogue.h»

void fill(Catalogue& catalogue);
void test(const Catalogue& catalogue);

int main()
{
    Catalogue catalogue;
    fill(catalogue);
    test(catalogue);

    return 0;
}

void fill(Catalogue& catalogue)          ◄─── Fills the catalogue with
{                                             test Book objects
    catalogue.add("Life of Pi", "Martel", "Yann");
    catalogue.add("The Call of the Wild", "London", "Jack");
    catalogue.add("To Kill a Mockingbird", "Lee", "Harper");
```

```
        catalogue.add("Little Women", "Alcott", "Louisa");
        catalogue.add("The Adventures of Sherlock Holmes",
                    "Doyle", "Conan");
        catalogue.add("And Then There Were None", "Christie", "Agatha");
        catalogue.add("Carrie", "King", "Stephen");
        catalogue.add("It: A Novel", "King", "Stephen");
        catalogue.add("Frankenstein", "Shelley", "Mary");
        catalogue.add("2001: A Space Odyssey", "Clarke", "Arthur");
        catalogue.add("Ender's Game", "Card", "Orson");
    }

void search(const Catalogue& catalogue, const Book& target)          ◄─────────┐
{                                                                              │  Searches the catalogue
    cout << endl << "Find " << target << endl;                                 │  for a target book

    vector<Book *> matches = catalogue.find(target);

    if (matches.size() == 0) cout << "No matches." << endl;
    else
    {
        cout << "Matches:" << endl;

        for (Book *book : matches)
        {
            cout << "  " << *book << endl;
        }
    }
}


void test(Catalogue& catalogue)          ◄────────  Test function
{
    Book target1("Life of Pi", "Martel", "Yann");
    search(catalogue, target1);

    Book target2("", "King", "");          ◄─────────┐  Don't care
    search(catalogue, target2);                       │  (wildcard) attributes

    Book target3("1984", "Orwell", "George");
    search(catalogue, target3);

    Book target4("", "", "");          ◄─────────┘
    search(catalogue, target4);
}
```

The output from the test run is

```
Find {TITLE: 'Life of Pi', LAST: 'Martel', FIRST: 'Yann'}
Matches:
  {TITLE: 'Life of Pi', LAST: 'Martel', FIRST: 'Yann'}

Find {TITLE: '', LAST: 'King', FIRST: ''}
Matches:
  {TITLE: 'Carrie', LAST: 'King', FIRST: 'Stephen'}
  {TITLE: 'It: A Novel', LAST: 'King', FIRST: 'Stephen'}
```

```
Find {TITLE: '1984', LAST: 'Orwell', FIRST: 'George'}
No matches.

Find {TITLE: '', LAST: '', FIRST: ''}
Matches:
   {TITLE: 'Life of Pi', LAST: 'Martel', FIRST: 'Yann'}
   {TITLE: 'The Call of the Wild', LAST: 'London', FIRST: 'Jack'}
   {TITLE: 'To Kill a Mockingbird', LAST: 'Lee', FIRST: 'Harper'}
   {TITLE: 'Little Women', LAST: 'Alcott', FIRST: 'Louisa'}
   {TITLE: 'The Adventures of Sherlock Holmes', LAST: 'Doyle', ➥
FIRST: 'Conan'}
   {TITLE: 'And Then There Were None', LAST: 'Christie', FIRST: 'Agatha'}
   {TITLE: 'Carrie', LAST: 'King', FIRST: 'Stephen'}
   {TITLE: 'It: A Novel', LAST: 'King', FIRST: 'Stephen'}
   {TITLE: 'Frankenstein', LAST: 'Shelley', FIRST: 'Mary'}
   {TITLE: '2001: A Space Odyssey', LAST: 'Clarke', FIRST: 'Arthur'}
   {TITLE: 'Ender's Game', LAST: 'Card', FIRST: 'Orson'}
```

Apparently, our application fulfills its requirements. Figure 2.3 depicts our progress thus far after one development iteration. We'll award ourselves a couple of gold coins.

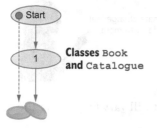

Figure 2.3   In our first development iteration, we created two classes: Book and Catalogue. The dotted line shows our development path. The application fulfills its current requirements.

2.3.2   *Iteration 2: Encapsulation, delegation, and loose coupling*

Now, suppose that we're given additional requirements to add two more book attributes—the publication year and the genre:

- The attributes for each fiction book shall include its publication year and its genre.
- The book genres shall be ADVENTURE, CLASSICS, DETECTIVE, FANTASY, HISTORIC, HORROR, ROMANCE, and SCIFI.

We need to make some code changes to accommodate the new requirements. Ostensibly, class Book needs two new member variables for the year and the genre. Because the requirements give a specific list for the genres, we can define enumeration constants for them.

At this point, we can see that any attribute changes we make to class `Book` will require corresponding changes to class `Catalogue`:

- Member function `add()` has book attributes as parameters (listing 2.2).
- The `if` statement in member function `find()` references the book attributes (listing 2.3).

Oops! Are the the changes we're making to class **Book** about to leak into class **Catalogue**?

Yes, and this unfortunate change leak will get worse if we add even more book attributes.

We can plug the leak by encapsulating the code that will vary by putting the attributes into a separate class `Attributes` (see listing 2.5).

The Encapsulate What Varies Principle

Good software design separates code that can vary from code that won't vary. Encapsulating the code that can vary isolates it from the rest of the program. Then, when changes occur to the encapsulated code, those changes won't leak out and cause other code to change. A common way to encapsulate code that can vary is to put it in a class by itself.

Because changing the book attributes necessitates changes to searching the attributes, we also need to encapsulate that behavior in class `Attributes`. Private member function `is_match()` explicitly compares attributes and returns `true` or `false`, respectively, if they do or do not match. Special `Genre` value `UNSPECIFIED` and `year` value 0 will be don't-care search target values. To perform the case-insensitive string comparisons, we must move static member function `equal_ignore_case()` from class `Catalogue` to class `Attributes`.

Listing 2.5 (Program 2.2 Books-2): `Attributes.h`

```cpp
#include <iostream>

using namespace std;

enum class Genre
{
    ADVENTURE, CLASSICS, DETECTIVE, FANTASY, HISTORIC,
    HORROR, ROMANCE, SCIFI, UNSPECIFIED
};
```

The genre attribute

```cpp
inline ostream& operator <<(ostream& ostr, const Genre& genre)
{
    switch (genre)
    {
        case Genre::ADVENTURE: ostr << "adventure"; break;
        case Genre::CLASSICS:  ostr << "classics";  break;
        case Genre::DETECTIVE: ostr << "detective"; break;
        case Genre::FANTASY:   ostr << "fantasy";   break;
        case Genre::HISTORIC:  ostr << "historic";  break;
        case Genre::HORROR:    ostr << "horror";    break;
        case Genre::ROMANCE:   ostr << "romance";   break;
        case Genre::SCIFI:     ostr << "scifi";     break;

        default: ostr << "unspecified"; break;
    }

    return ostr;
}

class Attributes
{
public:
    Attributes(const string ttl,
               const string lst, const string fst,
               const int yr, const Genre gen)
        : title(ttl), last(lst), first(fst),
          year(yr), genre(gen) {}

    string get_title() const { return title; }
    string get_last()  const { return last; }
    string get_first() const { return first; }
    int    get_year()  const { return year; }
    Genre  get_genre() const { return genre; }
```

Explicitly match attributes, including year and genre.

```cpp
    bool is_match(const Attributes& target_attrs) const
    {
        return equal_ignore_case(target_attrs.get_title(), title)
            && equal_ignore_case(target_attrs.get_last(),  last)
            && equal_ignore_case(target_attrs.get_first(), first)
            && (   (target_attrs.get_year()  == 0)
                || (target_attrs.get_year()  == year))
            && (   (target_attrs.get_genre() == Genre::UNSPECIFIED)
                || (target_attrs.get_genre() == genre));
    }
```

```
private:
    string title;
    string last;
    string first;
    int    year;
    Genre  genre;

    static bool equal_ignore_case(const string string1,
                                  const string string2) ...
};

inline ostream& operator <<(ostream& ostr, const Attributes& attrs)
{
    ostr << "{TITLE: '"   << attrs.get_title()
         << "', LAST: '"  << attrs.get_last()
         << "', FIRST: '" << attrs.get_first()
         << "', YEAR: "   << attrs.get_year()
         << ", GENRE: "   << attrs.get_genre() << "}";

    return ostr;
}
```

Static member function moved from class Catalogue

The added year and genre attributes

Also, output the year and genre attributes.

We replaced the overloaded << operator for a Book object with one for an Attributes object that outputs all the attributes, including the year and genre.

A Book object is now constructed from an Attributes object, as follows. Each Book object will point to its Attributes object.

Listing 2.6   (Program 2.2 Books-2): `Book.h`

```
#include "Attributes.h"

using namespace std;

class Book
{
public:
    Book(Attributes * const attrs) : attributes(attrs) {}
    virtual ~Book() { delete attributes; }

    Attributes *get_attributes() const { return attributes; }

private:
    Attributes *attributes;
};
```

Each Book object will point to its Attributes object.

Class Catalogue needs changes to its add() and find() member functions to handle the new Attributes class (listing 2.7). We pass a reference to an Attributes object to function add(), which uses the object to construct a Book object to add to the booklist vector. We pass a reference to the target Attributes object to function find().

Listing 2.7   (Program 2.2 Books-2): `Catalogue.h`

```cpp
#include <vector>
#include "Book.h"

using namespace std;

class Catalogue
{
public:
    void add(Attributes * const attrs)
    {
        booklist.push_back(new Book(attrs));
    }

    vector<Book *> find(const Attributes& target_attrs) const;

private:
    vector<Book *> booklist;
};
```

Construct a Book object from the Attributes object.

Member function `find()` becomes much simpler (listing 2.8). The function *delegates* attribute matching to class `Attributes` by calling the latter's `is_match()` member function, and thus `find()` is no longer affected by any changes to book attributes.

Delegation is a way for a class to ask another class to perform a task on its behalf.

Especially if the other class is better suited to perform the task.

Attribute matching does fit better in a cohesive `Attributes` class.

Listing 2.8   (Program 2.2 Books-2): `Catalogue.cpp`

```cpp
#include "Book.h"
#include "Catalogue.h"

vector<Book *>Catalogue::find(const Attributes& target_attrs) const
{
    vector<Book *> matches;

    for (Book *book : booklist)
    {
        Attributes *book_attrs = book->get_attributes();
        if (book_attrs->is_match(target_attrs))
        {
            matches.push_back(book);
        }
    }

    return matches;
}
```

Delegate attribute matching to class Attributes.

The Delegation Principle

Move functionality out of one class (the requester) into another more suitable class (the delegate) to make the two classes more cohesive. The requester class commonly has a member variable that points to the delegate class. A particular member function in the delegate class implements the work to be done on behalf of the requester class. The requester class generally should not have any dependencies on how the delegate class does that work. At run time, an object of the requester class can request the work by calling that member function on an object of the delegate class.

In our example, the requester is class `Catalogue`, and the delegate is class `Attributes`.

Class `Catalogue` is now *loosely coupled* with class `Attributes` because we've minimized the dependences of `Catalogue` on `Attributes`. Class `Catalogue` doesn't know the specific attributes that class `Attributes` maintains. Classes `Book` and `Attributes` are also loosely coupled with each other: class `Attributes` doesn't know that its objects are stored by `Book` objects, and class `Book` also doesn't need to know how class `Attributes` is implemented.

The Principle of Least Knowledge

Well-designed classes are *loosely coupled*, meaning that they ought to have little, if any, dependencies on each other. The less a class knows about how another class is implemented, the fewer dependencies it has on the other class. A class can hide its implementation by making its member variables and member functions private.

The Principle of Least Knowledge supports the Encapsulate What Varies Principle. If a class needs to change its implementation, the change can't affect any other code that doesn't depend on that implementation.

The test program `tester.cpp` must change whenever the book attributes change. Example code to add a book to the catalogue is now

```
catalogue.add(new Attributes("The Call of the Wild",
                             "London", "Jack",
                             1903, Genre::ADVENTURE));

catalogue.add(new Attributes("To Kill a Mockingbird",
                             "Lee", "Harper",
                             1960, Genre::CLASSICS));
```

and example code to search for books is now

```
Attributes target_attrs1("Life of Pi", "Martel", "Yann",
                         2003, Genre::ADVENTURE);
search(catalogue, target_attrs1);

Attributes target_attrs2("", "King", "", 0, Genre::HORROR);
search(catalogue, target_attrs2);
```

However, we won't consider that an encapsulation failure because the testing code is not intrinsically a part of the application. We must assume that any means to load the catalogue from outside the application (such as from a file) must know about the current book attributes.

The sample output is

```
Find {TITLE: '', LAST: 'King', FIRST: '', YEAR: 0, GENRE: horror}
Matches:
  {TITLE: 'Carrie', LAST: 'King', FIRST: 'Stephen', YEAR: 1974, ➥
GENRE: horror}
  {TITLE: 'It: A Novel', LAST: 'King', FIRST: 'Stephen', YEAR: 1986, ➥
GENRE: horror}
```

Figure 2.4 shows our progress after two iterations. We were able to handle a few more requirements, so let's award ourselves more gold coins.

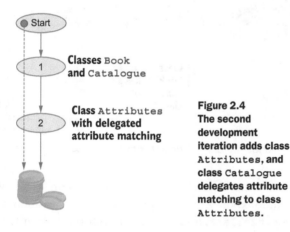

**Figure 2.4
The second
development
iteration adds class
Attributes, and
class Catalogue
delegates attribute
matching to class
Attributes.**

2.3.3 *Iteration 3: More kinds of books and their attributes*

We've been concerned with changes to the Book attributes. But the kinds of books we store in the catalogue can also change. Here are more requirements:

- It must be possible to add cookbooks and their attributes to the catalogue.
- The attributes for a cookbook must include its region.
- The regions shall be CHINA, FRANCE, INDIA, ITALY, MEXICO, US, and UNSPECIFIED.

This may also be an opportunity to show off our object-oriented programming skills! Our application now must store both fiction and cookbooks in the catalogue. It's reasonable to make Book a superclass and design two new subclasses for it, Fiction and Cookbook. In the next listing, the constructor for subclass Fiction calls the constructor of its superclass Book.

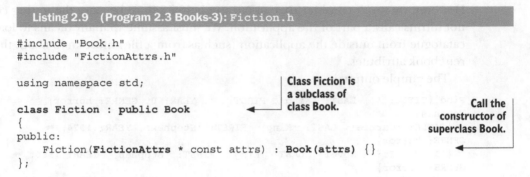

Listing 2.9   (Program 2.3 Books-3): `Fiction.h`

```
#include "Book.h"
#include "FictionAttrs.h"

using namespace std;                      Class Fiction is
                                          a subclass of
                                          class Book.          Call the
class Fiction : public Book                                   constructor of
{                                                             superclass Book.
public:
    Fiction(FictionAttrs * const attrs) : Book(attrs) {}
};
```

In the next listing, the constructor for subclass `Cookbook` also calls the superclass constructor.

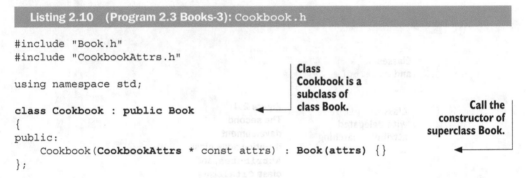

Listing 2.10   (Program 2.3 Books-3): `Cookbook.h`

```
#include "Book.h"
#include "CookbookAttrs.h"

using namespace std;                      Class
                                          Cookbook is a
                                          subclass of
                                          class Book.          Call the
class Cookbook : public Book                                  constructor of
{                                                             superclass Book.
public:
    Cookbook(CookbookAttrs * const attrs) : Book(attrs) {}
};
```

We can also make `Attributes` a superclass (listing 2.11) and design two new subclasses for it, `FictionAttrs` and `CookbookAttrs`. Superclass `Attributes` maintains the common member variables `title`, `last`, and `first`. Therefore, its member function `is_match()` only compares those common attributes.

Listing 2.11   (Program 2.3 Books-3): `Attributes.h`

```
#include <string>

using namespace std;

class Attributes
{
public:
    Attributes(const string ttl,
               const string lst, const string fst)
        : title(ttl), last(lst), first(fst) {}

    virtual ~Attributes() {}

    string get_title() const { return title; }
    string get_last()  const { return last; }
    string get_first() const { return first; }

protected:
```

```
    bool is_match(const Attributes& target_attrs) const
    {
        return equal_ignore_case(target_attrs.get_title(),  title)
            && equal_ignore_case(target_attrs.get_last(),   last)
            && equal_ignore_case(target_attrs.get_first(), first);
    }
private:
    string title;
    string last;
    string first;

    static bool equal_ignore_case(const string string1,
                                  const string string2) ...
};
```

Compare only the common attributes.

The common attributes

Subclass `FictionAttrs` contains the attributes unique to fiction books: genre and year (listing 2.12). Its constructor first calls the constructor of its superclass `Attributes` to initialize the inherited common member variables `title`, `last`, and `first`. Then, it initializes the `year` and `genre` member variables of the subclass. We also moved the definitions of the `Genre` enumeration constants and their overloaded `<<` operator physically closer to class `FictionAttrs`.

Member function `is_match()` first calls the superclass member function `Attributes::is_match()` to check the common `title`, `last`, and `first` attributes. If that passes, then the subclass can check the fiction book's `year` and `genre` attributes.

Listing 2.12 (Program 2.3 Books-3): `FictionAttrs.h`

```
#include <iostream>
#include <string>
#include "Attributes.h"

using namespace std;

enum class Genre ...

inline ostream& operator <<(ostream& ostr, const Genre& genre) ...

class FictionAttrs : public Attributes
{
public:
    FictionAttrs(const string title,
                 const string last, const string first,
                 const int yr, const Genre gen)
        : Attributes(title, last, first),
          Year(yr), genre(gen) {}

    int   get_year()  const { return year; }
    Genre get_genre() const { return genre; }

    bool is_match(const FictionAttrs& target_attrs) const
    {
        if (!Attributes::is_match(target_attrs)) return false;
```

First initialize the common attributes.

Then initialize the year and genre for fiction books.

First match the common attributes.

```
            return (    (target_attrs.get_year()   == 0)
                    || (target_attrs.get_year()   == year))
                && (    (target_attrs.get_genre() == Genre::UNSPECIFIED)
                    || (target_attrs.get_genre() == genre));
        }
```

> Then match the year and
> genre for fiction books.

```
    private:
        int    year;                    │ Fiction book year and
        Genre genre;                    │ genre attributes
    };

    inline ostream& operator <<(ostream& ostr, const FictionAttrs& attrs)
    {
        ostr << "{TITLE: '"    << attrs.get_title()
            << "', LAST: '"   << attrs.get_last()
            << "', FIRST: '" << attrs.get_first()
            << "', YEAR: "    << attrs.get_year()
            << ", GENRE: "    << attrs.get_genre() << "}";

        return ostr;
    }
```

Subclass `CookbookAttrs` contains the region attribute unique to cookbooks, as in the
following listing. Its constructor and `is_match()` member function behave similarly to
the ones in subclass `FictionAttrs`.

Listing 2.13   **(Program 2.3 Books-3):** `CookbookAttrs.h`

```
#include <iostream>
#include <string>
#include "Attributes.h"

using namespace std;

enum class Region
{
    CHINA, FRANCE, INDIA, ITALY, MEXICO, US, UNSPECIFIED
};

inline ostream& operator <<(ostream& ostr, const Region& region)
{
    switch (region)
    {
        case Region::CHINA:  ostr << "China";  break;
        case Region::FRANCE: ostr << "France"; break;
        case Region::INDIA:  ostr << "India";  break;
        case Region::ITALY:  ostr << "Italy";  break;
        case Region::MEXICO: ostr << "Mexico"; break;
        case Region::US:     ostr << "US";     break;

        default: ostr << "unspecified"; break;
    }

    return ostr;
}
```

```
class CookbookAttrs : public Attributes
{
public:
    CookbookAttrs(const string title,
                  const string last, const string first,
                  const Region reg)
        : Attributes(title, last, first),
          region(reg) {}

    Region get_region() const { return region; }

    bool is_match(const CookbookAttrs& target_attrs) const
    {
        if (!Attributes::is_match(target_attrs)) return false;

        return (target_attrs.get_region() == Region::UNSPECIFIED)
            || (target_attrs.get_region() == region);
    }
private:
    Region region;
};

inline ostream& operator <<(ostream& ostr, const CookbookAttrs& attrs)
{
    ostr << "{TITLE: '"   << attrs.get_title()
         << "', LAST: '"  << attrs.get_last()
         << "', FIRST: '" << attrs.get_first()
         << "', REGION: " << attrs.get_region() << "}";

    return ostr;
}
```

First initialize the common attributes.

Then initialize the region for cookbooks.

First match the common attributes.

Cookbook region attribute

Then match the region for cookbooks.

These are examples of the *Open-Closed Principle*. Once we've decided that class Attributes has captured the common member variables and functions for all attributes, we *closed* it for modification to provide code stability. We don't expect to make more changes to the class. But we *opened* the class for extensions in the form of subclasses such as FictionAttrs and CookbookAttrs to provide the flexibility to add more kinds of book attributes. Class Book and its subclasses are another example of this design principle.

The Open-Closed Principle

Closing a class to modification provides stability—programmers will always know what that code does and how to use it. But keeping it open for extensions in the form of subclasses allows adding functionality beyond what the closed superclass provides.

The Open-Closed Principle supports loose coupling and encapsulation. For example, a Shape superclass can hide how it stores coordinates. But it can have subclasses such as Rectangle and Circle that extend functionality by displaying the various shapes, but the subclasses are not dependent on how the coordinates are stored. If it ever becomes necessary to change the coordinates code in the superclass, the subclasses will inherit the changes but not require any code modifications.

Class Book has not changed (listing 2.14). As each Book object, whether Fiction or Cookbook, must point to its corresponding Attributes object, either FictionAttrs or CookbookAttrs, respectively, we'll put that common pointer in superclass Book. Therefore, Book contains a pointer to the superclass Attributes, rather than specifically to FictionAttrs or CookbookAttrs. This is an example of *coding to the interface*, because superclass Attributes serves as the interface of its subclasses.

The Code to the Interface Principle

If a class has several subclasses, our code should have the flexibility to work with any of the subclasses at run time. For example, if a Shape superclass has subclasses Rectangle and Circle, coding to a specific implementation is poor design:

```
Rectangle *rect = new Rectangle();  // poor design!
rect->display();
```

Variable rect can only work with Rectangle shapes. But we can code instead *to the interface* (superclass Shape in this example):

```
Shape *shape = new Rectangle();
shape->display();
```

Variable shape can work with Rectangle shapes, but it can also work with Circle shapes:

```
shape = new Circle();
shape->display();
```

Coding to the interface relies on polymorphism. Which display() member function is invoked at run time in this example depends on the type of object (Rectangle or Circle) that variable shape is pointing to.

Listing 2.14   (Program 2.3 Books-3): Book.h

```
#include "Attributes.h"

using namespace std;

class Book
{
public:
    Book(Attributes * const attrs) : attributes(attrs) {}
    virtual ~Book() { delete attributes; }

    Attributes *get_attributes() const { return attributes; }

private:
    Attributes *attributes;        ◀——————  Pointer to an Attributes
};                                           object, not specifically
                                             FictionAttrs or
                                             CookbookAttrs
```

Class `Catalogue` now needs overloaded `add()` member functions: one for `Fiction-Attrs` and one for `CookbookAttrs`. Similarly, it also needs overloaded `find()` member functions, as in the following listing. Member variable `booklist` remains a vector of pointers to `Book` objects, not pointers specifically to `Fiction` or `Cookbook` objects, another example of the Code to the Interface Principle.

> **Listing 2.15   (Program 2.3 Books-3):** `Catalogue.h`

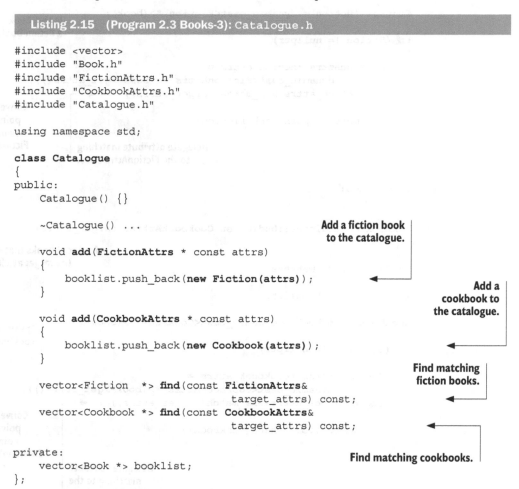

```
#include <vector>
#include "Book.h"
#include "FictionAttrs.h"
#include "CookbookAttrs.h"
#include "Catalogue.h"

using namespace std;

class Catalogue
{
public:
    Catalogue() {}

    ~Catalogue() ...

    void add(FictionAttrs * const attrs)          ◄──  Add a fiction book
    {                                                   to the catalogue.
        booklist.push_back(new Fiction(attrs));
    }
                                                   ◄──  Add a
    void add(CookbookAttrs * const attrs)               cookbook to
    {                                                   the catalogue.
        booklist.push_back(new Cookbook(attrs));
    }
                                                   ◄──  Find matching
    vector<Fiction  *> find(const FictionAttrs&          fiction books.
                             target_attrs) const;
    vector<Cookbook *> find(const CookbookAttrs&   ◄──
                             target_attrs) const;
private:                                            Find matching cookbooks.
    vector<Book *> booklist;
};
```

The two `add()` member functions are similar to each other, and the two `find()` member functions are similar to each other.

> **Listing 2.16   (Program 2.3 Books-3):** `Catalogue.cpp`

```
#include "Book.h"
#include "Fiction.h"
#include "FictionAttrs.h"
#include "Cookbook.h"
#include "CookbookAttrs.h"
#include "Catalogue.h"
```

```
vector<Fiction *>Catalogue::find(const FictionAttrs& target_attrs)
    const
{
    vector<Fiction *> matches;

    for (Book *book : booklist)
    {
        Fiction *fiction = dynamic_cast<Fiction *>(book);

        if (fiction != nullptr)
        {
            FictionAttrs *fiction_attrs =
                    dynamic_cast<FictionAttrs *>(book->get_attrs());
            if (fiction_attrs->is_match(target_attrs))
            {
                matches.push_back(fiction);
            }
        }
    }

    return matches;
}
```

Find fiction books that match the target attributes.

Is this book a fiction book?

Convert the pointer to point to a FictionAttrs object.

Delegate attribute matching to the FictionAttrs class.

```
vector<Cookbook *>Catalogue::find(const CookbookAttrs& target_attrs)
    const
{
    vector<Cookbook *> matches;

    for (Book *book : booklist)
    {
        Cookbook *cookbook = dynamic_cast<Cookbook *>(book);

        if (cookbook != nullptr)
        {
            CookbookAttrs *cookbook_attrs =
                    dynamic_cast<CookbookAttrs *>(book->get_attrs());
            if (cookbook_attrs->is_match(target_attrs))
            {
                matches.push_back(cookbook);
            }
        }
    }

    return matches;
}
```

Find cookbooks that match the target attributes.

Is this book a cookbook?

Convert the pointer to point to a CookbookAttrs object.

Delegate attribute matching to the CookbookAttrs class.

The overloaded add() member function with the FictionAttrs parameter appends a new Fiction book object to the booklist. The overloaded add() member function with the CookbookAttrs parameter appends a new Cookbook book object.

The overloaded find() member function with the FictionAttrs parameter must only check Fiction book objects. While iterating over each book object in the booklist, the statements

```
Fiction *fiction = dynamic_cast<Fiction *>(book);
if (fiction != nullptr) ...
```

check whether variable `book` is currently pointing to a `Fiction` book object. If it isn't a `Fiction` book object, pointer variable `fiction` is set to `nullptr`, and the function skips that object. But when it is a `Fiction` book object, the statements

```
FictionAttrs *fiction_attrs =
                dynamic_cast<FictionAttrs *>(book->get_attrs());
if (fiction_attrs->is_match(target_attrs))
```

first convert the `Attributes` pointer returned from `book->get_attrs()` to a pointer to a `FictionAttrs` object. Then, they delegate attribute matching to the `Fiction-Attrs` object by calling its `is_match()` member function. The `find()` function returns a vector of pointers to any matching `Fiction` book objects.

Checking and converting pointer types in C++

Consider the overloaded `Catalogue::find()` member function that receives the `FictionAttrs` parameter. We declared pointer variable `Book *book` in the `for` loop that iterates over `Book` objects in vector `booklist`. Because `booklist` contains pointers to `Book` objects, during each iteration of the loop, variable `book` will point to an object instantiated from one of the `Book` subclasses. If the variable is pointing to a `Fiction` book object, then the call to `dynamic_cast<>()` in the statements

```
Fiction *fiction = dynamic_cast<Fiction *>(book);
if (fiction != nullptr) ...
```

will convert the `Book` pointer to a `Fiction` pointer, and therefore pointer variable `fiction` will point to a `Fiction` object. But if variable `book` is pointing instead to a `Cookbook` object, the dynamic cast will return `nullptr`. Therefore, this call to `dynamic_cast<>()` performs both pointer type checking and pointer type conversion. We use the other call to `dynamic_cast<>()` to check and convert an `Attributes` pointer to a `FictionAttrs` pointer.

We can similarly define the overloaded `find()` member function with the `Cookbook-Attrs` parameter. When this function iterates over the booklist, it must check for `Cookbook` objects, and for those objects, it delegates attribute matching to `CookbookAttrs` objects. It returns a vector of pointers to matching `Cookbook` objects.

When the test program loads books into the catalogue, it calls the overloaded `Catalogue::add()` function either with a `FictionAttrs` object,

```
catalogue.add(new FictionAttrs("Little Women",
                        "Alcott", "Louisa",
                        1868, Genre::CLASSICS));
```

or with a `CookbookAttrs` object:

```
catalogue.add(new CookbookAttrs("The Woks of Life",
                        "Leung", "Bill", Region::CHINA));
```

I have a bad feeling about this code. Has it become more complex than it needs to be?

Yes, with all those runtime type checks and conversions and duplicated code, it can only get worse.

Indeed, what if the requirements change further, and the catalogue must store and search for other kinds of books, and each kind has unique attributes? We made our application more complex by attempting to handle requirement changes, namely new kinds of books and additional book attributes. Examples of the complexity include the following:

- Each kind of book requires a pair of `Book` and `Attributes` subclasses.
- Each kind of book requires an overloaded `add()` member function and an overloaded `find()` member function in class `Catalogue`. These functions have similar code.
- Each `find()` member function requires a `dynamic_cast<>()` call to ensure it will check the right kind of book, and another `dynamic_cast<>()` call to convert a pointer to the right kind of attributes. Otherwise, these member functions have similar code.

If our application needs to manage more kinds of books, we will have an increase of subclasses, duplicate code, and runtime type checks and conversions.

The Don't Repeat Yourself Principle

Repeated code is often a sign of poor design. Not only does repeated code enlarge the size of a program, but that code also makes the program harder to maintain. If you need to make a change to the code that's repeated, you'll need to make the same change to multiple copies of the code. You run the risk of missing a copy or inadvertently changing copies differently.

One way to eliminate repeated code is to share only one copy of it as a separate function or as a separate cohesive class.

Table 2.1 shows the current situation with fiction books and cookbooks, and what happens when we include how-to books.

Table 2.1   Our current design requires many classes to handle different kinds of books and their attributes.

Kind of book	Classes	Attributes
All books	`Book, Attributes`	title, last, first
Fiction	`Fiction, FictionAttrs`	year, genre
Cookbook	`Cookbook, CookbookAttrs`	region
How-to	`Howto, HowtoAttrs`	subject

Figure 2.5 shows a diagram of our application architecture as we've designed it thus far.

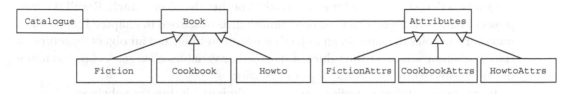

Figure 2.5 **A diagram of our application architecture as we've designed it thus far, showing our classes and subclasses and their relationships.**

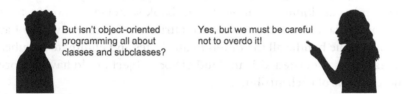

After the third iteration, we must admit that using subclasses to handle changes in the requirements for books and attributes was a poor design decision that won't scale well if there are more kinds of books. Figure 2.6 shows our progress after this iteration. We deserve those lumps of coal!

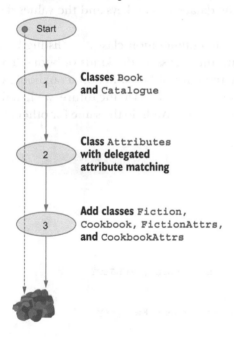

Figure 2.6   **The third development iteration added subclasses** Fiction, Cookbook, FictionAttrs, **and** CookbookAttrs. **This increase in the number of subclasses plus the added runtime type checking and type conversions tell us that we took a wrong decision path.**

2.3.4   *Iteration 4: A better design after backtracking*

Let's take a deep breath, backtrack, and take another decision branch. Recall the purposes of classes in object-oriented programming, as described in chapter 1. A class has member variables to maintain an object's state at run time, and an object undergoes a state transition whenever the values of its member variables change. A class has member functions to implement the object's behavior.

In our book catalogue application, as we've designed it thus far, subclasses `Fiction` and `Cookbook` have little to do with state or behavior. We don't need those subclasses. Class `Book` alone ought to be sufficient.

Subclasses `FictionAttrs` and `CookbookAttrs` represent very similar behaviors, primarily performing attribute matching during book searches. However, they have different member variables for their respective attributes. Is there a way to have the `Attributes` class alone handle all the different attributes and eliminate its subclasses? An `Attributes` object associated with any kind of `Book` object would have to store both the name and the value of each attribute.

Whenever there are name–value pairs in a C++ program, we should consider the `map` data structure from the standard template library (STL). An STL `map` contains *name–value* pairs, where the name serves as the key to retrieve the paired value. Therefore, the pairs in a `map` are usually called *key–value* pairs. When we declare a `map`, we must specify both the datatype of the keys and the datatype of the values. All the keys have the same datatype, and all the values have the same datatype. The keys and the values datatype can be different from each other.

For the keys datatype, we can define the enumeration class `Key` (listing 2.17). We need one enumeration constant per attribute across all the kinds of books. The map value paired with key `KIND` will indicate the kind of book: fiction, cookbook, etc. To make it easier to change the list of enumeration constants in the future, we'll define the enumeration class `Key` in its own `Key.h` source file. We'll do the same for other enumeration classes.

Listing 2.17   (Program 2.4 Books-4): `Key.h`

```
#include <iostream>

using namespace std;

enum class Key
{
    KIND, TITLE, LAST, FIRST, YEAR, GENRE, REGION, SUBJECT
};

inline ostream& operator <<(ostream& ostr, const Key& key)
{
    switch (key)
    {
        case Key::KIND:    ostr << "KIND";    break;
        case Key::TITLE:   ostr << "TITLE";   break;
```

```
        case Key::LAST:    ostr << "LAST";    break;
        case Key::FIRST:   ostr << "FIRST";   break;
        case Key::YEAR:    ostr << "YEAR";    break;
        case Key::GENRE:   ostr << "GENRE";   break;
        case Key::REGION:  ostr << "REGION";  break;
        case Key::SUBJECT: ostr << "SUBJECT"; break;
    }

    return ostr;
}
```

Our challenge will be the datatype of the values of the key–value pairs. The value can be a string, such as the value paired with key TITLE; an integer paired with key YEAR; or any of the enumeration attribute values, such as a Genre value paired with key GENRE. If we add more kinds of books and attribute keys, their attribute values can introduce even more datatypes. Table 2.2 shows the keys we have thus far and the datatype of the value paired with each key.

Table 2.2 Key–value pairs that represent book attributes.

Key	Datatype of paired value
KIND	enum class Kind
TITLE	string
LAST	string
FIRST	string
YEAR	int
GENRE	enum class Genre
REGION	enum class Region
SUBJECT	enum class Subject

The datatype of the key is enum class Key. The datatype of each paired value depends on the key.

It will be easy to add new kinds of books, such as how-to books to the Kind enumeration constants.

Listing 2.18   (Program 2.4 Books-4): Kind.h

```
#include <iostream>

using namespace std;

enum class Kind
{
    FICTION, COOKBOOK, HOWTO
};

inline ostream& operator <<(ostream& ostr, const Kind& kind)
{
    switch (kind)
    {
```

```
        case Kind::FICTION:  ostr << "fiction";  break;
        case Kind::COOKBOOK: ostr << "cookbook"; break;
        case Kind::HOWTO:    ostr << "howto";    break;
    }

    return ostr;
}
```

In the next listing, we define the Genre enumeration constants similarly.

Listing 2.19   (Program 2.4 Books-4): `Genre.h`

```
#include <iostream>

using namespace std;

enum class Genre
{
    ADVENTURE, CLASSICS, DETECTIVE, FANTASY, HISTORIC,
    HORROR, ROMANCE, SCIFI
};

inline ostream& operator <<(ostream& ostr, const Genre& genre)
{
    switch (genre)
    {
        case Genre::ADVENTURE: ostr << "adventure"; break;
        case Genre::CLASSICS:  ostr << "classics";  break;
        case Genre::DETECTIVE: ostr << "detective"; break;
        case Genre::FANTASY:   ostr << "fantasy";   break;
        case Genre::HISTORIC:  ostr << "historic";  break;
        case Genre::HORROR:    ostr << "horror";    break;
        case Genre::ROMANCE:   ostr << "romance";   break;
        case Genre::SCIFI:     ostr << "scifi";     break;
    }

    return ostr;
}
```

Likewise, in the following listing, we define the Region enumeration constants.

Listing 2.20   (Program 2.4 Books-4): `Region.h`

```
#include <iostream>

using namespace std;

enum class Region
{
    CHINA, FRANCE, INDIA, ITALY, MEXICO, PERSIA, US
};

inline ostream& operator <<(ostream& ostr, const Region& region)
{
    switch (region)
```

```
    {
        case Region::CHINA:  ostr << "China";  break;
        case Region::FRANCE: ostr << "France"; break;
        case Region::INDIA:  ostr << "India";  break;
        case Region::ITALY:  ostr << "Italy";  break;
        case Region::MEXICO: ostr << "Mexico"; break;
        case Region::PERSIA: ostr << "Persia"; break;
        case Region::US:     ostr << "US";     break;
    }

    return ostr;
}
```

And finally, we define the `Subject` enumeration constants.

Listing 2.21 (Program 2.4 Books-4): `Subject.h`

```
#include <iostream>

using namespace std;

enum class Subject
{
    DRAWING, PAINTING, WRITING
};

inline ostream& operator <<(ostream& ostr, const Subject& subject)
{
    switch (subject)
    {
        case Subject::DRAWING:  ostr << "drawing";  break;
        case Subject::PAINTING: ostr << "painting"; break;
        case Subject::WRITING:  ostr << "writing";  break;
    }

    return ostr;
}
```

We no longer need UNSPECIFIED values. In our new design, if an attribute is missing in a search target, that attribute will be a don't-care.

We need a common datatype for the paired values in the `AttributeMap`, even though there are several different underlying datatypes (table 2.2). Therefore, we can define each pair's `AttributeValue` to be a `variant` type that can have a value that is either an `int`, `string`, `Kind`, `Genre`, `Region`, or `Subject`, as shown in the following listing.

Listing 2.22 (Program 2.4 Books-4): `Attributes.h`

```
#include <string>
#include <map>
#include <variant>

#include "Key.h"
```

```
#include "Kind.h"
#include "Genre.h"
#include "Region.h"
#include "Subject.h"

using namespace std;

typedef variant<int, string,
                Kind, Genre, Region, Subject> AttributeValue;     │  The variant


typedef map<Key, AttributeValue> AttributeMap;         ◄──  The attribute map


enum type_indexes                                           ┌ Indexes that
{                                                           │ correspond to
    INT_INDEX, STRING_INDEX,                                │ the variant
    KIND_INDEX, GENRE_INDEX, REGION_INDEX, SUBJECT_INDEX    │ datatypes
};                                                          └


class Attributes
{
public:
    Attributes(AttributeMap *const pairs);
    ~Attributes() { delete attribute_map; }

    bool is_match(const Attributes& target_attrs) const;

    friend ostream& operator <<(ostream& ostr,
                        const Attributes& attrs);

private:
    AttributeMap *attribute_map;              ◄──  The attribute map

    bool is_matching_pair(const Key& target_key,
                        const AttributeValue& target_value) const;

    static bool equal_ignore_case(const string string1,
                            const string string2) ...
};
```

The enumeration type `type_indexes` has values that correspond to the variant datatypes: `INT_INDEX` for `int`, `STRING_INDEX` for `string`, `KIND_INDEX` for `Kind`, and so forth. These indexes allow us in the `Attributes` constructor (listing 2.23) to verify that the value of each key–value pair in the map has the correct datatype. This is an example of defensive programming—we don't ever want to create an invalid `Attributes` object.

Listing 2.23   (Program 2.4 Books-4): `Attributes.cpp` **(part 1 of 3)**

```
#include <iostream>
#include <string>
#include <cassert>
```

```
#include "Key.h"
#include "Kind.h"
#include "Genre.h"
#include "Region.h"
#include "Subject.h"
#include "Attributes.h"
```

The Attributes constructor

```
using namespace std;

Attributes::Attributes(AttributeMap *pairs) : attribute_map(pairs)
{
    for (AttributeMap::iterator it = pairs->begin();
         it != pairs->end(); it++)
    {
        Key key   = it->first;
        int index = it->second.index();

        switch (key)
        {
            case Key::YEAR:
                assert(index == INT_INDEX); break;

            case Key::TITLE:
            case Key::LAST:
            case Key::FIRST:
                assert(index == STRING_INDEX); break;

            case Key::KIND:
                assert(index == KIND_INDEX); break;

            case Key::GENRE:
                assert(index == GENRE_INDEX); break;

            case Key::REGION:
                assert(index == REGION_INDEX); break;

            case Key::SUBJECT:
                assert(index == SUBJECT_INDEX); break;
        }
    }
}
...
```

Iterate over the elements of the map to verify that the value of each pair has the correct datatype.

Defensive programming

Well-designed applications practice defensive programming to guard against programming errors. Functions should create only proper objects from their parameter values.

Perform runtime checks of function parameter values to ensure that no invalid values are being passed in. However, to keep the example programs in this book short, their functions generally do not have parameter checking.

Member function `is_match()` compares this `Attributes` object against the `target_attrs` object. The two `Attributes` objects match only if all the corresponding key–value elements in their maps compare equally. Iterator `target_it` iterates over the key–value elements of the `target_attrs` object's map. For each element

- The first test checks whether this attribute's map contains the target element's key.
- If the first test passes, then the second test checks the equality of their paired values.

If any test fails while iterating over the elements of the `target_attrs` object's map, the attributes objects do not match. If a particular attribute (such as the year) isn't in the target map, then that attribute is a don't-care during matching.

Listing 2.24   (Program 2.4 Books-4): `Attributes.cpp` **(part 2 of 3)**

```
...
bool Attributes::is_match(const Attributes& target_attrs) const
{
    AttributeMap *target_pairs = target_attrs.attribute_map;
    AttributeMap::iterator it;

    for (it = target_pairs->begin(); it != target_pairs->end(); it++)
    {
        Key            target_key   = it->first;
        AttributeValue target_value = it->second;

        if (!is_matching_pair(target_key, target_value))
        {
            return false;
        }
    }

    return true;
}

bool Attributes::is_matching_pair(
                        const Key& target_key,
                        const AttributeValue& target_value) const
{
    if (attribute_map->find(target_key) == attribute_map->end())
    {
        return false;
    }

    if ((*attribute_map)[target_key] == target_value)
    {
        return true;
    }

    if (target_value.index() == STRING_INDEX)
    {
```

```
        return equal_ignore_case(
                        get<string>((*attribute_map)[target_key]),
                        get<string>(target_value));
    }

    return false;
}
...
```

An example of what the overloaded operator << (listing 2.25) can print is

```
{KIND: fiction, TITLE: 'Carrie', LAST: 'King', FIRST: 'Stephen', ↪
YEAR: 1974, GENRE: horror}
```

Listing 2.25   (Program 2.4 Books-4): `Attributes.cpp` **(part 3 of 3)**

```
ostream& operator <<(ostream& ostr, const Attributes& attrs)
{
    AttributeMap *pairs = attrs.attribute_map;
    AttributeMap::iterator it;

    ostr << "{";

    for (it = pairs->begin(); it != pairs->end(); it++)   ◀──┐ Iterate over
    {                                                          │ the key–value
        Key            key   = it->first;                      │ pairs of the
        AttributeValue value = it->second;                     │ map.

        if (it != pairs->begin()) ostr << ", ";
        ostr << key << ": ";

        switch (key)
        {
            case Key::KIND:   ostr << get<Kind>(value); break;

            case Key::TITLE:
            case Key::LAST:
            case Key::FIRST:  ostr << "'" << get<string>(value)
                                   << "'"; break;

            case Key::GENRE:  ostr << get<Genre>(value);  break;
            case Key::YEAR:   ostr << get<int>(value);    break;

            case Key::REGION: ostr << get<Region>(value); break;

            default: break;
        }
    }

    ostr << "}";
    return ostr;
}
```

Class `Book` now has an overloaded operator << to print book attributes, but the class itself hasn't changed (listing 2.26).

Listing 2.26   (Program 2.4 Books-4): `Book.h`

```
#include <iostream>
#include <string>
#include "Attributes.h"

using namespace std;

class Book
{
    ...
};

inline ostream& operator <<(ostream& ostr, const Book& book)
{
    cout << *book.get_attributes();
    return ostr;
}
```

Class `Catalogue` is much simpler now, as shown in the following listing.

Listing 2.27   (Program 2.4 Books-4): `Catalogue.h`

```
#include <vector>
#include "Book.h"

using namespace std;

class Catalogue
{
public:
    void add(Attributes * const attrs);

    vector<Book *> find(const Attributes& target_attrs) const;

private:
    vector<Book *> booklist;
};
```

We've eliminated the duplicate code and now follow the Don't Repeat Yourself (DRY) Principle. There is only one `add()` member function and only one `find()` member function. We no longer need calls to `dynamic_cast<>()` to do runtime type checks and conversions. A bonus of this design is a book can have any attributes, not limited to certain ones based on the kind of book, as shown in the following listing.

Listing 2.28   (Program 2.4 Books-4): `Catalogue.cpp`

```
#include "Book.h"
#include "Catalogue.h"

void Catalogue::add(Attributes * const attrs)    ◄──── Only one add()
{                                                        member function
    booklist.push_back(new Book(attrs));
}
```

```
vector<Book *>Catalogue::find(const Attributes& target_attrs)
    const
{
    vector<Book *> matches;

    for (Book *book : booklist)
    {
        Attributes *book_attributes = book->get_attributes();
        if (book_attributes->is_match(target_attrs))
        {
            matches.push_back(book);
        }
    }

    return matches;
}
```

Only one find()
member function

In the test program `tester.cpp`, function `fill()` now enters a book into the catalogue with statements like

```
AttributeMap pairs3 =
{
    {Key::KIND,  Kind::FICTION},
    {Key::TITLE, string("To Kill a Mockingbird")},
    {Key::LAST,  string("Lee")},
    {Key::FIRST, string("Harper")},
    {Key::YEAR,  1960},
    {Key::GENRE, Genre::CLASSICS}
};
catalogue.add(new Attributes(new AttributeMap(pairs3)));
```

An example search is

```
AttributeMap target_pairs2 =
{
    {Key::KIND,  Kind::FICTION},
    {Key::LAST,  string("KING")},
    {Key::GENRE, Genre::HORROR}
};
search(catalogue, Attributes(new AttributeMap(target_pairs2)));
```

The string `"KING"` will match `"King"` in the catalogue. The output is

```
Find {KIND: fiction, LAST: 'KING', GENRE: horror}
Matches:
  {KIND: fiction, TITLE: 'Carrie', LAST: 'King', FIRST: 'Stephen', ➡
YEAR: 1974, GENRE: horror}
  {KIND: fiction, TITLE: 'It: A Novel', LAST: 'King', FIRST: ➡
'Stephen', YEAR: 1986, GENRE: horror}
```

Missing attributes are don't-cares, so this search will return all Chinese cookbooks:

```
AttributeMap target_pairsB =
{
    {Key::REGION, Region::CHINA}
};
search(catalogue, Attributes(new AttributeMap(target_pairsB)));
```

The output is

```
Find {REGION: China}
Matches:
  {KIND: cookbook, TITLE: 'The Wok of Life', LAST: 'Leung', FIRST: ➡
'Bill', REGION: China}
  {KIND: cookbook, TITLE: 'Chinese Cooking for Dummies', LAST: 'Yan', ➡
FIRST: 'Martin', REGION: China}
```

Figure 2.7 shows that after four iterations, we've arrived at an application design that successfully encapsulates changes to the kinds of books and their attributes. Only class `Attributes` will need modifications. Classes `Book` and `Catalogue` will not require modifications. We can award ourselves a pot of gold.

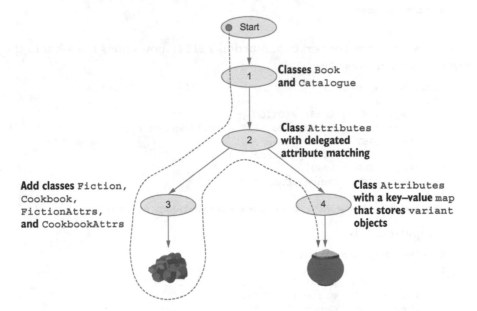

Figure 2.7   It took four iterations, including some backtracking, to find the development path to an application design that successfully encapsulates changes to the kinds of books and their attributes.

 OK, so the final design got rid of all the **Book** and **Attribute** subclasses. But what if I discover that other parts of my application need to use those subclasses?

Then, your design should keep the subclasses. Software design often requires making tradeoffs.

This chapter demonstrated developing the book application with four iterations. Virtually all significant applications will require multiple iterations, often many more than four. The following chapters will have shorter example programs, and we'll limit the number of iterations.

Summary

- It usually takes several development iterations to achieve a well-designed program. Be willing to backtrack from bad design decisions.

- The Single Responsibility Principle (SRP) states that a class should be cohesive and have only one primary responsibility.

- The Encapsulate What Varies Principle states that code that can vary should be isolated to keep its changes from causing other code to change.

- The Delegation Principle states that one class can perform work on the behalf of another class, where the work belongs to a more suitable cohesive class.

- The Principle of Least Knowledge states that classes should not know about each other's implementation, and so the classes are loosely coupled with few, if any, dependencies on each other.

- The Open-Closed Principle states that a class should be closed for modification but open for extension to provide both stability and flexibility.

- The Code to the Interface Principle states that for runtime flexibility, we should not write code that can work only with a specific subclass but use polymorphism and write code that can work with multiple subclasses.

- The Don't Repeat Yourself Principle states that well-designed code does not contain duplicate copies of code.

- OOP is important for good application design, but it's not a panacea to all design problems. Be smart about how to apply its concepts. For example, do not create too many subclasses unnecessarily and thereby make your application too complex.

- Using better data structures can simplify complex code.

Part 2

Design the right application

There are many benefits to having well-designed software. But an application, no matter how well designed, is a failure if it doesn't do what it is supposed to do: before we can design an *application right*, we must determine what is the *right application*. Therefore, we must first gather and analyze the application's requirements. Those are not easy tasks, and we must do them carefully.

Once we have sufficient requirements, we're ready to analyze them and to start designing the classes of the application. We can meet the challenges of change and complexity by using good design principles to build cohesive and loosely coupled classes. We can document our design with UML (Unified Modeling Language) diagrams.

Get requirements to build the right application

3

This chapter covers

- Functional and nonfunctional requirements of an application
- What are good requirements and how to obtain them
- Use cases
- The functional specification
- Analyzing the requirements to obtain the initial application classes

Before we start worrying about building an *application right* (make it well-designed), we must ensure that we're going to build the *right application*. An application that doesn't do what the client wants is a failed, unsuccessful application, no matter how well designed it may be. The *client* of an application can be a future end user (including yourself), your manager who requested you to write the application, the person who hired you as a software consultant or contractor, or any other stakeholder who wants a successful application.

Manning Comix

In this chapter, we'll learn how to get good requirements for an application. Then, we'll see how to analyze them to obtain the initial set of classes. Remember that requirements can change, and we must design accordingly and develop iteratively.

3.1   *The overture to application design*

Figure 3.1 shows a timeline of the major activities and milestones during the application development. The activities with the bold outlines, which are covered in this chapter, are the crucial overture to application design.

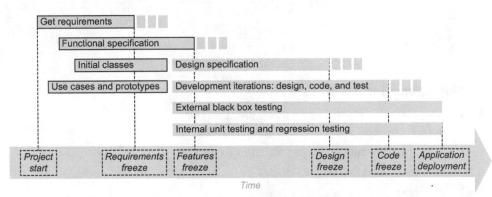

Figure 3.1   Timeline of the major activities while developing an application. The activities with the bold outlines are the crucial prelude to application design. The dotted time spans following Get Requirements and Functional Specification suggest that their freeze dates must be flexible.

Suppose a client has asked you to develop a more advanced version of the book catalogue application from chapter 2. The client has some ideas about a "book catalogue server" that stores book data in some sort of database, and library customers searching for books are provided a form interface where they fill in and submit their desired book attributes. Moreover, a special type of end user with a librarian role is responsible for adding new books to the catalogue and updating or removing existing books (figure 3.2). How can we convert these vague ideas into firm requirements to ensure that the application we eventually develop will fully satisfy the client? There are two kinds of requirements: functional and nonfunctional.

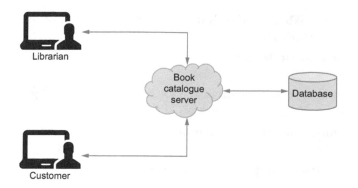

Figure 3.2   A more advanced version of the book catalogue application. A librarian interacts with the book catalogue server to enter new books into the catalogue and to update and remove existing books. A customer interacts with the server to search for books. The books are stored in a backend database.

3.2   *Functional requirements: What must the application do?*

A *functional requirement* states a specific operation that the application must do, or a specific operation that the application must allow an end user to do, to be a successful application. In chapter 2, we saw functional requirements for our example book catalogue application. Based on those requirements, a list of operations that the application must do includes

- Storing attributes for all books including the book title and the author's first and last names
- Storing year and genre attributes for fiction books, a region attribute for cookbooks, and a subject attribute for how-to books
- Performing case-insensitive string matches
- Allowing don't-care target attributes for book searches

Based on the functional requirements, a list of operations the application must allow its end users to do includes

- Adding fiction books, cookbooks, and how-to books to the catalogue
- Searching the catalogue for books that match a given set of target attributes

We can rewrite these operations as requirements using strong auxiliary verbs such as *must* and *shall*:

- A user *must* be able to add fiction books, cookbooks, and how-to books and their attributes to the catalogue.
- The attributes for each book *shall* be the book title and the author's last and first names.
- The attributes of a fiction book *shall* include its publication year and genre: adventure, classics, detective, fantasy, historic, horror, romance, or science fiction.

- The attributes of a cookbook *shall* include its region: China, France, India, Italy, Mexico, Iran, or the United States.
- The attributes of a how-to book *shall* include its subject: drawing, painting, or writing.
- A user *must* be able to search the catalogue for books that match a given set of target attributes.
- String comparisons while matching attributes during book searches *shall* be case-insensitive.
- A user *must* be able to specify don't-care attributes for book searches.

When we listen to what clients tell us and then translate their desires into written requirements, we should not create statements using weaker auxiliary verbs such as *should* or *could*.

What's wrong with the auxiliary verbs *should* and *could*?

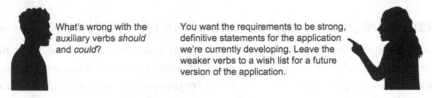

You want the requirements to be strong, definitive statements for the application we're currently developing. Leave the weaker verbs to a wish list for a future version of the application.

3.3   *Nonfunctional requirements: Constraints on the application*

A *nonfunctional requirement* imposes a specific restriction or constraint that the application must satisfy to be successful. These requirements involve issues such as performance, platforms, and maintainability.

We didn't list nonfunctional requirements in chapter 2 for our book catalogue application. Here's a list of nonfunctional requirements for the application:

- A book search must take under 2 seconds.
- The application must run on the Windows, macOS, and Linux platforms.
- The user interface shall be similar to the UI of the previous version.
- Displayed messages shall be customizable to be in English, Spanish, or Vietnamese.

Are the nonfunctional requirements less important than the functional requirements?

Absolutely not! The nonfunctional and functional requirements are equally important to build the right application.

Do not think that nonfunctional requirements are less important than functional requirements! A well-designed and fully functional application is a failure if its performance is unacceptable or if it doesn't run on the users' platforms.

Internationalization note

The last nonfunctional requirement listed above pertains to *internationalization*, sometimes abbreviated *I18N* (because, well, there are 18 letters between the initial *I* and the final *N* of the word). The process of adapting an application to a particular locale is called *localization* (*L10N*) and involves changing the natural language (English, Spanish, etc.) of text messages and making other text changes such as date, time, monetary formats, and character-encoding standards. If you're developing an internationalized application, encapsulate the affected parts of the application when the locales vary.

A requirement should not state how to design the application to meet the requirement. For example, the nonfunctional requirement about the user interface does not say to make forms of the old UI be included in the new UI. Requirements should not include design and implementation details.

Manning Comix

3.4 What are good requirements?

What makes an ideal set of requirements? Ideal requirements for developing a well-designed application themselves meet the following standards:

- *Clarity*—The requirements must be written clearly in nontechnical and jargon-free language to be understood by both the client and the software developers.
- *Consistency*—Requirements must not contradict each other. For example, we cannot have one requirement state that the application must run on Windows and macOS and another one state that the application must run only on Linux.
- *Correctness*—Each requirement must be correct. For example, a requirement for a medical application that states that the application must process pregnancy data from male patients is clearly wrong.
- *Completeness*—Any gaps in the requirements can lead to wrong guesses by the software developers and result in an application that doesn't do what the client wants.

- *Being realistic*—Do not include requirements that can't be satisfied, such as overly optimistic performance figures.
- *Being verifiable*—Will it be possible to test the application to ensure that it satisfies every requirement?
- *Traceability*—Can we trace each requirement to a functionality or constraint of the application? We don't want the application to miss satisfying any requirements. Conversely, can we trace each functionality or constraint to a requirement? We don't want to load the application with unwanted features.

Will we always get ideal requirements?

Rarely! We must expect that the requirements will change as we engage more with the client.

3.5   *How to get requirements*

How do we get requirements for an application? Where do they come from? Because requirements dictate what will make the application successful, an obvious start is to ask the client about the application. This may involve an extended set of interviews—unless it's a trivial application, it most certainly won't be a one-time interview. Ask questions and get clarifications. Is this what you want? What do you mean by that? Do you want the application to do this or that?

These requirements-gathering interviews require good interpersonal skills. We need to discover what our client wants and not introduce our own biases. We have a major bridge to gap—we assume that clients are experts in their domains (such as finance for a banking application), whereas we're the software development experts. Clients' expertise and vocabularies may not have much in common with ours.

But here's a major catch: *clients do not always know what they want!* Do not apply too much pressure to get requirements out of them, or they may start making things up. Your client may be thinking, "I'm paying these developers a lot, and they have a deadline. They won't get going unless I give them more requirements. I'd better give them *something* to make them start coding." This is a surefire way to get bad requirements, and bad requirements can only lead to bad applications.

Therefore, software developers must work hard to get requirements by other means. One way is to observe the ways people currently do their tasks and imagine how an application can improve their performance. Look at specific tasks being done manually or with legacy software and devise requirements for the application to better automate those tasks.

In some software organizations, team members such as project managers who may have better communication skills than the programmers are responsible for interviewing the client to get the initial lists of requirements. However, it's still important for the developers to have some hands-on contacts with the problems they are expected to solve.

Many meetings among the members of the development team may be necessary to decide upon the lists of functional and nonfunctional requirements. In an ideal situation, an application's client is made a virtual member of the development team to be always available to answer questions about requirements. Short of that situation, it is critical to maintain a communication channel between the developers and their client that is as open as possible. The feedback loop between the client and the development team must be tight and constantly active.

3.5.1 A short requirements case study

Figure 3.3 shows a simple scenario. Public libraries used to have card catalogues, which were physical banks of drawers that held index cards containing the attributes of the books in the library. The cards were alphabetized by book title, author's last name, and subject. Therefore, each book required at least three cards. Each drawer was labeled by the range of the alphabet of the cards it held. A library customer looking for a book would consult the card catalogue to see if the library had the book, and if so, the cards indicated where to find it. Librarians maintained the card catalogue. It was a very manual process for both the librarians and the customers. Therefore, our client, the head librarian, hired us to automate the catalogue.

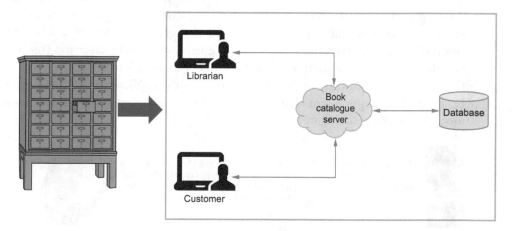

Figure 3.3 To automate a library's old-fashioned card catalogue with a software application, you must first get the requirements to develop the right application.

We must first get the requirements from the client to develop the right application. We interview the head librarian to learn how the librarians maintain the card catalogue and to ask what they think we can do to improve their work. We also interview the library's customers to understand how they search for books in the card catalogue and to ask what we can do to improve their searches. But perhaps the librarians may only be able to suggest incremental improvements to their work, such as an online form to create and print cards for the drawers. Similarly, the library's customers may not have the imagination to come up with better searching methods. Therefore, we must observe the librarians working and the customers searching and apply our experience with computer-based applications to come up with more requirements. We can create and show prototypes of the new application to inspire better requirements. Getting requirements is another iterative process.

The librarians only suggested incremental improvements to their current processes.

We'll get much better requirements after closely observing how the librarians work and showing them some prototypes of the application.

3.5.2 Stated and implied requirements

The librarians and customers provide *stated* application requirements. By reading between the lines, we can conceive *implied* requirements. Yes, our interviewees said that requirements A and C are needed. But we know from our own experience (or common sense) that they will also need requirement B to properly automate their operations.

On the timeline in figure 3.1, the client and the developers must agree on the date labeled "Requirements freeze." Presumably, there will be no more changes to the requirements after that date. But often, the collected requirements are less than ideal, so then we should expect they may still change, and there may still be additional requirements. However, the requirements must settle shortly after the freeze date to enable software design to stabilize and ultimately to complete the application on time. Good application design encapsulates the parts of the application that are most likely to be affected by requirement changes. A well-designed application is flexible enough to incorporate any resulting new code.

Why have freeze dates if we're just going to ignore them?

We don't ignore them! They are important milestone dates for our project. If we miss a milestone by too much, that's a warning that our project might be late.

Software engineering

Requirements gathering and analysis is a major topic within the broader subject of software engineering. Software engineering covers project-level topics, including project management and schedules; development methodologies (such as extreme programming and test-driven development); enterprise application architectures; tools for task management, bug tracking, and software revision control; testing strategies; project documentation; product deployment and maintenance; and other topics. Software engineering in general, other than the topic of software design, is outside the scope of this book.

Entire books have been written about how to gather and analyze software requirements. This book can only give a brief outline of the process.

3.6 Unified Modeling Language diagrams for creating and documenting design

The Unified Modeling Language (UML) is an industry-standard family of diagrams to help software developers design an application and document the design. The following section covers UML use case diagrams that describe to both the application's client and its developers how an end user will interact with the application. Chapter 4 covers UML class, state, and sequence diagrams that further document the application's design.

UML diagramming is a useful skill in every software developer's repertoire. Not only are the diagrams important for documenting an application's design, but their visual nature makes them very helpful during software designing and coding.

NOTE Most of the popular computer-based drawing tools provide palettes of the UML objects. During the development iterations, the diagrams are easy to create and manipulate to keep track of an application's evolving design.

3.7 Use cases provide context for the requirements

The lists of functional and nonfunctional requirements for an application are parts of the documentation that the development team writes to describe the application. Use cases provide context for the requirements and show how they determine the application's runtime behavior.

A use case describes how an end user of the application, often with a specified role (such as our book catalogue application's customer or librarian), will perform a sequence of actions to achieve a particular goal. Therefore, we write it from the point of view of that user. Since users can interact with the application in different ways to achieve various goals, we will need multiple use cases to cover the major goals.

Documentation of use cases typically consists of two parts. First, a UML *use case diagram* groups together several related use cases and shows which users interact with which use cases. The second part consists of a written *use case description* for each use case.

3.7.1 UML use case diagram

Figure 3.4 shows an example use case diagram for an advanced version of our book catalogue application. In this version, a backend database stores the books and their attributes.

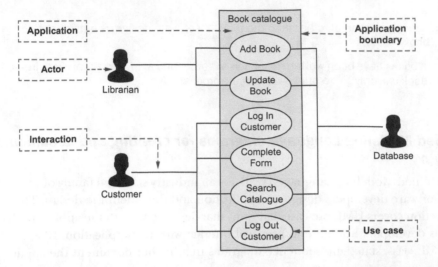

Figure 3.4 **A UML use case diagram containing the names of six use cases for an advanced version of our book catalogue application. The labels in the dashed boxes and the dashed arrows indicate the various components of the diagram. When drawing a use case diagram, do not include these labels and arrows.**

The diagram shows the names of several use cases and how various actors interact with them. The box that encloses the use cases represents the application and its boundary—it's important to know what's in the application and what's not. The name of each use case should be short and descriptive in a verb–noun form, such as "Add Book" and "Log in customer." The figures represent actors who interact with the use cases. An *actor* is any agent external to the application that interacts with the application, and it can be a person (such as the librarian and the customer) or another application or system (such as the database system). The interaction lines indicate which use cases each actor can interact with.

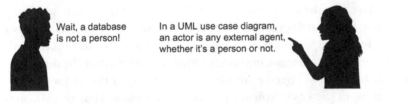

A large application may have many use case diagrams, each containing a small number (at most about a half dozen) of use cases.

3.7.2   *Use case description*

Use cases provide context for the application's requirements. They show how the functional requirements determine the functionality of the application, and they also show which nonfunctional requirements ensure that the functionality will be practical.

We write a separate use case description for each use case in the use case diagrams. This description provides detailed information about the use case:

- *Name of the use case*—It should be short and descriptive in a verb–noun form.
- *Goal*—What is the actor trying to achieve?
- *Summary of the use case*—A short (one or two sentences) description.
- *Actors*—Who or what interacts with this use case?
- *Preconditions*—What must be true, or what must have already happened, before this use case can go into action? References to other use cases can appear here.
- *Trigger*—What did an actor do to start this use case? Write the following sequence of action steps from the point of view of this actor.
- *Primary action sequence*—A sequence of action steps that occur during this use case between the triggering actor (and any other actors) and the application. There should be no more than about 10 steps. If you need more steps, the use case may be too complex and should be broken up. The steps can refer to other use cases.
- *Alternate action sequences*—What action steps should occur if something goes wrong during the primary sequence?
- *Postconditions*—What will be the situation when this use case is finished?
- *Nonfunctional requirements*—Which nonfunctional requirements apply to this use case?
- *Glossary*—Define any terms in this use case that a reader may find confusing.

Write each use case from the point of view of the actor that triggers the use case.

Here is an example of a use case description for the advanced version of our book catalogue application. The customer fills out an online form that includes a "Search" button to specify the desired target book attributes to do a book search.

- *Name of the use case*—Search Catalogue.
- *Goal*—Search the book catalogue for books that match the customer's target attributes.
- *Summary of the use case*—The customer searches the book catalogue using a set of target book attributes, and the catalogue returns a list of any books that match those attributes.
- *Actors*—The customer and the backend database.
- *Preconditions*—Books and their attributes are already loaded into the catalogue. See the use case Add Book. The customer has completed filling the Attributes form with the target book attributes. See the use case Complete Form.
- *Trigger*—The customer presses the "Search" button.
- *Primary action sequence:*
  1. The application verifies that the Attributes form is correctly filled out.

2. The application formulates a database query from the book attributes in the form.

3. The application sends the query to the backend database server.

4. The database returns a list of matching books to the application.

5. The application formats the list of matching books for presentation.

6. The customer sees the list of matching books.

- *Alternate action sequence 1*—Incorrectly filled form. Replace primary sequence steps 2–6.

2. Highlight the incorrect form field.

3. Display an explanatory error message.

4. The customer corrects the erroneous form field.

5. Return to primary sequence step 1.

- *Alternate action sequence 2*—No matching books. Replace primary sequence steps 4–6.

4. The database returns an empty list.

5. The application displays "No books found."

- *Postconditions*—The customer sees either a list of matching books or the message "No books found." There were no changes to the book catalogue.

- *Nonfunctional requirements:*
  - Search results must return in under 2 seconds.
  - The customer shall be on a Windows, macOS, or Linux platform.
  - The application must be usable by a customer whose native language is English, Spanish, or Vietnamese.

- *Glossary:*
  - *Catalogue*—A searchable repository of books and their attributes
  - *Attribute*—A feature of a book that can be matched during a search, such as the book title or the author's name
  - *Customer*—A user who searches the book catalogue

Use case descriptions should be short, simple, and informal. Both the application's clients and its developers need to understand them. Therefore, we should not use overly technical language. There should be no implementation details. We must concentrate on what the application needs to do in response to an actor's triggering action, not how the application will do it.

Requirements come from a continuous engagement with the client of the application. Write down the requirements that are known so far and create use cases. The use cases illustrate for the client how the application will behave under various scenarios. This can inspire more requirements. New requirements may, in turn, require new use cases. There may be several rounds of adding new requirements and creating new use cases. A substantial application with a rich set of actor interactions can have dozens of use cases.

A powerful way to elicit requirements is to show the client a prototype of the application. This can be some quick-and-dirty code that shows a few key use cases in action. Seeing a tangible piece of working code, however hacked together, will often inspire the client to point out what's missing or superfluous, or what doesn't work in a desired way. This prototype can be as simple as a deck of slides containing simulated screenshots of the application as it's being used. We then capture comments and observations by the client in new requirements, or we modify existing ones.

3.8 *The functional specification and software validation*

The development team writes a *functional specification* to document the application it's about to create. Its purpose is to inform both the application's client and the developers in nontechnical, jargon-free language.

> **NOTE** The format and contents of the functional specification are usually determined by the client's organization. Different organizations might give the document different names, such as External Reference Specification. It's external because this document views the application from the outside. It should contain no internal implementation details. Implementation details belong in the design specification covered in chapter 4.

The functional specification should include the following content:

- *Application name*—For example, Book Catalogue.
- *Clear problem statement*—What is the problem that this application addresses? For example, the ability to store and search for books.
- *Objectives*—What is the application supposed to accomplish? For example, to create a means to enter books into a repository and then search for them using target book attributes.
- *Functional requirements*—A list of the functional requirements. The requirements should be stated strongly with the auxiliary verbs *must* or *shall.*
- *Nonfunctional requirements*—A list of the nonfunctional requirements. The requirements should be stated strongly with the auxiliary verbs *must* or *shall.*
- *Use cases*—UML use case diagrams and a use description for each use case.

A functional specification can also include an external test plan, a deployment plan, and a maintenance plan. These are often separate documents.

If it's included, the external test plan should describe black-box tests. These are tests that are doable without knowing the internals of the application code. For each test, the test plan describes what the input data or user action should be and the expected result. Black-box testing helps to verify that an application meets its functional and nonfunctional requirements. Such tests are often run by test engineers who were not part of the development team.

"Black box" sounds ominous.

It simply means we should treat the code we're testing as something we can't look inside to see how it's implemented.

How elaborate should the functional specification be? That often depends on the client's organization and the development methodology. Some organizations and methodologies place less emphasis on documentation and favor prototyping and tighter engagement with the client. Other organizations regard the functional specification to be such an important document that they go to the extreme of considering it to be a contract between the client and the software developers. They may require multiple levels of management to sign off a complete functional specification and then deem it frozen before allowing the developers to move on to designing the application.

But ideally, as suggested in figure 3.1 by the dotted time span, we should be allowed to modify the functional specification when we need to tweak requirements or discover new ones during application design and coding. It should be modifiable up to a certain point in time, often called the "features freeze," agreed to by the developers and the client. Even though it's initially moveable, the functional specification serves as an important stake in the ground for both the developers and the client.

Regardless of whether it rises to the level of a contract, it is critical that the client of the application carefully read the functional specification, which should have no implementation details. By reading, understanding, and approving the functional specification, the client *validates* the application, that is, confirms that we are going to build the right application, one that meets the client's requirements.

Once the application is validated (remember that clients can still change their minds about the requirements), we can begin the design–code–test iterations. Testing is *verification* that we are building the software right—that we are implementing bug-free code to fulfill each and every requirement.

NOTE   Software verification and validation (software V&V) is a major topic in the fields of software engineering and software quality control.

3.9   *Where do classes come from?*

Once we have at least the first draft of the functional specification, we can start to think about the classes of the application. To create the initial set of classes, analyze the application's functional requirements. Requirements analysis, the process of carefully examining an application's requirements during design, is a major software engineering topic. The rest of this chapter covers its most important points.

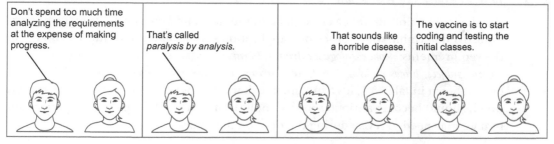

Here is an extended set of functional requirements for the more advanced version of our book catalogue application from chapter 2. Recall that functional requirements state what an application must do or allow a user to do:

- The book catalogue shall store different kinds of books and their attributes.
- A librarian must be able to add new books to the catalogue.
- A librarian must be able to update and delete existing books in the catalogue.
- The kinds of books shall include fiction, cookbooks, and how-to.
- All books must have title, author's last name, and author's first name attribute values.
- Fiction books must include the publication year and genre attributes.
- Genre must include adventure, classics, detective, fantasy, historic, horror, romance, and science fiction.
- Cookbooks must include the region attribute.
- How-to books must include the subject attribute.
- A customer must be able to search the catalogue by providing any number of desired target attribute values.
- A customer must complete a web browser-based form to specify target attribute values for book searches.
- A customer's input in the form must be verified for correct format and values.
- During searches, string attribute matches must be case-insensitive.
- A customer must be able to specify any number of don't-care (wildcard) target attributes.
- Each don't-care attribute must, by default, match the corresponding attribute in all books in the catalogue.
- A book in the catalogue shall match if it has all the attributes in the customer's target attributes and all the corresponding book and target attribute values are equal, or the target attribute is a don't-care.

3.9.1   *Textual analysis: Nouns can become classes*

Recall from section 1.8 that a class specifies the state and behavior of its objects at run time. To determine what classes our application should have, first find the nouns in the requirements: *book, catalogue, attribute, librarian, customer, kind, title, name, year, genre, region, subject, browser, form, input,* and *string.* The nouns represent potential classes, but as shown in table 3.1, it's a judgment call which nouns should become classes and which should become attributes in our application. This is the type of design decision that we may need to revisit during the development iterations.

Table 3.1   Decide whether each noun of the requirements should be a class.

Noun	Class?
catalogue	Yes. The application implements a book catalogue.
Book	Yes. The catalogue stores book objects.
attribute	Yes. Each book object has a set of attributes.
librarian	No. According to figure 3.4, a librarian is an agent outside of the application.
customer	No. According to figure 3.4, a customer is an agent outside of the application.
kind	No. It is an attribute value that is an enumeration constant.
title	No. It is an attribute value that is a string.
name	No. It is an attribute value that is a string.
year	No. It is an attribute value that is an integer.
genre	No. It is an attribute value that is an enumeration constant.
region	No. It is an attribute value that is an enumeration constant.
subject	No. It is an attribute value that is an enumeration constant.
browser	No. The application works with existing browsers.
form	Yes. The application manages a user input form.
input	No. It is an attribute value entered by a user into a form.
format	No. A format isn't a separate thing in the application.
value	No. An attribute value is an integer, string, or enumeration constant.
string	No. The application uses built-in C++ strings.

We are left with these nouns that can become the initial classes in our application: *catalogue, book, attribute,* and *form.* For each class, we must determine its member variables so that its objects can maintain state at run time. Table 3.2 can be the result after several design iterations like the ones described in chapter 2. Later iterations can discover more classes.

Table 3.2 The initial classes of the application

Class	State	Member variables
Catalogue	List of books	booklist (vector of pointers to Book objects)
Book	Book attributes	attributes (pointer to the book's attributes)
Attributes	Attribute values	attribute_map (map of key–value pairs)
Form	Input values	individual member variables for the book attributes

3.9.2 Textual analysis: Verbs can become member functions

Next, we must determine the runtime behavior of each class's objects from the verbs in the requirements: *store, add, update, delete, include, have, be, search, complete, verify, constitute, specify,* and *match.* We should consider only (transitive) verbs that perform some action on an object. Like table 3.2, table 3.3 can be the result after several design iterations.

Table 3.3 Determine the behavior of each class.

Verb	Class	Member function
add	Catalogue	add() a book to the booklist
update	Catalogue	update() a book in the booklist
delete	Catalogue	delete() a book from the booklist
search	Catalogue	find() matching books in the booklist
verify	Form	verify() user input in the form fields
match	Attributes	is_match() check if attribute pairs match

Each class's member functions work with that class's member variables. For example, in class Catalogue, the add() member function adds pointers to Book objects to the booklist member variable.

So, did the textual analysis give us all the classes that we'll need?

Absolutely not! These are just our initial classes. We'll come up with more classes during our development iterations.

Now that we have some initial classes, we need to make sure to design them and any subsequent classes well. That's the topic of the next chapters.

Summary

- Functional requirements state what an application must do, or allow a user to do, for the application to be successful.

- Nonfunctional requirements impose restrictions or constraints that the application must meet to be successful. They are just as important as functional requirements. Examples are performance or platform requirements.

- State requirements using the strong verbs *must* and *shall*.

- Getting good requirements is crucial. Interview the application's clients or observe how people currently perform their tasks. Create prototypes of the application to show to the clients. Imagine ways an application can improve their productivity.

- Requirements come from a continuous engagement with clients, who may not always know what they want. Be prepared for the requirements to change during application design and even during coding.

- Good requirements are clear, consistent, correct, complete, realistic, verifiable, and traceable.

- Use cases provide context for the requirements and show how they determine the application's functionality. Document the use cases with UML use case diagrams and use case descriptions. Use cases can inspire new requirements.

- A functional specification written in nontechnical, jargon-free language informs both the clients and the software developers what the application will do. It can include an external test plan for black-box testing. Some organizations consider this document to be a contract between clients and developers. Ideally, it should be modifiable (up until the features freeze milestone) to accommodate changes to the requirements.

- Clients validate that the software developers are going to build the right application by approving the functional specification. The developers verify that they are building the application right through testing. Software verification and validation (software V&V) is a major topic in the fields of software engineering and software quality control.

- Analyze the requirements to obtain the initial set of classes for the application. Determine which nouns become classes and which verbs become member functions that implement behavior. Assign member variables and member functions to the classes.

- Don't fall victim to paralysis by analysis. Create and show prototypes, start the development iterations, and more classes will arise.

Good class design to build the application right

This chapter covers

- The place of design in the application development process
- How to design classes well
- UML diagrams to aid class design
- The design specification

In chapter 3, we worked with our clients on the functional and nonfunctional requirements to ensure that we build the *right* application. Simple textual analysis produced our initial set of classes. In this chapter, we begin to design the classes well to ensure that we build the application *right*.

In chapter 1, we learned that design is a disciplined engineering approach to create a solution to a problem. For software development, that means applying good software design techniques to find the best development path to a well-designed application that meets its requirements. In chapter 2, we saw that the development path requires iterations and, most likely, backtracking.

This chapter discusses where application design fits within the overall development process. It covers some basic guidelines for good class design. Because most applications consist of multiple classes, we'll also examine how the classes can relate to each other. Chapter 3 introduced UML (Unified Modeling Language) use case diagrams. To document our class design, we'll use more of these industry-standard diagrams. Finally, a design specification pulls together all the design documentation for an application.

4.1   When do we do application design?

A major application is often created by several software developers working together as a team, with various activities overlapping over time. This chapter covers the design activities with the bold borders in figure 4.1.

Application design occurs during nearly the entire project. As we saw in chapter 3, we must first get the application's requirements. Creating use cases and prototypes help to elicit requirements. The Functional Specification documents the requirements and use cases. We can choose the application's initial classes from its requirements. Some of the prototypes may result in more classes. Most of the application design subsequently occurs during the development iterations, where we expand and refine the initial set of classes. This chapter covers how to document our class design for our own benefit and for the design specification.

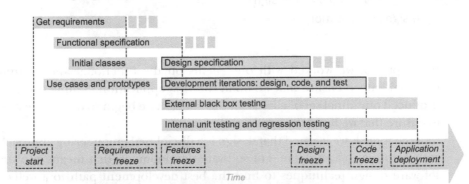

Figure 4.1   **Creating an application involves many activities. This diagram shows when the activities start relative to each other and how they overlap in time. However, it does not show their relative durations. The major project milestones are presented at the bottom. Most of the application design occurs during the development iterations. The design specification documents our design. This diagram shows these activities with heavy borders. Their dotted timespans suggest that their freeze dates must be flexible.**

Both external black box testing (described in chapter 3) and internal testing (described later in this chapter) occur in parallel with the development iterations.

The bottom of the diagram shows milestone dates, such as "Project Start," "Requirements Freeze," "Features Freeze," and so forth, that a project schedule maintains. These are goals that the project team should meet to get an application deployed on time. However, many projects slip their freeze milestones. For example, the project manager may agree that new requirements are important enough to be included in the project past the requirements' freeze milestone. If we allow a project to slip much past a milestone freeze date, we greatly increase the risk of not completing the project on time.

4.2 Two important goals for good class design

In chapter 3, we saw how performing a textual analysis of the requirements gives us a good start at determining our application's classes. But how can we be certain that we've put the member variables and member functions in the right classes? When we design classes, there are two important goals: cohesion and loose coupling.

4.2.1 Cohesion and the Single Responsibility Principle

A class is cohesive if it adheres to the Single Responsibility Principle (section 2.3.1). A well-designed class should have only one primary responsibility. Here's an example. Suppose that in an application about cars, we have a class `AutomobileApp`.

Listing 4.1 **(Program 4.1 Automobile-1):** `AutomobileApp.h` **(not cohesive)**

```
class AutomobileApp
{
public:
    void accelerate();
    void adjust_headlights();
    void apply_brakes();
    void change_oil();
    void change_tires();
    void check_brakes();
    void check_tires();
    void rotate_tires();
    void shut_off_engine();          Behaviors
    void start_engine();
    void tuneup_engine();
    void turn_left();
    void turn_right();
    void vacuum_car();
    void wash_car();
    void wax_car();

private:
    Brake brakes[4];
    Engine engine;
    Oil engine_oil;                  State information
    Direction heading;
    Headlight headlights[4];
```

```
    int speed;
    Soap soap;
    Tire tires[4];                          State information
    Vacuum vacuum_cleaner;
    CarWax wax;
};
```

This class is not cohesive because it has too many state and behavior responsibilities:

- automobile operation
  - *state*—brakes, engine, heading, speed
  - *behavior*—accelerate(), apply_brakes(), shut_off_engine(), start_engine(), turn_left(), turn_right()
- automobile maintenance
  - *state*—engine_oil, headlights, tires
  - *behavior*—adjust_headlights(), change_oil(), change_tires(), check_brakes(), check_tires(), rotate_tires(), tuneup_engine()
- automobile cleaning
  - *state*—soap, vacuum_cleaner, wax
  - *behavior*— vacuum_car(), wash_car(), wax_car()

We need to break class AutomobileApp into smaller classes, each of which has a single primary responsibility.

Listing 4.2   (Program 4.2 Automobile-2): Automobile.h (cohesive)

```
class Automobile
{
public:
    void accelerate();
    void apply_brakes();
    void shut_off_engine();              Automobile operation
    void start_engine();                 behaviors
    void turn_left();
    void turn_right();

private:
    Brake brakes[4];
    Direction heading;
    Headlight headlights[4];
    int speed;
    Tire tires[4];
};

class Garage
{
public:
    Garage(Automobile *c) : car(c) {}
```

```
    void adjust_headlights();
    void change_oil();
    void change_tires();                              Garage maintenance
    void check_brakes();                              behaviors
    void check_tires();
    void rotate_tires();
    void tuneup_engine();

private:
    Automobile *car;

    Oil new_oil;
    vector<Tire> new_tires;
};

class CarWash
{
public:
    CarWash(Automobile *c) : car(c) {}

    void vacuum_car();                                Carwash cleaning
    void wash_car();                                  behaviors
    void wax_car();

private:
    Automobile *car;

    Soap soap;
    Vacuum vacuum_cleaner;
    CarWax wax;
};
```

Each of these classes is cohesive with a single primary responsibility. Class `Automobile` is responsible for automobile operations. Class `Garage` is responsible for automobile maintenance. Class `CarWash` is responsible for automobile cleaning. The latter two classes each has a pointer to the `Automobile` object. The Single Responsibility Principle is important for good class design. If changes are necessary, a cohesive class should have only one reason to change.

Manning Comix

4.2.2   *Loose coupling and the Principle of Least Knowledge*

Loosely coupled classes have minimal dependencies on each other. Class A is dependent on class B if class A has references to class B. For example, class Garage depends on class Automobile because its member variable car points to an Automobile object.

Loosely coupled classes adhere to the Principle of Least Knowledge (section 2.3.2), which supports encapsulation. The less class A knows about the internal implementation details of class B, the less likely changes to class B will affect class A.

Manning Comix

We saw an example of the Principle of Least Knowledge in chapter 2. The dependency that class Catalogue (partially reproduced in listing 4.3) has on class Attributes was only through pointers and references to Attributes objects, and therefore class Catalogue has no knowledge of how class Attributes implements the book attributes.

Listing 4.3   (Program 2.4 Books-4): Catalogue.h

```
class Catalogue
{
public:                                                    Pointer to an
    void add(Attributes * const attrs);                    Attributes
                                                           object

    vector<Book *> find(const Attributes& target_attrs) const;

private:                                                   Reference to
    vector<Book *> booklist;                               an Attributes object
};
```

Class Attributes (partially reproduced in listing 4.4) has no dependencies at all on class Catalogue. It has no member variables, function parameters, or member functions with local variables that point to or refer to Catalogue objects. Therefore, Attributes objects do not know that they are ultimately stored in a Catalogue object. Even though class Catalogue delegates attribute matching to class Attributes by calling the latter's Boolean is_match() member function, class Attributes does not know who is calling that function.

Listing 4.4 (Program 2.4 Books-4): `Attributes.h`

```cpp
class Attributes
{
public:
    Attributes(AttributeMap *const pairs);
    ~Attributes() { delete attribute_map; }

    bool is_match(const Attributes& target_attrs) const;

    friend ostream& operator <<(ostream& ostr,
                                const Attributes& attrs);

private:
    AttributeMap *attribute_map;

    bool is_matching_pair(const Key& target_key,
                          const AttributeValue& target_value) const;

    static bool equal_ignore_case(const string string1,
                                  const string string2) ...
};
```

Classes `Catalogue` and `Attributes` are loosely coupled. We saw how loose coupling encapsulates any changes in class `Attributes` from affecting class `Catalogue`. Loose coupling and the Principle of Least Knowledge are important for good class design.

Manning Comix

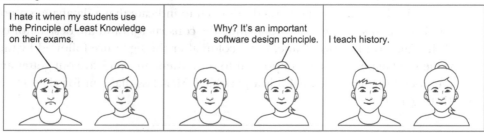

4.3 *UML class diagrams to document class design*

We saw UML use case diagrams in chapter 3. UML class diagrams document class design. A class diagram consists of at least the name of the class. Optionally, it includes the names and datatypes of the class's member variables and the *signature* of its member functions. A function's signature consists of the name of the function, the name and datatype of each parameter, and the datatype of the return value.

NOTE Google "UML drawing tools" for tools to draw these diagrams. Some of the tools are free.

Figure 4.2 shows four possible UML class diagrams for the class Catalogue (listing 4.3). The first diagram only shows the class name. The second diagram includes the member variables but not the member functions. The third diagram includes the member functions in the bottom section but not the member variables in the empty middle section. The fourth diagram includes the member variables (middle section) and the member functions (bottom section). The selection of diagram depends on how much detail about the class we need to show. A diagram in a high-level description of the application could show less than a diagram in a low-level description.

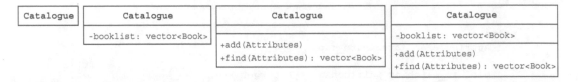

Figure 4.2   Possible UML class diagrams for class Catalogue **that include different amounts of information. A plus sign (+) indicates public, and a minus sign (-) indicates private. How much information to include in a class diagram depends on whether the diagram is in high-level or low-level design documentation of the application.**

The minus sign (-) in front of a name indicates that the member is private, and the plus sign (+) that the member is public. We can also use the hashtag (#) for protected members, which are only accessible by a class's subclasses. The datatype of a member variable follows the name and a colon. The signature of each member function does not need to include every detail about the parameters; we only show their datatypes. Unless it's important to show, we don't need to indicate that a datatype is a pointer or a reference. It's not necessary to include the constructors and the destructor of a class. If the function returns a value, put a colon after the signature followed by the return value's datatype. Unless it's important to show them, we can leave out getter and setter member functions. Figure 4.3 is a possible UML class diagram for class Attributes (listing 4.4).

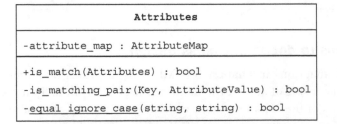

Figure 4.3   A UML class diagram for class Attributes **that includes all three parts: its name, member variables, and member functions. Private member** function equal_ignore_case() **is underlined to indicate that it is static. This diagram is suitable for detailed design documentation.**

4.4   Class relationships determine runtime interactions

Most applications consist of multiple classes, especially if they are well-designed, cohesive classes. The relationship between two classes determines how their objects can interact at run time. Therefore, it's important during class design to get the relationships right.

A class diagram that includes an application's classes should also indicate the relationships among them by connecting the diagrams with lines. Figure 2.5 in chapter 2, also reproduced in figure 4.4, is such a diagram.

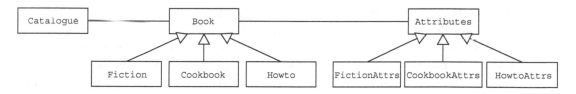

Figure 4.4   A UML class diagram that shows an application's multiple classes and their relationships. The relationship between two classes determines how their instantiated objects can interact at run time.

Table 4.1 at the end of section 4.4.4 will summarize the ways to specify the different relationships with class diagrams.

4.4.1   Dependency: The most basic relationship

A line connecting two classes, like the one between `Book` and `Attributes` in figure 4.4, represents a dependency relationship. Just as we can choose the amount of information to show for each class, we can also choose how much information to show about each relationship. A simple line between two classes indicates an unspecified dependency relationship. This gives the least amount of relationship information. An arrowhead clarifies who depends on whom. In figure 4.5, class `Catalogue` depends on class `Book`, but class `Book` does not depend on class `Catalogue`.

Figure 4.5   A UML diagram that shows (left to right) class `Catalogue`, a relationship, and class `Book`. The dependency relationship arrow going from class `Catalogue` to class `Book` indicates that class `Catalogue` depends on class `Book`. But class `Book` does not depend on class `Catalogue`.

If we want to include more information about a relationship between two classes, we can label the dependency arrows (figure 4.6). For example, member variable `booklist` of class `Catalogue` is a vector of pointers to `Book` objects (listing 4.3). When we label a relationship arrow with the member variable name, we don't include the name in the middle section of the class diagram. Figure 4.6 also indicates multiplicity: a single (1) `booklist` in a `Catalogue` object will contain zero or more (*) `Book` objects. A plus (+) means one or more. When it's appropriate, we can replace a * or a + with a specific number. At either end of the relationship, we can even indicate a range of numbers like 2..5.

Catalogue	1 -booklist *	Book
+add(Attributes) +find(Attributes) : vector<Book>		-attributes : Attributes
		+get_attributes() : Attributes

Figure 4.6   Diagrams that show more design detail. Class `Catalogue` **depends on class** `Book` **via its private** `booklist` **member variable. The multiplicity indicators show that a single (1)** `Catalogue` **object can contain zero or more (*)** `Book` **objects.**

A dependency relationship is *transient* if class A has a member function f that has a parameter or a local variable that references class B. However, class A does not have a member variable that references class B. The relationship is transient because it exists only during a call to function f. In class `Catalogue` (listing 4.3), the `add()` member function receives a pointer to an `Attributes` object, and the `find()` member function is passed a reference to an `Attributes` object. But class `Catalogue` does not have an `Attributes` member variable. Therefore, the dependency on class `Attributes` exists only during a call to `add()` or to `find()`. Figure 4.7 shows this transient dependency relationship with the dashed arrow.

Figure 4.7   Class `Catalogue` **has a transient dependency relationship on class** `Attributes`, **as shown by the dashed dependency arrow. The** `add()` **member function of class** `Catalogue` **receives a pointer to an** `Attributes` **object and the** `find()` **member function is passed a reference to an** `Attributes` **object. The dependency exists only during calls to these functions.**

4.4.2   Aggregation and composition: Objects that contain other objects

UML class diagrams can be more precise in terms of the nature of a dependency. When a class aggregates (contains) another class, such as by having a member variable that points to the other class, we can use the aggregation arrow that has an open diamond at the tail end next to the diagram for the container class (there is no arrowhead). Figure 4.8 explicitly shows that class `Catalogue` aggregates class `Book`. Each `Catalogue` object contains zero or more `Book` objects. In this example, we chose to include the information that `booklist` is a vector of `Book` objects.

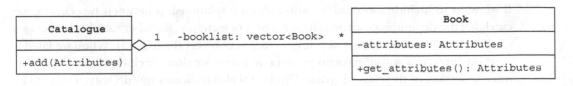

Figure 4.8   Class `Catalogue` **aggregates class** `Book`. **Each** `Catalogue` **object contains zero or more** `Book` **objects in a vector member variable named** `booklist`. **The open diamond at the tail of the dependency arrow is next to the diagram for the container class** `Catalogue`.

We can be even more precise about an aggregation relationship. A UML class diagram indicates a composition type of aggregation with a filled-in diamond at the tail of the arrow (figure 4.9).

Composition is a stronger form of aggregation. We can choose to specify composition if, according to the logic of the application, the object that's a part of the composition cannot exist outside of its container. In figure 4.9, an `Attributes` object cannot exist without its `Book` object. The destructor for a `Book` object should delete any `Attributes` object that it points to, so that when we delete a `Book` object, its `Attributes` object is deleted at the same time:

```
virtual ~Book() { delete attrs; }
```

In contrast, with the `Catalogue-Book` aggregation, a `Book` object can exist outside of a `Catalogue` object.

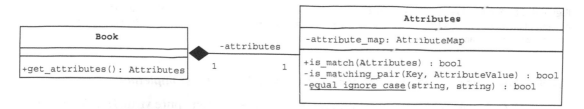

Figure 4.9 Class `Book` is composed of class `Attributes`. Each `Book` object has one `Attributes` object. According to the logic of the application, an `Attributes` object cannot exist without being a part of a `Book` object. The destructor for a `Book` object should delete any `Attributes` object that it points to.

Figure 4.10 shows both an aggregation relationship and a composition relationship to illustrate their difference. According to the logic of a hypothetical application, `Book` objects are contained by `Bookshelf` objects, but `Book` objects can exist outside of `Bookshelf` objects. A `Bookcase` object is composed of `Bookshelf` objects, but a `Bookshelf` object cannot exist without being a part of a `Bookcase` object.

Figure 4.10 The difference between aggregation and composition. In this diagram, each `Bookshelf` object can contain 0 through 25 `Book` objects, and `Book` objects can exist outside of `Bookshelf` objects. Each `Bookcase` object is composed of 1 through 5 `Bookshelf` objects, but a `Bookshelf` object cannot exist without being a part of a `Bookcase` object.

4.4.3 Generalization: Superclasses and their subclasses

The generalization relationship involves superclasses, subclasses, and inheritance. The general class is the superclass.

After three development iterations of our book catalogue application in chapter 2, we had designed (poorly, as it turned out) a `Book` superclass and `Fiction`, `Cookbook`, and `Howto` subclasses. A UML diagram shows a superclass–subclass relationship with an arrow going from the subclass to the superclass, and the arrowhead is an open triangle against the superclass. Figure 4.11 also shows superclass `Attributes` and its subclasses `FictionAttrs`, `CookbookAttrs`, and `HowtoAttrs` with a different way of drawing the arrows. We can choose the way to draw the arrows depending on which looks the best for a diagram.

Figure 4.11 Superclass `Book` has subclasses `Fiction`, `Cookbook`, and `Howto`. Also, superclass `Attributes` has subclasses `FictionAttrs`, `CookbookAttrs`, and `HowtoAttrs`. This figure shows two ways of drawing generalization diagrams.

4.4.4   *Abstract classes and interfaces: What subclasses must implement*

A C++ class is abstract if it contains at least one abstract (pure virtual) member function. Listing 4.5 shows abstract class `MotorVehicle` with two abstract member functions `start_engine()` and `stop_engine()`. We then must implement these two functions in subclasses such as `Car` and `Truck`. Class `MotorVehicle` provides default implementations of member functions `accelerate()`, `turn_left()`, `turn_right()`, `apply_brakes()`, and `drive()` that the subclasses can choose whether to override.

Listing 4.5   (Program 4.3 VehicleAbstract): `MotorVehicle.h`

```
#include <iostream>

using namespace std;

typedef int Brake;
typedef int Direction;
typedef int Engine;

class MotorVehicle
{
public:
    virtual ~MotorVehicle() {}

    virtual void start_engine() = 0;          Abstract member
    virtual void stop_engine() = 0;           functions

    virtual void accelerate()
    {
        cout << "vehicle accelerates" << endl;
    }
```

```
    virtual void turn_left()
    {
        cout << "vehicle turns left" << endl;
    }

    virtual void turn_right()
    {
        cout << "vehicle turns right" << endl;
    }

    virtual void apply_brakes()
    {
        cout << "vehicle applies brakes" << endl;
    }

    virtual void drive()
    {
        start_engine();
        accelerate();
        turn_left();
        turn_right();
        apply_brakes();
        stop_engine();

        cout << endl;
    }

private:
    Brake brakes[4];
    Engine engine;
    Direction heading;
    int speed;
};
```

Subclass `Car` privately implements member functions `start_engine()` and `stop_engine()`, and it inherits the remaining member functions from its superclass `MotorVehicle`.

> **Listing 4.6   (Program 4.3 VehicleAbstract):** `Car.h`

```
#include <iostream>
#include "MotorVehicle.h"

using namespace std;

class Car : public MotorVehicle
{
public:
    virtual ~Car() {}

private:
    virtual void start_engine() override
    {
        cout << "car starts engine" << endl;
    }
```

```
    virtual void stop_engine() override
    {
        cout << "car stops engine" << endl;
    }
};
```

Subclass `Truck` privately implements member functions `start_engine()` and `stop_engine()`. It also privately overrides the superclass implementations of member functions `turn_left()` and `turn_right()`.

Listing 4.7   (Program 4.3 VehicleAbstract): `Truck.h`

```cpp
#include <iostream>
#include "MotorVehicle.h"

using namespace std;

class Truck : public MotorVehicle
{
public:
    virtual ~Truck() {}

private:
    virtual void start_engine() override
    {
        cout << "truck starts engine" << endl;
    }

    virtual void stop_engine() override
    {
        cout << "truck stops engine" << endl;
    }

    virtual void turn_left() override
    {
        cout << "truck turns left" << endl;
    }

    virtual void turn_right() override
    {
        cout << "truck turns right" << endl;
    }
};
```

Figure 4.12 shows that in the UML class diagram for this example program, we indicate that a class is abstract by printing its name in italics or a slanted font. We also print the name of an abstract function in italics or a slanted font.

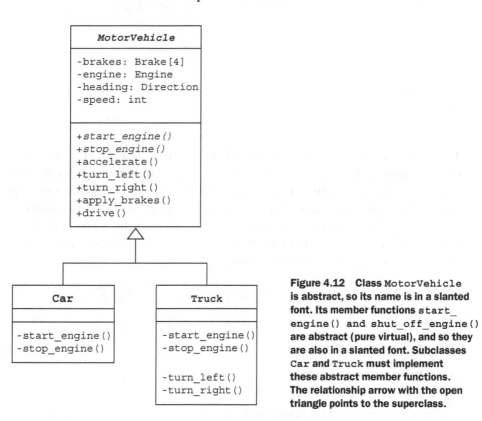

Figure 4.12 Class `MotorVehicle` **is abstract, so its name is in a slanted font. Its member functions** `start_ engine()` **and** `shut_off_engine()` **are abstract (pure virtual), and so they are also in a slanted font. Subclasses** `Car` **and** `Truck` **must implement these abstract member functions. The relationship arrow with the open triangle points to the superclass.**

The test program creates `Car` and `Truck` objects and calls the inherited `drive()` member function on each.

Listing 4.8   (Program 4.3 VehicleAbstract): `tester.cpp`

```cpp
#include "Car.h"
#include "Truck.h"

int main()
{
    Car car;
    car.drive();

    Truck truck;
    truck.drive();

    return 0;
}
```
The output from the program is

```
car starts engine
vehicle accelerates
vehicle turns left
vehicle turns right
```

```
vehicle applies brakes
car stops engine

truck starts engine
vehicle accelerates
truck turns left
truck turns right
vehicle applies brakes
truck stops engine
```

A C++ interface class is an abstract class that contains only abstract (pure virtual) member functions. It does not contain any member variables, although it can contain constants. The abstract member functions specify the behaviors any class that implements the interface must have, but it's up to each class to implement the behaviors by providing code for these member functions. An interface class differs from an abstract class by not providing any default member function implementations. The example `Motor-VehicalInterface` is an interface class.

Listing 4.9   (Program 4.4 VehicleInterface): `MotorVehicleInterface.h`

```
typedef int Brake;
typedef int Direction;
typedef int Engine;

class MotorVehicleInterface
{
public:
    virtual ~MotorVehicleInterface();

    virtual void start_engine() = 0;
    virtual void stop_engine() = 0;
    virtual void accelerate() = 0;            Only pure virtual
    virtual void apply_brakes() = 0;          member functions
    virtual void turn_left() = 0;
    virtual void turn_right() = 0;

    virtual void drive() = 0;
};
```

In this version, class `Car` must implement all the virtual member functions of the interface.

Listing 4.10   (Program 4.4 VehicleInterface): `Car.h`

```
#include <iostream>
#include "MotorVehicleInterface.h"

using namespace std;

class Car : public MotorVehicleInterface
{
public:
```

```cpp
        virtual ~Car() {}

        virtual void drive() override
        {
            start_engine();
            accelerate();
            turn_left();
            turn_right();
            apply_brakes();
            stop_engine();

            cout << endl;
        }

private:
        virtual void start_engine() override
        {
            cout << "car starts engine" << endl;
        }

        virtual void stop_engine() override
        {
            cout << "car stops engine" << endl;
        }

        virtual void accelerate() override
        {
            cout << "car accelerates" << endl;
        }

        virtual void turn_left() override
        {
            cout << "car turns left" << endl;
        }

        virtual void turn_right() override
        {
            cout << "car turns right" << endl;
        }

        virtual void apply_brakes() override
        {
            cout << "car turns applies brakes" << endl;
        }

        Brake brakes[4];
        Engine engine;
        Direction heading;
        int speed;
};
```

Similarly, class `Truck` must implement all the member functions.

Listing 4.11   (Program 4.4 VehicleInterface): `Truck.h`

```cpp
#include <iostream>
#include "MotorVehicleInterface.h"

using namespace std;

class Truck : public MotorVehicleInterface
{
public:
    virtual ~Truck() {}

    virtual void drive() override
    {
        start_engine();
        accelerate();
        turn_left();
        turn_right();
        apply_brakes();
        stop_engine();

        cout << endl;
    }

private:
    virtual void start_engine() override
    {
        cout << "truck starts engine" << endl;
    }

    virtual void stop_engine() override
    {
        cout << "truck stops engine" << endl;
    }

    virtual void accelerate() override
    {
        cout << "truck accelerates" << endl;
    }

    virtual void turn_left() override
    {
        cout << "truck turns left" << endl;
    }

    virtual void turn_right() override
    {
        cout << "truck turns right" << endl;
    }

    virtual void apply_brakes() override
    {
        cout << "truck turns applies brakes" << endl;
    }
```

```
    Brake brakes[4];
    Engine engine;
    Direction heading;
    int speed;
};
```

Figure 4.13 shows that in its UML class diagram, the label «interface» appears above the interface name MotorVehicleInterface. Dashed relationship arrows indicate that classes Car and Truck implement the interface. In a class diagram for an interface, italics or a slanted font is not necessary.

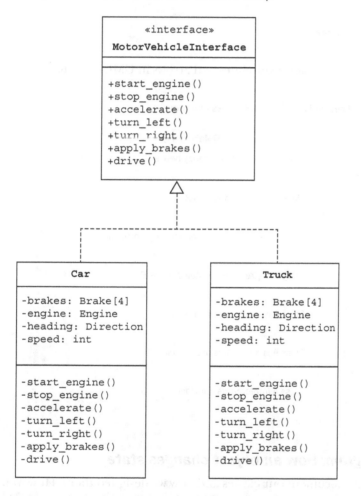

Figure 4.13 The label «interface» appears above the name of interface MotorVehicleInterface. All of its member functions are abstract, and it contains no member variables. The dashed relationship arrow with the open triangle indicates that subclasses Car and Truck implement the interface, and therefore, they must provide code for all the member functions of the interface.

Using the same test program, the output becomes

```
car starts engine
car accelerates
car turns left
car turns right
car turns applies brakes
car stops engine

truck starts engine
truck accelerates
truck turns left
truck turns right
truck turns applies brakes
truck stops engine
```

Table 4.1 summarizes the relationship lines and arrows in UML class diagrams.

Table 4.1　Relationship lines and arrows in UML class diagrams

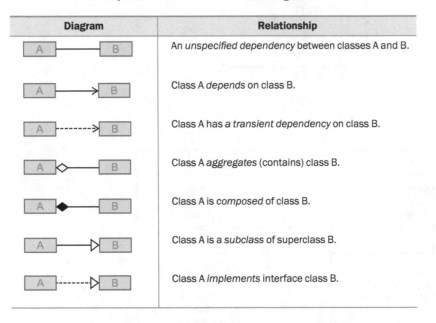

Diagram	Relationship
A —— B	An *unspecified dependency* between classes A and B.
A ——→ B	Class A *depends* on class B.
A ----→ B	Class A has a *transient dependency* on class B.
A ◇—— B	Class A *aggregates* (contains) class B.
A ◆—— B	Class A is *composed* of class B.
A ——▷ B	Class A is a *subclass* of superclass B.
A ----▷ B	Class A *implements* interface class B.

4.5　*UML state diagram: How an object changes state*

UML class diagrams document our classes and how we designed them. However, those diagrams are static—they don't show how objects instantiated from the classes interact with each other at run time.

A UML state diagram provides dynamic runtime information. It focuses on a single object and how it changes state at run time in response to events defined by its behaviors. Recall that an object's runtime state is determined by the unique values of its member variables, and its behaviors are implemented by its member functions. A state diagram allows us to visualize what happens to a particular object during run time and helps to ensure that we designed the class with the correct member variables and member functions.

Figure 4.14 is a UML state diagram for a `Car` object from figure 4.13. Each rounded box represents a state, and each arrow represents a transition from one state to another. Each arrow has a label that indicates the event that causes the transition. The object's behaviors define the kinds of events that can occur. In this example, the state of the `Car` object is characterized by the current values of the object's `speed` and `heading` member variables. The filled-in circle is the starting point, and the filled-in circle with a circle around it is an ending point.

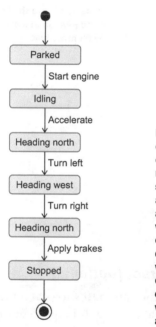

Figure 4.14 A UML state diagram that shows the state changes of a `Car` object during run time. Each box represents a state, and each arrow represents a transition from one state to another. Each transition is labeled with the behavior (event) that causes the transition. Such a diagram allows us to visualize what happens to a particular object during run time and helps to ensure that we designed the class with the correct member variables and member functions.

Each event in the diagram causes the `Car` object to change state. For example, starting the engine changes the object's initial state from parked to idling. Accelerating then changes the object's state to "heading north."

Figure 4.15 is a state diagram that will help to design a `Student` class in a hypothetical school simulation application. It includes more information about an object's runtime state transitions. The filled-in diamonds are the decision branch and merge points, and the decision conditions are the labels in square brackets. The heavy bars indicate where the transitions fork and join. The diagram shows the state changes of a student enrolling in a course.

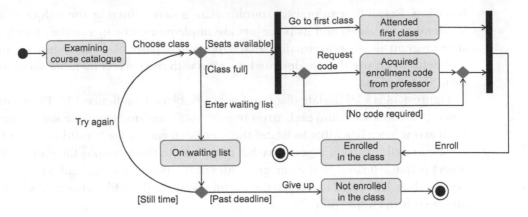

Figure 4.15   A state diagram for a student enrolling in a course. The filled-in diamonds are the decision branch and merge points. The heavy bars indicate where the transitions fork and join. Such a diagram would help to design a `Student` class with the correct member variables and member functions in a hypothetical school simulation application.

Manning Comix

4.6   *UML sequence diagram: How objects interact [optional]*

A UML sequence diagram also provides dynamic information. It shows at a high level the run-time interactions among the objects during a use case. It helps to ensure that we assigned the member functions and designed the class relationships correctly. Figure 4.16 is a sequence diagram for our book catalogue application in chapter 2.

The use case is a customer searching for books that match target book attributes. The figure at the top left represents the customer. The boxes along the top of the diagram to the right of the stick figure represent objects instantiated from the classes. By convention, each class name is underlined to indicate that it's an object instantiated from the class. Time proceeds from top to bottom. The customer and each object have a lifeline represented by a dashed vertical line. Each vertical rectangle on a lifeline represents the time during which the customer or object is active in the use case. The labeled horizontal arrows represent the interactions among the objects. The objects' behaviors (i.e., their member functions) determine the interactions. The objects implement these interactions with calls to member functions.

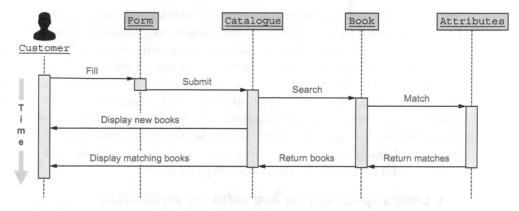

Figure 4.16   A UML sequence diagram for a customer searching for books that match target book attributes. At a high level, it shows the runtime interactions among objects involved in this use case as time goes from top to bottom. Such a diagram helps to ensure that we designed the class relationships correctly.

In this scenario, a customer first interacts with a `Form` object to fill in the target book attributes and then presses the "Submit" button. That notifies the `Catalogue` object to start a book search. In the meantime, the `Catalogue` object displays new books to the customer. The search interacts with `Book` objects, which in turn match against `Attributes` objects. The matching attributes cause a return of the corresponding `Book` objects. Finally, the `Catalogue` object displays these books to the customer.

Figure 4.17 is another example of a sequence diagram, and this one is for a hypothetical bank ATM (automatic teller machine) application.

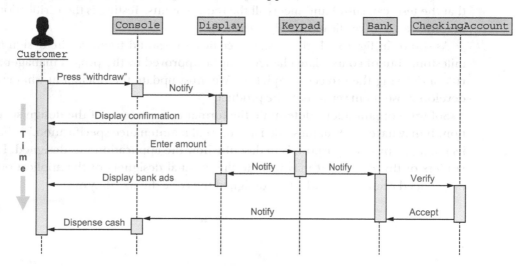

Figure 4.17   An example of a UML sequence diagram for the use case of a customer withdrawing cash from a bank ATM in a hypothetical banking application

The use case is a customer withdrawing cash. In this second scenario, an ATM customer first interacts with the `Console` object and presses the "Withdraw" option. That action notifies the `Display` object to display a confirmation message. Now the customer interacts with the `Keypad` object to enter the amount to withdraw. The `Keypad` object notifies the `Bank` object, and in the meantime, it also notifies the `Display` object to display bank ads. The `Bank` object asks the `CheckingAccount` object to verify the withdrawal amount. If the `CheckingAccount` object accepts the withdrawal, the `Bank` object notifies the `Console` object to initiate dispensing cash. As with the previous sequence diagram, this diagram helps to ensure us that we assigned the member functions and designed the class relationships correctly.

4.7   The design specification and software verification

The UML class, state, and sequence diagrams belong in the design specification. This is a technical document created by the development team that describes and justifies the design of the application. This document can contain implementation details, and it is meant to be read by the current and future developers of the application.

The design specification may include an Internal Test Plan. Unlike the black-box tests in an External Test Plan described in chapter 3, an internal unit test can target and stress a particular piece of code. For example, a unit test can pass different parameter values to a member function of a class and verify the return values. The developers should run unit tests. After a change to the code, and especially at the end of each development iteration, regression testing ensures that previously working code wasn't accidentally broken (i.e., the code hasn't regressed) by rerunning earlier unit tests. Internal testing verifies that we developed the application right—that it's bug-free (to the extent that the tests can show) and meets all the requirements. Testing is the verification part of software V&V (verification and validation).

As shown in figure 4.1, the design specification should freeze at the design freeze milestone, but of course, late changes may be approved by the project manager at the risk of delaying the project completion. We must update the document whenever we develop subsequent versions of the product.

Software organizations determine the format and contents of the design specification. It may have other names, such as "internal maintenance specification." Whatever its name, its primary purpose is to describe how the application was designed. Future readers of this document may include the original designers of the application who might need reminders of why they designed the code the way they did.

Summary

- A project to develop an application consists of multiple activities performed in parallel by a team of developers. Design occurs throughout nearly the entire project, and mostly during the design–code–test development iterations.

- Well-designed classes are cohesive and follow the Single Responsibility Principle.

- Well-designed classes are loosely coupled and follow the Principle of Least Knowledge.

- A UML class diagram provides information about an application's classes and their relationships. Each class diagram shows the class name and, optionally its member variables and member functions. The amount of information to show depends on whether the diagram is part of a high-level or a low-level description of the application's design.

- Different types of arrows drawn between two class diagrams indicate the relationship between the classes: dependency, aggregation, composition, or generalization.

- A UML state diagram focuses on the state changes of a single object at run time. An event causes an object to make a transition from one state to another, and the events are defined by the object's behavior. Visualizing what happens to a particular object during run time helps to ensure that the object's class is well-designed with correct member variables and member functions.

- A UML sequence diagram shows the high-level interactions among objects at runtime. How an object behaves during an interaction is determined by its member functions. Visualizing these dynamic interactions helps to ensure that the classes are well-designed with correct member functions and proper relationships.

- A design specification describes and justifies an application's design for its current and future developers. It contains the UML class, sequence, and state diagrams. Furthermore, it can include a test plan for internal testing.

- For the verification part of software V&V, software developers perform internal testing that includes unit and regression tests during the development iterations.

Part 3

Design the application right

Good design principles help us design the application right. These principles include minimizing dependencies among classes by hiding their implementations, leaving no surprises in our code, designing subclasses right, and choosing between "is-a" inheritance relationships and "has-a" aggregation relationships.

The design principles help us meet the challenges of change and complexity by creating cohesive and loosely coupled classes. We'll see in the next part of the book that good design principles form the foundation of design patterns.

Hide class 5
implementations

Well-designed applications incorporate proven design principles. Chapter 4 discussed the importance of loose coupling in class design. Two loosely coupled classes have minimal dependencies on each other, which helps ensure that changes in one class don't cause changes in another class.

Manning Comix

We can certainly be proud when other programmers admire and use the classes we wrote. But well-designed classes hide their implementations by making their member variables and functions private. A class should expose only those members that other programmers need to access by making them public.

This chapter covers design principles that support a strategy to minimize the dependencies among classes. Implementation hiding is an important part of encapsulation. If we hide the implementation of a class, other classes can't depend on what they can't access. Therefore, we can make changes to the implementation without forcing other classes to change in response.

The next chapter will cover more design principles. We'll see how the principles support each other and work together. Later chapters will cover design patterns that provide models we can use to develop custom solutions to common programming problems. The design principles are the foundation for the design patterns.

5.1   *The Principle of Least Knowledge and hidden implementations*

Recall that a class's member variables represent state—each state of an object at run time is characterized by a unique set of values of its member variables. A class's member functions represent an object's runtime behavior. A class's *implementation* is the way we code member variables and functions of the class.

For example, think again about the Book class from chapter 2 that represented a book in a catalogue. Its implementation may include components such as the book's title and author that represent inherent attributes of a book. No other class should be concerned about how we implement these attributes—they could be string values already assigned to the Book object or values dynamically looked up in a database when we ask for them. Certainly, a class from a customer application shouldn't be allowed to change a book's title or author. Therefore, these attributes should be private. However, the class should provide public means for another class to access a book's title and author, but without needing to know their implementation.

The primary way to minimize the dependencies that a class A has on class B is for class A to know as little as possible about the implementation of class B. This, of course, is the Principle of Least Knowledge (sections 2.3.2 and 4.2.2). This principle is also known as the *Law of Demeter*, named after the ancient Greek goddess of agriculture, with the allusion of growing software with loosely coupled classes. Class B should expose only as much of itself as necessary for other code to use the class, hiding the rest. In a C++ class, hiding is accomplished by declaring member variables and functions to be private. Private member functions, which can be called only by other member functions of the class, are often called *helper functions*.

Hidden doesn't necessarily mean *invisible*. Unless your classes are compiled and kept in a library, developers may be able to read their source code. *Hidden* means *inaccessible*. Private member variables and functions of a class are inaccessible by other code. A class can also partially hide its implementation by declaring members to be protected. Then only a class's subclasses can access the protected members. *Hidden implementation code is effectively encapsulated*. We can make changes to the hidden implementation of a class without affecting any other code that uses the class.

If you change a member function in your class from public to private, then, for sure, someone will have written code in another class that depended on calling that function.

That's Murphy's Law for programmers!

Indeed, a good rule of thumb is the following: when designing a class, make every member variable and member function private (or protected), except those that are necessary to be public to enable other code to use the class. There's an old saying: "Once public, always public." If you make a member variable or function public, you might not be able to change it to private later without forcing code rewrites.

5.2 *Public getter and setter functions access hidden implementation selectively*

In listing 5.1, the Item class hides how it implements state by making its member variables name, weight, and price private. Then, the class can have public *getter* and *setter* member functions, more formally known as *accessors* and *mutators*. These functions are meant to be called by any code that uses the class. A getter function allows code to probe an Item object's current state, such as by returning the value of private member variable weight, without revealing how the state is implemented. A setter function allows code to modify an Item object's state, such as by providing a new value for private member variable price, without revealing how the state is implemented.

Listing 5.1   (Program 5.1 DemeterItem): Item.cpp

```
#include <string>

using namespace std;

class Item
{
public:
    Item(const string n, const double w, const double p)
        : name(n), weight(w), price(p) {}
```

```
    string get_name()   const { return name; }
    double get_weight() const { return weight; }
    double get_price()  const { return price; }

    void set_price(const double p) { price = p; }

private:
    string name;
    double weight;
    double price;
};
```

Getter functions

← **Setter function**

Hidden state implementation

As suggested in figure 5.1, the caller of the public getter function `get_price()` does not know how the class implements state. The function returns the current value of a private `price` member variable. Or, the function could obtain the price by other hidden means, such as a dynamic lookup in a price database. Code that uses class `Item` should not depend on any particular implementation.

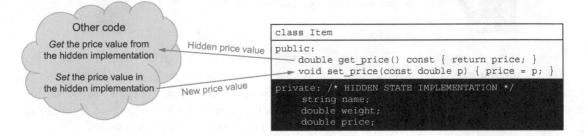

Figure 5.1   A getter function enables code to obtain the price value from an `Item` object's hidden state. A setter function enables code to modify the `price` value in an `Item` object's hidden state. Neither function reveals how the class implements state. For example, we might later decide to have member function `get_price()` dynamically look up the price from a database. We'll be able to make this change without making changes to the function's caller.

By hiding how the class implements state and then providing public getter and setter functions, we can control how code can probe or modify an object's state at run time. For example, a runtime check can prevent a setter function from corrupting an object's state with an invalid value:

```
    void Item::set_price(const double p)
    {
        assert(p > 0.00);
        price = p;
    }
```

A well-designed setter function won't allow an object to be put into an invalid state at run time.

That's just good defensive programming!

Of course, in a real application, we should handle a bad argument value much more gracefully than by immediately aborting the program.

If we don't change the signatures of the public getter and setter functions (i.e., if we don't change how to call them), we'll will be able to modify how the class implements state without forcing changes on code using the class. Section 5.4 discusses further the role of setter functions.

5.3   *Class Date: An example of implementation hiding*

The development iterations of the following example application demonstrate the importance of hiding a class implementation and the problems we can run into if we don't hide the implementation. Let's suppose the application maintains the dates of scheduled appointments by using a Date class. A calendar date consists of a year, a month, and a day of the month. Therefore, the Date class can hide its implementation by making its member variables year, month, and day private.

Day and date

Dates are important for many applications. Unfortunately, everyday terminology can be confusing. A *day* is any 24-hour period, which is midnight to midnight by convention. In the Gregorian calendar in use today throughout much of the world, a specific day is identified by a *date* consisting of three integer values: a *year*, a *month*, and a *day of the month*. An example date (written in the U.S. format) is 9/2/2025 for September 2, 2025.

In common use, the meanings of the words *day* and *date* often overlap. We refer to special days using only a month and a day of the month (e.g., to*day* is July 20, my birth*day* is September 2, New Year's *Day* is January 1). However, Don's birth*date* was January 10, 1938. To add to the confusion, the day of the month is itself called a *date* (e.g., today's *date* is the 12th). It should be clear from context which *day* is meant, such as Christmas *Day* is December 25, and there are 12 *days* of Christmas.

In our examples, class Date comprises three member variables—year, month, and day—where day is short for day of the month.

If we were to design a Day class, it would have a one-to-one aggregation with the Date class—each Day object would have a member variable that points to a Date object representing its identifying date.

Next, suppose that the application must perform date arithmetic with the Date objects:

- What is the date *n* days from this date, where *n* can be positive (for a date after this date) or negative (for a date before this date)?
- How many days are there from this date to another date?

Unfortunately, date arithmetic with the Gregorian calendar is notoriously difficult because of its rules:

- April, June, September, and November each has 30 days.
- February has 28 days, except for leap years when it has 29 days.
- All other months have 31 days.
- Years that are divisible by four are leap years, except that after 1582, years divisible by 100 but not 400 are not leap years.
- There is no year 0. Year 1 CE is preceded by year 1 BCE (year −1).
- During the switchover to the Gregorian calendar, 10 days were dropped. The next date after October 4, 1582, was October 15, 1582.

5.3.1   *Iteration 1: Date arithmetic with loops*

The following listing is class `Date` that does date arithmetic.

Listing 5.2   (Program 5.2 DateArithmetic-1): `Date.h`

```
#include <set>

using namespace std;

class Date
{
public:
    Date(const int y, const int m, const int d)
        : year(y), month(m), day(d) {}

    int get_year()  const { return year; }      │ Public getter functions
    int get_month() const { return month; }
    int get_day()   const { return day; }

    Date add_days(int n) const;                  │ Public date arithmetic
    int days_from(const Date& other) const;      │ functions

    void print();

private:
    static const set<int> LONG_MONTHS;

    static const int JANUARY  = 1;
    static const int FEBRUARY = 2;
    static const int DECEMBER = 12;              │ Private hidden
                                                 │ constants for the
    static const int GREGORIAN_START_YEAR = 1582;│ Gregorian calendar
    static const int GREGORIAN_START_MONTH = 10; │ rules
    static const int GREGORIAN_START_DATE = 15;
    static const int JULIAN_END_DATE = 4;

    int year, month, day;      ◄────── Private hidden state
                                       implementation
```

```
    static int days_in_month(const int year, const int month);
    static bool is_leap_year(const int year);

    int compare_to(const Date& other) const;
    Date next_date() const;
    Date previous_date() const;
};
```

Private hidden helper functions

The following listing shows one way to implement date arithmetic, but it is very inefficient.

Listing 5.3 (Program 5.2 DateArithmetic-1): `Date.cpp` **(very inefficient)**

```
#include <iostream>
#include <set>
#include "Date.h"

using namespace std;

Date Date::add_days(int n) const
{
    Date date = *this;

    while (n > 0)
    {
        date = date.next_date();
        n--;
    }

    while (n < 0)
    {
        date = date.previous_date();
        n++;
    }

    return date;
}

int Date::days_from(const Date& other) const
{
    Date date = *this;
    int n = 0;

    while (date.compare_to(other) > 0)
    {
        date = date.previous_date();
        n++;
    }

    while (date.compare_to(other) < 0)
    {
        date = date.next_date();
        n--;
    }
```

Start with a copy of this date.

Loop n days into the future.

Loop n days into the past.

Start with a copy of this date.

Loop to count days in the past.

Loop to count days in the future.

```
      return n;
}

const set<int> Date::LONG_MONTHS { 1, 3, 5, 7, 8, 10, 12 };

int Date::days_in_month(const int year, const int month)
{
   if (LONG_MONTHS.find(month) != LONG_MONTHS.end()) return 31;
   if (month == 2) return is_leap_year(year) ? 29 : 28;
   return 30;
}

bool Date::is_leap_year(const int year)
{
   if (year%4 != 0) return false;
   if (year < GREGORIAN_START_YEAR) return true;

   return (year%100 != 0) || (year%400 == 0);
}

int Date::compare_to(const Date& other) const
{
   if (year > other.year)   return 1;
   if (year < other.year)   return -1;
   if (month > other.month) return 1;
   if (month < other.month) return -1;

   return day - other.day;
}
```

Return a positive value if this date comes after the other date. Return a negative value if this date comes before the other date. Return 0 if both dates are the same.

```
Date Date::next_date() const
{
   int y = year;
   int m = month;
   int d = day;

   if (   y == GREGORIAN_START_YEAR
       && m == GREGORIAN_START_MONTH
       && d == JULIAN_END_DATE)        d = GREGORIAN_START_DATE;
   else if (d < days_in_month(y, m)) d++;
   else
   {
       d = 1;
       m++;

       if (m > DECEMBER)
       {
           m = JANUARY;
           y++;
           if (y == 0) y++;   // no year 0
       }
   }

   return Date(y, m, d);
}
```

Apply Gregorian calendar rules to return the next date.

```
Date Date::previous_date() const
{
    int y = year;
    int m = month;
    int d = day;

    if (   y == GREGORIAN_START_YEAR
        && m == GREGORIAN_START_MONTH
        && d == GREGORIAN_START_DATE) d = JULIAN_END_DATE;
    else if (d > 1)                   d--;
    else
    {
        m--;

        if (m < JANUARY)
        {
            m = DECEMBER;
            y--;
            if (y == 0) y--;   // no year 0
        }

        d = days_in_month(y, m);
    }

    return Date(y, m, d);
}

void Date::print()
{
    cout << month << "/" << day << "/";
    if (year > 0) cout <<  year;
    else          cout << -year << " BCE";
}
```

> Apply Gregorian calendar rules to return the previous date.

Member function add_days() starts with this date and iterates day-by-day n days into the future if the value of argument n is positive, or n days into the past if the value of n is negative. Member function days_from() starts with this date and iterates day-by-day to count days either into the past or into the future, depending on whether this date falls after or before the Date argument, respectively. Both member functions call helper functions previous_date() and next_date() in their loops.

Helper function compare_to() compares this date with the Date argument. It returns a negative value if this date comes before the argument, a positive value if this date comes after the argument, or 0 if both dates are the same. Only the sign of the value matters.

Helper functions previous_date() and next_date() each must apply the difficult Gregorian calendar rules to calculate and return the date that is one before or one after, respectively, this date.

Member function print() prints a date in the U.S. format, that is, month/day/year. For example, 9/2/2025 for September 2, 2025.

If the dates are far apart, the program will do a lot of looping!

Also, the calls to the member functions `previous_date()` and `next_date()` are expensive due to the Gregorian calendar rules.

It's even worse than that. Each iteration in the member functions `add_days()` and `days_from()` gets a new `Date` object when it calls `previous_date()` or `next_date()`. Function `add_days()` returns only the `Date` object created by the last iteration. The following listing is a simple test program.

Listing 5.4   (Program 5.2 DateArithmetic-1): `tester.cpp`

```
#include <iostream>
#include "Date.h"

using namespace std;

int main()
{
    Date date1(2025, 9, 2);  // September 2, 2025
    Date date2(2027, 4, 3);  // April 3, 2027

    cout << "date1 = "; date1.print(); cout << endl;
    cout << "date2 = "; date2.print(); cout << endl;

    int count = date2.days_from(date1);
    cout << "count = " << count << endl;

    cout << "should be date2: ";
    date1.add_days(count).print(); cout << endl;
    return 0;
}
```

The output is

```
date1 = 9/2/2025
date2 = 4/3/2027
count = 578
should be date2: 4/3/2027
```

The application is functional and appears to perform the date arithmetic correctly. However, it is terribly inefficient. Member function `add_days()` must loop as many times as the value of argument n. Member function `days_from()` must loop as many times as there are days from this date to the `Date` argument and call member function `compare_to()` at the beginning of each loop. Calls to helper functions `next_date()` and `previous_date()` inside the loops are expensive because of the Gregorian calendar rules, and each call creates and returns a `Date` object. This is clearly a poor design (figure 5.2). We need to backtrack and come up with a better design.

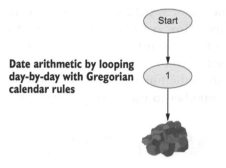

Date arithmetic by looping
day-by-day with Gregorian
calendar rules

Figure 5.2   The version of
class Date from iteration
1 performs date arithmetic
correctly, but it does it poorly
because of expensive looping
day-by-day with the Gregorian
calendar rules. This version
deserves a lump of coal.

5.3.2   *Iteration 2: Julian day numbers simplify date arithmetic*

A much more efficient way to perform date arithmetic is to use a *Julian day number* to identify each day instead of the Gregorian year, month, and day of the month. The Julian day number of a particular day is the number of days since noon on January 1, 4713 BCE, of the Gregorian calendar. We'll use a Julian day number only at noon so that the number is always a whole number. Date arithmetic is trivial with Julian day numbers.

Julian day number

Do not be puzzled by the various calendar uses of the name "Julian." Astronomers use *Julian day numbers* to identify days rather than using the year, month, and day of the month. A Julian day number counts the *number of days* since noon on January 1, 4713 BCE, of the Gregorian calendar, so that day at noon has Julian day number 0. Because it takes hours of the day into account, a Julian day number can have a fractional part, but it's whole at noon. The 16th-century historian Josephus Justus Scaliger invented the concept and named it after his father Julius.

There are complicated algorithms for converting between a day's Julian day number and its corresponding Gregorian year, month, and day of the month. The algorithms in the following application are from *Numerical Recipes, the Art of Scientific Computing*, 3rd edition, by William H. Press et al., Cambridge University Press, 2007.

A useful conversion milepost is Julian day number 2,440,000, which corresponds to the Gregorian date May 23, 1968.

Julian day numbers are not related to the Julian *calendar* introduced by the Roman emperor Julius Caesar in 45 BCE.

A day's Julian *date* is a combination of the year and the day of the year. For example, the Julian date of January 1, 2024, is 2024-01, and the Julian date of December 31, 2024, is 2024-366 (2024 is a leap year). This is also not related to the Julian day number.

The second design iteration of class Date (listing 5.5) uses Julian day numbers. Like in the previous version of the class, we want to hide how we implement the state of its objects, so member variable julian is private. We no longer need private member variables `year`, `month`, and `day`. Helper function `to_julian()` converts a year, month, and day of the month to a Julian day number. How we call the public constructor function hasn't changed—we still pass it a trio of year, month, and day-of-the-month values. The constructor calls `to_julian()` to compute the corresponding Julian day number from the trio. A private constructor initializes the Julian day number directly. Helper function `to_ymd()` converts a Julian day number to the corresponding year, month, and day of the month.

Listing 5.5   (Program 5.3 DateArithmetic-2): `Date.h`

```
#include <set>

using namespace std;

class Date
{
public:
    Date(const int year, const int month, const int day)
        : julian(to_julian(year, month, day)) {}

    ...

private:
    static const set<int> LONG_MONTHS;

    static const int JANUARY  = ...
    ...

    static const int MAX_MONTH_DAYS  = 31;
    static const int MONTHS_PER_YEAR = 12;

    Date(int j) : julian(j) {}

    int julian;

    static int days_in_month(const int year, const int month);
    static bool is_leap_year(const int year);

    static int to_julian(const int year, const int month,
                         const int day);
    static void to_ymd(const int julian, int& year, int& month,
                                          int& day);
};
```

The public constructor calls to_julian() to initialize private member variable julian from the year, month, and day of the month.

The private constructor initializes the Julian day number directly.

Hidden state implementation

Hidden helper function to convert year, month, and day of the month to a Julian day number

Hidden helper function to convert a Julian day number to year, month, and day of the month

---

Listing 5.6 shows that date arithmetic is much more efficient with Julian day numbers. Member function `add_days()` simply adds the value of argument n to this date's Julian day number to obtain the Julian day number for the new date. Member function `days_from()` subtracts the Julian day number of the other date from this date's Julian day number to obtain the number of days.

Because we hid the implementation of class Date, we were able to change the implementation radically without causing code that uses the class to change. We can call the Date constructor to create a Date object like before and call the public getter functions get_year(), get_month(), and get_day() without change to get the date's year, month, and day of the month. Furthermore, we can call the public member functions add_days() and days_from() the same way as before and get the same expected results.

Listing 5.6   (Program 5.3 DateArithmetic-2): Date.cpp (could be better)

```cpp
#include <iostream>
#include <set>
#include <math.h>
#include "Date.h"

int Date::get_year() const
{
    int year, month, day;
    to_ymd(julian, year, month, day);
    return year;
}

int Date::get_month() const
{
    int year, month, day;
    to_ymd(julian, year, month, day);
    return month;
}

int Date::get_day() const
{
    int year, month, day;
    to_ymd(julian, year, month, day);
    return day;
}

Date Date::add_days(const int n) const
{
    return Date(julian + n);
}

int Date::days_from(const Date& other) const
{
    return julian - other.julian;
}

const set<int> Date::LONG_MONTHS { 1, 3, 5, 7, 8, 10, 12 };

int Date::days_in_month(const int year, const int month) ...

bool Date::is_leap_year(const int year) ...
```

Convert a Julian day number to year, month, and day of the month.

Return a new Date after a simple addition to the Julian day number.

Simple subtraction of Julian day numbers

```
int Date::to_julian(const int year, const int month, const int day)
{
    int y = year;
    if (year < 0) y++;

    int m = month;
    if (month > 2) m++;
    else
    {
        y--;
        m += 13;
    }

    long j = static_cast<long>(floor(365.25*y) + floor(30.6001*m))
                    + day + 1720995;

    const long GREGORIAN_CUTOFF =
        GREGORIAN_START_DATE +
        MAX_MONTH_DAYS*(GREGORIAN_START_MONTH +
                            MONTHS_PER_YEAR*GREGORIAN_START_YEAR);

    if (day + MAX_MONTH_DAYS*(month + MONTHS_PER_YEAR*year) >=
                                            GREGORIAN_CUTOFF)
    {
        int x = static_cast<int>(0.01*y);
        j += 2 - x + static_cast<int>(0.25*x);
    }

    return j;
}

void Date::to_ymd(int julian, int& year, int& month, int& day)
{
    long ja = julian;

    const long GREGORIAN_CUTOFF = 2299161;

    if (julian >= GREGORIAN_CUTOFF)
    {
        long jalpha = static_cast<long>(
            (static_cast<float>(julian - 1867216) - 0.25)/36524.25);
        ja += 1 + jalpha - static_cast<long>(0.25*jalpha);
    }

    long jb = ja + 1524;
    long jc = static_cast<long>(
        6680.0 + (static_cast<float>(jb - 2439870) - 122.1)/365.25);
    long jd = static_cast<long>(365*jc + (0.25*jc));
    long je = static_cast<long>((jb - jd)/30.6001);

    day = jb - jd - static_cast<long>(30.6001*je);

    month = je - 1;
    if (month > 12) month -= 12;

    year = jc - 4715;
```

Conversion algorithms from Numerical Recipes, the Art of Scientific Computing (3rd ed., Cambridge University Press, 2007)

```
        if (month > 2) year--;
        if (year <= 0) year--;
}

void Date::print()
{
    int year, month, day;
    to_ymd(julian, year, month, day);

    cout << month << "/" << day << "/";
    if (year > 0) cout <<  year;
    else          cout << -year << " BCE";
}
```

> Convert from the Julian day number to print the year, month, and day of the month.

The same test program (listing 5.4) produces the same output.

While it may do date arithmetic very efficiently, the second iteration of class Date introduced a different inefficiency. Helper function to_julian() computes the Julian day number corresponding to a Gregorian year, month, and day of the month. Conversely, member function to_ymd() computes the year, month, and day of the month to a corresponding Julian day number. Both are complicated due to the Gregorian calendar rules.

The public constructor calls to_julian() to initialize julian from the year, month, and day of the month values (listing 5.5). Each of the getter functions get_year(), get_month(), and get_day() must first call to_ymd() before it can return the year, month, or day of the month, respectively. The public member function print() also must call to_ymd().

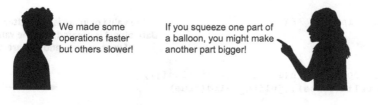

We still don't have a good design (figure 5.3). But we can improve the efficiency of class Date with a third iteration.

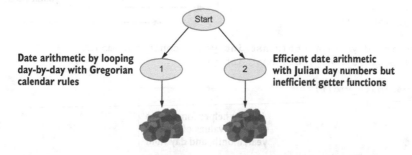

Figure 5.3 The version of class Date from iteration 2 performs data arithmetic very efficiently using Julian day numbers, but getter functions for the year, month, or day of the month must each call an expensive conversion algorithm. We get yet another lump of coal.

5.3.3   *Iteration 3: A hybrid approach with lazy evaluation*

How can we have fast access to the year, month, and day of the month along with efficient date arithmetic? This third iteration of class Date takes a hybrid approach. This version has all four private member variables: year, month, day, and julian.

> **Listing 5.7   (Program 5.4 DateArithmetic-3):** Date.h (efficient hybrid version)

```
#include <set>

using namespace std;

class Date
{
public:
    Date(const int y, const int m, const int d)
        : year(y), month(m), day(d), julian(0),
          ymd_valid(true), julian_valid(false) {}

    int get_year();
    int get_month();
    int get_day();

    Date add_days(const int n);
    int days_from(Date& other);

    void print();

private:
    static const set<int> LONG_MONTHS;

    static const int JANUARY  = ...
...

    Date(int j)
        : year(2000), month(1), day(1), julian(j),
          ymd_valid(false), julian_valid(true) {}

    int year, month, day;
    int julian;

    bool ymd_valid;
    bool julian_valid;

    static int days_in_month(const int year, const int month);
    static bool is_leap_year(const int year);

    void validate_ymd();
```

The values of year, month, and day are valid after the Date object is created, but the value of julian is not.

The value of julian is valid after the Date object is created, but the values of year, month, and day are not.

Are values of the trio year, month, and day valid?

Is the value of julian valid?

Hidden helper function to make the values of the trio year, month, and day valid

```
    void validate_julian();

    static int to_julian(const int year, const int month,
                         const int day);
    static void to_ymd(const int julian, int& year, int& month,
                                          int& day);
};
```

Hidden helper function to make the value of julian valid.

Boolean member variables `ymd_valid` and `julian_valid` help to ensure that, whenever necessary, the value of `julian` and the values of the trio `year`, `month`, and `day` are synchronized. Helper function `validate_ymd()` synchronizes the values of the trio with the current value of `julian`. Helper function `validate_julian()` synchronizes the value of `julian` with the current values of the trio.

Listing 5.8 **(Program 5.4 DateArithmetic-3):** `Date.cpp` **(efficient hybrid version)**

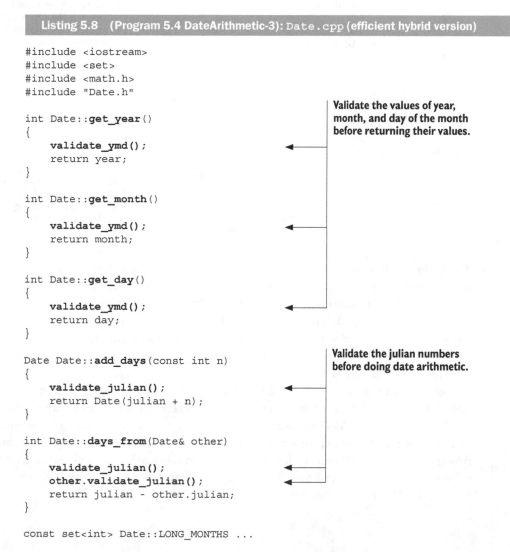

```
#include <iostream>
#include <set>
#include <math.h>
#include "Date.h"

int Date::get_year()
{
    validate_ymd();
    return year;
}

int Date::get_month()
{
    validate_ymd();
    return month;
}

int Date::get_day()
{
    validate_ymd();
    return day;
}

Date Date::add_days(const int n)
{
    validate_julian();
    return Date(julian + n);
}

int Date::days_from(Date& other)
{
    validate_julian();
    other.validate_julian();
    return julian - other.julian;
}

const set<int> Date::LONG_MONTHS ...
```

Validate the values of year, month, and day of the month before returning their values.

Validate the julian numbers before doing date arithmetic.

```
int Date::days_in_month(const int year, const int month) ...

bool Date::is_leap_year(const int year) ...

void Date::validate_ymd()
{
    if (!ymd_valid)
    {
        to_ymd(julian, year, month, day);
        ymd_valid = true;
    }
}
```

> Synchronize the values of the trio year, month, and day of the month with the current value of julian.

```
void Date::validate_julian()
{
    if (!julian_valid)
    {
        julian = to_julian(year, month, day);
        julian_valid = true;
    }
}
```

> Synchronize the value of julian with the current values of the trio year, month, and day of the month.

```
int Date::to_julian(const int year, const int month, const int day) ...

void Date::to_ymd(int julian, int& year, int& month, int& day) ...

void Date::print()
{
    validate_ymd();

    cout << month << "/" << day << "/";
    if (year > 0) cout <<  year;
    else          cout << -year << " BCE";
}
```

> ◄── Validate the values of year, month, and day of the month before printing their values.

The public getter functions get_year(), get_month(), and get_year() each must first call helper function validate_ymd() to ensure that the value it returns is synchronized with the current value of julian. Public member function print() must also call validate_ymd() before printing. Public member functions add_days() and days_from(), both of which perform date arithmetic with Julian day numbers, must each call helper function validate_julian() to ensure that the value of julian is synchronized with the current values of year, month, and day.

Helper function validate_ymd() calls the expensive helper function to_ymd() only if the values of year, month, and day are not already synchronized with the value of julian. The private Boolean member variable ymd_valid keeps track of this synchronization. Similarly, helper function validate_julian() calls the expensive helper function to_julian() only if the value of julian is not already synchronized with the values of year, month, and day. The private Boolean member variable julian_valid keeps track of the synchronization.

We call helper function `to_ymd()` only when we're about to access the values of `year`, `month`, and `day`. We call helper function `to_julian()` only when we're about to perform date arithmetic using the value of `julian`. This is an example of the *Lazy Evaluation Principle*, where we delay performing a calculation until we need the result, which makes our code more efficient by preventing unnecessary calculations.

The Lazy Evaluation Principle

If at run time we don't need the result of a calculation immediately, then we should be lazy and postpone the calculation until we need the result. The Lazy Evaluation Principle is especially useful to improve performance if the calculation is expensive or time-consuming.

 A **Date** object in effect caches the values of **year**, **month**, and **day** and the value of **julian**. It recomputes them only when necessary.

So it pays to be lazy and wait until the last possible moment to do an expensive calculation!

Because we hid the implementation of the `Date` class with private member variables and provided public getter functions, we were again able to refactor the code to further improve its efficiency. We encapsulated the implementation changes. Code that uses the `Date` class only needs to know that a `Date` object's state is characterized by its year, month, and day of the month, and that `Date` objects can perform date arithmetic efficiently. We've hidden the use of Julian day numbers to support date arithmetic (figure 5.4).

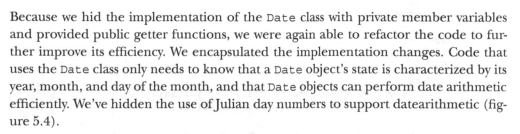
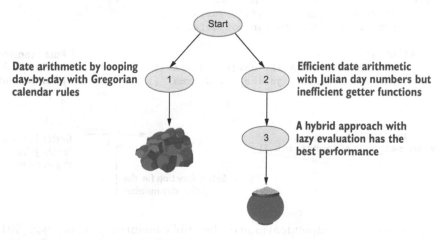

Date arithmetic by looping day-by-day with Gregorian calendar rules

Efficient date arithmetic with Julian day numbers but inefficient getter functions

A hybrid approach with lazy evaluation has the best performance

Figure 5.4 The version of class `Date` from iteration 3 is a hybrid that uses lazy evaluation. It has the best performance of the three versions. This version deserves the pot of gold.

5.4   *Public setter functions carefully modify hidden implementation*

A public getter function allows code to probe an object's state without revealing how the state is implemented. On the other hand, a public setter function allows code to modify an object's state, also without revealing how the state is implemented.

None of the three versions of class `Date` in this chapter provided any public setter functions. Therefore, once we've constructed a `Date` object at run time with year, month, and day of the month values, the object is *immutable*—there is no way to change its state. Immutable objects are often justified by an application's logic. We'll learn more about immutable objects in section 5.7.

Listing 5.9 shows another version of class `Date`. This version selectively allows access to another part of its implementation—its Julian day number. We now make public the constructor that takes an integer value to initialize member variable `julian`. Public getter function `get_julian()` returns the value of the private `julian` data member. Public setter function `set_julian()` sets `julian` to its argument value, thus changing the state of a `Date` object. Therefore, in this version, `Date` objects are mutable.

Listing 5.9   (Program 5.5 DateArithmetic-4): `Date.h`

```
#include <set>

using namespace std;

class Date
{
public:
    Date()
        : year(2000), month(1), day(1), julian(0),
          ymd_valid(false), julian_valid(false) {}

    Date(const int y, const int m, const int d)
        : year(y), month(m), day(d), julian(0),
          ymd_valid(true), julian_valid(false) {}

    Date(int j)                                          Public constructor
        : year(2000), month(1), day(1), julian(j),       to initialize the
          ymd_valid(false), julian_valid(true) {}         Julian day number

    ...

    int get_julian();                                    Getter function
    void set_julian(const int j);                        for the Julian
                                                          day number
    ...                          Setter function for the
};                               Julian day number
```

Listing 5.10 shows the implementation of the public member functions `get_julian()` and `set_julian()`. Function `set_julian()` allows code to modify the value of private member variable `julian` in a safe manner. It checks the value of its argument before using it and aborts the program if the value is negative. A real application should handle this error more gracefully than immediately aborting. Similarly, each constructor function should also check its argument values.

Listing 5.10　(Program 5.5 DateArithmetic-4): `Date.cpp` (optimal hybrid version)

```
...

int Date::get_julian()
{
    validate_julian();
    return julian;
}

void Date::set_julian(const int j)
{
    assert(j >= 0);

    julian = j;
    julian_valid = true;
    ymd_valid = false;
}


...
```

The new test program exercises accessing and setting a `Date` object's Julian day number.

Listing 5.11　(Program 5.5 DateArithmetic-4): `tester.cpp`

```
#include <iostream>
#include <iomanip>
#include "Date.h"

using namespace std;

int main()
{
    Date date1(2025, 9, 2);  // September 2, 2025
    Date date2(2027, 4, 3);  // April 3, 2027

    cout << "date1 = "; date1.print(); cout << endl;
    cout << "date2 = "; date2.print(); cout << endl;

    int count = date2.days_from(date1);
    cout << "count = " << count << endl;

    cout << "should be date2: ";
    date1.add_days(count).print(); cout << endl << endl;

    int j1 = date1.get_julian();
    cout << "date1 Julian day number = " << j1 << endl << endl;

    Date d;
```

```
        int js[] = { 0, 2440000, 3000000 };

        for (int j : js)
        {
            d.set_julian(j);
            cout << setw(8) << d.get_julian();
            cout << «: «; d.print(); cout << endl;
        }

        cout << endl;

        d.set_julian(j1);
        cout << "should be date1: "; d.print(); cout << endl;

        return 0;
    }
```

The printed results are

```
date1 = 9/2/2025
date2 = 4/3/2027
count = 578
should be date2: 4/3/2027

date1 Julian number = 2460921

      0: 1/1/-4713
2440000: 5/23/1968
3000000: 8/15/3501

should be date1: 9/2/2025
```

5.5   *Beware of dangerous setter functions*

Should we always favor providing setter functions? What about the values of the trio year, month, and day of the month in the hidden implementation? Let's see what can happen if we provide additional setter functions.

Listing 5.12   (Program 5.6 DateArithmetic-5): `Date.cpp` (poorly designed)

```
void Date::set_year(const int y)
{
    assert(y != 0);

    validate_ymd();
    year = y;
    julian_valid = false;
}

void Date::set_month(const int m)
{
    assert((m >= 1) && (m <= 12));

    validate_ymd();
    month = m;
```

```
        julian_valid = false;
}

void Date::set_day(const int d)
{
    assert((d >= 1) && (d <= 31));  // needs more checking!

    validate_ymd();
    day = d;
    julian_valid = false;
}
```

In an actual application, setter function `set_day()` will need a much more comprehensive validation of its argument value that takes into consideration the current month and year. The following listing is a test program for this poorly designed version of class `Date`.

Listing 5.13 (Program 5.6 DateArithmetic-5): `tester.cpp`

```
#include <iostream>
#include <iomanip>
#include "Date.h"

using namespace std;

int main()
{
    Date d(2030, 1, 31);  // January 31, 2030
    cout << "starting date: "; d.print(); cout << endl;
    cout << "Julian day number = " << d.get_julian() << endl << endl;

    d.set_month(2);                                    ◄──── Problematic
    cout << "modified date: "; d.print(); cout << endl;       setting of the
    int j = d.get_julian();                                   month
    d.set_julian(j);
    cout << "surprise date: "; d.print(); cout << endl;

    return 0;
}
```

The output is

```
starting date: 1/31/2030
Julian day number = 2462533

modified date: 2/31/2030
surprise date: 3/3/2030
```

By providing setter functions to set a `Date` object's private `year`, `month`, and `day` member variables individually, we were able to put the object into an invalid state, the nonexistent date February 31, 2030. Then, by setting the Julian day number of that nonexistent date, we ended up with March 3, 2030, a nasty surprise. We must never allow a setter function to put an object into an invalid state. The next chapter will discuss code surprises.

Poorly designed setter functions can get us into a lot of trouble!

We must practice defensive programming with setter functions. Also, not every private member variable should have a public setter function.

If we want to allow setting the year, month, and day of the month of an existing `Date` object, a much safer alternative is to provide a setter function that modifies all three at once:

```
void Date::set_ymd(const int y, const int m, const int d)
{
    ...
}
```

Then, it would be much easier in an actual application for the setter function to check the arguments to ensure that the combination of all three values results in a valid `Date` object. Of course, the `Date` constructor that takes year, month, and day of the month argument values should also check the argument values.

5.6   *Rules from the Law of Demeter*

The Law of Demeter prescribes several rules that help us design proper loosely coupled classes. By following these rules, we avoid designing a class that has certain problematic dependencies on another class. Specifically, they tell whether a member function `afunc` of class `A` can call a member function `bfunc` of another class `B`:

A Function `afunc` can call function `bfunc` on a class `B` object if class `A` aggregates the object (i.e., class `A` has a member variable whose value is that of class `B` object or a pointer to that class `B` object).

B Function `afunc` can call function `bfunc` on a class `B` object if the object was passed as an argument to `afunc`.

C Function `afunc` can call function `bfunc` on a class `B` object if `afunc` instantiated the object.

D Function `afunc` should not call function `bfunc` on a class `B` object that was returned by a call on another object's member function.

The Law of Demeter basically says that a class should only call member functions of objects that are close to it. Classes `DemeterAuto`, `Engine`, and `Sparkplug` provide examples that obey and disobey the law's rules.

Listing 5.14   (Program 5.7 DemeterAuto): `DemeterAuto.h`

```
class Sparkplug
{
public:
    void replace() { /* replace sparkplug */ }
};
```

```
class Engine
{
public:
    Sparkplug *get_sparkplug() const { return plug; }

    void replace_sparkplug()
    {
        plug->replace();
    }
private:
    Sparkplug *plug;
};
```

> ◄ Obeys: plug is a member variable of class Engine (rule A).

```
class DemeterAuto
{
public:
    void service_sparkplug(Sparkplug *plug)
    {
        plug->replace();
    }

    void maintain_auto()
    {
        engine.replace_sparkplug();

        Sparkplug *plug1 = engine.get_sparkplug();
        plug1->replace();

        Sparkplug *plug2 = new Sparkplug();
        plug2->replace();
    }
private:
    Engine engine;
};
```

> Obeys: plug is a parameter of member function service_sparkplug() (rule B).

> Obeys: engine is a member variable of class DemeterAuto (rule A).

> DISOBEYS: the value of plug1 points to an object returned by the Engine object (rule D).

> Obeys: the value of plug2 points to an object instantiated by member function maintain_auto() (rule C).

5.7 But is the implementation really hidden?

To write an application that stores employee records, we could have a class `Employee` that records an employee's birthdate via a one-to-one aggregation with class `Date` (listing 5.15). We want an `Employee` object to be immutable by a regular user of the application—after we've created an object, the employee's id, name, and birthdate should not be changeable by such a user. All three private member variables, `employee_id`, `name`, and `birthdate` are in the hidden state implementation, and the class itself has no setter functions.

However, we'll use the mutable version of class `Date` (listings 5.9 and 5.10) with its public `set_julian()` setter function. We'll assume that a different class of the application, say `EmployeeForAdmin`, also aggregates class `Date` but has setter functions to allow an administrative user to correct an error in an employee's birthdate. However, a regular user should not be able to modify an employee's birthdate. Is making `birthdate` private sufficient?

Listing 5.15   (Program 5.8 HiddenDate-1): `Employee.h` **(faulty design)**

```
#include <iostream>
#include <string>
#include "Date.h"

using namespace std;

class Employee
{
public:
    Employee(long id, string name, Date *bdate)
        : employee_id(id), name(name), birthdate(bdate) {}

    Date *get_birthdate() const { return birthdate; }

    friend ostream& operator <<(ostream& os, const Employee& emp);

private:
    long employee_id;
    string name;

    Date *birthdate;
};

inline ostream& operator <<(ostream& os, const Employee& emp)
{
    os << "Employee #" <<emp.employee_id << endl;
    os << "  Name: " << emp.name << endl;
    os << "  Birthdate: "; emp.birthdate->print(); os << endl;

    return os;
}
```

Since class `Employee` has no setter functions, is an `Employee` object truly immutable? Listing 5.16 is a test program.

Listing 5.16   (Program 5.8 HiddenDate-1): `tester.cpp`

```
#include <iostream>
#include "Employee.h"

using namespace std;

int main()
{
    Date *date1 = new Date(2000, 1, 10);
    Employee mary(1234567890, "Mary", date1);       ◄──┐ Is this Employee
    cout << mary << endl;                               │ object immutable?

    int julian1 = date1->get_julian();
    date1->set_julian(julian1 + 366);               ◄──┐ Changes the birthdate
    cout << mary << endl;                               │ year to 2001

    Date *date2 = mary.get_birthdate();
```

```
int julian2 = date2->get_julian();
date2->set_julian(julian2 + 365);
cout << mary << endl;

return 0;
}
```

Changes the birthdate year to 2002

Here's the output:

```
Employee #1234567890
  Name: Mary
  Birthdate: 1/10/2000

Employee #1234567890
  Name: Mary
  Birthdate: 1/10/2001

Employee #1234567890
  Name: Mary
  Birthdate: 1/10/2002
```

Obviously, the `Employee` object is not immutable. There were several design failures:

- We first dynamically created a new `Birthday` object and assigned its pointer to variable `date1`. We used `date1` to create the `Employee` object.

- Because we had a pointer to the `Birthday` object that is now embedded in the `Employee` object, we were able to use that pointer to change the employee's birth year.

- Using the getter function of the `Employee` class, we obtained a pointer to the `Employee` object's embedded `Birthday` object. We used that pointer to change the employee's birth year again.

 Those sneaky pointers exposed my hidden implementation.

 This is a subtle design fault that is often overlooked.

This surely is a subtle design fault. If a class whose objects are supposed to be immutable provides pointers into its hidden state implementation, we can inadvertently use those pointers to modify an object's state at run time.

There are remedies to ensure that the `Employee` objects are immutable, as shown in listing 5.17. The class constructor should store a copy of the `Date` object that is passed to it. The getter function should return a pointer to a copy of the embedded `Date` object. Then, it will not be possible to change the birthdate embedded in the `Employee` object.

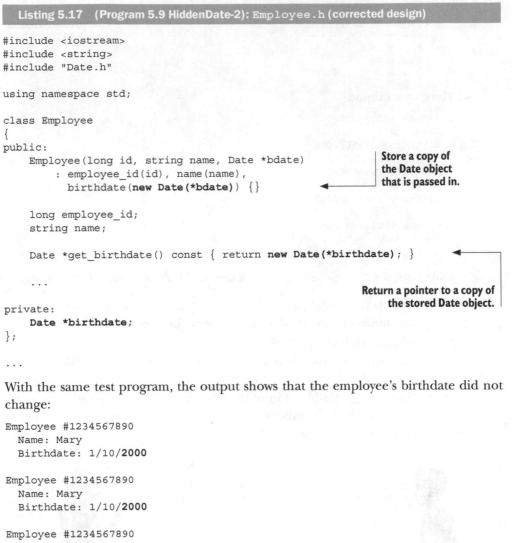

Listing 5.17   (Program 5.9 HiddenDate-2): `Employee.h` **(corrected design)**

```
#include <iostream>
#include <string>
#include "Date.h"

using namespace std;

class Employee
{
public:
    Employee(long id, string name, Date *bdate)
        : employee_id(id), name(name),
          birthdate(new Date(*bdate)) {}

    long employee_id;
    string name;

    Date *get_birthdate() const { return new Date(*birthdate); }

    ...

private:
    Date *birthdate;
};

...
```

Store a copy of the Date object that is passed in.

Return a pointer to a copy of the stored Date object.

With the same test program, the output shows that the employee's birthdate did not change:

```
Employee #1234567890
  Name: Mary
  Birthdate: 1/10/2000

Employee #1234567890
  Name: Mary
  Birthdate: 1/10/2000

Employee #1234567890
  Name: Mary
  Birthdate: 1/10/2000
```

5.8   *The Open-Closed Principle supports code stability*

In chapter 2, during the third development iteration of the book catalogue application, we created several subclasses for the superclass `Attributes`. Figure 5.5 shows that ill-fated design.

Although we ultimately determined that having many subclasses was a poor design for the application, figure 5.5 is a good example of the Open-Closed Principle, according to which we should close a class against modification but open it for subclassing (section 2.3.3). It assumes that we are confident that a class has captured all the common attributes and behaviors of a set of objects, and therefore, the design of that class should not change. That supports code stability. However, we allow extending the class for objects that have attributes and behaviors beyond the common ones. In other words, the closed class is the superclass, and the extensions are its subclasses.

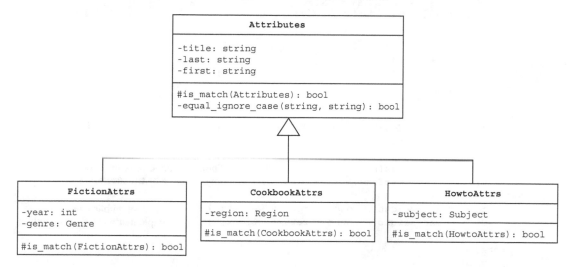

Figure 5.5   **A design of the book catalogue application with superclass** `Attributes` **and its subclasses. In the class diagram for** `Attributes`**, the symbol # indicates the member function** `is_match(Attributes)` **is protected—it is visible to the subclasses but hidden to other code.**

The Open-Closed Principle is another way to design classes with hidden implementation. By making the member variables and member functions of the superclass private, we can hide how we implement the common parts of the state and behavior inherited by its subclasses. In class `Attributes`, member variables `title`, `last`, and `first` are private. `FictionAttrs` extends `Attributes`, so how that class implements the book title, so the subclass objects hide how they implement the `title`, `last`, and `first` parts of their state. The class extends its hidden state implementation with its private `year` and `genre` member variables.

Manning Comix

The following listing is another example of the Open-Closed Principle. Suppose that class `Mammal` has all the common attributes and behaviors of mammals that a particular application needs. Therefore, we can close this class.

Listing 5.18   (Program 5.10 Mammals): `Mammal.h`

```cpp
#include <iostream>

using namespace std;

class Mammal
{
public:
    Mammal(const double w, const double h) : weight(w), height(h) {}
    virtual ~Mammal() {}

    virtual void eat() = 0;                              Common public behavior to be
    virtual void perform() = 0;                          implemented by the subclasses

    double get_weight() const { return weight; }         Common public behavior
    double get_height() const { return height; }         implemented by this superclass

protected:
    void sleep()
    {                                                    Hidden common behavior
        cout << "close eyes" << endl;                    accessible only by the subclasses
        snore();
    }

private:
    double weight, height;              ◄───── Hidden common state implementation

    void snore()
    {                                                    Hidden common behavior
        cout << "Zzzz" << endl;                          implementation
    }
};
```

We close class `Mammal`, but we can keep it open for extension. Subclasses `Human` and `Cat` each extends the class by adding its member variables and functions. Each subclass must define member functions `eat()` and `perform()`. Protected member function `sleep()` is visible to `Mammal` subclasses but is hidden from other code.

Listing 5.19   (Program 5.10 Mammals): `Mammals.h`

```cpp
#include <iostream>
#include "Mammal.h"

class Human : public Mammal
{
public:
    Human(const double w, const double h, const bool ng)
        : Mammal(w, h), needs_glasses(ng) {};
```

```
    ~Human() {};

    void eat()      { cout << "eat with knife and fork"
                            << endl; }
    void perform() { read_book(); sleep(); }
private:
    bool needs_glasses;

    void read_book()
    {
        if (needs_glasses) cout << "squint" << endl;
        cout << «turn pages» << endl;
    }
};

class Cat : public Mammal
{
public:
    Cat(const double w, const double h, const double ff)
        : Mammal(w, h), fur_factor(ff) {};

    ~Cat() {}

    void eat()      { cout << "eat from a bowl" << endl; }
    void perform() { shed(); }
private:
    double fur_factor;

    void shed()
    {
        cout << "shed ";
        if (fur_factor > 1.0) cout << "a lot";
        else                  cout << "a little";
        cout << endl;
    }
};
```

- **Public implementation of common behavior for humans** — `void eat()` / `void perform()`
- Hidden extended state implementation for humans ← `bool needs_glasses;`
- **Hidden extended behavior implementation for humans** — `void read_book()`
- **Public implementation of common behavior for cats** — `void eat()` / `void perform()`
- Hidden extended state implementation for cats ← `double fur_factor;`
- **Hidden extended behavior implementation for cats** — `void shed()`

Subclass Human keeps the implementation of its part of the state (member variable needs_glasses) and behavior (member function read_book()) hidden. Likewise, subclass Cat keeps the implementation of its part of the state (member variable fur_factor) and behavior (member function shed()) hidden. Because they are declared to be pure virtual in superclass Mammal, both subclasses must implement the public member functions eat() and perform(). The implementation of the common parts of the state (height and weight) and behavior (snoring) of each subclass are hidden by their superclass Mammal. The following listing is a test program.

Listing 5.20   (Program 5.10 Mammals): `tester.cpp`

```cpp
#include "Mammals.h"

int main()
{
    Human ron(77.11, 1.85, true);
    cout << "Human Ron" << endl;
    cout << "weight: " << ron.get_weight() << " kg" << endl;
    cout << "height: " << ron.get_height() << " m" << endl;
    ron.eat();
    ron.perform();

    cout << endl;

    Cat buddy(5.55, 0.30, 1.25);
    cout << "Cat Buddy" << endl;
    cout << "weight: " << buddy.get_weight() << " kg" << endl;
    cout << "height: " << buddy.get_height() << " m" << endl;
    buddy.eat();
    buddy.perform();

    return 0;
}
```

The output is

```
Human Ron
weight: 77.11 kg
height: 1.85 m
eat with knife and fork
squint
turn pages
close eyes
Zzzz

Cat Buddy
weight: 5.55 kg
height: 0.3 m
eat from a bowl
shed a lot
```

We implement a common core implementation in a superclass and lock it from further changes to support code stability, but we can extend the implementation in subclasses. We can hide the common and the extended implementations.

Summary

- Minimize dependencies on a class by hiding how the class implements state to support encapsulation. Hide member variables and member functions by making them private. When the hidden implementation of a class is encapsulated, we can refactor the implementation to improve it without causing changes to any code using the class.

- Public getter and setter member functions allow controlled access to hidden object state. The getter functions return values from an object's state without revealing how the state is implemented. The setter functions modify an object's state without revealing how the state is implemented.

- A setter member function should not put an object into an invalid state. We must be careful what setter functions to provide.

- An immutable class creates objects that cannot be modified after we've constructed them. Such a class should not provide public setter functions.

- A class whose objects are supposed to be immutable must not provide pointers to its hidden state implementation because that would allow other code to use the pointers to modify the object's state at run time.

- According to the Lazy Evaluation Principle, runtime performance should be improved by delaying an expensive calculation until its results are needed.

- The Law of Demeter prescribes rules to guide designing classes that have no problematic dependencies on other classes.

- The Open-Closed Principle says to close a superclass for modification but open it for extensions by subclasses. The superclass can hide and encapsulate the implementation of the common parts of the state and behavior inherited by its subclasses. This principle supports code stability.

Don't surprise your users

6

This chapter covers

- The Principle of Least Astonishment and how to avoid surprising your users
- Preventing unexpectedly poor runtime performance
- Careful coding with C++ vectors to avoid performance problems
- Applying Programming by Contract to a class and its member functions

We all love surprise parties, but being surprised by the results of a function call is a definite sign of poor design. Well-designed software should not contain any surprises that can cause runtime logic errors or poor performance.

Ideally, when we design a class, its objects will behave and perform just the way its users expect. A user can be another programmer who uses the class or an end user who interacts with the application. Unexpected behavior can lead to runtime logic errors or applications that don't perform well.

This chapter covers some common unwanted surprises regarding our code and ways to eliminate them. Some bad surprises are simply how C++ works. However, some surprises in our code are a result of preventable coding faults, such as the common off-by-one error. A well-named function won't mislead another programmer to believe that the function does something other than what its name suggests. We can avoid the surprise of poor performance with more efficient programming or a better choice of data structures. Even code from the Standard Template Library (STL) such as the vector can lead our code to execute many unexpected operations if we don't understand how it works. The concept of Programming by Contract can eliminate many surprises by making explicit what another programmer can expect from a class we wrote.

6.1   *No surprises and the Principle of Least Astonishment*

There are many ways in which poor design can cause surprises. The *Principle of Least Astonishment* states that there should be few, if any, surprises in our code.

> **The Principle of Least Astonishment**
>
> There should be few, if any, surprises for programmers (including ourselves later) who use our code. Surprises can cause logic and runtime errors and make code difficult to maintain.

This section covers two sources of surprises, off-by-one errors and misnamed functions. The common off-by-one error can cause hard-to-find logic errors in a program, but it is easily preventable as long as we are careful about such matters as how many times a loop executes. A function that we wrote and misnamed may cause another programmer to experience perplexing logic errors by assuming the function does something other than what its name suggests. Section 6.2 is devoted to another insidious source of surprises—poor performance.

Manning Comix

6.1.1 *Off-by-one errors*

It's easy, even for an experienced programmer, to make an off-by-one error, where a computed value is one more or one less than expected, or an operation occurs one more or one fewer time than expected. These deceptive errors are hard to find, and they can cause surprising runtime logic errors. A classic off-by-one error is a loop that goes around one too few or one too many times.

Listing 6.1   (Program 6.1 SurpriseLoop): `loop.cpp`

```cpp
#include <iostream>

using namespace std;

int main()
{
    int count = 0;

    for (int i = 5; i <= 10; i++)
    {
        count++;
        cout << "count = " << count << ", i = " << i << endl;
    }
}
```

> Potential off-by-one error: the loop executes not 10 − 5 = 5 times, but 10 − 5 + 1 = 6 times.

Indeed, this loop executes six times:

```
count = 1, i = 5
count = 2, i = 6
count = 3, i = 7
count = 4, i = 8
count = 5, i = 9
count = 6, i = 10
```

Of course, if the loop termination is instead `i < 10`, then the loop will indeed iterate five times. But then `i` will not reach the value 10.

I can see how off-by-one errors are common with loops.

Here's a sneakier example. Suppose we have an application that maintains the dates of scheduled appointments. Listing 6.2 shows a Date class that the application can use. Its private member variables year, month, and day record a date's year, month, and day of the month, respectively, and we pass integer values to the constructor to initialize those variables. Therefore, if we pass the values 2025, 2, and 4, we ought to expect to create a Date object that represents the date February 4, 2025. To keep this example short, we'll leave off checking the constructor's parameter values.

Listing 6.2   (Program 6.2 SurpriseDate-1): `Date.h`

```cpp
#include <iostream>
#include <string>

using namespace std;

class Date
{
public:
    Date(const int y, const int m, const int d)
        : year(y), month(m), day(d) {}

    friend ostream& operator <<(ostream& ostr, const Date& date);

private:
    static const string MONTH_NAMES[12];          // Private static
                                                  // constant string array
    int year, month, day;                         // of month names
};
```

Member variable MONTH_NAMES is a private static constant string array of month names. The overloaded << operator prints a date object in the form "month day, year" where the month is a capitalized three-letter abbreviation, such as

```
FEB 4, 2025
```

Listing 6.3   (Program 6.2 SurpriseDate-1): `Date.cpp` **(off-by-one error)**

```cpp
#include <iostream>
#include "Date.h"

const string Date::MONTH_NAMES[12] =
{
    "JAN", "FEB", "MAR", "APR", "MAY", "JUN",
    "JUL", "AUG", "SEP", "OCT", "NOV", "DEC"
};

ostream& operator <<(ostream& ostr, const Date& date)
{
    ostr << date.MONTH_NAMES[date.month]
        << " " << date.day << ", " << date.year;

    return ostr;
}
```

The following listing is a short test program.

Listing 6.4   (Program 6.2 SurpriseDate-1): `tester.cpp`

```cpp
#include <iostream>
#include "Date.h"

using namespace std;

int main()
{
    Date date(2025, 2, 4);  // February 4, 2025
    cout << date << endl;

    return 0;
}
```

The output from this program is

```
MAR 4, 2025
```

A nasty surprise! We expected FEB, not MAR.

This is only one example of the ubiquitous off-by-one error caused by array index values beginning with 0 and not 1. This surprise is compounded by the Date class having a major inconsistency: year and day of the month values are exact, but a month value apparently must be one less. This is not obvious to the programmer who uses the Date class, and hence the runtime logic error.

A well-designed class needs to remove the surprise. The following listing shows one way to do so. The output << operator silently subtracts 1 from date.month when indexing into the MONTH_NAMES string array.

Listing 6.5   (Program 6.3 SurpriseDate-2): `Date.cpp`

```cpp
#include <iostream>
#include "Date.h"

const string Date::MONTH_NAMES[12] = ...

ostream& operator <<(ostream& ostr, const Date& date)
{
    ostr << date.MONTH_NAMES[date.month - 1]        ◄──────  Subtract 1 from the
        << " " << date.day << ", " << date.year;            month value.

    return ostr;
}
```

This simple fix removes the surprise, and the output is correct:

```
FEB 4, 2025
```

Subtracting 1 from month has a tiny runtime cost. But if the cost is a concern, then there is another solution.

Listing 6.6   (Program 6.4 SurpriseDate-3): `Date.cpp`

```cpp
#include <iostream>
#include "Date.h"

const string Date::MONTH_NAMES[13] =              ◄────── 13 elements
{
    "",                                           ◄────── Dummy first element
    "JAN", "FEB", "MAR", "APR", "MAY", "JUN",
    "JUL", "AUG", "SEP", "OCT", "NOV", "DEC"
};

ostream& operator <<(ostream& ostr, const Date& date)
{
    ostr << date.MONTH_NAMES[date.month]          ◄──┐ No longer needs
         << " " << date.day << ", " << date.year;    │ to subtract 1

    return ostr;
}
```

Now, there are 13 `MONTH_NAMES` elements. `MONTH_NAMES[0]` is a dummy first element and operator `<<` no longer needs to subtract 1 from `month`. We've eliminated this runtime cost at the expense of one unused array element. Then, in class `Date`, we must change the declaration of the private static array:

```cpp
static const string MONTH_NAMES[13];
```

Again, the `Date` class behaves as expected, and the test program produces the correct output.

6.1.2   *Misnamed functions can mislead their callers*

A frequent source of unwanted surprises for a programmer using another programmer's code is a poorly named function that does something unexpected when called. Often, we know what we intend a function to do as we write it, and therefore, we may not realize that the name we chose is ambiguous or misleading. Or, the name may have been appropriate when we wrote the function, but we subsequently modified the function without changing its name.

Here's an example of how a poorly named function called by an unwary user can lead to a runtime logic error. Class `SortedList` is a subclass of `vector<int>`. The class has a static function `merge()` that takes three `SortedList` parameters—`list1` and `list2` to merge and `merged_list` to contain the merged elements. An overloaded `<<` operator prints the contents of a `SortedList` object.

Listing 6.7   (Program 6.5 SurpriseMerge-1): `SortedList.h`

```cpp
#include <iostream>
#include <vector>

using namespace std;
```

```cpp
class SortedList : public vector<int>
{
public:
    SortedList() {}

    SortedList(const initializer_list<int> init_list)
        : vector<int>(init_list) {}

    static void merge(const SortedList& list1,
                      const SortedList& list2,
                            SortedList& merged_list);
};

inline ostream& operator <<(ostream& ostr, const SortedList& list)
{
    for (int i : list) cout << " " << i;
    return ostr;
}
```

The public static function `SortedList::merge()` merges the elements of its first two parameters `list1` and `list2` and stores the merged elements into its third parameter `merged_list`. But the function also removes duplicate values from `merged_list`. This latter operation is not at all obvious from the function's name.

Listing 6.8   (Program 6.5 SurpriseMerge-1): `SortedList.cpp` **(bad surprises)**

```cpp
#include "SortedList.h"

void SortedList::merge(const SortedList& list1,
                       const SortedList& list2,
                             SortedList& merged_list)
{
    size_t size1 = list1.size();
    size_t size2 = list2.size();

    int i1 = 0;
    int i2 = 0;

    while ((i1 < size1) || (i2 < size2))
    {
        if (    (i1 < size1)
            && ((i2 == size2) || (list1[i1] <= list2[i2])))       // Merge
        {                                                          // SortedList list1
            merged_list.push_back(list1[i1]);                      // and list2 into
            i1++;                                                  // SortedList
        }                                                          // merged_list.
        else
        {
            merged_list.push_back(list2[i2]);
            i2++;
        }
    }

    int i = 0;
```

```
    while (i < merged_list.size())
    {
        int j = i + 1;      B

        while (j < merged_list.size())
        {
            if (merged_list[i] == merged_list[j])
            {
                merged_list.erase(merged_list.begin() + j);
            }
            else j++;
        }

        i++;
    }
}
```

Remove duplicate values from merged_list.

Our test program creates and initializes two sorted `SortedList` objects `list1` and `list2` and creates the `SortedList` object `merged_list` (listing 6.9). In an actual application, we should check that the values in the two lists are indeed sorted. The program passes the three lists to function `SortedList::merge()`. Based on the function name, we expect upon return that `merged_list` will contain all the merged values from `list1` and `list2`. The program then calls function `print_frequencies()`, which uses an STL `map` to compute and print the frequency of each value in `merged_list`.

Listing 6.9   (Program 6.5 SurpriseMerge-1): `tester.cpp`

```cpp
#include <iostream>
#include <iomanip>
#include <map>
#include "SortedList.h"

using namespace std;

void print_frequencies(const SortedList& merged_list);

int main()
{
    SortedList list1 {2, 5, 5, 5, 7, 11, 11, 11, 13, 13};
    SortedList list2 {0, 1, 2, 2, 2, 2, 4, 4, 5, 6, 7, 7, 9, 11};

    cout << "List 1:" << list1 << endl;
    cout << "List 2:" << list2 << endl;

    SortedList merged_list;
    SortedList::merge(list1, list2, merged_list);
    cout << "Merged:" << merged_list << endl;

    cout << endl;
    print_frequencies(merged_list);

    return 0;
}
```

```
void print_frequencies(const SortedList& merged_list)
{
    map<int, int> freqs;                                    ← Map of the
                                                              merged values
    cout << "Frequency table" << endl;                        and their
                                                              frequencies
    for (int i : merged_list)
    {
        if (freqs.find(i) == freqs.end()) freqs[i] = 1;     ← Computes
        else                              freqs[i]++;          frequencies
    }

    for (map<int, int>::iterator it = freqs.begin();
         it != freqs.end(); it++)
    {
        cout << setw(7) << it->first << ": " << it->second << endl;
    }
}
```

The output is

```
List 1: 2 5 5 5 7 11 11 11 13 13
List 2: 0 1 2 2 2 2 4 4 5 6 7 7 9 11
Merged: 0 1 2 4 5 6 7 9 11 13

Frequency table
      0: 1
      1: 1
      2: 1
      4: 1
      5: 1
      6: 1
      7: 1
      9: 1
     11: 1
     13: 1
```

Surprise! We have a serious logic error. Because the function unexpectedly removed all the duplicate values, each frequency is at most 1. A better name for the function that won't mislead a programmer might be `merge_and_deduplicate`.

Manning Comix

6.2 *Poor performance is an unwelcome surprise*

Poor runtime performance is another bad surprise, caused by often hidden, inefficient programming. Poor performance can even come from using a data structure from the STL, such as the STL vector, if we don't fully understand how the data structure operates.

Poor performance can cause longer running time or using too much memory or other resources. An application that does what it's supposed to do (i.e., it meets its functional requirements) but performs poorly (i.e., it fails to meet a nonfunctional performance requirement) is an unwelcome surprise. Poor performance can result from careless use of a data structure. When we call a function written for an application or a standard library function, we do not expect that call to result in unwanted surprises.

6.2.1 *Bad design can cause unexpected performance problems*

Choosing the right algorithms is an important part of good design. A function that implements a poorly chosen algorithm can lead to unexpected performance problems, such as long running time for the unwary caller of the function.

Consider the function `merge()` in listing 6.8. As the lengths of the two vectors grow linearly, the running time of the function grows exponentially.

The growing running times are due to the way we removed the duplicate values from `merged_list`. The second `while` loop contains a nested third `while` loop, but a much better design would not require nested loops. In the first `while` loop that performs the merge, we can include tests to prevent duplicate values from entering `merged_list`, as in the following listing. By taking advantage of the sorted lists, we simply don't append a value to `merged_list` if it equals the last appended value.

Listing 6.10 (Program 6.6 SurpriseMerge-2): `SortedList.cpp` **(improved performance)**

```cpp
#include "SortedList.h"

void SortedList::merge_and_deduplicate(const SortedList& list1,
                                       const SortedList& list2,
                                       SortedList& merged_list)
{
    size_t size1 = list1.size();
    size_t size2 = list2.size();

    size_t merged_size = 0;

    int i1 = 0;
    int i2 = 0;

    while ((i1 < size1) || (i2 < size2))
    {
        if (    (i1 < size1)
            && ((i2 == size2) || (list1[i1] <= list2[i2])))
        {
```

```
            if (    (merged_size == 0)
                 || (list1[i1] != merged_list[merged_size-1]))          ◄─────────┐
            {                                                           ◄─────────┤
                merged_list.push_back(list1[i1]);                                 │
                merged_size++;                                                    │
            }                                                                     │
            i1++;                                                                 │
        }                                                                         │
        else                                                                      │
        {                                                                         │
            if (    (merged_size == 0)                                   ◄─────────┤
                 || (list2[i2] != merged_list[merged_size-1]))          ◄─────────┤
            {                                                                     │
                merged_list.push_back(list2[i2]);                                 │
                merged_size++;                                                    │
            }                                                                     │
            i2++;                                                                 │
        }                                                                         │
    }                                                                             │
}
```

Don't append a duplicate value (a value equal to the last appended value).

This improved version of the merge function scales well. As the lengths of the two SortedList objects increase linearly, the function's run time increases approximately linearly in proportion.

> **NOTE**   We *refactor* code by redesigning it to improve it in some way, such as making it perform more efficiently, but without changing its functionality or how to use it. Refactoring is a common operation during development iterations.

6.2.2   *The vexatious performance of C++ vectors*

Many object-oriented languages have object variables that can be assigned only pointers or references to objects at run time. However, C++ variables can be assigned object values directly. C++ variables whose values are objects can cause runtime performance surprises for programmers who do not use them carefully.

C++ programmers learn that vectors from the STL are more convenient to use than arrays. An STL vector internally manages a hidden dynamic array to store its elements. We can insert an element anywhere into a vector or append elements at its end. We can delete any element from the vector. We don't need to write code to keep track of a vector's storage requirements because the vector automatically adjusts the size of its internal dynamic array as we insert, append, and delete elements. However, we can inadvertently incur some nasty performance.

C++ vectors are so easy to use! They're powerful, too. I can append, insert, and delete elements and not have to maintain a dynamic array.

Yes, they're powerful. They do a lot for you automatically at run time. But if you're not careful, vectors can have surprising performance problems.

Here's an example of how careless use of STL vectors can lead to performance problems. Suppose we're writing an application that keeps track of the dates of appointments. We can reuse the Date class (listing 6.6). Class Appointments keeps the dates in private member variable dates, which is an STL vector of Date objects (listing 6.11). Public member functions at() returns the Date object in the vector at a given index, append() appends a new Date object to the end of the vector, insert() inserts a Date object into the vector at a given index, and remove() removes a Date object at a given index from the vector.

To keep this example short, we won't do the runtime checking such as making sure that a vector index is within the valid range that a real application must do. The code for the class appears to be simple and straightforward, but it has serious hidden performance problems.

Listing 6.11   (Program 6.7 SurpriseVector-1): `Appointments.h` **(poor performance)**

```cpp
#include <vector>
#include "Date.h"

using namespace std;

class Appointments
{
public:
    vector<Date> get_dates() const { return dates; }

    Date at(const int index) const { return dates[index]; }
    void append(const Date date)    { dates.push_back(date); }

    void insert(const int index, const Date date)
    {
        dates.insert(dates.begin() + index, date);
    }

    void remove(const int index)
    {
        dates.erase(dates.begin() + index);
    }

private:                                      Private vector
    vector<Date> dates;        ◄───────────   of Date objects
};
```

A test program (listing 6.12) performs the following operations:

- Construct Date objects.
- Append Date objects to the vector.
- Initialize a Date variable from an existing Date object.
- Assign an existing Date object to a Date variable.
- Insert a Date object into the vector.
- Remove a Date object from the vector.

The program prints messages to indicate what operations it's about to perform, and it prints the contents of the vector to confirm the results of the operations. The statements that perform the operations are set in bold.

Listing 6.12   (Program 6.7 SurpriseVector-1): `tester.cpp`

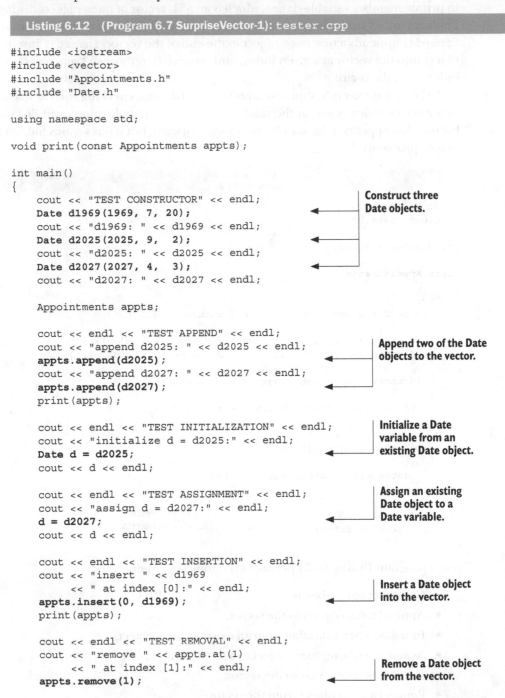

```cpp
#include <iostream>
#include <vector>
#include "Appointments.h"
#include "Date.h"

using namespace std;

void print(const Appointments appts);

int main()
{
    cout << "TEST CONSTRUCTOR" << endl;
    Date d1969(1969, 7, 20);
    cout << "d1969: " << d1969 << endl;
    Date d2025(2025, 9,  2);
    cout << "d2025: " << d2025 << endl;
    Date d2027(2027, 4,  3);
    cout << "d2027: " << d2027 << endl;

    Appointments appts;

    cout << endl << "TEST APPEND" << endl;
    cout << "append d2025: " << d2025 << endl;
    appts.append(d2025);
    cout << "append d2027: " << d2027 << endl;
    appts.append(d2027);
    print(appts);

    cout << endl << "TEST INITIALIZATION" << endl;
    cout << "initialize d = d2025:" << endl;
    Date d = d2025;
    cout << d << endl;

    cout << endl << "TEST ASSIGNMENT" << endl;
    cout << "assign d = d2027:" << endl;
    d = d2027;
    cout << d << endl;

    cout << endl << "TEST INSERTION" << endl;
    cout << "insert " << d1969
         << " at index [0]:" << endl;
    appts.insert(0, d1969);
    print(appts);

    cout << endl << "TEST REMOVAL" << endl;
    cout << "remove " << appts.at(1)
         << " at index [1]:" << endl;
    appts.remove(1);
```

Construct three Date objects.

Append two of the Date objects to the vector.

Initialize a Date variable from an existing Date object.

Assign an existing Date object to a Date variable.

Insert a Date object into the vector.

Remove a Date object from the vector.

```
    print(appts);

    cout << endl << "Done!" << endl;
    return 0;
}

void print(const Appointments appts)
{
    int i = 0;

    cout << "printing vector ..." << endl;
    for (Date date : appts.get_dates())
    {
        cout << "[" << i << "] " << date << endl;
        i++;
    }
}
```

The program's output:

```
TEST CONSTRUCTOR
d1969: JUL 20, 1969
d2025: SEP 2, 2025
d2027: APR 3, 2027

TEST APPEND
append d2025: SEP 2, 2025
append d2027: APR 3, 2027
printing vector ...
[0] SEP 2, 2025
[1] APR 3, 2027

TEST INITIALIZATION
initialize d = d2025:
SEP 2, 2025

TEST ASSIGNMENT
assign d = d2027:
APR 3, 2027

TEST INSERTION
insert JUL 20, 1969 at index [0]:
printing vector ...
[0] JUL 20, 1969
[1] SEP 2, 2025
[2] APR 3, 2027

TEST REMOVAL
remove SEP 2, 2025 at index [1]:
printing vector ...
[0] JUL 20, 1969
[1] APR 3, 2027

Done!
```

The output is what we expect and appears unremarkable.

However, the performance surprise is what C++ automatically does behind our backs at run time during this short test. We'll see later that this program is poorly designed and causes many extra operations. To reveal these operations, we can add special output statements to class `Date`. We can instrument each call to the default constructor, regular constructor, copy constructor, and copy assignment operator, and destructor to write a message.

> ### The Big Three
>
> A C++ class's destructor, copy constructor, and copy assignment operator are known as The Big Three. The rule of thumb says that if you need to explicitly implement any one of them rather than use the default, you should implement all three.
>
> With the addition of the move constructor and the move assignment operator, we get The Big Five. (See http://mng.bz/5lpD.)

Because we're overriding the default copy constructor and the default copy assignment operator, our implementations must explicitly perform the member-by-member copies and assignments, respectively.

Listing 6.13   (Program 6.8 SurpriseVector-2): `Date.h` (instrumented)

```
#include <iostream>
#include <string>

using namespace std;

class Date
{
public:
    Date() : year(2000), month(1), day(1)
    {
        cout << "(default constructor) " << endl;
    }

    Date(const int y, const int m, const int d)
        : year(y), month(m), day(d)
    {
        cout << "(regular constructor) "; print(); cout << endl;
    }

    Date(const Date& other)
    {
        cout << "(copy constructor) "; other.print(); cout << endl;

        year  = other.year;                    Explicit member-by-
        month = other.month;                   member copying
        day   = other.day;
    }
```

```
    Date& operator =(const Date& other)
    {
        cout << "(assignment operator) "; other.print();
        cout << endl;

        if (this == &other) return *this;

        year  = other.year;                          Explicit member-by-
        month = other.month;                         member assignments
        day   = other.day;

        return *this;
    }

    ~Date()
    {
        cout << «(destructor) «; print(); cout << endl;
    }

    void print() const;

private:
    static const string MONTH_NAMES[13];

    int year, month, day;
};
```

The instrumented program output shows all the calls to the regular and copy constructors, destructor, and assign operator:

```
TEST CONSTRUCTOR
(regular constructor) JUL 20, 1969
d1969: JUL 20, 1969
(regular constructor) SEP 2, 2025
d2025: SEP 2, 2025
(regular constructor) APR 3, 2027
d2027: APR 3, 2027


TEST APPEND
append d2025: SEP 2, 2025
(copy constructor) SEP 2, 2025
(copy constructor) SEP 2, 2025
(destructor) SEP 2, 2025
append d2027: APR 3, 2027
(copy constructor) APR 3, 2027
(copy constructor) APR 3, 2027
(copy constructor) SEP 2, 2025
(destructor) SEP 2, 2025
(destructor) APR 3, 2027
(copy constructor) SEP 2, 2025
(copy constructor) APR 3, 2027
printing vector ...
```

Pass Date object d2027 by value to function append().

Vector member function push_back() makes a copy of its Date argument d2027.

The vector allocated a new longer internal dynamic array, so copy its Date object d2025 from the old array to the new array.

Deallocate Date object d2025 in the old dynamic array and then deallocate the old array.

Date argument d2027 to function append() goes out of scope, so deallocate it.

Pass the Appointments argument by value to function print(), so copy the vector's Date elements d2025 and d2027.

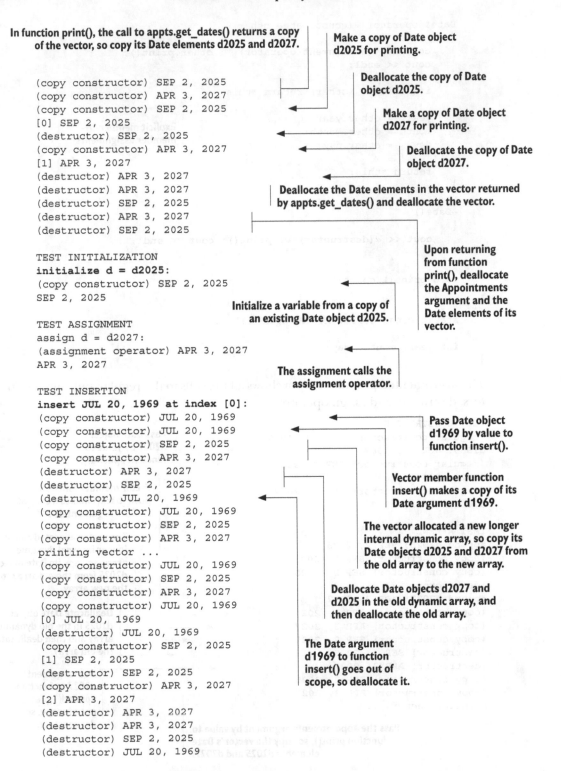

In function print(), the call to appts.get_dates() returns a copy of the vector, so copy its Date elements d2025 and d2027.

Make a copy of Date object d2025 for printing.

```
(copy constructor) SEP 2, 2025
(copy constructor) APR 3, 2027
(copy constructor) SEP 2, 2025
[0] SEP 2, 2025
(destructor) SEP 2, 2025
(copy constructor) APR 3, 2027
[1] APR 3, 2027
(destructor) APR 3, 2027
(destructor) APR 3, 2027
(destructor) SEP 2, 2025
(destructor) APR 3, 2027
(destructor) SEP 2, 2025
```

Deallocate the copy of Date object d2025.

Make a copy of Date object d2027 for printing.

Deallocate the copy of Date object d2027.

Deallocate the Date elements in the vector returned by appts.get_dates() and deallocate the vector.

Upon returning from function print(), deallocate the Appointments argument and the Date elements of its vector.

```
TEST INITIALIZATION
initialize d = d2025:
(copy constructor) SEP 2, 2025
SEP 2, 2025
```

Initialize a variable from a copy of an existing Date object d2025.

```
TEST ASSIGNMENT
assign d = d2027:
(assignment operator) APR 3, 2027
APR 3, 2027
```

The assignment calls the assignment operator.

```
TEST INSERTION
insert JUL 20, 1969 at index [0]:
(copy constructor) JUL 20, 1969
(copy constructor) JUL 20, 1969
(copy constructor) SEP 2, 2025
(copy constructor) APR 3, 2027
(destructor) APR 3, 2027
(destructor) SEP 2, 2025
(destructor) JUL 20, 1969
(copy constructor) JUL 20, 1969
(copy constructor) SEP 2, 2025
(copy constructor) APR 3, 2027
printing vector ...
(copy constructor) JUL 20, 1969
(copy constructor) SEP 2, 2025
(copy constructor) APR 3, 2027
(copy constructor) JUL 20, 1969
[0] JUL 20, 1969
(destructor) JUL 20, 1969
(copy constructor) SEP 2, 2025
[1] SEP 2, 2025
(destructor) SEP 2, 2025
(copy constructor) APR 3, 2027
[2] APR 3, 2027
(destructor) APR 3, 2027
(destructor) APR 3, 2027
(destructor) SEP 2, 2025
(destructor) JUL 20, 1969
```

Pass Date object d1969 by value to function insert().

Vector member function insert() makes a copy of its Date argument d1969.

The vector allocated a new longer internal dynamic array, so copy its Date objects d2025 and d2027 from the old array to the new array.

Deallocate Date objects d2027 and d2025 in the old dynamic array, and then deallocate the old array.

The Date argument d1969 to function insert() goes out of scope, so deallocate it.

```
(destructor) APR 3, 2027
(destructor) SEP 2, 2025
(destructor) JUL 20, 1969

TEST REMOVAL
remove (copy constructor) SEP 2, 2025
SEP 2, 2025 at index [1]:
(destructor) SEP 2, 2025
(assignment operator) APR 3, 2027
(destructor) APR 3, 2027
(copy constructor) JUL 20, 1969
(copy constructor) APR 3, 2027
printing vector ...
(copy constructor) JUL 20, 1969
(copy constructor) APR 3, 2027
(copy constructor) JUL 20, 1969
[0] JUL 20, 1969
(destructor) JUL 20, 1969
(copy constructor) APR 3, 2027
[1] APR 3, 2027
(destructor) APR 3, 2027
(destructor) APR 3, 2027
(destructor) JUL 20, 1969
(destructor) APR 3, 2027
(destructor) JUL 20, 1969

Done!
(destructor) APR 3, 2027
(destructor) APR 3, 2027
(destructor) JUL 20, 1969
(destructor) APR 3, 2027
(destructor) SEP 2, 2025
(destructor) JUL 20, 1969
```

The call to appts.at(1) returns a copy of the Date object d2025 from the vector at index 1.

Deallocate Date object d2025 from the vector at index 1.

Replace the Date object removed from the vector at index 1 by assigning the Date object d2027 at index 2.

Deallocate the old Date object d2027 at index 2

Deallocate the local Appointments object appts and the Date objects in its vector.

Deallocate local Date objects d2027, d2025, and dl969.

This alarming output shows operations that C++ automatically performed on our behalf when we ran the test program. Applications where many automatic and hidden operations occur at run time can result in appallingly poor performance. In this example, not only is the running time longer, but there are many memory allocations and deallocations.

To understand this output that was generated by our instrumentation of class `Date`, we can analyze some of the calls made by the test program and identify the automatic operations performed by C++ at run time (figures 6.1–6.7). When we call `appts.append(d2027)` after (a copy of) `Date` object `d2025` is already in the vector:

1 Pass the `Date` object `d2027` argument by value to call `appts.append()`, so make a copy of the object by calling the copy constructor.
2 Vector member function `push_back()` appends a copy of its `Date` object `d2027` argument, so call the copy constructor.
3 The vector must grow by one, so it allocates a new longer internal dynamic array.
4 Copy `Date` object `d2025` from the old dynamic array to the new array, so call the copy constructor:

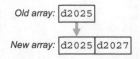

Figure 6.1

5 Deallocate the elements of the old dynamic array, and call the destructor of Date element d2025 in the old array:

Figure 6.2

6 Upon returning from the call to function appts.append(), its copy of d2027 goes out of scope, so call the destructor of Date object d2027.

When we call function print() with Date objects d2025 and d2027 already in the vector,

1 Pass the Appointments argument by value, so copy each of the vector's Date objects by calling their copy constructors.
2 In function print(), the call to appts.get_dates() returns a copy of the vector, so call the copy constructor for each of its Date objects.
3 Make a copy of Date object d2025 in the vector for printing.
4 Deallocate the copy of Date object d2025.
5 Make a copy of Date object d2027 in the vector for printing.
6 Deallocate the copy of Date object d2027.
7 Deallocate each Date object in the vector returned by appts.get_dates().
8 Upon return from function print(), its Appointments copy goes out of scope, so deallocate the argument and each Date object in its vector.

Similar operations occur when we insert a Date object into the vector as when we appended an object. The vector must grow by one, so it allocates a new longer internal dynamic array and deallocates the old array. When we call appts.insert(0, d1969) with Date objects d2025 and d2027 already in the vector,

1 Pass the Date object d1969 argument by value to call appts.append(), and copy the object by calling the copy constructor.
2 Vector member function insert() appends a copy of its Date argument, so call the copy constructor.
3 The vector must grow by one, so it allocates a new longer internal dynamic array.

4 Copy `Date` objects `d2025` and `d2027` from the old dynamic array to the new array, so call their copy constructors:

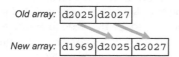

Figure 6.3

5 Deallocate the elements of the old dynamic array, and call the destructors of `Date` objects `d2025` and `d2027` in the old array:

Figure 6.4

6 Upon returning from the call to function `appts.insert()`, its argument goes out of scope, so call the destructor of `Date` object `d1969`.

When we call function `appts.remove()` to remove the object from the vector at index 1,

1 The call to `appts.at(1)` returns a copy of the `Date` object `d2025` at index 1.

2 Deallocate the `Date` object `d2025` being removed from the vector at index 1:

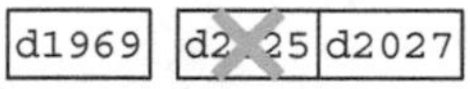

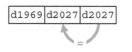

Figure 6.5

3 Replace the removed object by assigning it the `Date` object `d2027` at index 2, and call the copy assignment operator:

Figure 6.6

4 Deallocate the old `Date` object `d2027` at index 2. These last three steps moved each object that follows the removed object up one position to fill in the newly emptied position:

d1969 d2027 d2027

Figure 6.7

The C++ standard vector class

A standard C++ `std::vector` class manages an internal dynamic array whose storage automatically grows at run time as needed, which makes vectors convenient for programmers to use. The `vector` class uses strategies to reduce the need to create a new dynamic array every time new elements are added. We can call its `reserve()` member function to pre-allocate a vector of a given size. When the vector must create a new internal dynamic array to accommodate the addition of new elements, it chooses an optimal amount to make the new array's size longer than the old array's size. Then, subsequent additions of elements might not require creating new arrays.

To mitigate much of our application's bad performance, we need to redesign the `Appointments` class to use pointers to `Date` objects rather than `Date` objects directly. Member variable `dates` is now a vector of pointers to `Date` objects. Member functions `append()` and `insert()` are each passed a pointer to the `Date` object, and member function `at()` returns a pointer to a `Date` object.

Listing 6.14   (Program 6.9 SurpriseVector-3): `Appointments.h`

```cpp
#include <vector>
#include "Date.h"

using namespace std;

class Appointments
{                                               Use pointers to Date objects.
public:
    vector<Date *> get_dates() const { return dates; }

    Date *at(const int index) const { return dates[index]; }
    void append(Date * const date)  { dates.push_back(date); }

    void insert(const int index, Date * const date)
    {
        dates.insert(dates.begin() + index, date);
    }

    void remove(const int index)
    {
        dates.erase(dates.begin() + index);
    }

private:                          A vector of pointers
    vector<Date *> dates;         to Date objects
};
```

A new version of the test program dynamically creates new `Date` objects. The values of its variables and the values of the arguments that it passes are pointers to those `Date` objects. Additionally, it passes the `Appointments` argument `appts` more sensibly by reference to the `print()` function, as shown in the following listing.

Listing 6.15   (Program 6.9 SurpriseVector-3): `tester.cpp`

```cpp
#include <iostream>
#include <vector>
#include "Appointments.h"
#include "Date.h"

using namespace std;

void print(const Appointments& appts);

int main()
{
    cout << "TEST CONSTRUCTOR" << endl;
    Date *d1969 = new Date(1969,  7, 20);
    cout << "d1969: " << *d1969 << endl;
    Date *d2025 = new Date(2025,  9,  2);
    cout << "d2025: " << *d2025 << endl;
    Date *d2027 = new Date(2027,  4,  3);
    cout << "d2027: " << *d2027 << endl;

    Appointments appts;

    cout << endl << "TEST APPEND" << endl;
    cout << "append d2025: " << *d2025 << endl;
    appts.append(d2025);
    cout << "append d2027: " << *d2027 << endl;
    appts.append(d2027);
    print(appts);

    cout << endl << "TEST INITIALIZATION" << endl;
    cout << "initialize d = d2025:" << endl;
    Date *d = d2025;
    cout << *d << endl;

    cout << endl << "TEST ASSIGNMENT" << endl;
    cout << "assign d = d2027:" << endl;
    d = d2027;
    cout << *d << endl;

    cout << endl << "TEST INSERTION" << endl;
    cout << "insert " << *d1969
         << " at index [0]:" << endl;
    appts.insert(0, d1969);
    print(appts);

    cout << endl << "TEST REMOVAL" << endl;
    cout << "remove " << *appts.at(1)
         << " at index [1]:" << endl;
    appts.remove(1);
    print(appts);

    cout << endl << "TEST DESTRUCTOR" << endl;
```

Reference parameter
Appointments&

Dynamically create Date
objects and initialize the
variables with pointers
to the objects.

```
        delete d1969;                    Explicitly delete the dynamically
        delete d2025;                    created Date objects.
        delete d2027;


        cout << endl << "Done!" << endl;
        return 0;
}

void print(const Appointments& appts)
{
        int i = 0;

        cout << "printing vector ..." << endl;
        for (Date *date : appts.get_dates())
        {
            cout << "[" << i << "] " << *date << endl;
            i++;
        }
}
```

The output from this version of the program shows that, even with the instrumented Date class (listing 6.13), there are no longer any extra calls to the copy constructor, the copy assignment operator, and destructor. If allowed by the application logic, using pointers to objects rather than the objects directly can eliminate many performance surprises.

```
TEST CONSTRUCTOR
(regular constructor) JUL 20, 1969
d1969: JUL 20, 1969
(regular constructor) SEP 2, 2025
d2025: SEP 2, 2025
(regular constructor) APR 3, 2027
d2027: APR 3, 2027

TEST APPEND
append d2025: SEP 2, 2025
append d2027: APR 3, 2027
printing vector ...
[0] SEP 2, 2025
[1] APR 3, 2027

TEST INITIALIZATION
initialize d = d2025:
SEP 2, 2025

TEST ASSIGNMENT
assign d = d2027:
APR 3, 2027

TEST INSERTION
insert JUL 20, 1969 at index [0]:
printing vector ...
[0] JUL 20, 1969
[1] SEP 2, 2025
[2] APR 3, 2027
```

```
TEST REMOVAL
remove SEP 2, 2025 at index [1]:
printing vector ...
[0] JUL 20, 1969
[1] APR 3, 2027

TEST DESTRUCTOR
(destructor) JUL 20, 1969
(destructor) SEP 2, 2025
(destructor) APR 3, 2027

Done!
```

That last bit of refactoring made a huge difference!

In C++, you often can get performance gains by working with objects not directly but via pointers instead.

By working with objects via pointers or references instead of accessing them directly, we can greatly reduce the number of calls to copy constructors, copy assignment operators, and destructors. Especially with large objects, copying can be an expensive, time-consuming operation.

6.3 *Programming by Contract helps to eliminate surprises [optional]*

The bottom line: Never leave surprises in your code! One way to eliminate surprises in a class that we write is to include a contract for programmers who use the class. The contract for a member function states explicitly what *preconditions* must be true when a caller calls the function and what *postconditions* the caller can expect to be true when the function returns. The contract also states the *class invariant*. A class invariant must remain true for the class's objects at run time before and after every call to a member function. (It may be violated temporarily by an object undergoing mutation.) The invariant ensures that there are never any objects left in an invalid state.

By defining the preconditions and postconditions of member functions of a class and the class invariant, both the programmers and the users of a class can be confident that objects of the class will behave correctly as expected at run time and therefore not have surprises.

Programming by Contract

The concept of *programming by contract* was first proposed by the object-oriented programming pioneer Bertrand Meyer. His Eiffel programming language had constructs that allowed a programmer to define preconditions, postconditions, and invariants, and the language checked at run time that they were true. This was especially helpful while debugging a program. The checks could be turned off when the application is deployed so that they don't hurt performance.

The C++ language doesn't have native support for programming by contract. However, we can still implement its concepts using existing features of the language. While it's probably overkill to use contracts on every class of an application, it may be wise to use them on the most critical classes.

Manning Comix

This section shows how we can program a circular buffer class by contract. We'll add preconditions and postconditions to its member functions and devise a class invariant. We'll see how the contract helps ensure that the class is correctly designed.

6.3.1   *Programming a circular buffer by contract*

The following example demonstrates programming by contract on a class that implements a circular buffer (listing 6.16). A dynamic array of a given capacity holds integer contents, and private member variable `buffer` points to it. Public member function `add()` inserts an integer element at the tail of the buffer, and public member function `remove()` removes an integer element from the head of the buffer and returns the element's value. Member variable `capacity` is the maximum number of elements the buffer can hold. Member variables `head` and `tail` are the indexes of the head and tail elements, respectively. Member variable `count` keeps track of how many elements are currently in the buffer. Private member function `class_invariant()` computes the class invariant and returns true if the invariant holds or false otherwise.

Listing 6.16   (Program 6.10 CircularBuffer-1): `CircularBuffer.h`

```
class CircularBuffer
{
public:
    CircularBuffer(const int cap);
    ~CircularBuffer() { delete[] buffer; }

    int get_count() const { return count; }

    void add(const int value);
    int remove();

private:
    int capacity;
    int head, tail;
```

```
    int count;

    int *buffer;

    bool class_invariant() const;
};
```

In the implementation of the circular buffer (listing 6.17), member function add()
increments member variable tail after adding a new value to the buffer. The value of
tail wraps around to the other end of the buffer when it exceeds the buffer capacity.
Member function remove() increments member variable head after removing a value
from the buffer. Its value also wraps around to the other end of the buffer when it
exceeds the buffer capacity.

　　In this example, we've documented each member function by a header comment—a
highly recommended practice but generally not done in this book's examples to save
space. The comment tags @precondition, @postcondition, and @invariant specify
function preconditions, function postconditions, and the class invariant, respectively.
Helper function class_invariant() implements the class invariant.

Listing 6.17　(Program 6.10 CircularBuffer-1): `CircularBuffer.cpp`

```
#include <cassert>
#include "CircularBuffer.h"                            Private member function to
                                                        test the class invariant
/**
 * @invariant (0 <= head < capacity) and (0 <= tail < capacity)
 */
bool CircularBuffer::class_invariant() const
{
    return (0 <= head) && (head < capacity)            Class invariant
        && (0 <= tail) && (tail < capacity);
}


/**
 * Constructor
 * @parm cap the capacity of the buffer.
 * @postcondition the buffer is empty.
 */
CircularBuffer::CircularBuffer(const int cap)
    : capacity(cap), head(0), tail(0), count(0),
      buffer(new int[capacity])
{
    assert(class_invariant());                 Check the class invariant.
}


/**
 * Add a new value to the tail of the buffer.
 * @parm value the value to add.
 * @precondition the buffer is not full.
 * @postcondition the buffer is not empty.
 */
void CircularBuffer::add(const int value)
```

```
{
    assert(count < capacity);  // not full          ◄──── Check the precondition.

    buffer[tail] = value;
    tail = (tail + 1)%capacity;
    count++;
                                                          Check the
    assert(count > 0);  // not empty          ◄──────     postcondition.
    assert(class_invariant());          ◄────────────
}                                                         Check the class invariant.

/**
 * Remove a value from the head of the buffer.
 * @return the removed value.
 * @precondition the buffer is not empty.
 * @postcondition the buffer is not full.
 */
int CircularBuffer::remove()
{
    assert(count > 0);  // not empty          ◄──── Check the precondition.

    int value = buffer[head];
    head = (head + 1)%capacity;
    count--;

    assert(count < capacity);  // not full          ◄──── Check the postcondition.
    assert(class_invariant());          ◄───────────
                                                         Check the class invariant.
    return value;
}
```

The test program exercises the circular buffer.

Listing 6.18   (Program 6.10 CircularBuffer-1): `tester.cpp`

```cpp
#include <iostream>
#include "CircularBuffer.h"

using namespace std;

const int SIZE = 5;

int main()
{
    CircularBuffer buffer(SIZE);
                                                         Check the
    for (int value = 10; value < 100; value+=10)         precondition
    {                                                    before calling
        if (buffer.get_count() < SIZE)          ◄─────   buffer.add().
        {
            buffer.add(value);
            cout << "added " << value << endl;
        }
    }
```

```
for (int i = 1; i < 10; i++)
{
    if (buffer.get_count() > 0)
    {
        int value = buffer.remove();
        cout << "removed " << value << endl;
    }
}

int value = buffer.remove();

return 0;
}
```

Check the precondition before calling buffer.remove().

Call function remove() without first checking its precondition.

The output of the test program is:

```
added 10
added 20
added 30
added 40
added 50
removed 10
removed 20
removed 30
removed 40
removed 50
Assertion failed: (count > 0), function remove, ➡
file CircularBuffer.h, line 51.
```

The following sections explain the preconditions, postconditions, class invariant, and output of this program.

6.3.2   *Precondition: What must be true before calling a function*

A function's precondition must be true when a function is called. *It is the caller's responsibility to check the precondition before making the call.*

> **The Precondition Principle**
>
> The *precondition* of a function is a condition (a Boolean expression) that must be true when we call the function. According to programming by contract, if the precondition of a function is true and we call the function, the function must guarantee that it will behave properly. It is the responsibility of the caller to check the precondition before making the call. If the precondition is false, but we call the function anyway, the function is not required to behave in a manner suitable or convenient for the caller.
>
> If the precondition is for a member function of a class, then the class must provide some public means for the caller to check the validity of the precondition. Because it's the caller's responsibility to do so, the function has no obligation to check whether the precondition is met.

In class `CircularBuffer` (listing 6.17), the precondition to calling member function `add()` is that the buffer is not full. Therefore, the test program (listing 6.18) first calls member function `get_count()` to check that the count is less than `SIZE`. It doesn't try to add if the buffer is full. The precondition to calling member function `remove()` is that the buffer is not empty, and the test program again first calls `get_count()`, this time to check that the count is not 0. It doesn't try to remove if the buffer is empty.

If the precondition of a function is true, and we call the function, the function must guarantee that it will behave properly. For function `add()`, that means it must properly add the value to the tail of the buffer and advance member variable `tail`. Function `remove()` must properly remove a value from the head of the buffer, advance member variable `head`, and return the removed value.

Because it's the caller's responsibility to check the precondition of a function, the function is relieved of the need to check it. What happens if the precondition of a function is not met, but we call the function anyway? The function is not required to behave in a manner suitable to the caller. For example, if we call member function `add()`, and the buffer is already full, ways that function can behave include the following:

- Assumes the caller checked the precondition and proceeds to add the new value to the buffer, thereby overwriting an existing value. This also causes the value of member variable `tail` cross the value of member variable `head` and the value of member variable `count` to exceed the capacity of the buffer.
- Checks the precondition and if it's not met, it does not add the new value, but instead does nothing or prints an error message.
- Checks the precondition, and if it's not met, aborts the program.

If we don't check the precondition of member function `remove()` and call it when the buffer is empty, ways that function can behave include the following:

- Assumes the caller checked the precondition and proceed to remove a value from the buffer, thereby potentially returning a value that had previously been returned. This also causes the value of member variable `head` to cross the value of member variable `tail` and the value of member variable `count` to go negative.
- Checks the precondition and if it's not met, it does not remove a value, but instead does nothing, prints an error message, or returns a dummy value.
- Checks the precondition, and if it's not met, aborts the program.

In class `CircularBuffer`, we chose the abort option for both member functions. In each function, the `assert()` checks the value of the function's precondition and immediately aborts the program if the precondition is not met. Programming by contract allows a function's programmer to code a behavior that may not necessarily be convenient for the caller.

The test program (listing 6.18) made its last call to `remove()` without first checking the function's precondition. The buffer was empty, so the function aborted the program with an assertion failure.

That's too brutal! If you call a function despite its precondition not being met, you're at the mercy of its programmer as to what happens.

Good software design puts responsibilities on the caller of the function, too.

If the precondition of a function includes the fact that the function will throw an exception for bad argument values, we consider the exception to be part of the contract with the caller. Then, the caller is no longer obligated to check the argument values before calling the function.

6.3.3 *Postcondition: What must be true after returning from a function*

However, if a function was called when its precondition was met, then *it is the responsibility of the function to meet its postcondition* before returning.

> **The Postcondition Principle**
>
> The *postcondition* of a function is a condition (a Boolean expression) that must be true when the function returns. According to programming by contract, if a function was called when its precondition was met, *it is the responsibility of the function to meet its postcondition before returning*.
>
> We can assume that if we called a function and it returned, it behaved properly, and the postcondition is true. This relieves us from the obligation to do an error check after the call. (Of course, we still can check.)

In class `CircularBuffer` (listing 6.17), if we call member function `add()` after confirming that its precondition is met, then the function must successfully add the new value to the buffer, and thereafter, the buffer cannot be empty. Before the function returns, it checks its postcondition that member variable `count` must be greater than zero. For this example, the function aborts the program if the postcondition isn't met.

If we call member function `remove()` after confirming that its precondition is met, then the function must successfully remove a value from the buffer and return it, and thereafter, the buffer cannot be full. Before the function returns, it checks its postcondition that member variable `count` must be less than member variable `capacity`. In this example, the function aborts the program if the postcondition isn't met.

In an actual application, a function would somehow try a different way to meet its postcondition rather than simply abort the program. A possible remedy is to throw an exception if a problem occurred. That would change the function's contract. The postcondition would then be that the function either succeeded or it threw an exception.

So, if a function has a postcondition returned, does that mean I don't need to write code to check any part of the postcondition after returning?

No, you don't. But if you want to practice defensive programming, you might still want to write code to perform some runtime checking.

6.3.4   *Class invariant: What must remain true of object states*

A class invariant ensures that no invalid objects are created at run time and that each of its objects never enters an invalid state.

> **The Class Invariant Principle**
>
> The *class invariant* is a condition (a Boolean expression) involving the class's state implementation that must be true after each object is created at run time (i.e., after each constructor call). It must remain true each time after an object is mutated by a setter function or any other function that changes the object's state. The class invariant ensures that no invalid objects are created and that no object ever enters an invalid state. Typically, the class invariant consists of the class's member variables.

In class `CircularBuffer` (listing 6.17), the class invariant says that the values of member variables `head` and `tail` are both always greater than or equal to 0 and less than the buffer capacity:

```
(0 <= head < capacity) and (0 <= tail < capacity)
```

The Boolean helper function `class_invariant()` performs this test, and we must call it before the constructor returns and before each of the member functions `add()` and `remove()` returns. The constructor sets an object's initial state, and the two functions modify the object's state. Like with the function preconditions and postconditions in this example class, the program aborts if the class invariant is ever false.

Is this a valid class invariant? When an object is first created, member variables `head` and `tail` are each set to 0, which satisfies the `>= 0` parts of the invariant. Member functions `add()` and `remove()` each increments `tail` and `head` by 1 and then performs the modulo operation with member variable `capacity` on the sum:

```
(tail + 1)%capacity
```

and

```
(head + 1)%capacity
```

The result of a modulo operation is always a value from 0 up to but not including the value of the divisor (`capacity` in this case), and so the values of `head` and `tail` each remains `>= 0` and `< capacity`. Therefore, we have a valid invariant.

The class invariant can be violated while an object's state is changing. For example, in function `add()`, had we written

```
tail = tail + 1;
tail = tail%capacity
```

the value of `tail` can briefly equal the value of `capacity` before the modulo operation occurs. However, the class invariant must be true again before the function returns.

Finding an appropriate invariant for a class can be challenging. The class invariant we chose for class `CircularBuffer` alone is not sufficient to ensure that the buffer will operate correctly. For example, it does not guarantee that the values of member variables `head` and `tail` do not cross each other. The class invariant works together with the preconditions and postconditions of the member functions to guarantee that the buffer will operate correctly.

Proving a program to be correct

Theoretically, if we can specify the proper class invariants and the preconditions and postconditions for each member function in every class of a program, we can prove that the program is correct. However, this is very difficult in practice for all but the simplest programs.

Famous computer scientist Don Knuth once said about a program he had written, "Beware of bugs in the above code; I have only proved it correct, not tried it" (https://www-cs-faculty.stanford.edu/~knuth/faq.html).

Summary

- Code should behave as expected by its users.
- The Principle of Least Astonishment states that there should be few, if any, surprises in well-designed software. Some surprises are due to the way C++ operates. We can also inadvertently put surprises in our code.
- Off-by-one errors are common, and they can lead to insidious runtime logic errors that are hard to find.
- A poorly named function can mislead a caller of the function to believe that it does something other than its name suggests.
- Poorly designed code can have unexpected bad runtime performance, which includes longer than expected running times or excessive use of memory and other resources.
- The C++ STL vector is easy to use and very powerful. However, using objects directly with vector code can cause many automatic calls to copy constructors, copy assignment operators, and destructors behind our backs at run time and thereby cause performance problems. Using pointers to objects instead can eliminate many of these automatic calls.
- Programming by contract ensures users of a class that we wrote won't be surprised by how its objects behave at run time.

- The Precondition Principle states that the caller of a function must ensure that the function's precondition is true before making the call. If the precondition is true, the function must guarantee that it will perform correctly.
- The Postcondition Principle states that the function must ensure that its postcondition is true before returning.
- The Class Invariant Principle involves a condition that must remain true at run time. It ensures that none of the class's objects are left in an invalid state.

Design subclasses right 7

As described in section 1.8, inheritance is one of the main concepts of object-oriented programming. When we create an application with class hierarchies of superclasses and subclasses, we must design the subclasses right to achieve a well-designed application.

We should know when to use function overriding or overloading. There are several design principles we can use. The Liskov Substitution Principle states that we should be able to substitute a superclass object by one of its subclass objects, and it provides additional rules to help ensure that we designed the subclasses correctly. The Favor Composition over Inheritance Principle involves making design tradeoffs between *is-a* relationships and *has-a* relationships among classes to avoid hardcoding object behaviors in the source code and instead provide the flexibility to make behavior decisions at run time. We can increase flexibility of our code further by using factory classes. If we use Programming by Contract (introduced in section 6.3) with subclasses, we must set the preconditions and postconditions of any overriding member functions correctly.

7.1   *When to use function overriding or overloading*

This section describes function overriding and overloading, used by the example programs in this and the previous chapters. Good class design can use both concepts, so we should know how to use them properly when designing classes.

7.1.1   *Override superclass member functions to get subclass behavior*

Function overriding involves superclasses and their subclasses. A member function of a subclass overrides a member function of the superclass if the two functions have the same signature. The *signature* of a function consists of its function name and the number, datatype, and order of its parameters. The names of the parameters and the datatype of the return value are not included in the signature.

   We should use function overriding when we want a subclass object to have similar but not exactly the same behavior as a superclass object. The subclass's overriding member function implements the desired subclass behavior.

   In our code, we can call a subclass's overriding function directly on an object of the subclass. But more likely, we'll be using the Code to the Interface Principle (section 2.3.3). Then, polymorphism determines at run time whether the program calls the overridden function in the superclass or the overriding function in the subclass. It depends on whether the object we're calling the function on is from the superclass or the subclass, respectively.

   Figure 7.1 shows an example of function overriding. Calling `amount_owed()` on a `GeneralTax` object will invoke the member function in superclass `GeneralTax`. The function uses the value of private constant GENERAL_RATE and the value of parameter income to compute and return the tax amount owed. Member function amount_owed() in subclass LocalTax has the same signature as the corresponding member function in superclass Tax; therefore, the subclass function overrides the superclass function. Calling the function on a LocalTax object will invoke the subclass's member function. The subclass function uses the value of private constant LOCAL_RATE and the value of parameter earnings to compute and return the tax amount owed.

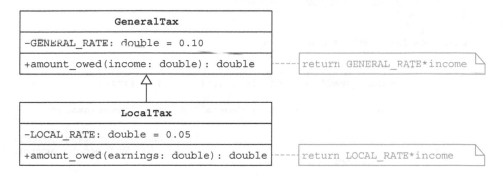

Figure 7.1 Member function amount_owed() in subclass LocalTax overrides the member function amount_owed() in superclass GeneralTax. Both functions have the same signature despite the different parameter names, income and earnings. The functions must be virtual for polymorphism to work.

Function amount_owed() must be virtual for polymorphism to work. Suppose we declared a variable a_tax to be a pointer to a GeneralTax object and then we have the expression a_tax>amount_owed(10000.00). Polymorphism determines at run time whether to call the superclass function or the subclass function depending on whether a_tax currently points to a GeneralTax object or to a LocalTax object, respectively.

The following listing shows the superclass GeneralTax, its subclass LocalTax, and yet another subclass MaxTax. Each subclass overrides the virtual member function amount_owed() of the superclass.

Listing 7.1 (Program 7.1 Taxes): Taxes.h

```
class GeneralTax
{
public:
    virtual ~GeneralTax() {}

    virtual double amount_owed(const double income) const
    {
        return GENERAL_RATE*income;
    }

private:
    const double GENERAL_RATE = 0.10;
};
```

Virtual member function amount_owed() in superclass Tax

```
class LocalTax : public GeneralTax
{
public:
    double amount_owed(const double earnings) const override
    {
        return LOCAL_RATE*earnings;
    }
private:
    const double LOCAL_RATE = 0.5;
};

class MaxTax : public GeneralTax
{
public:
    double amount_owed(const double amount) const override
    {
        return LOCAL_RATE*amount + GeneralTax::amount_owed(amount);
    }
private:
    const double LOCAL_RATE = 0.5;
};
```

Overriding member functions amount_owed() in subclasses LocalTax and MaxTax

Invoke the overridden superclass member function GeneralTax::amount_owed().

Keyword override

The optional keyword `override` at the end the header of each of the overriding member functions tells the C++ compiler that we meant the member function to override a virtual member function in the superclass. The compiler will check that the function in the superclass is indeed virtual and that the signatures of the overridden and overriding functions are the same. If this is not true, the compiler will issue an error message. The overridden function must be virtual to enable polymorphism.

We can use the optional keyword `override` at the end of the header of each of the overriding member functions `amount_owed()` in subclasses `LocalTax` and `MaxTax` to tell the C++ compiler our intent. The names of the function parameters `income`, `earnings`, and `amount` are not considered parts of the function signatures.

The overriding member function `amount_owed()` in subclass `MaxTax` demonstrates that it is possible to invoke an overridden member function of the superclass by using the scope resolution operator `::` with the name of the superclass.

The following listing is a test program that demonstrates the results of the function overriding.

Listing 7.2   (Program 7.1 Taxes): `tester.cpp`

```
#include <iostream>
#include "Taxes.h"

using namespace std;
```

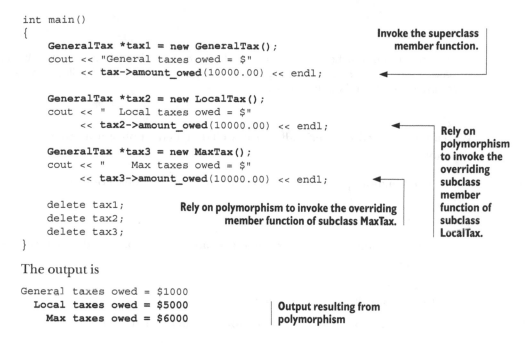

```
int main()
{
    GeneralTax *tax1 = new GeneralTax();
    cout << "General taxes owed = $"
        << tax->amount_owed(10000.00) << endl;

    GeneralTax *tax2 = new LocalTax();
    cout << "  Local taxes owed = $"
        << tax2->amount_owed(10000.00) << endl;

    GeneralTax *tax3 = new MaxTax();
    cout << "    Max taxes owed = $"
        << tax3->amount_owed(10000.00) << endl;

    delete tax1;
    delete tax2;
    delete tax3;
}
```

Invoke the superclass member function.

Rely on polymorphism to invoke the overriding subclass member function of subclass LocalTax.

Rely on polymorphism to invoke the overriding member function of subclass MaxTax.

The output is

```
General taxes owed = $1000
  Local taxes owed = $5000
    Max taxes owed = $6000
```

Output resulting from polymorphism

Declaring the superclass member function to be virtual enables polymorphism, as demonstrated by the `tax2` and `tax3` variables in the test program and the last two lines of the output. We declared variable `tax2` to be a pointer to a `GeneralTax` object, but at run time, it points to a `LocalTax` object. With polymorphism, the program calls the overriding `amount_owed()` member function of class `LocalTax`. Similarly, variable `tax3` points to a `MaxTax` object at run time, and the program calls the overriding `amount_owed()` member function of class `MaxTax`.

7.1.2 Overload functions that have similar or equivalent behaviors

Function overloading occurs when two or more functions in the same scope have the same name but different signatures. We should overload a set of functions when they are so strongly related that it doesn't make sense to invent a different name for each function. We can overload member functions of a class and standalone functions. The C++ compiler knows which overloaded function to invoke based on the call's arguments.

Function overloading is very common

Function overloading is very common in C++ programs. For example, if we consider the + operator as a function, then we have operator overloading. If its two arguments are integer or real values, the operator returns their sum by performing arithmetic addition. However, if the two arguments are string values, the operator returns a string value equal to the value of the second string added to the end of the value of the first string by performing string concatenation.

(continued)

The square root function `sqrt()` in the standard math library is overloaded. We can pass it a `double`, `float`, or `long double` argument value, and it will compute and return the argument's square root as a `double`.

We can use function overloading for well-designed applications in the following situations:

- The functions perform conceptually similar operations. For example,

```
void print(Textfile f);            // print to standard out
void print(Textfile f, PDF p);  // print to a PDF
```

- The functions perform the same operation and produce identical results. For example,

```
void draw_circle(int x, int y, double radius);
void draw_circle(Point p, double radius);
```

In this example, the second function can call the first, as in

```
draw_circle(p.x, p.y, radius);
```

- The functions perform equivalent operations. For example,

```
vector<Book *> search(Genre g, int year, string title);
vector<Book *> search(Region r, string title);
```

C++ also allows operators to be overloaded. Commonly overloaded operators include the arithmetic operators and the output << operator. Operator << is already overloaded to enable it to output values of different datatypes such as `int`, `double`, and `string`. We can overload it further. For example, in listing 2.18, we overloaded operator << to print `Kind` values:

```
enum class Kind
{
    FICTION, COOKBOOK, HOWTO
};

inline ostream& operator <<(ostream& ostr, const Kind& k)
{
    switch (k)
    {
        case Kind::FICTION:  ostr << "fiction";  break;
        case Kind::COOKBOOK: ostr << "cookbook"; break;
        case Kind::HOWTO:    ostr << "howto";    break;
    }

    return ostr;
}
```

Then, we can use the << operator to output the value of a `Kind` variable `k` to `cout`:

```
cout << k << endl;
```

Depending on the value of `k`, the output will be the string "`fiction`", "`cookbook`", or "`howto`".

7.2 *The Liskov Substitution Principle and proper subclasses*

Inheritance is one of the main concepts of object-oriented programming (section 1.8). When we create applications with a class hierarchy of superclasses and their subclasses, we must design the subclasses right to achieve a well-designed application. The Liskov Substitution Principle helps to ensure that we designed proper subclasses for a superclass.

The Liskov Substitution Principle

Wherever there is a superclass object in a program, we should be able to substitute an object from one of its subclasses. In other words, we should be able to replace each occurrence of a superclass object in the source code with an object from one of its subclasses. This substitution should be possible because an object that is an instance of a subclass object is also an instance of the superclass.

The Liskov Substitution Principle states that if we designed the subclasses properly, after we make such a substitution, the program should run without logic or runtime errors, although it may produce different but meaningful results. Subclasses that violate this design principle were designed improperly.

The principle was named after object-oriented programming pioneer and professor Barbara Liskov of the Massachusetts Institute of Technology (MIT).

In the test program in listing 7.2, we were able to substitute a subclass `LocalTax` object (variable `tax2`) for the superclass `GeneralTax` object (variable `tax1`) in the second output statement, and the program still ran properly, although with different output:

```
GeneralTax *tax1 = new Tax();
cout << "Taxes owed = $"
     << tax1->amount_owed(50000.00) << endl;

GeneralTax *tax2 = new LocalTax();
cout << "Local taxes owed = $"
     << tax2->amount_owed(50000.00) << endl;
```

The `GeneralTax` superclass and its `LocalTax` and `MaxTax` subclasses follow the Liskov Substitution Principle.

The next example shows how a program can fail if we disregard the principle. In another version of the `CircularBuffer` class (section 6.3), we'll implement the buffer as a vector—a very bad idea as we'll soon see, but we'll do it to demonstrate a point—and so `CircularBuffer` is a subclass of `vector<int>` (listing 7.3).

How convenient! We can use inheritance and say that our circular buffer is a vector.

 That's a very object-oriented thing to do. But violating the Liskov Substitution Principle often leads to serious logic errors.

As in the previous version of the class, public member function add() enters an integer element at the tail of the buffer, and public member function remove() removes an integer element from the head of the buffer. Member variables head and tail are the indexes of the head and tail elements, respectively. Member variable count keeps track of how many elements are currently in the buffer.

Listing 7.3   (Program 7.2 CircularBuffer-2): CircularBuffer.h **(poorly designed)**

```
#include <vector>

using namespace std;

class CircularBuffer : public vector<int>          ◄——
{
public:
    CircularBuffer(const int cap);

    void add(const int value);
    int remove();

    friend ostream& operator <<(ostream& ostr,
                                CircularBuffer& buffer);

private:
    int capacity;
    int head, tail;
    int count;
};
```

Implement a circular buffer as a vector (bad design!)

As in our previous version of class CircularBuffer, member function add() increments member variable tail after adding a new value to the buffer (listing 7.4). Variable tail wraps around to the other end of the buffer when its value exceeds the buffer capacity. Member function remove() increments member variable head after removing a value from the buffer. Variable head also wraps around to the other end of the buffer when its value exceeds the buffer capacity. To keep this version of the class short, we'll leave out the pre- and postconditions and the class invariant. The overloaded << operator prints the contents of the buffer in order from head to tail.

Listing 7.4   (Program 7.2 CircularBuffer-2): CircularBuffer.cpp

```
#include <iostream>
#include "CircularBuffer.h"

using namespace std;
```

```
CircularBuffer::CircularBuffer(const int cap)
    : capacity(cap), head(0), tail(0), count(0)
{
    reserve(capacity);
    for (int i = 0; i < capacity; i++) push_back(0);
}

void CircularBuffer::add(const int value)
{
    at(tail) = value;
    tail = (tail + 1)%capacity;
    count++;
}
```

◀——— **Increment tail and wrap it around to the other end if its value reached the buffer capacity.**

```
int CircularBuffer::remove()
{
    int value = at(head);
    head = (head + 1)%capacity;
    count--;

    return value;
}
```

◀——— **Increment head and wrap it around to the other end if its value reached the buffer capacity.**

```
ostream& operator <<(ostream& ostr, CircularBuffer& buffer)
{
    int i = buffer.head;
    int c = buffer.count;

    cout << "Contents: ";

    while (c > 0)
    {
        cout << buffer.at(i) << " ";
        i = (i + 1)%buffer.capacity;
        c--;
    }

    return ostr;
}
```

Print the buffer contents in order from head to tail.

The following listing is a test program. It performed two invalid operations because we violated the Liskov Substitution Principle.

Listing 7.5　(Program 7.2 CircularBuffer-2): `tester.cpp`

```
#include <iostream>
#include "CircularBuffer.h"

using namespace std;

const int SIZE = 5;

int main()
{
    CircularBuffer buffer(SIZE);
```

```
        for (int value = 10; value <= 50; value+=10)
        {
            buffer.add(value);
        }
        cout << buffer << endl;

        buffer.at(1) = 99;  // INVALID!!!       ◄────┐ Invalid modification of
        cout << buffer << endl;                       a value in the buffer

        cout << "Remove " << buffer.remove() << endl;
        cout << "Remove " << buffer.remove() << endl;
        cout << buffer << endl;

        buffer.erase(buffer.begin() + 1);  // INVALID!!!    ◄──┐
        cout << buffer << endl;

        return 0;                                Invalid removal of a
}                                                value from the buffer
```

Output from the program is

```
Contents: 10 20 30 40 50
Contents: 10 99 30 40 50
Remove 10
Remove 99
Contents: 30 40 50
Contents: 40 50 libc++abi.dylib: terminating with uncaught exception
➥of type std::out_of_range: vector
```

A circular buffer is logically not a vector. We should not use vector operations to modify a value in the buffer using the vector's `at()` member function, nor should we remove a value using the vector's `erase()` member function. These operations corrupt the circular buffer and will result in runtime logic errors, causing the program to crash. The program failed because subclass `CircularBuffer` violated the Liskov Substitution Principle—we cannot substitute a subclass `CircularBuffer` object for a superclass `vector<int>` object because we can't use vector operations on a circular buffer.

We can fix the program by not making `CircularBuffer` a subclass of `vector<int>`, but instead, the `CircularBuffer` class can have a member variable that is a `vector<int>`. In other words, class `CircularBuffer` has a vector. This is the difference between the is-a (inheritance) relationship and the has-a (aggregation) relationship. The Liskov Substitution Principle can help us decide which one to use. We can rewrite `CircularBuffer` as a standalone class that has private member variable `buffer` that aggregates a `vector<int>`.

Listing 7.6   (Program 7.3 CircularBuffer-3): `CircularBuffer.h`

```
#include <vector>

using namespace std;

class CircularBuffer       ◄──── Not a subclass of vector
{
```

```
public:
    CircularBuffer(const int cap);

    void add(const int value);
    int remove();

    friend ostream& operator <<(ostream& ostr,
                                CircularBuffer& buffer);

private:
    int capacity;
    int head, tail;
    int count;

    vector<int> buffer;              ◄────── Aggregated vector
};
```

Class `CircularBuffer` hides its aggregated vector. The public member `functions`
`add()` and `remove()` control access to the vector, and the class does not enable other
behaviors with the vector.

Listing 7.7   (Program 7.3 CircularBuffer-3): `CircularBuffer.cpp`

```
#include <iostream>
#include "CircularBuffer.h"

using namespace std;
```
Operate on the private aggregated vector.
```
CircularBuffer::CircularBuffer(const int cap)
    : capacity(cap), head(0), tail(0), count(0)
{
    buffer.reserve(capacity);                              ◄──────
    for (int i = 0; i < capacity; i++) buffer.push_back(0);  ◄────
}

void CircularBuffer::add(const int value)
{
    buffer.at(tail) = value;                              ◄──────
    tail = (tail + 1)%capacity;
    count++;
}

int CircularBuffer::remove()
{
    int value = buffer.at(head);                          ◄──────
    head = (head + 1)%capacity;
    count--;

    return value;
}

ostream& operator <<(ostream& ostr, CircularBuffer& cb)
{
    int i = cb.head;
    int c = cb.count;
```

```
    cout << "Contents: ";

    while (c > 0)
    {
        cout << cb.buffer.at(i) << " ";
        i = (i + 1)%cb.capacity;
        c--;
    }

    return ostr;
}
```

Operate on the private aggregated vector.

The test program cannot perform vector operations on a circular buffer, as shown in the following listing.

Listing 7.8   (Program 7.3 CircularBuffer-3): `tester.cpp`

```
#include <iostream>
#include "CircularBuffer.h"

using namespace std;

const int SIZE = 5;

int main()
{
    CircularBuffer cb(SIZE);

    for (int value = 10; value <= 50; value+=10)
    {
        cb.add(value);
    }
    cout << cb << endl;

    cout << "Remove " << cb.remove() << endl;
    cout << "Remove " << cb.remove() << endl;
    cout << cb << endl;

    return 0;
}
```

The program no longer crashes, and it runs properly. Its output is

```
Contents: 10 20 30 40 50
Remove 10
Remove 20
Contents: 30 40 50
```

7.3   *Choosing the is-a and has-a relationships*

An object-oriented application often contains multiple superclasses and their subclasses, and classes with member variables that are pointers to other classes. Therefore, designing such an application well requires choosing between is-a (inheritance) and has-a (aggregation) relationships, or using a good combination of the two.

Consider an application involving children's toys. This application includes several different toys: toy car, model airplane, and train set. For each toy, we want to model its play action behavior (roll it on the floor or fly it in the air) and its sound behavior (engine noises or the choo-choo sound). Our first version of the application architecture involves primarily is-a relationships between the abstract superclass Toy and its subclasses (figure 7.2). The Toy subclasses can have different behaviors, but each implements the what(), play(), and sound() member functions.

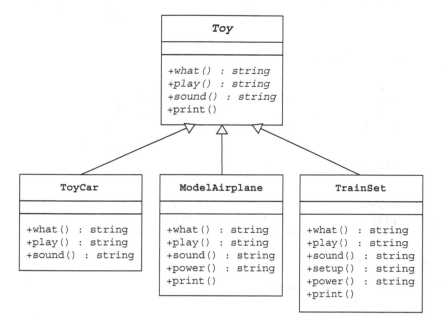

Figure 7.2 **This version of the application uses is-a relationships between the Toy subclasses and their superclass. Two design faults are the duplicated code, which violates the Don't Repeat Yourself Principle, and the hardcoded play action and sound behavior of each toy.**

We can imagine that in a real application, each toy could have more behaviors, and each behavior would involve more than simply returning a string, as shown in the following listing.

> **Listing 7.9** **(Program 7.4 Toys-1):** Toy.h **(poorly designed)**

```
#include <iostream>
#include <string>

using namespace std;

class Toy
{
public:
    virtual ~Toy() {}
```

```
        virtual string what()   const = 0;
        virtual string play()   const = 0;
        virtual string sound() const = 0;

    virtual void print() const
    {
        cout << endl;
        cout << what() << endl;
        cout << "   play: " << play() << endl;
        cout << "   sound: " << sound() << endl;
    }
};


class ToyCar : public Toy
{
public:
    string what()   const override { return "TOY CAR"; }
    string play()   const override { return "roll it"; }
    string sound() const override { return "RRrr RRrr"; }
};


class ModelAirplane : public Toy
{
public:
    string what()   const override { return "MODEL AIRPLANE"; }
    string play()   const override { return "fly it"; }
    string sound() const override { return "RRrr RRrr"; }

    string power() const { return "wind up"; }

    void print() const override
    {
        Toy::print();
        cout << "   power: " << power() << endl;
    }
};


class TrainSet : public Toy
{
public:
    string what()   const override { return "TRAIN SET"; }
    string play()   const override { return "roll it"; }
    string sound() const override { return "choo choo"; }

    string setup() const { return "lay down track"; }
    string power() const { return "insert batteries"; }

    void print() const override
    {
        Toy::print();
        cout << "   setup: " << setup() << endl;
        cout << "   power: " << power() << endl;
    }
};
```

Common behaviors to be
implemented by each subclass

As figure 7.2 clearly shows, this version of the application uses is-a relationships. For example, a `TrainSet` is a `Toy`.

A serious fault of this design is the duplicated code among the subclasses, which violates the Don't Repeat Yourself Principle (section 2.3.3). For example, both `ToyCar` and `TrainSet` have the same code that implements their `play()` member functions, and both `ToyCar` and `ModelAirplane` have the same code for their `sound()` member functions. This will be a more serious problem if the code that implements each member function does more or if we add more subclasses and behaviors.

Another fault is that each toy's play action and sound behavior are hardcoded in the source code for each `Toy` subclass. For example, the source code that implements class `TrainSet` hardcodes that a train set is played by rolling it and that it makes the choo-choo sound. The following test program exercises the behaviors.

Listing 7.10 (Program 7.4 Toys-1): `tester.cpp`

```cpp
#include "Toy.h"

using namespace std;

int main()
{
    ToyCar car;
    car.print();

    ModelAirplane plane;
    plane.print();

    TrainSet train;
    train.print();

    return 0;
}
```

The output is

```
TOY CAR
    play: roll it
   sound: RRrr RRrr

MODEL AIRPLANE
    play: fly it
   sound: RRrr RRrr
   power: wind up

TRAIN SET
    play: roll it
   sound: choo choo
   setup: lay down track
   power: insert batteries
```

One way to avoid duplicating code among the member functions of the Toy subclasses is to make each unique play action and sound behavior an individual class. Then, we can share those behavior classes by having the Toy subclasses inherit them (figure 7.3).

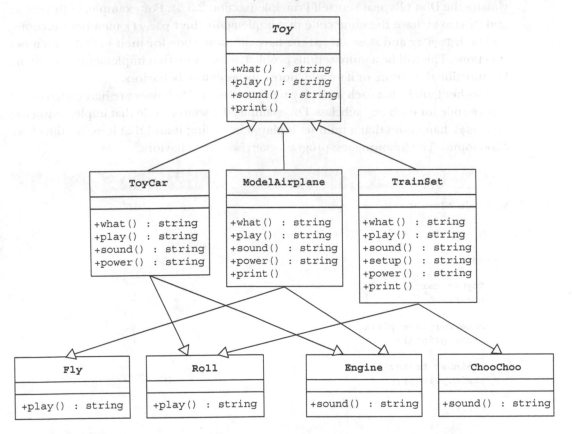

Figure 7.3   The play action and sound behaviors are each a separate class. Each Toy subclass has an is-a relationship with the Toy superclass and s-a relationships with the play action and sound classes. By sharing these classes, we've eliminated some code duplication, but each toy still has hardcoded behaviors.

The figure shows that both the ToyCar and TrainSet subclasses inherit and share the Roll play action class and that both the ToyCar and ModelAirplane subclasses inherit and share the Engine sound class. ModelAirplane also inherits the Fly play action class, and TrainSet also inherits the ChooChoo sound class.

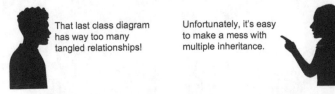

That last class diagram has way too many tangled relationships!

Unfortunately, it's easy to make a mess with multiple inheritance.

The following listing shows the play actions as individual classes.

Listing 7.11   (Program 7.5 Toys-2): `PlayAction.h`

```cpp
#include <string>

using namespace std;

class Fly
{
public:
    string play() const { return "fly it"; }
};
class Roll
{
public:
    string play() const { return "roll it"; }
};
```

The following listing shows the sounds as individual classes.

Listing 7.12   (Program 7.5 Toys-2): `Sound.h`

```cpp
#include <string>

using namespace std;

class Engine
{
public:
    string sound() const { return "RRrr RRrr"; }
};

class ChooChoo
{
public:
    string sound() const { return "choo choo"; }
};
```

With this design, each toy can inherit its play action and sound behaviors (figure 7.3). Because each `Toy` subclass already inherits from superclass `Toy`, we must use multiple inheritance, as shown in the following listing. The scope resolution operator lets us explicitly call member functions `Roll::play()`, `Fly::play()`, `Engine::sound()`, and `ChooChoo::sound()` from the inherited behavior classes.

Listing 7.13   (Program 7.5 Toys-2): `Toy.h` (poorly designed)

```cpp
#include <iostream>
#include <string>
#include "PlayAction.h"
#include "Sound.h"

using namespace std;
```

```
class Toy
{
    ...
};
```

Multiple inheritance

Use the scope resolution operator to call the appropriate behaviors.

```
class ToyCar : public Toy, public Roll, public Engine
{
public:
    string what()  const override { return "TOY CAR"; }
    string play()  const override { return Roll::play(); }
    string sound() const override { return Engine::sound(); }
};
```

```
class ModelAirplane : public Toy, public Fly, public Engine
{
public:
    string what()  const override { return "MODEL AIRPLANE"; }
    string play()  const override { return Fly::play(); }
    string sound() const override { return Engine::sound(); }

    ...
};
```

Multiple inheritance

Use the scope resolution operator to call the appropriate behaviors.

```
class TrainSet : public Toy, public Roll, public ChooChoo
{
public:
    string what()  const override { return "TRAIN SET"; }
    string play()  const override { return Roll::play(); }
    string sound() const override { return ChooChoo::sound(); }

    ...
};
```

Multiple inheritance

Use the scope resolution operator to call the appropriate behaviors.

The same test program (listing 7.10) generates the same output as before.

For each subclass of Toy, our second version of the application added is-a relationships with the classes for the play action and sound behaviors, in addition to its previous is-a relationship with the Toy superclass. For example, a ModelAirplane is a Toy, and it also is a Fly play action and an Engine sound. This version solved the code duplication problem because there is only one sharable copy of each play action and each sound. However, the source code for each toy's subclass still hardcoded the toy's behaviors, only this time using multiple inheritance.

To have more flexibility in how the toys behave, we want to avoid hardcoding each toy's play and sound behaviors in the source code of its subclass and instead be able to determine each toy's behaviors at run time. To accomplish this, our final version of the toy application replaces the is-a relationships between the toys and their behaviors with has-a relationships. Figure 7.4 diagrams both the is-a and has-a relationships of this final version of the application.

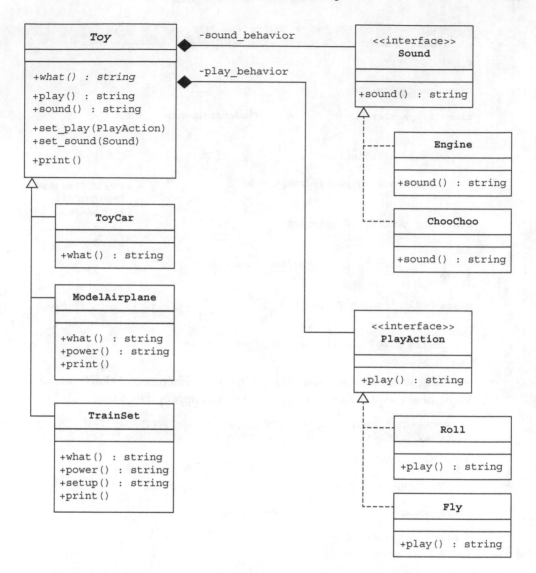

Figure 7.4 Each `Toy` subclass has an is-a relationship to the `Toy` superclass. The `Toy` superclass has has-a relationships to the `PlayAction` and `Sound` behaviors, which allows the `Toy` subclasses to access and share play action and sound behaviors. This design is more flexible and has loose coupling between the toys and their play action and sound behaviors. The toy behaviors are no longer hardcoded in the source code but can be specified whenever a toy object is created at run time. A toy's behaviors can also be modified at run time by calling the setter functions `set_play()` and `set_sound()`.

First, we make each play action implement interface `PlayAction`. Each `PlayAction` class must implement member function `play()` in a way appropriate for the subclass.

Listing 7.14 (Program 7.6 Toys-3): `PlayAction.h`

```cpp
#include <string>

using namespace std;

class PlayAction                    ◄──── PlayAction superclass
{
public:
    virtual ~PlayAction() {}

    virtual string play() const = 0;              ◄──  Play behavior to be
};                                                      implemented by
                                                        each subclass
class Fly : public PlayAction
{
public:
    string play() const override { return "fly it"; }
};

class Roll : public PlayAction
{
public:
    string play() const override { return "roll it"; }
};
```

Similarly, we make each sound implement interface `Sound`. Each `Sound` class must implement member function `sound()` in a way appropriate for the subclass.

Listing 7.15 (Program 7.6 Toys-3): `Sound.h`

```cpp
#include <string>

using namespace std;

class Sound              ◄──── Sound superclass
{
public:
    virtual ~Sound() {}

    virtual string sound() const = 0;          ◄──  Sound behavior to
};                                                   be implemented by
                                                     each subclass
class ChooChoo : public Sound
{
public:
    string sound() const override { return "choo choo"; }
};

class Engine : public Sound
{
public:
    string sound() const override { return "RRrr RRrr"; }
};
```

We've applied the Open-Closed Principle (sections 2.3.3 and 5.8) to both interfaces `PlayAction` and `Sound`. We can add new play action and sound behaviors without changing their interfaces.

Superclass `Toy` maintains has-a relationships to the play action and sound behaviors via its private `play_behavior` and `sound_behavior` member variables. We initialize these member variables in the constructor.

Listing 7.16   (Program 7.6 Toys-3): `Toy.h`

```cpp
#include <iostream>
#include <string>
#include "PlayAction.h"
#include "Sound.h"

using namespace std;

class Toy
{
public:
    Toy(PlayAction * const p, Sound * const s)
        : play_behavior(p), sound_behavior(s) {}        ◄──  Initialize the play
                                                              action and sound
    virtual ~Toy()                                            behaviors.
    {
        delete play_behavior;
        delete sound_behavior;
    }                                                   Delegate the play action behavior
                                                         to a PlayAction object to be
    virtual string what() const = 0;                      determined at run time.

    void set_play(PlayAction * const p) { play_behavior  = p; }
    void set_sound(Sound * const s)     { sound_behavior = s; }

    string play()  const { return play_behavior->play(); }    ◄──
    string sound() const { return sound_behavior->sound();}   ◄──

    virtual void print() const                          Delegate the sound behavior
    {                                                     to a Sound object to be
        cout << endl;                                     determined at run time.
        cout << what() << endl;
        cout << "   play: " << play() << endl;
        cout << "   sound: " << sound() << endl;
    }

private:
    PlayAction *play_behavior;              Implement the has-a relationships
    Sound      *sound_behavior;            with a play action and a sound.
};

class ToyCar : public Toy
{
public:
```

```
    ToyCar(PlayAction * const p, Sound * const s) : Toy(p, s) {}

    ...
};

class ModelAirplane : public Toy
{
public:
    ModelAirplane(PlayAction * const p, Sound * const s)
        : Toy(p, s) {}

    ...
};

class TrainSet : public Toy
{
public:
    TrainSet(PlayAction * const p, Sound * const s) : Toy(p, s) {}

    ...
};
```

Pass the PlayAction and Sound objects to the superclass Toy constructor.

In this version of the application, class `Toy` follows the Delegation Principle (section 2.3.2) and delegates the play action and sound behaviors to the `PlayAction` and `Sound` classes. None of the `Toy` subclasses has hardcoded these behaviors. Instead, `PlayAction` and `Sound` objects representing these behaviors are passed to each `Toy` subclass's constructor when a `Toy` object is created at run time.

Object-oriented programming is about classes and subclasses, but we must be very careful how we design them and determine their relationships.

Good class design is critical if we want our code to be flexible and maintainable.

The test program in the following listing creates each `Toy` object and creates and passes the appropriate `PlayAction` and `Sound` objects to the constructors. To demonstrate further behavior flexibility, the test program uses the `Toy` class's setter function `set_sound()` to change the sound behavior of the `TrainSet` object at run time.

Listing 7.17   (Program 7.6 Toys-3): `tester.cpp`

```
#include <iostream>
#include <vector>
#include "Toy.h"

int main()
{
    Toy *car   = new ToyCar(new Roll(), new Engine());
    Toy *plane = new ModelAirplane(new Fly(), new Engine());
    Toy *train = new TrainSet(new Roll(), new ChooChoo());
```

Determine each toy's behaviors when constructing a toy object.

```
    car->print();
    plane->print();
    train->print();

    train->set_sound(new Engine());        ◄─────   Modify a toy's
    train->print();                                 sound behavior.

    delete car;
    delete plane;
    delete train;

    return 0;
}
```

Output from this final version of the application is

```
TOY CAR
    play: roll it
  sound: RRrr RRrr

MODEL AIRPLANE
    play: fly it
  sound: RRrr RRrr
  power: wind up

TRAIN SET
    play: roll it
  sound: choo choo
  setup: lay down track
  power: insert batteries

TRAIN SET
    play: roll it
  sound: RRrr RRrr
  setup: lay down track
  power: insert batteries
```

Using the has-a relationship instead of the is-a relationship between the toys and their play action and sound behaviors is an example of the Favor Composition over Inheritance Principle.

The Favor Composition over Inheritance Principle

A design that uses composition (has-a relationships where classes aggregate other classes) is often better than inheritance (is-a relationships of subclasses to superclasses). Inheritance is determined by the source code, and therefore, it hardcodes behavior. Composing behaviors at run time is much more flexible. Composition also makes it easier to share code and reduce duplication.

Because has-a relationships often involve delegation, the principle is also known as the Favor Delegation over Inheritance Principle.

Using this design principle gives us several benefits:

- *Flexibility*—The behaviors are not hardcoded in the source code and can be assigned and modified at run time.
- *Code sharing*—The behaviors are shared, thereby reducing code duplication.
- *Delegation*—The behaviors are delegated to the PlayAction and Sound subclasses.
- *Loose coupling*—Class Toy and its subclass have no knowledge of the implementation of the PlayAction and Sound subclasses. The PlayAction and Sound subclasses have no dependencies on the Toy subclasses.
- *Encapsulation*—We can add and modify toy behaviors in the future without the need to change the Toy superclass or any of its subclasses.
- *Reduced complexity*—The class hierarchies are simplified. No multiple inheritance is needed.

Manning Comix

7.4   *Use a factory function with the Code to the Interface Principle*

Code such as

```
TrainSet *toy = new TrainSet(new Roll(), new ChooChoo());
```

is inherently inflexible because variable toy is hardcoded to only point to a TrainSet object. One solution is to use the Code to the Interface Principle (section 2.3.3), where the interface in this case is the superclass Toy:

```
Toy *toy = new TrainSet(new Roll(), new ChooChoo());
```

Now, variable toy can later point to a different Toy object.

However, this code still isn't as flexible as it could be. What if, during a different run of the application, we need to initialize variable toy to a different Toy object? To obtain even more flexibility, where we hardcode less and allow more to be determined at run time, we can use a factory function that encapsulates calls to new. The purpose of a factory function is to encapsulate creating and returning objects from different subclasses of a superclass. A parameter value determines which subclass object to create and return. The factory functions are often static members of a factory class. Our `ToyFactory` class encapsulates creating and returning `Toy` objects in factory function `make()`.

Listing 7.18   (Program 7.7 Toys-4) `ToyFactory.h`

```
#include "Toy.h"

enum class Kind { CAR, AIRPLANE, TRAIN };          ◀────── Kinds of toys

class ToyFactory                    ◀────── The factory class
{
public:
    static Toy *make(const Kind kind)        ◀────── The static factory function
    {
        switch (kind)          ◀──┐ Create and return a toy object based
        {                         │ on the value of parameter kind.
            case Kind::CAR:
                return new ToyCar(new Roll(), new Engine());

            case Kind::AIRPLANE:
                return new ModelAirplane(new Fly(), new Engine());

            case Kind::TRAIN:
                return new TrainSet(new Roll(), new ChooChoo());

            default: return nullptr;
        }
    }
};
```

The Factory Principle

If a program creates different objects at run time, we can encapsulate calls to `new` in a factory function. The value of a parameter passed to the factory function determines which object to create and return. The objects that a factory function can create are usually from subclasses of a common supertype. Using a factory function gives us the flexibility to determine at run time what type of object to create.

We can implement a factory function as a function of a factory class that is related to the supertype, or the factory function can be a function of the supertype itself. The factory function can be static.

The test program in the following listing shows that now we have the flexibility to determine at run time which `Toy` object to create depending on the value of variable `kind`.

Listing 7.19   (Program 7.7 Toys-4): `tester.cpp`

```cpp
#include <iostream>
#include "Toy.h"
#include "ToyFactory.h"

using namespace std;

int main()
{
    Kind kind = Kind::AIRPLANE;

    Toy *toy = ToyFactory::make(kind);
    toy->print();

    delete toy;
    return 0;
}
```

◄—— **Determine at run time which Toy object to create.**

This program's output is only

```
MODEL AIRPLANE
    play: fly it
    sound: Rrrr RRrr
    power: wind up
```

 Hardcoding behaviors is inherently inflexible. We won't be able to make changes later without rewriting the source code.

For greater flexibility, write code that allows choosing and changing behaviors at run time.

7.5   *Programming by Contract with subclasses [optional]*

We need to be extra careful with subclasses if we use Programming by Contract (section 6.3), especially when adhering to the Code to the Interface Principle (section 7.4). If a subclass overrides member functions of its superclass, and if the overridden superclass member functions have pre- and postconditions, then what pre- and postconditions are appropriate for the subclass's member functions?

Consider class `Shipment` and its subclasses `Expedited` and `International` (listing 7.20). Class `Shipment` (for shipping a package by regular mail) has two member functions. Setter function `set_cost()` sets the cost of shipping. Its precondition is simply that the cost is greater than 0. Member function `calculate_days()` calculates how many days it will take the package to arrive at its destination. In an actual application, the function would use the shipping method and other factors to make this calculation. Its postcondition is the number of days must be between 0 and 14. For this example, we'll simply hardcode the number of days to 5, which satisfies the postcondition.

Member function `set_cost()` of subclass `Expedited` (for expedited shipping) has the precondition that the cost is greater than 5. Its member function `calculate_days()`

has the postcondition that the number of days will be either 1 or 2, which it checks before returning. For this example, it's hardcoded to 2 days, which satisfies the postcondition. These two functions override the corresponding functions in the superclass `Shipment`.

Member function `set_cost()` of subclass `International` (for international shipping) has the precondition that the cost is greater than 0. Its member function `calculate_days()` has the postcondition that the number of days will be greater than 12, which it checks before returning. For this example, it's hardcoded to 20 days, which satisfies the postcondition. These two functions override the corresponding functions in the superclass `Shipment`.

Listing 7.20   (Program 7.8 ContractShipment): `Shipment.h` **(poorly designed)**

```cpp
#include <string>

using namespace std;

class Shipment
{
public:
    virtual ~Shipment() {}

    virtual string get_type() const { return "REGULAR"; }
    virtual double get_cost() const { return cost; }
    virtual int    get_days() const { return days; }

    /**
     * @precondition c > 0
     */
    virtual void set_cost(const double c)
    {
        if (!(c > 0)) throw c;
        cost = c;
    }

    /**
     * @postcondition (days > 0) && (days < 14)
     */
    virtual int calculate_days()
    {
        days = 5;

        if (!((days > 0) && (days < 14))) throw days;
        return days;
    }

protected:
    double cost;
    int days;
};

class Expedited : public Shipment
```

Virtual
functions that
can be
overridden by
the subclasses

```
    {
    public:
        string get_type() const override { return "EXPEDITED"; }

        /**
         * @precondition (c > 5)  INVALID!          ◀──── Invalid precondition
         */
        void set_cost(const double c) override
        {
            if (!(c > 5)) throw c;
            cost = c;
        }

        /**
         * @postcondition (days == 1) || (days == 2)
         */
        int calculate_days() override
        {
            days = 2;

            if (!((days == 1) || (days == 2))) throw days;
            return days;
        }
    };

class International : public Shipment
{
public:
    string get_type() const override { return "INTERNATIONAL"; }

        /**
         * @precondition c > 0
         */
        void set_cost(const double c) override
        {
            if (!(c > 0)) throw c;
            cost = c;
        }

        /**
         * @postcondition days > 12  INVALID!        ◀──── Invalid postcondition
         */
        int calculate_days() override
        {
            days = 20;
            return days;
        }
    };
```

Recall that the caller has the responsibility to ensure the precondition of a function is met before calling it and that the function can do whatever is convenient if it is called, even if the precondition is false. In this example, we made each set_cost() member function throw an exception if its precondition is violated. (Throwing an exception isn't declared by the function header, so it's not part of the contract.) Also, recall that it's the function's responsibility to meet its postcondition before returning, so the hardcoded number of days in each `calculate_days()` member function satisfies its postcondition.

The test program (listing 7.21) creates `Shipment`, `Expedited`, and `International` objects and passes each one in turn to function `ship_it()`. The function receives its argument as a pointer to a `Shipment` object. It calls `set_cost()` on the object with argument value 2.00, which satisfies the precondition `c > 0` for the `Shipment` member function. After returning from calling `calculate_days()` on the `Shipment` object, for defensive programming, it verifies that the postcondition `(days > 0) && (days < 14)` was satisfied for the `Shipment` member function. Both member functions `set_cost()` and `calculate_days()` are virtual, so polymorphism determines which class's member functions to call.

> ### Listing 7.21 (Program 7.8 ContractShipment): `tester.cpp`

```cpp
#include <iostream>
#include "Shipment.h"

using namespace std;

void ship_it(Shipment * const s);

int main()
{
    Shipment *shipment      = new Shipment();
    Shipment *expedited      = new Expedited();
    Shipment *international = new International();

    ship_it(shipment);
    ship_it(expedited);
    ship_it(international);

    delete shipment;
    delete expedited;
    delete international;

    return 0;
}

void ship_it(Shipment * const s)
{
    try
    {
        cout << endl << "Shipping " << s->get_type();

        s->set_cost(2.00);

        s->calculate_days();
        int days = s->get_days();
        if (!((days > 0) && (days < 14))) throw days;
    }
```

Argument value 2.00 meets the precondition to call set_cost() on a Shipment object.

Verify that the postcondition is met after a call to calculate_days() on a Shipment object.

```
    catch (double cost)
    {
        cout << " *** Invalid cost: " << cost;
    }
    catch (int days)
    {
        cout << " *** Invalid days: " << days;
    }
}
```

The output of the program is

```
Shipping REGULAR
Shipping EXPEDITED *** Invalid cost: 2
Shipping INTERNATIONAL *** Invalid days: 20
```

Regular shipping had no problems. However, expedited shipping violated the precondition for the `set_cost()` member function, and international shipping apparently violated the postcondition for the `calculate_days()` member function. What went wrong?

Function `ship_it()` uses the pre- and postconditions of a `Shipping` object. But because the argument of `ship_it()` is a pointer to a `Shipping` object, we have no guarantee that at run time, the caller won't pass a pointer to an `Expedited` object or a pointer to an `International` object, which can then violate the pre- or postconditions.

Here are some guidelines when designing subclasses and using Programming by Contract:

- The range of the values allowed by the precondition of a subclass's overriding member function must include the range of the values allowed by the precondition of the overridden superclass member function. In the example, the precondition `cost > 5` for member function `set_cost()` in subclass `Expedited` did not include the range of `cost > 0` for member function `set_cost()` in superclass `Shipment`. Therefore, when superclass `Shipment` set the cost to 2, it violated the precondition of subclass `Expedited` (figure 7.5).

Preconditions

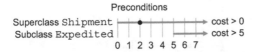

Superclass `Shipment`   cost > 0
Subclass `Expedited`   cost > 5

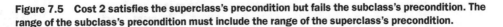

0 1 2 3 4 5 6 7

Figure 7.5   Cost 2 satisfies the superclass's precondition but fails the subclass's precondition. The range of the subclass's precondition must include the range of the superclass's precondition.

- The range of the values allowed by the postcondition of a superclass's overridden member function must include the range of the values allowed by the postcondition of the overriding subclass member function. In the example, the postcondition `(days > 0) && (days < 14)` for member function `calculate_days()` in superclass `Shipping` did not include the range of `days > 12` for member function `calculate_days()` in subclass `International`. Therefore, when subclass

`International` set the value of days to 20, it violated the postcondition of super-class `Shipping` (figure 7.6).

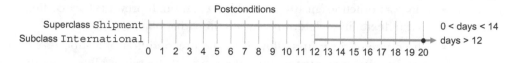

Figure 7.6 **Days 20 satisfies the subclass's postcondition but fails the superclass's postcondition. The range of the superclass's postcondition must include the range of the subclass's postcondition.**

Programming by Contract is messy with overriding member functions.

Like all contracts, they must be very carefully written.

Summary

- A well-designed application should contain only well-designed subclasses that support good design principles.

- The signature of a function consists of its name and the number, datatypes, and order of its parameters. It does not include the names of its parameters or the datatype of its return value.

- A member function of a subclass overrides a member function with the same signature in its superclass. At run time, we want to call the overriding function if the object was instantiated from the subclass.

- Overloaded functions have the same name but otherwise different signatures. In a well-designed application, a set of overloaded functions have operations that are conceptually similar, the same, or equivalent.

- It is important to understand when to use the is-a (inheritance) and the has-a (aggregation) relationship between classes.

- The Liskov Substitution Principle says that if subclasses are designed properly with the is-a relationship, then a subclass object can substitute for a superclass object in the code. The program will still be logically correct and continue to run. A subclass that violates this principle can cause the program to run with logic errors or crash.

- The Favor Composition over Inheritance Principle says that there are software design situations, where using the has-a relationship instead of the is-a relationship results in classes and subclasses that are more flexible, better encapsulated against changes, less complex, and more loosely coupled.

- The has-a relationship can prevent hardcoding behaviors in the source code of classes. It provides the flexibility to set object behaviors when creating the objects at run time and to later modify the behaviors.

- A factory function encapsulates object creation. It prevents hardcoding by giving us the flexibility to determine at run time what objects to create.

- The range of the values allowed by the precondition of a subclass's overriding member function must include the range of the values allowed by the precondition of the overridden superclass member function. The range of the values allowed by the postcondition of a superclass's overridden member function must include the range of the values allowed by the postcondition of the overriding subclass member function.

Part 4

Design patterns solve application architecture problems

Design patterns take our object-oriented software design skills up to the next level. They are models from which we can create well-designed solutions to many common software architecture problems. Software architecture refers to how we structure the code of our application—the classes and subclasses we design and how they relate to one another and interact at run time. Developers over many years and across different industries have proven that these patterns model reliable and flexible solutions that adhere to good design principles.

Some example architecture problems that design patterns can help solve are the following:

- An application uses a family of algorithms. Can we encapsulate each algorithm and make them interchangeable?
- An application needs to create different sets of objects. These objects can be organized into several categories or families. Can it be flexible about object creation but not mix up objects from different families?
- An application manages several different sequences of objects. Can the application process the objects one at a time from a sequence without needing to know how any of the sequences are implemented?
- One object of the application produces a stream of data at run time that other objects of the application consume. Can we design the application so that the producer doesn't need to know who the consumers are or what each consumer does with the data, and be able to add or remove consumers at run time?

The design patterns covered in these chapters are based on the object-oriented concepts and design principles covered in the previous chapters. Common goals among the patterns include encapsulating what varies and designing classes that are cohesive and loosely coupled. Design patterns can reduce hardcoding options so that applications can flexibly make choices at run time.

Design patterns are not copy-and-paste source code, nor are they code we import from libraries. We adapt a pattern by using it as a model to write custom code designed to solve a particular architecture problem in our application. These models involve cooperating classes and are not about creating elementary data structures such as vectors, maps, trees, or linked lists.

Design patterns were not invented; instead, they were discovered. Over many years, experienced developers encountered common software architecture problems in many software projects. From the best solutions to these problems, they saw patterns in the design of the classes, the relationships among the classes, and the runtime interactions of their objects.

An experienced programmer can recognize an architecture problem that can be solved with an appropriate design pattern and then decide whether to use the pattern as the model to create a solution to the problem. The four computer scientists who first conceived the idea of software design patterns wrote a book that described 23 original patterns. The chapters of this part will cover 13 of them.

Design Patterns and the Gang of Four

The concept of design patterns was first popularized by the book *A Pattern Language: Towns, Building, Construction* by Christopher Alexander et al. (Oxford University Press, 1977). This book contained patterns for solving common architectural problems of physical buildings (where to put doors and windows, how many stories, etc.) and how to design neighborhoods.

Four computer scientists, Erich Gamma, Richard Helm, Ralph Johnson, and John Vlissides, adapted the concept to solve common architectural problems of object-oriented software. They wrote *Design Patterns: Elements of Reusable Object-Oriented Software* (Addison-Wesley, 1995). This book is often called the *Gang of Four* (GoF) book. It contains 23 software design patterns organized into three categories: creational, structural, and behavioral patterns. This chapter and the following ones describe 13 of the most common patterns. In sidebars, I've quoted the intent of each pattern directly from the GoF book, and these quotes are attributed with the notation (GoF *nnn*), where *nnn* is the page number of the book.

Numerous authors have since discovered and written about other software design patterns. These new patterns are often used in specialized software fields, such as networking and web, database, and GUI programming. Programming paradigms other than object oriented, such as functional programming, have their own design patterns.

The benefits of design patterns

Whenever we encounter a software architecture problem while developing an application, we should not assume that the problem is unique. If we can use a design pattern, we won't have to reinvent the wheel.

Design meetings will be much more productive if all the application developers are well-versed in design patterns. For example, during a meeting, one developer might say, "We should use the Strategy Design Pattern to solve this problem." Every other developer in the meeting will know what that means and how the code should be written. Design patterns are a design vocabulary that keeps meetings at a high level and not bogged down by the coding details of how to implement a solution. A pattern prescribes the relationships among the solution's classes and the runtime interactions of their objects. A well-designed application can be modeled from multiple design patterns.

Explaining the design patterns

The following chapters explain each design pattern according to this outline:

1   Before using the design pattern
    a   A description of the software architecture problem the design pattern solves
    b   A description of a short application that has the architecture problem
    c   A UML diagram and "before" application code that demonstrates the problem
    d   A list of faults with that solution before using the design pattern
2   After using the design pattern
    a   A UML diagram and "after" application code modeled from the design pattern
    b   A list of benefits of that second solution
3   The design pattern's generic model
    a   A UML diagram of the design pattern's generic model
    b   A table that relates the components of the pattern's generic model with components of our second solution of the application

Steps 1.c and 1.d are omitted if a chapter teaches more than one design pattern, and the example application is an extension of the solution from step e of the preceding pattern.

A common question is, "How do I know when to use a design pattern?" It takes some experience and practice to recognize when to use a pattern and to know which one.

A design pattern is not a thing but an abstract model from which we can create a custom solution to a software architecture problem. Therefore, to explain the patterns, the chapters in this part contain many before and after UML diagrams and code examples. *It's important to study the examples carefully and understand the faults of the before solution and the benefits of the after solution modeled from each pattern.*

The sports examples

The application examples for the design patterns involve a school athletics department and the sports of baseball, volleyball, and football, and generating reports about the games. For readers unfamiliar with baseball and volleyball, here are highly simplified explanations of how the games are played and scored.

Baseball

Baseball is played by two teams, each with nine players. The teams take turns batting (offense) and fielding (defense). The game is played on a field containing a baseball diamond, consisting of home plate at one corner, and counterclockwise, first, second, and third base at the other corners. The sides of the diamond are 90 feet (approximately 27 meters). The playing field extends beyond the diamond.

The batting team sends its players one at a time, in a preassigned order, to be the batter and stand by home plate with a baseball bat. One player on the fielding team designated the pitcher stands at the center of the diamond and throws the baseball over home plate, which the batter attempts to hit with the bat.

A batter who manages to hit the ball attempts to run counterclockwise around the bases. Depending on how well the other team fields the ball and how well the batter runs, the batter can safely reach first base (hits a single), second base (hits a double), third base hits a triple), or all the way around (hits a homer). Any players currently at the bases also attempt to advance. Each player who crosses home plate scores a run (a point) for the team.

If, after several attempts, the batter fails to hit the ball thrown by the pitcher, the batter is out. The batter who hits the ball but fails to successfully reach one of the bases is also out. After every three outs by the batting team's players, the teams switch roles. Each team taking a turn batting and fielding constitutes an inning of play, and after nine innings, the game is over. Therefore, in this greatly simplified version of the game, a game is over after each team has made 27 outs.

Volleyball

Volleyball is played by two teams, each with six players, on a rectangular court separated by a net that is approximately 2.5 meters tall.

A round of play starts when a player on one team serves the ball by hitting it over the net with his or her hands. Thereafter, the teams hit the ball back and forth over the net until one team fails to do so, thereby giving the other team a point and ending the round.

The game ends when a team wins by attaining 15 points.

The Template Method and
Strategy Design Patterns

This chapter covers
- The Template Method Design Pattern
- The Strategy Design Pattern

Each design pattern is an industry-proven model from which we can create a well-designed solution to a common software architecture problem. A design pattern is only a model because it is rarely a solution we can use directly—we use it as the basis to create a custom solution to an architecture problem in our application. This chapter covers two design patterns.

Manning Comix

Application development, and programming in general, involve algorithms and data. The data are the ingredients, and the algorithms are the steps of the recipe. The two design patterns in this chapter, the Template Method Design Pattern and the Strategy Design Pattern, are models for a software architecture that must manage multiple algorithms.

Our example application for the Template Method Design Pattern generates sports reports. The basic outline of the reports is the same, but parts of the report differ. The example application for the Strategy Design Pattern shows how to deploy strategies to recruit players and reserve venues for different sports. The strategies are interchangeable, and at run time, the application can determine which one to deploy, depending on the sport.

For each of the two patterns, we'll have example code that doesn't use the pattern, followed by example code modeled by the pattern. Then, we'll see the improvement the pattern makes.

NOTE   Be sure to read the introduction to part 4 for important information about design patterns in general and to learn how this and subsequent chapters teach each pattern. In addition, in case you're unfamiliar with the games of baseball and volleyball, which were used in some of the examples, the introduction includes the basics of how the games are scored.

8.1   The Template Method Design Pattern defines the steps of an algorithm

We often use templates in real life that define the algorithms we perform daily. For example, consider the steps to back out of a parking space in a parking lot:

1 Step on the brake.
2 Start the car.
3 Shift into reverse.
4 Step on the accelerator to back out slowly.
5 Turn the steering wheel.
6 Step on the brake.
7 Shift into drive.
8 Step on the accelerator to move forward.

No matter what make or model of car you're driving, these are the steps and the order in which you must follow them. Steps 1, 4, 5, 6, and 8 are likely the same for all cars. But steps 2, 3, and 7 might be different, depending on the car. Starting the car may involve turning a key in the ignition or pressing a start button. The gear shift level might be located behind the steering wheel or by your side, or shifting gears might entail a set of push buttons.

Similarly, an application might use an algorithm that has several steps in a fixed order. Some of the steps may be constant, but other steps may vary. The first several code examples in this section will demonstrate how the Template Method Design Pattern can help solve a software architecture problem that defines an algorithm with steps in a prescribed order, where some of the steps are common and implemented by a superclass, but others are implemented by subclasses.

Suppose a school's athletics department wants an application that prints a short report after each baseball and volleyball game. The baseball report includes some statistics with a simple bar chart about the performance of one team during game. An example of such a report is

```
BASEBALL GAME REPORT

11 singles
 7 doubles
 1 triples
 1 homers

          ....5...10...15...20...25...30
Singles: SSSSSSSSSSS
Doubles: DDDDDDD
Triples: T
 Homers: H

End of report
```

The volleyball report includes the winner, the winning score, and how each team scored its points during the rounds of the game. An example of such a report is

```
VOLLEYBALL GAME REPORT

Winner was Team 2
The winning score was 15 to 11

      ....5...10...15
  1: 2
  2:  2
  3:   2
  4: 1
  5:  1
  6:    2
  7:   1
  8:     2
  9:    1
 10:     1
 11:       2
 12:      1
 13:        2
 14:       1
 15:         2
 16:          2
```

```
17:       1
18:             2
19:       1
20:             2
21:       1
22:             2
23:             2
24:             2
25:       1
26:             2
```

```
End of report
```

The report shows which team scored during each of the 26 rounds and the running score. For example, team 2 scored during the sixth round, after which team 1 had 2 points and team 2 had 4 points. The game ends as soon as a team has scored 15 points, so team 2 won, while team 1 ended with only 11 points. Therefore, the winning score was 15 to 11.

NOTE The introduction to part 4 briefly describes how baseball and volleyball games are scored.

8.1.1   Desired design features

An application that produces the baseball and volleyball reports should have the following features:

- *DF 1*—The report generation steps are in a fixed order.
- *DF 2*—Corresponding steps between the two reports that are executed the same way should be coded the same.
- *DF 3*—Corresponding steps between the two reports that are executed differently will have custom code for those steps in each report.
- *DF 4*—There is little or no duplicated code.

8.1.2   Before using the Template Method Design Pattern

Generating a game report consists of the following steps:

1 Print the report header.
2 Acquire data from the game.
3 Analyze the data.
4 Print the report.
5 Print the report footer.

Class `BaseballReport` has private member functions that implement these steps (figure 8.1). It depends on class `BaseballData`, which uses a random number generator to generate test data for the report.

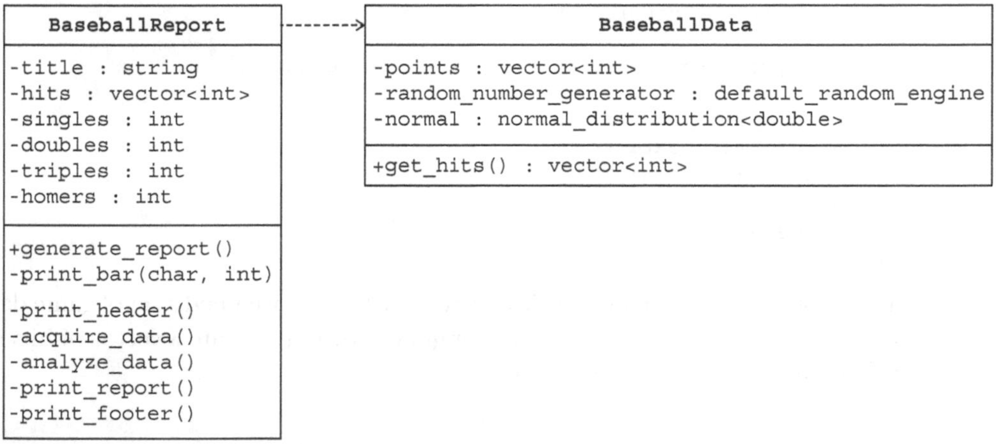

Figure 8.1 The public member function `generate_report()` of class `BaseballReport` **calls its private member functions, which perform the steps to generate a baseball game report. It depends on class** `BaseballData` **to generate random test data for the report.**

Public member function `generate_report()` of class `BaseballReport` calls its private member functions to execute the steps in the correct order to generate a game report.

Listing 8.1   (Program 8.1 Reports): `BaseballReport.h` **(before the design pattern)**

```
#include <string>
#include <vector>
#include "BaseballData.h"

using namespace std;

class BaseballReport
{
public:
    BaseballReport() : title("BASEBALL GAME REPORT")
    {
        singles = doubles = triples = homers = 0;
    }

    void generate_report()
    {
        print_header();
        acquire_data();
        analyze_data();
        print_report();
        print_footer();
```

Invoke the steps to generate a report.

```
    }

private:
    string title;
    vector<int> hits;
    int singles, doubles, triples, homers;

    void print_bar(const char ch, const int count) const;

    void print_header() const;
    void acquire_data();
    void analyze_data();
    void print_report() const;
    void print_footer() const;
};
```

To test our implementation of class `BaseballReport`, we need a set of game data. Class `BaseballData` uses a random number generator to generate a vector of hits made by the players of one team during a game.

Listing 8.2   (Program 8.1 Reports): `BaseballData.h` **(before the design pattern)**

```
#include <vector>
#include <random>
#include <time.h>

using namespace std;

class BaseballData
{
public:
    BaseballData()
        : normal(normal_distribution<double>(0.0, 1.75))
    {
        random_number_generator.seed(time(NULL));
        generate_hits();
    }

    vector<int> get_hits() const { return hits; }

private:                                    ◄─────┐  Accumulated hits
    vector<int> hits;                             │  during a game

    default_random_engine random_number_generator;      │ Random number
    normal_distribution<double> normal;                 │ generator

    void generate_hits();
};
```

Private member function `generate_hits()` uses the random number generator to generate normally distributed integer values that represent hits (singles, doubles, triples, homers) and outs for the team's player during the game. It appends each hit to the vector `hits` and stops after 27 outs.

Listing 8.3   (Program 8.1 Reports): `BaseballData.cpp` (before the design pattern)

```cpp
#include <vector>
#include <random>
#include "BaseballData.h"

using namespace std;

void BaseballData::generate_hits()
{
    int outs = 0;

    while (outs < 27)
    {
        double r   = normal(random_number_generator);      // Randomly generate
        int    hit = static_cast<int>(abs(r));             // a hit or an out.

        if (hit > 4) hit = 4;

        if (hit != 0) hits.push_back(hit);
        else          outs++;
    }
}
```

Now we can implement class `BaseballReport` (listing 8.4). Member functions `print_header()` and `print_footer()` print the report's header and footer, respectively. Member function `acquire_data()` gets the vector of hits from the `BaseballData` object. Member function `analyze_data()` tallies the number of singles, doubles, triples, and homers. Member function `print_report()` prints the game report.

Listing 8.4   (Program 8.1 Reports): `BaseballReport.cpp` (before the design pattern)

```cpp
#include <iostream>
#include <iomanip>
#include "BaseballData.h"
#include "BaseballReport.h"

using namespace std;

void BaseballReport::print_header() const
{
    cout << title << endl;
    cout << endl;
}

void BaseballReport::acquire_data()
{
    BaseballData data;
    hits = data.get_hits();
}
```

```
void BaseballReport::analyze_data()
{
    singles = doubles = triples = homers = 0;

    for (int hit : hits)
    {
        switch (hit)
        {
            case 1: singles++; break;
            case 2: doubles++; break;
            case 3: triples++; break;
            case 4: homers++;  break;

            default: break;
        }
    }
}

void BaseballReport::print_bar(const char ch, const int count) const
{
    for (int i = count; i > 0; i--) cout << ch;
    cout << endl;
}

void BaseballReport::print_report() const
{
    cout << setw(2) << singles << " singles" << endl;
    cout << setw(2) << doubles << « doubles» << endl;
    cout << setw(2) << triples << " triples" << endl;
    cout << setw(2) << homers  << " homers"  << endl;
    cout << endl;
    cout << "          ....5...10...15...20...25...30" << endl;
    cout << "Singles: "; print_bar('S', singles);
    cout << "Doubles: "; print_bar('D', doubles);
    cout << "Triples: "; print_bar('T', triples);
    cout << " Homers: "; print_bar('H', homers);
}

void BaseballReport::print_footer() const
{
    cout << endl;
    cout << "End of report" << endl;
}
```

Class `VolleyballReport` follows the same steps to print a volleyball game report (figure 8.2), and it depends on class `VolleyballData`, which uses a random number generator to generate test data for the report.

```
┌─────────────────────────────┐              ┌──────────────────────────────────────────────────────┐
│      VolleyballReport        │ ----------→  │                  VolleyballData                        │
├─────────────────────────────┤              ├──────────────────────────────────────────────────────┤
│ -title : string             │              │ -points : vector<int>                                  │
│ -points : vector<int>       │              │ -random_number_generator : default_random_engine       │
│ -team1_is_winner : bool     │              │ -uniform : uniform_int_distribution<int>               │
│ -losers_score : int         │              ├──────────────────────────────────────────────────────┤
├─────────────────────────────┤              │ +get_points() : vector<int>                            │
│ +generate_report()          │              └──────────────────────────────────────────────────────┘
│                             │
│ -print_header()            │
│ -acquire_data()            │
│ -analyze_data()            │
│ -print_report()            │
│ -print_footer()            │
└─────────────────────────────┘
```

Figure 8.2 **The public member function** `generate_report()` **of class** `VolleyballReport` **calls its private member functions, which perform the steps to generate a volleyball game report. It depends on class** `VolleyballData` **to generate random test data for the report.**

Public member function `generate_report()` in class `VolleyballReport` calls its private member functions to execute the steps in the correct order to generate a game report, as in the following listing.

Listing 8.5 **(Program 8.1 Reports):** `VolleyballReport.h` **(before the design pattern)**

```cpp
#include <string>
#include <vector>
#include "VolleyballData.h"

using namespace std;

class VolleyballReport
{
public:
    VolleyballReport()
        : title("VOLLEYBALL GAME REPORT"),
          team1_is_winner(false), losers_score(0) {}

    void generate_report()
    {
        print_header();
        acquire_data();          Invoke the steps to
        analyze_data();          generate a report.
        print_report();
        print_footer();
    }

private:
    string title;
    vector<int> points;
    bool team1_is_winner;
    int  losers_score;

    void print_header() const;
```

```
    void acquire_data();
    void analyze_data();
    void print_report() const;
    void print_footer() const;
};
```

Like the baseball game report, class VolleyballData uses a random number generator to generate a vector of points made by both teams during a simulated game.

```
#include <vector>
#include <random>
#include <time.h>

using namespace std;

class VolleyballData
{
public:
    VolleyballData() : uniform(uniform_int_distribution<int>(1, 2))
    {
        generator.seed(time(NULL));
        generate_points();
    }

    vector<int> get_points() const { return points; }

private:
    vector<int> points;                    ◄─────  Accumulated points
                                                   during a game

    default_random_engine random_number_generator;    Random number
    uniform_int_distribution<int> uniform;            generator

    void generate_points();
};
```

Private member function generate_points() uses the uniform random number generator to decide whether to add each round's point to either team 1 or to team 2 (member variables score1 and score2), and then it appends that team's score at the end of the round to vector points. To distinguish the two teams' points, the points of the second team are negative. The simulated game ends when one team attains 15 points.

```
#include <vector>
#include <random>
#include "VolleyballData.h"

using namespace std;

void VolleyballData::generate_points()
```

```
{
    int score1 = 0;
    int score2 = 0;

    while ((score1 < 15) && (score2 < 15))
    {
        int which_team = uniform(random_number_generator);       ◄──┐

        if (which_team == 1)                              Randomly add the point to
        {                                                       team 1 or to team 2.
            score1++;
            points.push_back(score1);
        }
        else
        {
            score2++;
            points.push_back(-score2);
        }
    }
}
```

Now, we can implement class `VolleyballReport` (listing 8.8). Member functions `print_header()` and `print_footer()` print the report's header and footer, respectively. Member function `acquire_data()` gets the vector of points from the `VolleyballData` object. Member function `analyze_data()` determines which team won the game (is the final entry in the `points` vector positive or negative?) and the final score. Member function `print_report()` prints the game report.

Listing 8.8   (Program 8.1 Reports) `VolleyballReport.cpp` **(before the design pattern)**

```cpp
#include <iostream>
#include <iomanip>
#include "VolleyballData.h"
#include "VolleyballReport.h"

using namespace std;

void VolleyballReport::print_header()
{
    cout << title << endl;
    cout << endl;
}

void VolleyballReport::acquire_data() const
{
    VolleyballData data;
    points = data.get_points();
}

void VolleyballReport::analyze_data()
{
    int final_index = points.size() - 1;
    team1_is_winner = points[final_index] > 0;       ◄──┐ Determine which
                                                          team won the game.
```

```
    for (int i = final_index; i > 0; i--)        ◄──────    Loop backwards to find
    {                                                        the losing team's score.
        if (    ( team1_is_winner && (points[i] < 0))
           || (!team1_is_winner && (points[i] > 0)))
        {
            losers_score = abs(points[i]);
            break;
        }
    }
}


void VolleyballReport::print_report() const
{
    cout << "Winner was Team ";
    cout << (team1_is_winner ? "1" : "2") << endl;
    cout << "The winning score was 15 to " << losers_score << endl;
    cout << endl;
    cout << "       ....5...10...15" << endl;

    int i = 0;
    for (int s : points)              ◄──────   Loop over the points to
    {                                            print a simple line graph.
        cout << setw(3) << ++i << ":";

        char ch = s > 0 ? '1' : '2';
        for (int k = 0; k < abs(s); k++) cout << " ";
        cout << ch << endl;
    }
}


void VolleyballReport::print_footer() const
{
    cout << endl;
    cout << "End of report" << endl;
}
```

The test program can generate either a volleyball game report or a baseball game report, depending on whether we started the program on the command line with the -v or -b option, respectively.

Listing 8.9   (Program 8.1 Reports): `tester.cpp` **(before the design pattern)**

```
#include <iostream>
#include "VolleyballReport.h"
#include "BaseballReport.h"

using namespace std;

int main(int argc, char *args[])
{
    if (argc < 2)
    {
        cout << "Usage: report -b | -v" << endl;
        return -1;
    }
```

```
if (string(args[1]) == "-b")
{
    BaseballReport baseball;
    baseball.generate_report();
}

if (string(args[1]) == "-v")
{
    VolleyballReport volleyball;
    volleyball.generate_report();
}

    return 0;
}
```

If we wanted to produce a football game report later, we would create class `Football-Report`, which would then follow the same steps.

 It's pretty obvious what the problem is with this design. There's too much duplicated code! That violates DF 4.

 This is the architecture problem that we'll be able to solve with the model that the Template Method Design Pattern gives us.

Indeed, the main fault with this solution is

- *Duplicated code*—In classes `VolleyballReport` and `BaseballReport`, we duplicated the code for member functions `print_header()` and `print_footer()` that represent common report generation operations. Report generation follows the same steps for each sport, so we've also duplicated the code for member function `generate_report()` in each class.

8.1.3　*After using the Template Method Design Pattern*

The Template Method Design Pattern comes to the rescue with this architecture problem to reduce code duplication. A superclass outlines the steps of an algorithm (to produce a game report in our example application), and it can implement shared common steps. Subclasses manage the different ways to implement the remaining steps. A member function in the superclass, known as the *template method*, calls the member functions that perform the steps in the proper order (figure 8.3).

The Template Method Design Pattern

"Define the skeleton of an algorithm in an operation, deferring some steps to subclasses. Template Method lets subclasses redefine certain steps of an algorithm without changing the algorithm's structure" (GoF 325).

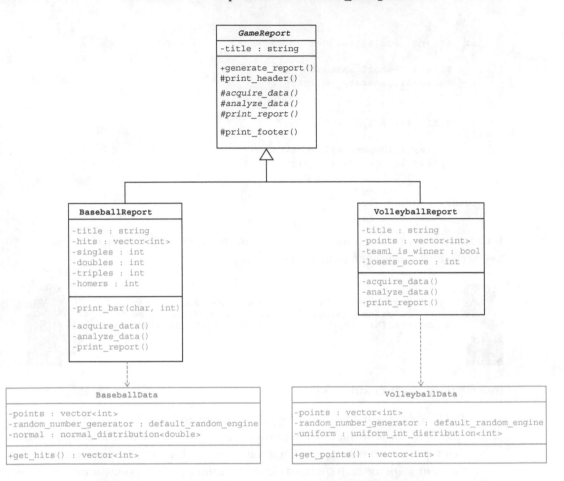

Figure 8.3   This version of the application is modeled from the Template Method Design Pattern. The superclass `GameReport` outlines the steps in the proper order for the algorithm to generate a report. It implements the common steps `print_header()` and `print_footer()` and delegates the remaining steps `acquire_data()`, `analyze_data()`, and `print_report()` to the `BaseballReport` and `VolleyballReport` subclasses. The public template method `generate_report()` in the superclass calls the step member functions in the proper order. The grayed-out portions of the diagram haven't changed logically from figures 8.1 and 8.2.

Using the Template Method Design Pattern to model our architecture gives us some major benefits:

- *Algorithm outline*—The `GameReport` superclass sets the standard for game report generation by declaring member functions that implement the steps of the algorithm. The template method `generate_report()` calls the step member functions steps in the proper order.

- *Reduced code duplication*—Step functions `print_header()` and `print_footer()` in the superclass define common behavior, which eliminates code duplication. This supports the Don't Repeat Yourself Principle (section 2.3.3). The subclasses define the remaining step functions.

- *Open-Closed Principle*—Superclass `GameReport` follows the Open-Closed Principle (section 2.3.3). We won't modify it, but we can extend it with the report subclasses.
- *Encapsulated steps*—The report subclasses follow the Encapsulate What Varies Principle (section 2.3.2) to encapsulate the varying steps to generate game reports.
- *Cohesive and decoupled classes*—Each report subclass is cohesive and decoupled from the other report subclasses.

In superclass `GameReport`, member function `generate_report()` is the template method.

Listing 8.10   (Program 8.2 Reports-TemplateDP): `GameReport.h`

```cpp
#include <iostream>
#include <string>

using namespace std;

class GameReport
{
public:
    GameReport(const string t) : title(t) {}
    virtual ~GameReport() {}

    void generate_report()                    ◄──── The template
    {                                                method
        print_header();
        acquire_data();
        analyze_data();
        print_report();
        print_footer();
    }

protected:
    void print_header() const                 ◄──── Common implementation
    {                                                of the print header step
        cout << title << endl;
        cout << endl;
    }

    virtual void acquire_data() = 0;                 Steps for the subclasses
    virtual void analyze_data() = 0;                 to implement
    virtual void print_report() const = 0;

    void print_footer() const                 ◄──── Common implementation
    {                                                of the print footer step
        cout << endl;
        cout << "End of report" << endl;
    }

private:
    string title;
};
```

Class `BaseballReport` is now a subclass of `GameReport`. It only needs to implement member functions `acquire_data()`, `analyze_data()`, and `print_report()` which are specific for baseball game reports. The implementations of these functions are unchanged from listing 8.4.

Listing 8.11   (Program 8.2 Reports-TemplateDP): `BaseballReport.h`

```cpp
#include <vector>
#include "BaseballData.h"
#include "GameReport.h"

using namespace std;

class BaseballReport : public GameReport
{
public:
    BaseballReport() : GameReport("BASEBALL REPORT")
    {
        singles = doubles = triples = homers = 0;
    }

private:
    vector<int> hits;
    int singles, doubles, triples, homers;

    void acquire_data() override;
    void analyze_data() override;          // Steps specific to
    void print_report() const override;    // baseball game reports

    void print_bar(const char ch, const int count);
};
```

The same is true for class `VolleyballReport`. The implementations of functions `acquire_data()`, `analyze_data()`, and `print_report()` are unchanged from listing 8.8.

Listing 8.12   (Program 8.2 Reports-TemplateDP): `VolleyballReport.h`

```cpp
#include <vector>

#include "GameReport.h"
#include "VolleyballData.h"

using namespace std;

class VolleyballReport : public GameReport
{
public:
    VolleyballReport()
        : GameReport("VOLLEYBALL REPORT"),
          team1_is_winner(false), losers_score(0) {}

private:
```

```
        vector<int> points;
        bool team1_is_winner;
        int  losers_score;

        void acquire_data() override;
        void analyze_data() override;            Steps specific to
        void print_report() const override;      volleyball game reports
};
```

Classes `VolleyballData` and `BaseballData` are unchanged. The same test program (listing 8.9) prints the same reports as in the previous version.

8.1.4   Template Method's generic model

Figure 8.4 shows the generic model of the Template Method Design Pattern. It is from a design pattern's generic model that we can create a custom solution to an architecture problem.

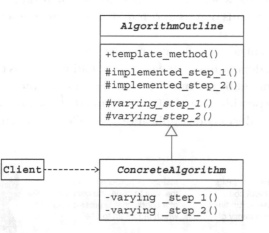

Figure 8.4   The generic model of the Template Method Design Pattern. We can compare it with figure 8.3. The member functions of the abstract superclass `AlgorithmOutline` outlines the steps of the algorithm. Member function `template_method()` calls the member functions representing the steps in the correct order. The superclass implements the common steps and delegates implementing the varying steps to its concrete subclasses. Table 8.1 shows how the example application applies the pattern.

Table 8.1   The Template Method Design Pattern as applied by the example application

Design pattern	Applied by the example application
`Client` class	Main
Superclass `AlgorithmOutline`	Superclass `GameReport`
Subclass `ConcreteAlgorithm`	Subclasses `VolleyballReport` and `BaseballReport`
`template_method()`	`generate_report()`
Common steps	`print_header()` and `print_footer()`
Varying steps	`acquire_data()`, `analyze_data()`, and `print_report()`

Manning Comix

8.2   *The Strategy Design Pattern encapsulates algorithms*

With the next design pattern, we continue the theme of an application that must manage multiple algorithms, but we'll do it in a somewhat different way. The Strategy Design Pattern provides a model for a software architecture problem that involves a family of algorithms, or several variants of an algorithm, that need to be interchangeable at run time.

For example, in a game program, a character may use different algorithms or strategies to determine its next move, depending on the current situation, such as choosing a move randomly or one determined by machine learning. For this architecture problem, the Strategy Design Pattern provides a model for a solution that encapsulates each algorithm or algorithm variant, reduces code duplication, and allows us to modify the algorithms independently.

Interchangeable means that we design the application so that, without code modifications, it can choose at run time one of the algorithms from a family of algorithms.

Instead of hardcoding the choice in the source code, the computed value of a conditional expression selects which algorithm to use.

Hardcoding vs. runtime flexibility

Hardcoding refers to the code we've written it in the source file. When we hardcode, we make decisions when we write the code about how the program will behave at run time. Once we've hardcoded, we can't make changes to the program's behavior without modifying the code. This may also require extensive retesting and rewriting documentation.

Many of the design patterns provide models for software architectures that have runtime flexibility so that the application can make behavior decisions when running. For example, the Strategy Design Pattern enables an application to choose which algorithm to use based on a logical decision. Our testing and documentation should cover all the algorithms before we deploy the application. A well-designed architecture can also minimize code changes if we later add new algorithms or modify existing ones.

To demonstrate the Strategy Design Pattern with a concrete example, we'll start with an application that involves three sports: baseball, football, and volleyball. For each sport, we need to execute an algorithm to recruit players and an algorithm to reserve a venue.

8.2.1 Desired design features

An application that has different algorithms for recruiting players and reserving venues for the three sports should have the following features:

- *DF 1*—Each sport should implement code for both algorithms.
- *DF 2*—It should be straightforward to add or delete sports.
- *DF 3*—It should be straightforward to add, delete, or modify algorithms for the sports.
- *DF 4*—It should be possible to make algorithm choices at run time.
- *DF 5*—It should be possible for sports to share algorithms, such as one for reserving a particular venue.

8.2.2 Before using the Strategy Design Pattern

The first version of the application is simple and straightforward (figure 8.5).

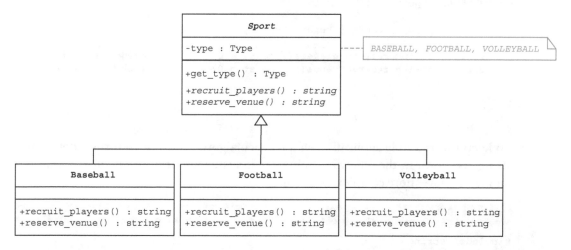

Figure 8.5   The first version of our sports application. Abstract class `Sport` **has pure virtual member functions representing algorithms that each of the subclasses** `Baseball`, `Football`, **and** `Volleyball` **must implement to recruit players and reserve a venue.**

Class `Sport` is abstract with pure virtual member functions `recruit_players()` and `reserve_venue()` that invoke the two algorithms. Subclasses `Baseball`, `Football`, and `Volleyball` each must implement these functions.

Listing 8.13   (Program 8.3 Sports): `Sport.h` **(before the design pattern)**

```
#include <iostream>
#include <string>

using namespace std;

enum class Type { BASEBALL, FOOTBALL, VOLLEYBALL };

inline ostream& operator <<(ostream& ostr, const Type& type)
{
    switch (type)
    {
        case Type::BASEBALL   : ostr << "baseball";   break;
        case Type::FOOTBALL   : ostr << "football";   break;
        case Type::VOLLEYBALL : ostr << "volleyball"; break;
    }

    return ostr;
}

class Sport
{
public:
    Sport(const Type t) : type(t) {}
    virtual ~Sport() {}

    Type get_type() const { return type; }

    virtual string recruit_players() const = 0;      To be implemented
    virtual string reserve_venue()   const = 0;      by subclasses

private:
    Type type;
};
```

To keep this example application simple, each algorithm simply returns a descriptive string, as shown in the following listing. In an actual application, the algorithms of a family can have more complex behaviors.

Listing 8.14   (Program 8.3 Sports): `Sports.h` **(before the design pattern)**

```
#include <string>
#include "Sport.h"

using namespace std;

class Baseball : public Sport
{
public:
    Baseball() : Sport(Type::BASEBALL) {}

    string recruit_players() const override
```

```
    {
        return "baseball players";
    }

    string reserve_venue() const override { return "stadium"; }
};

class Football : public Sport
{
public:
    Football() : Sport(Type::FOOTBALL) {}

    string recruit_players() const override
    {
        return "football players";
    }

    string reserve_venue() const override { return "stadium"; }
};

class Volleyball : public Sport
{
public:
    Volleyball() : Sport(Type::VOLLEYBALL) {}

    string recruit_players() const override
    {
        return "volleyball players";
    }

    string reserve_venue() const override { return "open field";}
};
```

Our test program generates a report for each sport.

Listing 8.15 (Program 8.3 Sports) `tester.cpp` **(before the design pattern)**

```cpp
#include <iostream>
#include "Sport.h"
#include "Sports.h"

using namespace std;

void generate_report(const Sport& sport);

int main()
{
    generate_report(Baseball());
    generate_report(Football());
    generate_report(Volleyball());

    return 0;
}
```

```
void generate_report(const Sport& sport)
{
    cout << sport.get_type() << endl;
    cout << "  players: " << sport.recruit_players()  << endl;
    cout << "    venue: " << sport.reserve_venue() << endl;

    cout << endl;
}
```

The output is

```
baseball
  players: baseball players
    venue: stadium

football
  players: football players
    venue: stadium

volleyball
  players: volleyball players
    venue: open field
```

This solution relies on inheritance—Baseball, Football, and Volleyball each is-a Sport. We can spot some serious shortcomings in this architecture design:

- *Duplicated code*—For example, the statement block { return "stadium"; } representing a venue algorithm is repeated several times. This will be a major problem with more sports or if the algorithms have more complex behaviors.
- *Lack of encapsulation*—If, for example, the stadium is unavailable and the sports that use it must have a different venue, we'll need to change the code in multiple places.
- *Hard-to-reuse code that ought to be shared*—If another sport needs the stadium venue, we can't easily reuse that code without duplicating it.
- *Hardcoded players and venues*—We will have to rewrite code to change them.

8.2.3   *After using the Strategy Design Pattern*

The Strategy Design Pattern provides a model that we can use to solve this architecture problem (figure 8.6). This solution relies on composition—has-a relationships—for the two families of algorithms. The algorithms are organized as superclasses and subclasses. Class Sport uses aggregation and the Code to the Interface Principle (section 2.3.3) with the PlayerStrategy and VenueStrategy interfaces. Class Sport has-a player algorithm family pointed to by member variable player_strategy, and it has-a venue algorithm family pointed to by member variable venue_strategy. The Strategy Design Pattern calls each algorithm a strategy, so these names are appropriate. Each of the Sport subclasses Baseball, Football, and Volleyball is now much simpler.

The Strategy Design Pattern

"Define a family of algorithms, encapsulate each one, and make them interchangeable. Strategy lets the algorithm vary independently from clients that use it" (GoF 315).

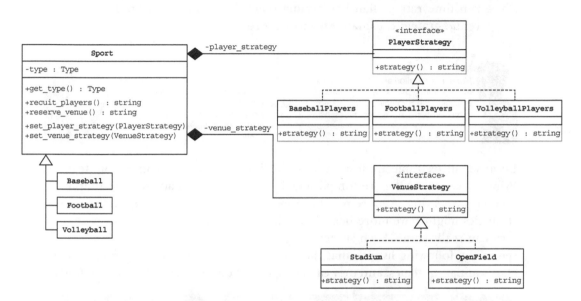

Figure 8.6 **This version of the application is modeled from the Strategy Design Pattern for the sport teams and venues. The player family of algorithms implement the `PlayerStrategy` interface, and the venue family of algorithms implement the `VenueStrategy` interface. Class `Sport` uses has-a relationships to aggregate the algorithms. Each player and venue algorithm has a `strategy()` member function. The `Baseball`, `Football`, and `Volleyball` subclasses are now much simpler, and each one sets the `player_strategy` and `venue_strategy` member variables of the `Sport` superclass.**

Advantages of applying the Strategy Design Pattern include the following:

- *Reusable shared code*—For example, subclass `Stadium` follows the Don't Repeat Yourself Principle (section 2.2.3). Both the baseball and football teams play in the stadium.

- *Encapsulated algorithms*—It will be possible to make changes to the interchangeable algorithms in the classes that implement `PlayerStrategy` and `VenueStrategy` interfaces without modifying the other classes. This is the Encapsulates What Varies Principle (section 2.3.2).

- *The Open-Closed Principle*—Superclass `Sport` is closed to changes, but we can extend it with subclasses. We can add and remove sports without affecting the superclass.

- *Favor has-a over is-a*—Class `Sport` aggregates the strategy classes such as `BaseballPlayers` and `Stadium` rather than rely on its subclasses to implement the strategies (section 7.3). Class `Sport` uses the Code to the Interface Principle (section 2.3.3) since its member variables `player_strategy` and `venue_strategy` point to the strategy interfaces `PlayerStrategy` and `VenueStrategy`, respectively.

- *Runtime flexibility*—The application can supply strategies for the sports during run time rather than hardcoding them. For example, a `Volleyball` object's venue strategy can change from `OpenField` to `Stadium`.

Has-a aggregation allows our code to make strategy decisions at run time. But using the Strategy Design Pattern in this version required more classes than in the previous version. It seems more complicated!

Design often requires making tradeoffs and compromises. Use a design pattern if you want its benefits. It may not be worth the effort for a trivial application or an application that's used only once.

Because our example application is so small to begin with, using the Strategy Design Principle can make it more complicated by adding classes. Each strategy simply returns a descriptive string. A more realistic application might have more strategies, and the strategies might have more behaviors. Then, the benefits of the Strategy Design Pattern can really shine. Each strategy might include multiple member functions. We'll see in the following listings that the creators of `Sport` objects determine the superclass's initial strategies, and they can change the behaviors later during run time.

Listing 8.16   (Program 8.4 Sports-StrategyDP): `Sport.h`

```cpp
#include <iostream>
#include <string>

#include "PlayerStrategy.h"
#include "VenueStrategy.h"

using namespace std;

enum class Type ...

class Sport
{
public:
    Sport(const Type t,
          PlayerStrategy * const ps, VenueStrategy * const vs)
        : type(t), player_strategy(ps), venue_strategy(vs) {}

    ~Sport()
    {
        delete player_strategy;
        delete venue_strategy;
    }

    Type get_type() const { return type; }
```

Set the initial player and venue strategies.

```
    string recruit_players() const
    {
        return player_strategy->strategy();           ◄———  Execute the
    }                                                        player strategy.

    string reserve_venue() const
    {
        return venue_strategy->strategy();            ◄———  Execute the
    }                                                        venue strategy.

    void set_player_strategy(PlayerStrategy * const ps)
    {
        player_strategy = ps;                  ◄———  Set the player
    }                                                strategy.

    void set_venue_strategy(VenueStrategy * const vs)
    {
        venue_strategy = vs;              ◄———  Set the venue
    }                                           strategy.

private:
    Type type;
    PlayerStrategy *player_strategy;       Aggregated
    VenueStrategy  *venue_strategy;        strategies
};
```

Each `Sport` class sets the initial strategies appropriately. For example, when we instantiate a `Baseball` object, its constructor calls the constructor of superclass `Sport` to set `player_strategy` to `BaseballPlayers` and `venue_strategy` to `Stadium`. In this example application, each player and venue strategy consists of only a member function that returns a descriptive string.

Listing 8.17   (Program 8.4 Sports-StrategyDP): `Sports.h`

```
#include "Sport.h"
#include "PlayerStrategy.h"
#include "VenueStrategy.h"

using namespace std;

class Baseball : public Sport
{
public:
    Baseball() : Sport(Type::BASEBALL,
                        new BaseballPlayers(),          Initial baseball
                        new Stadium()) {}               strategies
};

class Football : public Sport
{
public:
    Football() : Sport(Type::FOOTBALL,
                        new FootballPlayers(),          Initial football
                        new Stadium()) {}               strategies
```

```
};

class Volleyball : public Sport
{
public:
    Volleyball() : Sport(Type::VOLLEYBALL,
                         new VolleyballPlayers(),              Initial volleyball
                         new OpenField()) {}                   strategiess
};
```

Class Sport will not need to change if we add new Sport subclasses. We can use the Open-Closed Principle (section 2.3.3) and close superclass Sport for modification.

As figure 8.6 shows, each strategy to recruit players implements interface Player-Strategy, and each must implement the strategy() member function to allow superclass Sport to execute the algorithm to recruit players. Because its subclasses set its member variable player_strategy, class Sport follows the Delegation Principle (section 2.3.2) by delegating to its subclasses the choice of which player recruitment algorithm to execute.

Listing 8.18   (Program 8.4 Sports-StrategyDP): PlayerStrategy.h

```
#include <string>

using namespace std;

class PlayerStrategy
{
public:
    virtual ~PlayerStrategy() {}

    virtual string strategy() const = 0;
};

class BaseballPlayers : public PlayerStrategy
{
public:
    string strategy() const override
    {
        return "baseball players";
    }
};

class FootballPlayers : public PlayerStrategy
{
public:
    string strategy() const override
    {
        return "football players";
    }
};

class VolleyballPlayers : public PlayerStrategy
```

```
{
public:
    string strategy() const override
    {
        return "volleyball players";
    }
};
```

Similarly, each strategy to reserve a venue implements interface `VenueStrategy`, and each must implement the `strategy()` member function that allows the superclass `Sport` to execute the strategy to reserve a venue. Like with the player strategy, class `Sport` delegates to its subclasses the choice of which algorithm to execute when they set member variable `venue_strategy`.

Listing 8.19 (Program 8.4 Sports-StrategyDP): `VenueStrategy.h`

```
#include <string>

using namespace std;

class VenueStrategy
{
public:
    virtual ~VenueStrategy() {}

    virtual string strategy() const = 0;
};

class Stadium : public VenueStrategy
{
public:
    string strategy() const override
    {
        return "sports stadium";
    }
};

class OpenField : public VenueStrategy
{
public:
    string strategy() const override
    {
        return "open field";
    }
};
```

Each `Sport` subclass initializes the strategies, but now we have the flexibility to change a strategy at run time by calling a setter function. For example, if the test program contains the code

```
Volleyball volleyball;
volleyball.set_venue_strategy(new Stadium());
generate_report(volleyball);
```

the output is

```
baseball
  players: baseball players
    venue: sports stadium

football
  players: football players
    venue: sports stadium

volleyball
  players: volleyball players
    venue: open field

volleyball
  players: volleyball players
    venue: sports stadium
```

I love how the Strategy Design Pattern is built on top of good design principles.

It does neatly package the principles for us.

Indeed, design patterns help ensure that we use good design principles. The patterns simplify the software design process and facilitate design meetings among the developers.

8.2.4 *Strategy's generic model*

Figure 8.7 shows the generic model of the Strategy Design Pattern. Recall that it is from the design pattern's generic model that we can create a custom solution to an architecture problem (section 8.1.3).

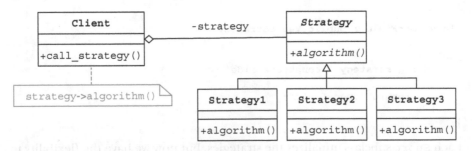

Figure 8.7   The generic model of the Strategy Design Pattern. Compare to figure 8.6. Table 8.2 shows how the example application applies the pattern.

Design pattern generic model

It is from a design pattern's generic model that we can create a custom solution to an architecture problem. Remember that a design pattern is not copy-and-paste code or code included from a library. Once we've identified a problem for which an appropriate design pattern can model a solution, we must tailor the solution to solve the specific problem in our application.

Experience teaches us to recognize whether an architecture problem can be solved by a design pattern and whether its benefits make its use worthwhile.

Table 8.2 The Strategy Design Pattern as applied by the example application

Design pattern	Applied by the example application
Class `Client`	Superclass `Sport`
Superclass `Strategy`	Interfaces `PlayerStrategy` and `VenueStrategy`
Subclasses `Strategy1`, `Strategy2`, etc.	Classes `BaseballPlayers`, `FootballPlayers`, `VolleyballPlayers`, `Stadium`, and `OpenField`
`algorithm()`	`strategy()` member functions
`strategy->algorithm()`	`player_strategy->strategy()` `venue_strategy->strategy()`

8.3   Choose between Template Method and Strategy

The Template Method Design Pattern and the Strategy Design Pattern have a similar goal—to encapsulate algorithms. Their main differences are the following:

- Template Method relies on inheritance. The outline of algorithm is in the super-class, and the encapsulated parts of the algorithm are in subclasses. Template Method allows the superclass to implement common steps of the algorithm.
- Strategy aggregates whole algorithms and makes them interchangeable. It uses composition—the `Strategy` subclasses (the `PlayerStrategy` and `VenueStrategy`) are composed by the `Client` class (superclass `Sport`).
- In the Strategy model, the `Client` class is loosely coupled from the `Strategy` subclasses. We can add, remove, or update the subclasses later.

We must decide which design pattern to use, depending on the application's needs and architecture.

The Strategy Design Pattern and the Template Method Design Pattern seem to solve the same architecture problem.

Yes, they are quite similar. We, software designers, must decide which pattern is more appropriate for our application.

Summary

- The Template Method Design Pattern defines the skeleton or outline of an algorithm and defers the implementation of some of the steps to subclasses. It lets subclasses redefine certain steps of an algorithm without changing the algorithm's structure.

- The Template Method Design Pattern relies on inheritance.

- The Strategy Design Pattern encapsulates each algorithm in a family of algorithms and makes them interchangeable. At run time, an application can choose which algorithm to use.

- The Strategy Design Pattern uses composition. The client class is loosely coupled from the strategy subclasses.

The Factory Method and Abstract Factory Design Patterns

Chapter 8 mentioned that applications development is about algorithms and data. The two design patterns in this chapter model the ways applications can deploy software factories to create objects during run time.

Manning Comix

235

The Factory Method Design Pattern provides a model for creating a group of related objects. Our example application shows how the design pattern allows a school athletic department to delegate responsibilities to the varsity sports and intramural sports organizations. The Abstract Factory Design Pattern goes further and provides a model for creating families of objects, preventing mixing objects from different families. We'll expand the example application to ensure that the varsity and intramural sports organizations keep their responsibilities apart.

In this chapter, we'll develop another example application incrementally. We'll adapt the appropriate patterns one at a time to model solutions to the architecture design problems as we encounter them.

> **NOTE**   Be sure to read the introduction to part 4 for important information about design patterns in general and to learn how this and subsequent chapters teach each pattern.

9.1   *The Factory Method Design Pattern lets subclasses create objects*

A common software architecture problem involves a group of related objects. For example, suppose we're developing an application for a manufacturer of automobile engines for Ford and GM cars. The manufacturer only works on engines for one type of car at a time. But it doesn't always know ahead of time which type it will work on. Then, there's the possibility that another car manufacturer may later ask it to make engines. Should we have an `EngineManufacturer` class that manages the engines for all types of cars and decides which ones to make? Should it have subclasses? How easy would it be to add another type of car and its engines? The Factory Method Design Pattern provides a model for encapsulating object creation by delegating their creation to subclasses.

For a concrete example, let's expand our example sports application to include an `AthleticsDept` class that manages two categories of sports: varsity and intramural. The class will also be responsible for generating the sport report.

9.1.1   *Desired design features*

An application that relies on each individual sport to generate its report should have the following features:

- *DF 1*—Similar to our Strategy Design Pattern example in chapter 8, each sport will be responsible for recruiting players and acquiring a venue.
- *DF 2*—The `AthleticsDept` class manages the sports teams without the danger of accidentally mixing up its responsibilities for the varsity and intramural teams.
- *DF 3*—It should be easy to add categories and sports, such as club sports.

9.1.2 Before using the Factory Method Design Pattern

Figure 9.1 shows our first design for the application. Classes `PlayerStrategy` and `VenueStrategy` don't change from the Strategy Design Pattern example (program 8.4, figure 8.6). But now we have varsity and intramural sports with varsity and intramural players.

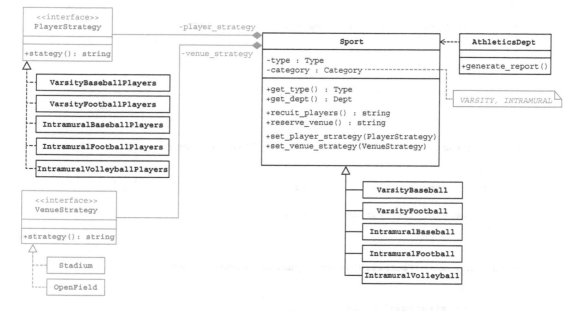

Figure 9.1 Class `AthleticsDept` generates the report for varsity and intramural sports. The grayed-out portions of the diagram haven't changed logically from figure 8.6.

Interface `PlayerStrategy` hasn't changed, but it has new varsity and intramural player classes that implement it. Each must implement member function `strategy()`. There are no changes to interface `VenueStrategy` and the classes that implement it.

Listing 9.1   **(Program 9.1 Provisions): `PlayerStrategy.h` (before the design pattern)**

```
#include <string>

using namespace std;

class PlayerStrategy
{
public:
    virtual ~PlayerStrategy() {}

    virtual string strategy() const = 0;
};
```

```cpp
class VarsityBaseballPlayers : public PlayerStrategy
{
public:
    string strategy() const override
    {
        return "varsity baseball players";
    }
};

class VarsityFootballPlayers : public PlayerStrategy
{
public:
    string strategy() const override
    {
        return "varsity football players";
    }
};

class IntramuralBaseballPlayers : public PlayerStrategy
{
public:
    string strategy() const override
    {
        return "intramural baseball players";
    }
};

class IntramuralFootballPlayers : public PlayerStrategy
{
public:
    string strategy() const override
    {
        return "intramural football players";
    }
};

class IntramuralVolleyballPlayers : public PlayerStrategy
{
public:
    string strategy() const override
    {
        return "intramural volleyball players";
    }
};
```

Class `Sport` now has a member variable `category` that keeps track of which athletic department the sport belongs to.

Listing 9.2   (Program 9.1 Provisions): `Sport.h` (before the design pattern)

```cpp
#include <iostream>
#include <string>

#include "PlayerStrategy.h"
#include "VenueStrategy.h"
```

```
using namespace std;

enum class Type ...

enum class Category { VARSITY, INTRAMURAL };

inline ostream& operator <<(ostream& ostr, const Category category)
{
    switch (category)
    {
        case Category::VARSITY:    ostr << "varsity";    break;
        case Category::INTRAMURAL: ostr << "intramural"; break;
    }

    return ostr;
}

class Sport
{
public:
    Sport(const Type t, const Category c,
          PlayerStrategy * const ps, VenueStrategy * const vs)
        : type(t), category(c),
          player_strategy(ps), venue_strategy(vs) {}

    ~Sport()
    {
        delete player_strategy;
        delete venue_strategy;
    }

    Type     get_type()     const { return type; }
    Category get_category() const { return category; }

    string recruit_players() const
    {
        return player_strategy->strategy();
    }

    string reserve_venue() const
    {
        return venue_strategy->strategy();
    }

    void set_player_strategy(PlayerStrategy * const ps)
    {
        player_strategy = ps;
    }

    void set_venue_strategy(VenueStrategy * const vs)
    {
        venue_strategy = vs;
    }
```

```
private:
    Type type;
    Category category;
    PlayerStrategy *player_strategy;
    VenueStrategy  *venue_strategy;
};
```

Class Sport has new subclasses, one for each varsity and intramural sport. The varsity teams play in the stadium, but unfortunately, the intramural teams are relegated to the open field.

Listing 9.3   (Program 9.1 Provisions): Sports.h (before the design pattern)

```
#include "Sport.h"
#include "PlayerStrategy.h"
#include "VenueStrategy.h"

using namespace std;

class VarsityBaseball : public Sport
{
public:
    VarsityBaseball() : Sport(Type::BASEBALL, Category::VARSITY,
                             new VarsityBaseballPlayers(),
                             new Stadium()) {}
};

class VarsityFootball : public Sport
{
public:
    VarsityFootball() : Sport(Type::FOOTBALL, Category::VARSITY,
                             new VarsityFootballPlayers(),
                             new Stadium()) {}
};

class IntramuralBaseball : public Sport
{
public:
    IntramuralBaseball() : Sport(Type::BASEBALL,
                               Category::INTRAMURAL,
                               new IntramuralBaseballPlayers(),
                               new OpenField()) {}
};

class IntramuralFootball : public Sport
{
public:
    IntramuralFootball() : Sport(Type::FOOTBALL,
                                Category::INTRAMURAL,
                                new IntramuralFootballPlayers(),
                                new OpenField()) {}
};

class IntramuralVolleyball : public Sport
```

```
{
public:
    IntramuralVolleyball() : Sport(Type::VOLLEYBALL,
                                   Category::INTRAMURAL,
                                   new IntramuralVolleyballPlayers(),
                                   new OpenField()) {}
};
```

Class `AthleticsDept.` is responsible for generating the sport report.

Listing 9.4   (Program 9.1 Provisions): `AthleticsDept.h` **(before the design pattern)**

```
#include "Sport.h"

class AthleticsDept
{
public:
    void generate_report(const Category& category, const Type& type);
};
```

Member function `generate_report()` does its job with nested `switch` statements to handle all the sports in the two categories.

Listing 9.5   (Program 9.1 Provisions): `AthleticsDept.cpp` **(before the design pattern)**

```
#include <iostream>
#include "Sport.h"
#include "Sports.h"
#include "AthleticsDept.h"

void AthleticsDept::generate_report(const Category& category,
                                    const Type& type)
{
    Sport *sport;

    switch (dept)
    {
        case Category::VARSITY:              | Varsity sports
            switch (type)
            {
                case Type::BASEBALL:
                {
                    sport = new VarsityBaseball();
                    break;
                }

                case Type::FOOTBALL:
                {
                    sport = new VarsityFootball();
                    break;
                }

                case Type::VOLLEYBALL:
                {
```

```
                    sport = nullptr;
                    break;
            }
        }

        cout << "varsity ";
        break;

    case Category::INTRAMURAL:                    Intramural sports
        switch (type)
        {
            case Type::BASEBALL:
            {
                sport = new IntramuralBaseball();
                break;
            }

            case Type::FOOTBALL:
            {
                sport = new IntramuralFootball();
                break;
            }

            case Type::VOLLEYBALL:
            {
                sport = new IntramuralVolleyball();
                break;
            }
        }

        cout << "intramural ";
        break;
    }

    cout << sport->get_category() << " "
         << sport->get_type() << endl;
    cout << "  players: " << sport->recruit_players() << endl;
    cout << "    venue: " << sport->reserve_venue()   << endl;
    cout << endl;
}
```

Nested switch statements! Smells like trouble to me. This could violate DF 2 if we're not careful.

I would hate to add more categories and sports to this code. This violates DF 3.

Nested `switch` statements often make complicated code that's error prone. The following listing is the test program for this version of the application.

Listing 9.6   **(Program 9.1 Provisions):** `tester.cpp` **(before the design pattern)**

```cpp
#include <iostream>
#include "Sport.h"
#include "Sports.h"
#include "AthleticsDept.h"

using namespace std;

int main()
{
    AthleticsDept dept;

    dept.generate_report(Category::VARSITY, Type::BASEBALL);
    dept.generate_report(Category::VARSITY, Type::FOOTBALL);

    dept.generate_report(Category::INTRAMURAL, Type::BASEBALL);
    dept.generate_report(Category::INTRAMURAL, Type::FOOTBALL);
    dept.generate_report(Category::INTRAMURAL, Type::VOLLEYBALL);

    return 0;
}
```

The output is

```
varsity baseball
  players: varsity baseball players
    venue: sports stadium

varsity football
  players: varsity football players
    venue: sports stadium

intramural baseball
  players: intramural baseball players
    venue: open field

intramural football
  players: intramural football players
    venue: open field

intramural volleyball
  players: intramural volleyball players
    venue: open field
```

We can readily recognize some notable shortcomings of this architecture:

- *Nested switch statements*—These are awkward and error prone.
- *Not encapsulating the potentially changing code*—We would have to modify the `AthleticsDept` class's `generate_report()` member function if we add or remove sports or add a new sports category, such as club sports.
- *Multiple responsibilities*—Besides generating the report, class `AthleticsDept` must also create the `Sport` objects.

9.1.3   After using the Factory Method Design Pattern

The Factory Method Design Pattern helps to alleviate these and other shortcomings. It uses the Factory Principle (section 7.4) in a specific architectural pattern. We want to encapsulate creating the `Sport` objects and remove that responsibility from class `AthleticsDept`. Following the pattern, we make `AthleticsDept` abstract with two subclasses, `VarsityDept` and `IntramuralDept` (figure 9.2). It has a pure virtual function `create_sport()` and private member variable `sport` that points to a `Sport` object. Each of the two subclasses serves as a factory class. Subclass `VarsityDept` implements `create_sport()`, which creates and returns a varsity `Sport` object. Subclass `IntramuralDept` implements `create_sport()`, which creates and returns an intramural `Sport` object. Therefore, each `create_sport()` is a factory function, also known as a *factory method*.

> ### The Factory Method Design Pattern
>
> "Define an interface for creating an object, but let subclasses decide which class to instantiate. Factory Method lets a class defer instantiation to subclasses" (GoF 107).

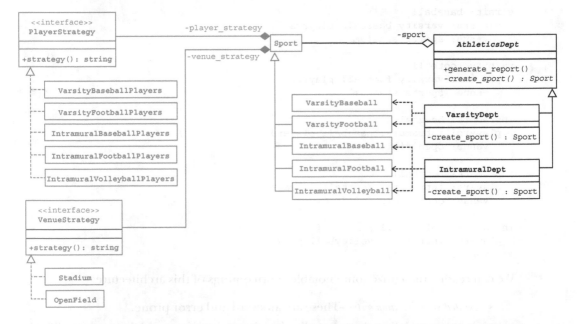

Figure 9.2   This version of the application is modeled from the Factory Method Design Pattern. Superclass `AthleticsDept` **delegates creating** `Sport` **objects to its subclasses. Subclasses** `VarsityDept` **and** `IntramuralDept` **are factory classes. Each implements the factory function** `create_sport()`**, which creates and returns an appropriate varsity or intramural** `Sport` **object. The grayed-out portions of the diagram have not changed logically from figure 9.1.**

Figure 9.2 shows some of the advantages of this revised architecture:

- *Encapsulated changes*—They make it easier to add new categories, such as club sports. This is the Encapsulate What Varies design principle (section 2.3.2).

- *The Open-Closed Principle*—Class `AthleticsDept` remains stable (section 2.3.3). We can extend the class by adding more subdepartments such as club sports, but the class is closed to further modification.

- *Use of factory classes*—Subclasses `VarsityDept` and `IntramuralDept` are the factories that handle the varsity and intramural sports categories, respectively. Class `AthleticsDept` follows the Delegation Principle (section 2.3.2) by delegating creating `Sport` objects to these subclasses. It will be easier to vary the sports of the two categories.

- *Cohesive classes*—Each of the `AthleticsDept` subclasses follows the Single Responsibility Principle (section 2.3) and is responsible only for creating its sport objects. This also eliminates the need for nested `switch` statements.

- *Loosely coupled classes*—The `AthleticsDept` subclasses are no longer dependent on the implementation of the `Sport` subclasses. This is the Principle of Least Knowledge (section 2.3.2).

 Subclasses **VarsityDept** and **IntramuralDept** are the factory classes, and **AthleticsDept** delegates creating the **Sport** objects to its subclasses.

 We used the Factory Method Design Pattern to model a custom solution to our architecture problem.

Abstract class `AthleticsDept` has two concrete subclasses `VarsityDept` and `IntramuralDept`, which are factory classes. Each subclass implements the virtual member function `create_sport()`, the factory method, to create and return a varsity or an intramural `Sport` object, respectively. Member variable `sport` keeps track of the `Sport` object that was created.

> **Listing 9.7   (Program 9.2 Provisions-FactoryDP):** `AthleticDept.h`

```
#include <string>
#include "Sport.h"

using namespace std;

class AthleticsDept
{
public:
    virtual ~AthleticsDept() { delete sport; }

    void generate_report(const Type& type);

private:
```

```
    Sport *sport;                          ◄——— The created Sport object

    virtual Sport *create_sport(const Type& type) = 0;
};

class VarsityDept : public AthleticsDept
{
private:
    Sport *create_sport(const Type& type) override;
};

class IntramuralDept : public AthleticsDept
{
private:
    Sport *create_sport(const Type& type) override;
};
```

The following listing shows the implementation of class AthleticsDept and its sub-classes VarsityDept and IntramuralDept. Each subclass creates and returns an appropriate Sport object. Therefore, superclass AthleticsDept delegates creating a Sport object to its subclasses. When its member function generate_report() calls the factory method create_sport() at run time, which sport object is created depends on whether generate_report() was called on a VarsityDept object or an IntramuralDept object.

Listing 9.8   (Program 9.2 Provisions-FactoryDP): AthleticsDept.cpp

```
#include <iostream>
#include "Sport.h"                          Generate a report on whichever
#include "Sports.h"                          Sport object was created
#include "AthleticsDept.h"                   by the factory subclass.

void AthleticsDept::generate_report(const Type& type)   ◄
{
    sport = create_sport(type);      ◄——   Delegate creating a Sport
                                            object to the factory method
    cout << sport->get_category() << " "    in an AthleticsDept subclass.
         << sport->get_type() << endl;
    cout << "  players: " << sport->recruit_players() << endl;
    cout << "    venue: " << sport->reserve_venue()    << endl;
    cout << endl;
}


Sport *VarsityDept::create_sport(const Type& type)      ◄
{
    switch (type)                           Factory method to create and
    {                                       return a varsity Sport object
        case Type::BASEBALL:   return new VarsityBaseball();
        case Type::FOOTBALL:   return new VarsityFootball();
        case Type::VOLLEYBALL: return nullptr;

        default: return nullptr;
    }
}
```

```cpp
Sport *IntramuralDept::create_sport(const Type& type)
{
    switch (type)
    {
        case Type::BASEBALL:   return new IntramuralBaseball();
        case Type::FOOTBALL:   return new IntramuralFootball();
        case Type::VOLLEYBALL: return new IntramuralVolleyball();

        default: return nullptr;
    }
}
```

Factory method to create and return an intramural Sport object

Our application uses delegation and factory classes.

Factory classes and the Delegation Principle together constitute the Factory Method Design Pattern.

The test program for this version of the application calls member function `generate_report()` either on a `VarsityDept` object or on an `IntramuralDept` object. If it's a `VarsityDept` object, `generate_report()` calls the factory method `create_sport()`, which uses polymorphism to create a varsity `Sport` object. But if it's an `IntramuralDept` object, the factory method uses polymorphism to create an intramural `Sport` object.

Listing 9.9   **(Program 9.2 Provisions-FactoryDP):** `tester.cpp`

```cpp
#include <iostream>
#include "Sport.h"
#include "Sports.h"
#include "AthleticsDept.h"

using namespace std;

int main()
{
    VarsityDept varsity;

    varsity.generate_report(Type::BASEBALL);
    varsity.generate_report(Type::FOOTBALL);

    IntramuralDept intramural;

    intramural.generate_report(Type::BASEBALL);
    intramural.generate_report(Type::FOOTBALL);
    intramural.generate_report(Type::VOLLEYBALL);

    return 0;
}
```

The output is unchanged from the previous version of the application.

9.1.4   *Factory Method's generic model*

Figure 9.3 shows the generic model of the Factory Method Design Pattern. Recall that it is from the design pattern's generic model that we can create a custom solution to an architecture problem (section 8.1.3).

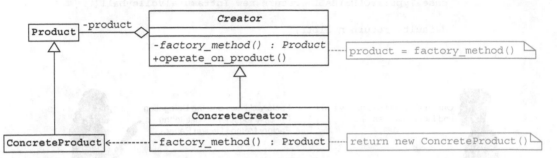

Figure 9.3   The generic model of the Factory Method Design Pattern (compare to figure 9.2)

Table 9.1 shows how the example application applies the pattern.

Table 9.1   The Factory Method Design Pattern as applied by the example application

Design pattern	Applied by the example application
Class `Product`	Superclass `Sport`
Class `ConcreteProduct`	`Sport` subclasses `VarsityBaseball`, `VarsityFootball`, `Intramural-Baseball`, `IntramuralFootball`, and `IntramuralVolleyball`
Class `Creator`	Superclass `AthleticsDept`
Class `ConcreteCreator`	Subclasses `VarsityDept` and `IntramuralDept`
`factory_method()`	Member functions `VarsityDept::create_sport()` and `IntramuralDept::create_sport()`
`operate_on_product()`	Member function `AthleticsDept::generate_report()`

9.2   *The Abstract Factory Design Pattern creates families of objects*

Let's think back to our example of the automobile engine manufacturer and consider how an engine is made of many parts; thus, the manufacturer is a creator of families of engine parts. A Ford engine consists of one family of parts and a GM engine of another family of parts. Some parts are standard and belong to both families. But the manufacturer must neither include Ford-only parts in a GM engine nor GM-only parts in a Ford engine. If our engine manufacturing application must include the concept of families of objects, the Abstract Factory Design Pattern provides a model to solve this architecture problem.

9.2.1   Before using the Abstract Factory Design Pattern

We saw in the previous version of our sports application that the `VarsityDept` subclass and the `IntramuralDept` subclass are factory classes that create `Sport` objects for their superclass `AthleticsDept`. But logically, there is no way to prevent us from making a coding error that mixes up the objects the factories created. The varsity baseball team does not want to play in the open field, and it would not be wise to have football players on the volleyball team. Can we further refine the application to help prevent such logic errors?

If we reexamine figure 9.2, we can consider the players and venue for varsity sports to be one family of objects, and the players and venue for intramural sports to be another family. We don't want to mix up families—the varsity player and venue objects belong together for a varsity sport, and the intramural player and venue objects belong together for an intramural sport.

9.2.2   After using the Abstract Factory Design Pattern

The Abstract Factory Design Pattern provides a model for an architecture design that creates families of objects (figure 9.4). We've added use of the pattern as an increment to the previous version of the application.

The abstract `ProvisionsFactory` class is the superclass of factory subclasses. Factory subclass `VarsityFactory` creates player and venue objects from the varsity family, and factory subclass `IntramuralFactory` creates player and venue objects from the intramural family. The `VarsityDept` subclass of superclass `AthleticsDept` requires the varsity family of `Sport` objects, and so it must use `VarsityFactory`. Similarly, the `IntramuralDept` subclass requires the intramural family of `Sport` objects, and so it must use `IntramuralFactory`. The two abstract factory classes relieve `VarsityDept` and `IntramuralDept` of the responsibility of creating objects within the appropriate families, and neither subclass needs to have knowledge of how the factories accomplish their tasks.

> ### The Abstract Factory Design Pattern
> "Provide an interface for creating families of related or dependent objects without specifying their concrete classes" (GoF 87).

It's all about families: the Strategy Design Pattern models a software architecture that manages a family of algorithms, while the Abstract Factory Design Pattern models a software architecture that creates families of objects.

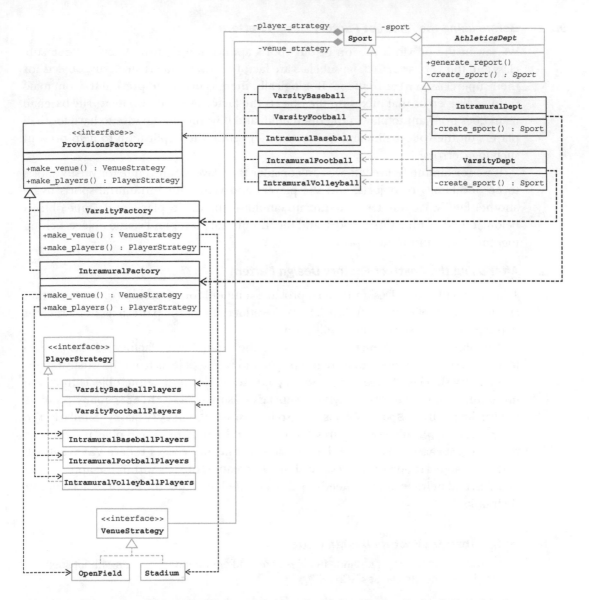

Figure 9.4   This version of the application is modeled from the Abstract Factory Design Pattern. Interface `ProvisionsFactory` **is the abstract factory. Implementor class** `VarsityFactory` **creates the varsity family of player and venue objects, and therefore,** `VarsityDept` **uses** `VarsityFactory`**. Implementor class** `IntramuralFactory` **creates the intramural family of player and venue objects, and therefore,** `IntramuralDept` **uses** `IntramuralFactory`**. The grayed-out portions of the diagram have not changed logically from figure 9.2.**

How will this work? As before, the `AthleticsDept` subclass `VarsityDept` creates varsity `Sport` objects. In this version of the application, the `create_sport()` member function passes a `VarsityFactory` object to the `Sport` constructor. The `Sport` constructor then uses the `VarsityFactory` object to create appropriate player and venue objects from the varsity family. Similarly, the `AthleticsDept` subclass `IntramuralDept` creates intramural `Sport` objects. Its `create_sport()` member function passes an `IntramuralFactory` object to the `Sport` constructor. The latter then uses the `IntramuralFactory` object to create appropriate player and venue objects from the intramural family.

Figure 9.4 shows some of the benefits of using the Abstract Factory Pattern.

- *Families kept together*—Each factory subclass guarantees that the objects it creates are from a single family.
- *Flexible to choose which family*—There is less hardcoding, which makes it possible to decide at run time whether to create the varsity or the intramural family of objects.
- *Encapsulated object creation*—Object creation is encapsulated in the factory subclasses. This is the Encapsulate What Varies Principle (section 2.3.2). Each `Sport` object delegates player and venue object creation to either the varsity factory or the intramural factory.
- *Cohesive classes*—Subclasses `VarsityDept` and `IntramuralDept` are each responsible only to create `Sport` objects. By passing a `VarsityFactory` or `IntramuralFactory` object, respectively, to the `Sport` constructor, they delegate creating player and venue objects from the appropriate families. This is the Single Responsibility Principle (section 2.3).
- *Loosely coupled classes*—Subclasses `VarsityDept` and `IntramuralDept` are not dependent on how the object families are created. This is the Principle of Least Knowledge (section 2.3.2).

Both the Factory Method and the Abstract Factory design patterns encapsulate object creation. But Abstract Factory adds the capability to ensure objects are created in the proper families. That's critical for DF 2.

Both design patterns make your code more flexible by reducing hardcoding. They allow making object creation decisions at run time. That satisfies DF 3.

The following listing is the abstract factory class `ProvisionsFactory` and the classes `VarsityFactory` and `IntramuralFactory` that implement the interface. These classes must implement member functions `make_players()` and `make_venue()` to create player and venue objects, respectively, within each family.

Listing 9.10 (Program 9.3 Provisions-AbsFactoryDP): `ProvisionsFactory.h`

```
#include <string>
#include "PlayerStrategy.h"
#include "VenueStrategy.h"

using namespace std;
                                          ┌─ Abstract
class ProvisionsFactory       ◄─────────┘   factory class
{
public:
```

Factory functions to be implemented
by the factory subclasses

```
    virtual ~ProvisionsFactory() {}

    virtual PlayerStrategy *make_players(const Type& type) = 0;
    virtual VenueStrategy  *make_venue() = 0;
};


class VarsityFactory : public ProvisionsFactory
{
public:
    PlayerStrategy *make_players(const Type& type) override
    {
        switch (type)
        {
            case Type::BASEBALL:
                return new VarsityBaseballPlayers();
            case Type::FOOTBALL:
                return new VarsityFootballPlayers();
            case Type::VOLLEYBALL:
                return nullptr;

            default: return nullptr;
        }
    }

    VenueStrategy *make_venue() override
    {
        return new Stadium();
    }
};


class IntramuralFactory : public ProvisionsFactory
{
public:
    PlayerStrategy *make_players(const Type& type) override
    {
        switch (type)
        {
            case Type::BASEBALL:
                return new IntramuralBaseballPlayers();
            case Type::FOOTBALL:
                return new IntramuralFootballPlayers();
            case Type::VOLLEYBALL:
                return new IntramuralVolleyballPlayers();

            default: return nullptr;
        }
    }

    VenueStrategy *make_venue() override
    {
        return new OpenField();
    }
};
```

Create and
return the
varsity family of
objects.

Create and return the
intramural family of objects.

Each `Sport` subclass delegates creating the sport's family of player and venue objects
to the `ProvisionsFactory` object passed to its constructor.

Listing 9.11   (Program 9.3 Provisions-AbsFactoryDP): `Sports.h`

```cpp
#include "Sport.h"
#include "PlayerStrategy.h"
#include "VenueStrategy.h"
#include "ProvisionsFactory.h"

using namespace std;

class VarsityBaseball : public Sport
{
public:
    VarsityBaseball(ProvisionsFactory& factory)
        : Sport(Type::BASEBALL, Category::VARSITY,
                factory.make_players(get_type()),
                factory.make_venue()) {}
};

class VarsityFootball : public Sport
{
public:
    VarsityFootball(ProvisionsFactory& factory)
        : Sport(Type::FOOTBALL, Category::VARSITY,
                factory.make_players(get_type()),
                factory.make_venue()) {}
};

class IntramuralBaseball : public Sport
{
public:
    IntramuralBaseball(ProvisionsFactory& factory)
        : Sport(Type::BASEBALL, Category::INTRAMURAL,
                factory.make_players(get_type()),
                factory.make_venue()) {}
};

class IntramuralFootball : public Sport
{
public:
    IntramuralFootball(ProvisionsFactory& factory)
        : Sport(Type::FOOTBALL, Category::INTRAMURAL,
                factory.make_players(get_type()),
                factory.make_venue()) {}
};

class IntramuralVolleyball : public Sport
{
public:
    IntramuralVolleyball(ProvisionsFactory& factory)
        : Sport(Type::VOLLEYBALL, Dept::INTRAMURAL,
                factory.make_players(get_type()),
                factory.make_venue()) {}
};
```

In each `AthleticsDept` subclass `VarsityDept` and `IntramuralDept`, member function `create_sport()` passes the appropriate factory to the constructors of the `Sport` subclasses.

Listing 9.12   (Program 9.3 Provisions-AbsFactoryDP): `AthleticsDept.cpp`

```cpp
#include <iostream>
#include "Sport.h"
#include "Sports.h"
#include "AthleticsDept.h"
#include "ProvisionsFactory.h"

void AthleticsDept::generate_report(const Type& type) ...

Sport *VarsityDept::create_sport(const Type& type)
{
    VarsityFactory varsity_factory;                    ◄──────  For the varsity family of
                                                               player and venue objects
    switch (type)
    {
        case Type::BASEBALL:
            return new VarsityBaseball(varsity_factory);
        case Type::FOOTBALL:
            return new VarsityFootball(varsity_factory);
        case Type::VOLLEYBALL:
            return nullptr;

        default: return nullptr;
    }
}


Sport *IntramuralDept::create_sport(const Type& type)
{
    IntramuralFactory intramural_factory;              ◄──────  For the intramural family of
                                                               player and venue objects
    switch (type)
    {
        case Type::BASEBALL:
            return new IntramuralBaseball(intramural_factory);
        case Type::FOOTBALL:
            return new IntramuralFootball(intramural_factory);
        case Type::VOLLEYBALL:
            return new IntramuralVolleyball(intramural_factory);

        default: return nullptr;
    }
}
```

There are no changes to the test program in this version of the application, and the output remains the same:

```
varsity baseball
  players: varsity baseball players
    venue: sports stadium
```

```
varsity football
   players: varsity baseball players
     venue: sports stadium

intramural baseball
   players: intramural baseball players
     venue: open field

intramural football
   players: intramural baseball players
     venue: open field

intramural volleyball
   players: intramural baseball players
     venue: open field
```

9.2.3 Abstract Factory's generic model

Figure 9.5 shows the generic model of the Abstract Factory Design Pattern. Recall that
it is from the design pattern's generic model that we can create a custom solution to an
architecture problem (section 8.1.3).

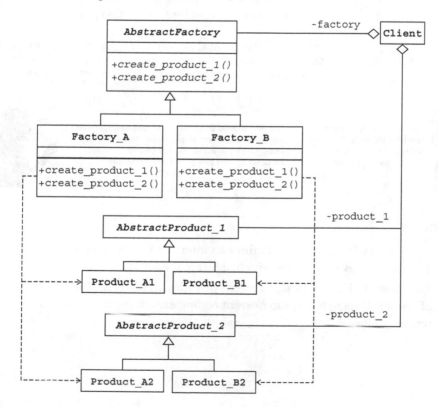

Figure 9.5   The generic model of the Abstract Factory Design Pattern (compare to figure 9.4)

The factory classes are key. Each one creates objects from only one family.

Using tested factory classes lessens the chance of making coding errors that mix up the objects from different families.

Table 9.2 shows how the example application applies the pattern.

Table 9.2　The Abstract Factory Design Pattern as applied by the example application

Design pattern	Applied by the example application
Client	Superclass `AthleticsDept`
Superclass `AbstractFactory`	Interface `ProvisionsFactory`
Factory subclasses `Factory_A`, `FactoryB`, etc.	Factory classes `VarsityFactory` and `IntramuralFactory`
Member functions `create_product_1()`, `create_product_2()`, etc.	Member functions `VarsityFactory::make_players()`, `VarsityFactory::make_venue()`, `IntramuralFactory::make_players()`, and `IntramuralFactory::make_venue()`
Classes `AbstractProduct_1`, `AbstractProduct_2`, etc.	Interfaces `PlayerStrategy` and `VenueStrategy`
Subclasses `Product_A1`, `Product_B1`, `Product_A2`, `Product_B2`, etc	Classes `VarsityBaseballPlayers`, `VarsityFootballPlayers`, `IntramuralBaseballPlayers`, `IntramuralFootballPlayers`, `IntramuralVolleyballPlayers`, `Stadium`, and `OpenField`

Our example application used the Strategy, Factory Method, and Abstract Factory design patterns!

A well-designed application may use several patterns, some multiple times. Applications modeled from design patterns will be more cohesive, have less hardcoding, and use good design principles.

Summary

- The Factory Design Pattern defines an interface for creating an object but delegates to subclasses to decide which object to create.
- The Abstract Factory Design Pattern provides an interface for creating families of related objects. It helps to prevent coding errors that mix up objects from different families.

The Adapter and Façade
Design Patterns
10

This chapter covers

- The Adapter Design Pattern
- The Façade Design Pattern

In this chapter, we tackle an all-too-common problem: working with legacy software. This code can be from a library that we can't modify, or it can be other external code that we don't have access to or otherwise cannot modify.

The Adapter Design Pattern provides a model for a software architecture that needs to integrate external code, such as from a library, with code in an existing application. However, the external and application codes weren't originally designed to work together, and we cannot change either of them. The pattern can also help to isolate an application from interface changes in the external code that may be beyond our control. Our example application must generate a report about the attendance and venue of various school sports, but the sports report that data differently.

The Façade Design Pattern provides a simpler higher-level interface that makes complex code that we can't modify easier to use. Our example application must interact with multiple organizations to raise funds for school sports.

> **NOTE**   Be sure to read the introduction to part 4 for important information about design patterns in general and to learn how this and subsequent chapters teach each pattern.

10.1 *The Adapter Design Pattern integrates code*

When we develop an application, we may need to incorporate some external code, such as code from a library or code that was previously written for some other application. We might not have access to the code's source files or know how it was implemented, and we might not be able to or allowed to change that code. Unfortunately, the external code isn't compatible with our application because it has a different interface. We may also be unable to change our application code because it has many dependents. The Adapter Design Pattern provides a model for solving this classic architecture problem of integrating codes that were never designed to work together.

An application often needs to import code from libraries and other external sources, but you can't modify the external code.

The Adapter Design Pattern saves the day if the external code's design isn't compatible with the application's code design.

For an example of a code integration challenge, consider developing a drawing application that includes various shape objects, such as lines, rectangles, and circles. The shape interface supports drawing operations such as setting the color, size, and orientation of a shape. Now we're asked to add a text object to the application. We found some existing code that edits and displays text and has an interface that supports operations such as setting the text color, font size, and font face. But the text interface isn't compatible with the shape interface, and the text code wasn't designed to work with the shape code. The Adapter Design Pattern provides a model to integrate the shape and text interfaces.

For our concrete example, we'll develop another example application involving sports reporting. As a demonstration, the first version will not use the Adapter Design Pattern, and we'll point out its faults. Then, we'll design a second version that uses the Adapter Design Pattern and see that pattern's benefits.

In our example application, a college's athletics department needs to know the venue and average number of fans attending each varsity baseball, varsity football, and intramural volleyball game. It gets this information from the baseball, football, and volleyball organizations.

10.1.1 Desired design features

An application that needs to work with existing external code should have the following features:

- *DF 1*—We should not need to modify our application code or the external code to make them work together.
- *DF 2*—Our application code should be isolated from any interface changes by the external code.
- *DF 3*—It should be straightforward to add another sport to the report.

10.1.2 Before using the Adapter Design Pattern

Suppose that, due to lack of coordination, each sport organization reports its information differently, and they don't want to change how they report. Therefore, class `AttendanceReport` requires three overloaded public `print()` member functions (figure 10.1), one for each sport. Each of these `print()` functions calls the private `legacy_print()` function that does the actual printing, but it can only accept an `AttendanceData` parameter. Because it's legacy and other parts of the application may depend on it, we don't want to change the function.

What follows is the example output from this attendance report application:

```
Baseball
  stadium: 500
Football
  stadium: 2000
Volleyball
  open field: 150
```

The report requires some enumeration constants and an overloaded operator `<<` function (listing 10.1).

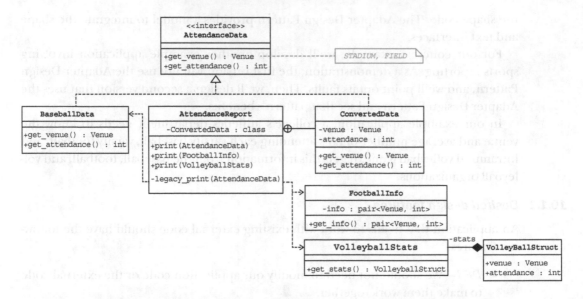

Figure 10.1   In the first version of the application, classes `BaseballData`, `FootballInfo`, **and**
`VolleyballStats` **present their venue and attendance data in different ways. Therefore, class**
`AttendanceReport` **requires nested private class** `ConvertedData` **and three overloaded public** `print()`
member functions. Each function calls the private `legacy_print()` **member function. The** `print()` **function**
for the football and volleyball sports uses class `ConvertedData` **to convert data from** `FootballInfo` **and**
`VolleyballStats`, **respectively, to the** `AttendanceData` **format.** `BaseballData` **is already in that format.**

Listing 10.1   (Program 10.1 Fans): `Enums.h` **(before the design pattern)**

```cpp
#include <iostream>

using namespace std;

enum class Venue { STADIUM, FIELD };

inline ostream& operator <<(ostream& ostr, const Venue& venue)
{
    switch (venue)
    {
        case Venue::STADIUM: ostr << "stadium";    break;
        case Venue::FIELD:   ostr << "open field"; break;
    }

    return ostr;
}
```

The legacy `legacy_print()` member function of class `AttendanceReport` expects
venue and attendance data in the form of an `AttendanceData` object (listing 10.2).
We don't want to modify `legacy_print()`.

Listing 10.2 (Program 10.1 Fans): `AttendanceData.h` (before the design pattern)

```
#include "Enums.h"

class AttendanceData
{
public:
    virtual ~AttendanceData() {}

    virtual Venue get_venue()      const = 0;
    virtual int   get_attendance() const = 0;
};
```

Class `BaseballData` is the only one that conforms to this interface (listing 10.3).

Listing 10.3 (Program 10.1 Fans): `BaseballData.h` (before the design pattern)

```
#include "Enums.h"
#include "AttendanceData.h"

class BaseballData : public AttendanceData
{
public:
    Venue get_venue()      const override { return Venue::STADIUM; }
    int   get_attendance() const override { return 500; }
};
```

Classes `FootballInfo` and `VolleyballStats` do not conform to the `Attendance-Data` interface. Perhaps the football and volleyball sports obtained their code from a library, and we have no access to their source files. Class `FootballInfo` presents its venue and attendance data as a `pair` object from the Standard Template Library.

Listing 10.4 (Program 10.1 Fans): `FootballInfo.h` (before the design pattern)

```
#include <utility>
#include "Enums.h"

using namespace std;

class FootballInfo   // cannot change!
{
public:
    FootballInfo()
    {
        info.first  = Venue::STADIUM;
        info.second = 2000;
    }

    pair<Venue, int> get_info() const { return info; }

private:
    pair<Venue, int> info;
};
```

Class `VolleyballStats` presents its venue and attendance data as a `struct` (listing 10.5).

Listing 10.5   (Program 10.1 Fans): `VolleyballStats.h` (before the design pattern)

```cpp
#include "Enums.h"

typedef struct
{
    Venue venue;
    int   attendance;
} VolleyballStruct;

class VolleyballStats  // cannot change!
{
public:
    VolleyballStats()
    {
        stats.venue      = Venue::FIELD;
        stats.attendance = 150;
    }

    VolleyballStruct get_stats() const { return stats; }

private:
    VolleyballStruct stats;
};
```

In class `AttendanceReport`, we require three overloaded public `print()` member functions that take the `AttendanceReport`, `FootballInfo`, and `VolleyballStats` parameters, respectively. Each `print()` function calls the private legacy `legacy_print()` function, which can only accept an `AttendanceData` object. We don't want to modify the legacy code. Therefore, two of the `print()` function must use class `ConvertedData` to convert its parameter data to an `AttendanceData` object.

Listing 10.6   (Program 10.1 Fans): `AttendanceReport.h` (before the design pattern)

```cpp
#include <string>
#include "AttendanceData.h"
#include "FootballInfo.h"
#include "VolleyballStats.h"

using namespace std;

class AttendanceReport
{
public:
    void print(const AttendanceData& data,
            const string title) const;

    void print(const FootballInfo& info,
            const string title) const;

    void print(const VolleyballStats& stats,
            const string title) const;
```

```
private:
    class ConvertedData : public AttendanceData
    {
    public:
        ConvertedData(const Venue v, const int a)
            : venue(v), attendance(a) {}

        Venue get_venue()        const override { return venue; }
        int   get_attendance() const override { return attendance; }

    private:
        Venue venue;
        int   attendance;
    };

    // Legacy: Cannot change!
    void legacy_print(const AttendanceData& data) const;
};
```

Internal private ConvertedData class for converting to an AttendanceData object

Legacy printing function that cannot change

Incompatible software is an all-too-common problem!

The software may have been written by multiple programmers at various times for different purposes. Some of the programmers may no longer be around.

One `print()` member function obtains `FootballInfo` venue and attendance count from the class's `pair` object, and another `print()` member function obtains `VolleyballStats` venue and attendance count from the class's `struct`. Each must convert their data using the internal `ConvertedData` class. Because class `Baseball-Data` implements the `AttendanceData` interface, its data does not require conversion.

Listing 10.7   (Program 10.1 Fans): `AttendanceReport.cpp` **(before the design pattern)**

```cpp
#include <iostream>
#include <string>
#include "AttendanceData.h"
#include "BaseballData.h"
#include "FootballInfo.h"
#include "VolleyballStats.h"
#include "AttendanceReport.h"

using namespace std;

void AttendanceReport::print(const AttendanceData& data,
                             const string title) const
{
    cout << title << endl;
    legacy_print(data);
}
```

```
void AttendanceReport::print(const FootballInfo& info,
                             const string title) const
{
    Venue venue      = info.get_info().first;        | Obtain data from the
    int   attendance = info.get_info().second;       | FootballInfo pair object.

    cout << title << endl;
    legacy_print(ConvertedData(venue, attendance));  ◄─────────┐
}                                                              |
          Convert FootballInfo data to AttendanceData by using ConvertedData. |

void AttendanceReport::print(const VolleyballStats& stats,
                             const string title) const
{
    Venue venue      = stats.get_stats().venue;      | Obtain data from the
    int   attendance = stats.get_stats().attendance; | VolleyballStats struct.

    cout << title << endl;
    legacy_print(ConvertedData(venue, attendance));  ◄─────────┐
}                                                              |
                                    Convert VolleyballStats data to |
                              AttendanceData by using ConvertedData. |
// Legacy: Cannot change!
void AttendanceReport::legacy_print(const AttendanceData& data) const
{
    cout << "  " << data.get_venue()
         << ": " << data.get_attendance() << endl;
}
```

This is already starting to look ugly! We needed a private internal class **ConvertedData** to convert data. That violates DF 1. If any sport changes the way it reports its data, we'll have to modify a **print()** member function in class **AttendanceReport**. That violates DF 2.

This code will get even uglier if we get more sports and then we must print venue and attendance data stored in other incompatible ways. That violates DF 3.

The test program produces the desired reports, as shown in the following listing.

Listing 10.8   (Program 10.1 Fans): `tester.cpp` (before the design pattern)

```
#include "BaseballData.h"
#include "FootballInfo.h"
#include "VolleyballStats.h"
#include "AttendanceReport.h"

int main()
{
    BaseballData     baseball_data;
    FootballInfo     football_info;
    VolleyballStats  volleyball_stats;

    AttendanceReport report;
```

```
    report.print(baseball_data,    "Baseball");
    report.print(football_info,    "Football");
    report.print(volleyball_stats, "Volleyball");

    return 0;
}
```

This version of our attendance report application has several major faults, including

- *Class with multiple responsibilities*—Class `AttendanceReport` is responsible both for converting data and for printing reports.
- *Classes not loosely coupled*—Class `AttendanceReport` must know the internal implementations of classes `FootballInfo` and `VolleyballStats` to obtain their venues and attendance numbers.
- *Inflexible architecture design*—If there is another source of venue and attendance data, such as for basketball games, it will require changes to class `AttendanceReport`.

10.1.3 *After using the Adapter Design Pattern*

Let's see how the Adapter Design Pattern removes these faults. It encapsulates the data conversion code and thereby removes that responsibility from class `Attendance-Report`. The pattern introduces two classes, `FootballData` and `VolleyballData`, that implement the `AttendanceData` interface (figure 10.2). Class `FootballData` is the adapter that wraps (aggregates) class `FootballInfo`. Similarly, class `Volley-ballData` is the adapter that wraps class `VolleyballStats`. Then, class `Attendance-Report` needs only the one public `print()` member function, which is always passed an `AttendanceData` object.

> **The Adapter Design Pattern**
>
> "Convert the interface of a class into another interface clients expect. Adapter lets classes work together that couldn't otherwise because of incompatible interfaces" (GoF 139).

Adapter `FootballData` implements the `AttendanceData` interface. It wraps class `FootballInfo` and performs the data conversion. Member variable `football_info` points to the `FootballInfo` object being wrapped. Member functions `get_venue()` and `get_attendance()` extract the venue and attendance data from the `Football-Info` class's `info` member variable, which is a `pair` object (listing 10.9).

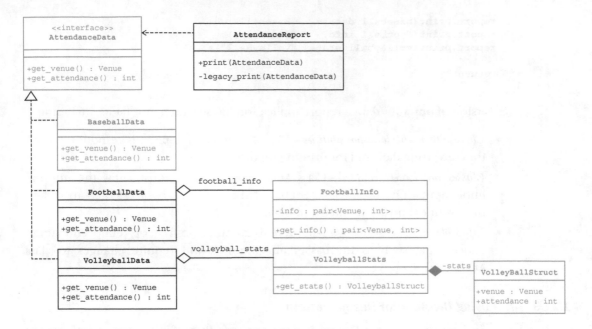

Figure 10.2   This version of the application uses the Adapter Design Pattern. Adapters `FootballData` **and** `VolleyballData` **each implements the** `AttendanceData` **interface. They wrap classes** `FootballInfo` **and** `VolleyballStats`, **respectively, and encapsulate the data conversion code. The grayed-out portions of the diagram have not changed logically from figure 10.1.**

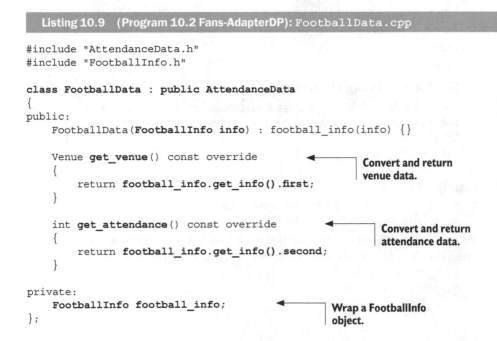

Listing 10.9   (Program 10.2 Fans-AdapterDP): `FootballData.cpp`

```cpp
#include "AttendanceData.h"
#include "FootballInfo.h"

class FootballData : public AttendanceData
{
public:
    FootballData(FootballInfo info) : football_info(info) {}

    Venue get_venue() const override          ◀──────  Convert and return
    {                                                   venue data.
        return football_info.get_info().first;
    }

    int get_attendance() const override       ◀──────  Convert and return
    {                                                   attendance data.
        return football_info.get_info().second;
    }

private:
    FootballInfo football_info;                ◀──────  Wrap a FootballInfo
};                                                      object.
```

Similarly, adapter `VolleyballData` implements the `AttendanceData` interface, wraps class `VolleyballStats`, and performs the data conversion. Member variable `volleyball_stats` points to the `VolleyballStats` object being wrapped. Member functions `get_venue()` and `get_attendance()` extract the venue and attendance data from the `VolleyballStats` class's stats member variable, which is a `struct` (listing 10.10).

Listing 10.10 (Program 10.2 Fans-AdapterDP): `VolleyballData.cpp`

```cpp
#include "AttendanceData.h"
#include "VolleyballStats.h"

class VolleyballData : public AttendanceData
{
public:
    VolleyballData(VolleyballStats stats)
        : volleyball_stats(stats) {}

    Venue get_venue() const override          ◄─── Convert and return
    {                                              venue data.
        return volleyball_stats.get_stats().venue;
    }
                                              Convert and return
    int get_attendance() const override       ◄─── attendance data.
    {
        return volleyball_stats.get_stats().attendance;
    }

private:                                       Wrap a VolleyballStats
    VolleyballStats volleyball_stats;         ◄─── object.
};
```

Class `AttendanceReport` now only needs one public `print()` member function, and it takes an `AttendanceData` parameter. It no longer does any data conversions.

Listing 10.11 (Program 10.2 Fans-AdapterDP): `AttendanceReport.h`

```cpp
#include <iostream>
#include <string>
#include "AttendanceData.h"

using namespace std;

class AttendanceReport
{
public:                                        Only one public
    void print(const AttendanceData& data,    ◄─── print function
               const string title) const;

                                              Legacy printing function
private:                                       that cannot change
    // Legacy: Cannot change!
    void legacy_print(const AttendanceData& data) const;   ◄───
};
```

The test program creates the two adapter classes and arranges each one to adapt its corresponding object. The output is the same as before.

Listing 10.12   (Program 10.2 Fans-AdapterDP): `tester.cpp`

```cpp
#include "BaseballData.h"
#include "FootballData.h"
#include "VolleyballData.h"
#include "FootballInfo.h"
#include "VolleyballStats.h"
#include "AttendanceReport.h"

int main()
{
    BaseballData     baseball_data;
    FootballInfo     football_info;                        Adapt a FootballInfo
    VolleyballStats volleyball_stats;                             object.

    FootballData    football_data(football_info);
    VolleyballData volleyball_data(volleyball_stats);

    AttendanceReport report;                               Adapt a VolleyballStats
                                                                  object.
    report.print(baseball_data,    "Baseball");
    report.print(football_data,    "Football");
    report.print(volleyball_data, "Volleyball");

    return 0;
}
```

Each class that provides attendance data is paired with an adapter class if it doesn't already conform to the **AttendanceData** interface.

We can add new attendance data classes and their adapters without modifying either the data classes or the legacy printing code.

Using the Adapter Design Pattern to model the architecture of the attendance report application has several important benefits:

- *Encapsulated data conversions*—The `FootballData` and `VolleyballData` adapter classes encapsulate data conversions from the `FootballInfo` and `Volleyball-Stats` classes, respectively. This is the Encapsulate What Varies Principle (section 2.3.2).

- *Single class responsibility*—Class `AttendanceReport` now has only the responsibility to print the report. It no longer has data conversion responsibilities. This is the Single Responsibility Principle (section 2.3). Each of the adapter classes `FootballData` and `VolleyballData` has the single responsibility to convert data.

- *Loosely coupled classes*—By applying the Principle of Least Knowledge (section 2.3.2), class `AttendanceReport` is loosely coupled with the data classes `FootballInfo` and `VolleyballStats`. We can add new data classes and their adapters without changing class `AttendanceReport`.

10.1.4 Adapter's generic model

Figure 10.3 shows the generic model of the Adapter Design Pattern. Recall from section 8.1.3 that it is from a design pattern's generic model that we can create a custom solution to an architecture problem.

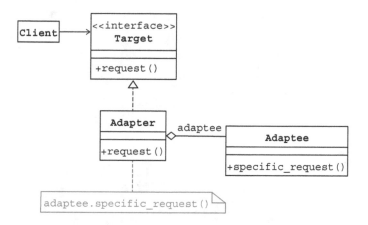

Figure 10.3   The generic model of the Adapter Design Pattern. Compare with figure 10.2. The `Adapter` class implements the `Target` interface. It adapts an `Adaptee` class by wrapping it so that the latter can work with the `Target` interface.

Table 10.1 shows how the example application applies the pattern.

Table 10.1   The Adapter Method Design Pattern as applied by the example application

Design pattern	Applied by the example application
Interface `Target`	Interface `AttendanceData`
Class `Adapter`	Classes `FootballData` and `VolleyballData`
Class `Adaptee`	Class `FootballInfo` and `VolleyballStats`
Function `request()`	Functions `get_venue()` and `get_attendance()`

Function `specific_request()`	`FootballInfo::get_info().first`
	`FootballInfo::get_info().second`
	`VolleyballStats::get_stats().venue`
	`VolleyballStats::get_state().attendance`

10.1.5 An alternative Adapter Design Pattern model

The Adapter Design Pattern has an alternative model that simplifies the adapter classes by relying on multiple inheritance instead of wrapping (figure 10.4).

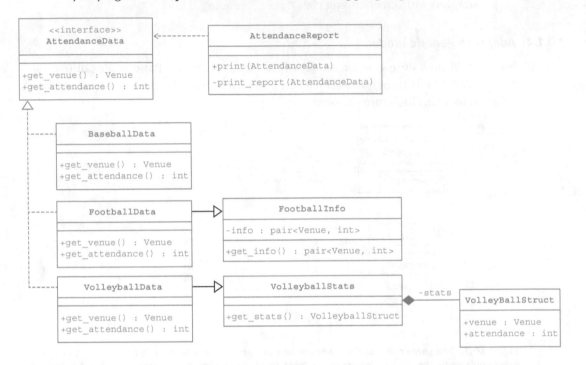

Figure 10.4 **In the alternative version of the Adapter Design Pattern, adapter class** FootballData **implements the** AttendanceData **interface and inherits from (rather than aggregates) the** FootballInfo **class. Adapter class** VolleyballData **implements the** AttendanceData **interface and inherits from the** VolleyballStats **class. Neither adapter class does wrapping. The grayed-out portions of the diagram have not changed logically from figure 10.2.**

Adapter class FootballData implements the AttendanceData interface and inherits from the FootballInfo class.

Listing 10.13 **(Program 10.3 Fans-AdapterDPx):** FootballData.h

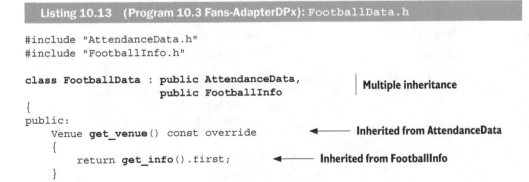

```
    int get_attendance() const override          ◄──── Inherited from AttendanceData
    {
        return get_info().second;              ◄──── Inherited from FootballInfo
    }
};
```

Similarly, adapter class `VolleyballData` implements the `AttendanceData` interface and inherits from the `VolleyballStats` class.

Listing 10.14   (Program 10.3 Fans-AdapterDPx): `VolleyballData.h`

```
#include "AttendanceData.h"
#include "VolleyballStats.h"

class VolleyballData : public AttendanceData,          │ Multiple inheritance
                       public VolleyballStats
{
public:
    Venue get_venue() const override          ◄──── Inherited from AttendanceData
    {
        return get_stats().venue;            ◄──── Inherited from VolleyballStats
    }

    int get_attendance() const override          ◄──── Inherited from AttendanceData
    {
        return get_stats().attendance;       ◄──── Inherited from VolleyballStats
    }
};
```

The test program is simpler because it doesn't have to know about classes `Football-Info` and `VolleyballStats`, only their adapters.

Listing 10.15   (Program 10.3 Fans-AdapterDPx): `tester.cpp`

```
#include "BaseballData.h"
#include "FootballData.h"
#include "VolleyballData.h"
#include "AttendanceReport.h"

int main()
{
    BaseballData    baseball_data;
    FootballData    football_data;
    VolleyballData  volleyball_data;

    AttendanceReport report;

    report.print(baseball_data,   "Baseball");
    report.print(football_data,   "Football");
    report.print(volleyball_data, "Volleyball");

    return 0;
}
```

Figure 10.5 shows the model of the alternative version of the Adapter Design Pattern.

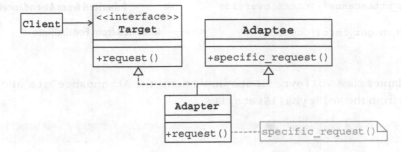

Figure 10.5 The model of the alternative version of the Adapter Design Pattern. Compare it with figure 10.4. The `Adapter` **class relies on multiple inheritance.**

The `Adapter` class in figure 10.5 relies on multiple inheritance and is called a *class adapter*. The `Adapter` class in figure 10.3 relies on object composition (wrapping) and is called an *object adapter*.

There are two types of adapters! How do I know which type to use?

It depends on what your application needs. Often it doesn't matter which type you use, so use whichever one is more convenient for you to program.

We should decide which type of adapter to use based on the needs of our application. We can share an object adapter. If several adaptee classes have the same interface, multiple instances of the same object adapter can each wrap an adaptee. Because it aggregates the adaptee class, an object adapter also wraps any adaptee subclasses. In contrast, with a class adapter, the client doesn't have to know about the adaptee class. Because it uses inheritance, a class adapter can override an adaptee's member functions. If these features of the two types of adapters don't matter for an application, then either type of adapter will do.

10.2 *The Façade Design Pattern hides a subsystem of interfaces*

Another common problem that we may encounter with a body of existing code is that it's complex and hard to use. The Façade Design Pattern provides a model for an application architecture that hides a subsystem of multiple interfaces. The application accomplishes this feat by fronting the subsystem interfaces with a simpler interface. This is a pattern we often use in our daily lives.

Consider starting a trip by car. We must interact with several components of the car:

1 Open the car door.
2 Sit in the driver's seat.
3 Close the car door.
4 Step on the brake.
5 Start the ignition.

6 Shift the gear.

7 Release the parking brake.

8 Step on the accelerator.

But we normally don't think of each step every time we start a trip. Instead, we have a start-the-car habit that allows us to do all the steps in order without thinking. This habit is our façade that hides all the steps. We simply start the car.

For our concrete programming example of using the Façade Design Pattern, consider a college athletics department that must do fund raising for its sports several times a year. It must solicit alumni for money, schedule fund-raising meetings with booster clubs, and collect student fees. Let's suppose that the university administration also helps with the fund raising. We'll design two versions of this fund-raising application. The first version doesn't use the Façade Design Pattern, and it will have several faults. The second version will use the pattern, and we'll see the benefits.

10.2.1 Desired design features

Design features for such an application should include

- *DF 1*—The application should not depend on the interfaces or the implementations of any of its multiple components.
- *DF 2*—The application should not be concerned with the order that its components perform their tasks.
- *DF 3*—The application needs to interact with only a single interface to manage its components.

10.2.2 Before using the Façade Design Pattern

Classes `AthleticsDept` and `Administration` each performs fundraising, and so each class must interact with classes `Alumni`, `BoosterClubs`, and `Students` (figure 10.6). Classes `AthleticsDept` and `Administration` each calls the `send_solicitations()` member function of class `Alumni`, the `schedule_meetings()` member function of class `BoosterClubs`, and the `collect_fees()` member function of class `Students`.

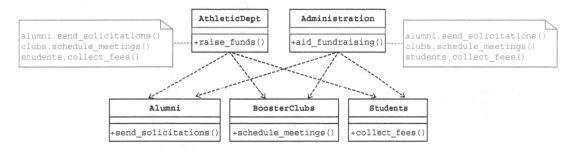

Figure 10.6   To perform fund raising, classes `AthleticsDept` **and** `Administration` **each must call the appropriate member functions of classes** `Alumni`, `BoosterClubs`, **and** `Students`.

Member function `send_solicitations()` of class `Alumni` is part of fundraising.

```
#include <iostream>

using namespace std;

class Alumni
{
public:
    void send_solicitations()
    {
        cout << "Send solicitations to alumni." << endl;
    }
};
```

Member function `schedule_meetings()` of class `BoosterClubs` is also part of fundraising.

```
#include <iostream>

using namespace std;

class BoosterClubs
{
public:
    void schedule_meetings()
    {
        cout << " Schedule meetings with booster clubs." << endl;
    }
};
```

Finally, member function `collect_fees()` of class `Students` is another part of fundraising.

```
#include <iostream>

using namespace std;

class Students
{
public:
    void collect_fees()
    {
        cout << " Collect student fees." << endl;
    }
};
```

To perform fundraising, member function `raise_funds()` of class `AthleticsDept` calls the member functions of classes `Alumni`, `BoosterClubs`, and `Students`.

Listing 10.19   (Program10.4 Funds): `AthleticsDept.h` **(before the design pattern)**

```cpp
#include <iostream>
#include "Alumni.h"
#include "BoosterClubs.h"
#include "Students.h"

using namespace std;

class AthleticsDept
{
public:
    void raise_funds()
    {
        Alumni alumni;
        BoosterClubs clubs;
        Students students;

        cout << endl << "ATHLETICS DEPARTMENT" << endl;

        alumni.send_solicitations();
        clubs.schedule_meetings();
        students.collect_fees();
    }
};
```

To help with fund raising, member function `aid_fundraising()` of class `Adminis-`
`tration` calls the same member functions.

Listing 10.20   (Program10.4 Funds): `Administration.h` **(before the design pattern)**

```cpp
#include <iostream>
#include "Alumni.h"
#include "BoosterClubs.h"
#include "Students.h"

using namespace std;

class Administration
{
public:
    void aid_fundraising()
    {
        Alumni alumni;
        BoosterClubs clubs;
        Students students;

        cout << endl << "SCHOOL ADMINISTRATION" << endl;

        alumni.send_solicitations();
        clubs.schedule_meetings();
        students.collect_fees();
    }
};
```

Each of the classes `Alumni`, `BoosterClub`, and `Students` has its own fund-raising interface. Therefore, classes `AthleticsDept` and `Administration` must know how to call call the different fund-raising functions. That violates DF 1 and DF 3

Also, classes `AthleticsDept` and `Administration` each must know in what order to call call the fund-raising functions. That violates DF 2.

The test program calls upon classes `AthleticsDept` and `Administration` to do fundraising.

> **Listing 10.21   (Program10.4 Funds):** `tester.cpp` **(before the design pattern)**

```cpp
#include "AthleticsDept.h"
#include "Administration.h"

int main()
{
    AthleticsDept athletics;
    athletics.raise_funds();

    Administration administration;
    administration.aid_fundraising();

    return 0;
}
```

The output of the application is

```
ATHLETICS DEPARTMENT
Send solicitations to alumni.
Schedule meetings with booster clubs.
Collect student fees.

SCHOOL ADMINISTRATION
Send solicitations to alumni.
Schedule meetings with booster clubs.
Collect student fees.
```

Faults of this version of the fund-raising application include

- *Duplicated code*—Classes `AthleticsDept` and `Administration` both call the fund-raising member functions of classes `Alumni`, `BoosterClubs`, and `Students`.
- *Inflexible code*—If we add more classes for fund raising, both the `AthleticsDept` and `Administration` classes will need to change.

10.2.3   *After using the Façade Design Pattern*

The Façade Design Pattern reduces the duplicated code and hides the fund-raising interfaces behind façade class `FundRaiser`. The façade class presents a simpler and higher-level interface than the interfaces provided by classes `Alumni`, `BoosterClubs`, and `Students`.

The Façade Design Pattern

"Provide a unified interface to a set of interfaces in a subsystem. Façade defines a higher-level interface that makes the interface easier to use" (GoF 183).

The `raise_funds()` member function of class `AthleticsDept` and the `aid_fundraising()` member function of class `Administration` each only has to call member function `do_fund_raising()` of class `FundRaiser` (figure 10.7).

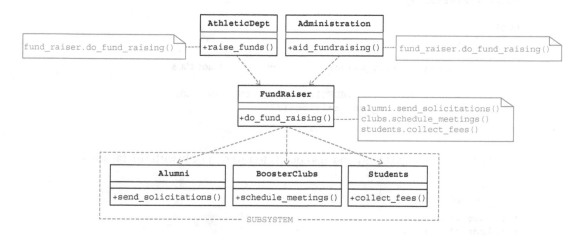

Figure 10.7 **The architecture modeled from the Façade Design Pattern hides the details of fundraising behind the façade class** `FundRaiser`, **which presents a higher-level interface that simplifies using the subsystem consisting of classes** `Alumni`, `BoosterClubs`, **and** `Students`.

Member function `do_fund_raising()` of the façade class `FundRaiser` interacts with classes `Alumni`, `BoosterClubs`, and `Students` by calling their member functions.

Listing 10.22 **(Program 10.5 Funds-FaçadeDP):** `FundRaiser.h`

```cpp
#include "Alumni.h"
#include "BoosterClubs.h"
#include "Students.h"

class FundRaiser
{
public:
    void do_fund_raising()
    {
        Alumni alumni;
        BoosterClubs clubs;
        Students students;

        alumni.send_solicitations();
        clubs.schedule_meetings();
        students.collect_fees();
    }
};
```

Class `AthleticsDept` needs to interact only with the façade class by calling its do_fund_raising() member function.

```
#include <iostream>
#include "FundRaiser.h"

using namespace std;

class AthleticsDept
{
public:
    void raise_funds()
    {
        FundRaiser fund_raiser;           ◄──── Façade class

        cout << endl << "ATHLETICS DEPARTMENT" << endl;
        fund_raiser.do_fund_raising();
    }
};
```

Similarly, class `Administration` also needs to interact only with the façade class.

```
#include <iostream>
#include "FundRaiser.h"

using namespace std;

class Administration
{
public:
    void raise_funds()
    {
        FundRaiser fund_raiser;           ◄──── Façade class

        cout << endl << "SCHOOL ADMINISTRATION" << endl;
        fund_raiser.do_fund_raising();
    }
};
```

Very nice! Now the **AthleticsDept** and the **Administration** classes only need to interact with the **FundRaiser** class.

We can create another façade class if the athletics department and the administration want to send out thank-you messages.

Modeling the architecture from the Façade Design Pattern has several key benefits:

- *Reduced code duplication*—The façade class encapsulates all the fundraising operations, and that code needs to appear only once. This is the Don't Repeat Yourself Principle (section 2.3.3).
- *Loosely coupled classes*—The AthleticsDept and Administration classes have no dependencies on the `Alumni`, `BoosterClubs`, and `Students` classes. This is the Principle of Least Knowledge (section 2.3.2).
- *More flexible code*—If we add another class for fund raising, such as `Corporate-Sponsors`, only the façade class needs to change. This is the Encapsulate What Varies Principle (section 2.3.2).
- *Easier to use subsystem*—The façade class makes the `Alumni`, `BoosterClubs`, and `Students` subsystem easier to use with a simple interface that hides the subsystem interfaces.

10.2.4 *Façade's generic model*

Figure 10.8 shows the generic model of the Façade Design Pattern. Recall that it is from the design pattern's generic model that we can create a custom solution to an architecture problem (section 8.1.3).

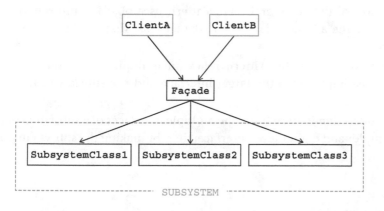

**Figure 10.8   The generic model of the Façade Design Pattern. Compare it with figure 10.7. The `Façade`
class hides the interfaces of the subsystem classes and makes the subsystem consisting of classes
`Alumni`, `BoosterClubs`, and `Students` easier to use.**

Table 10.2 shows how the example application applies the pattern. Recall that it is from the design pattern's generic model that we can create a custom solution to an architecture problem (section 8.1.3).

Table 10.2   The Façade Method Design Pattern as applied by the example application

Design pattern	Applied by the example application
Classes `ClientA, ClientB`, etc.	Casses `AthleticsDept` and `Administration`
Class `Façade`	Class `FundRaiser`
Classes `SubsystemClass1, SubsystemClass 2`, etc.	Classes `Alumni, BoosterClubs,` and `Students`

The Adapter Design Pattern models an architecture where an adaptee interface is adapted to be compatible with a target interface. It's the pattern for integrating library code with legacy application code.

The Façade Design Pattern models an architecture where a simpler higher-level interface hides a subsystem of interfaces. Both make an application with multiple components easier to use.

Summary

- The Adapter Design Pattern models a software architecture that converts the interface of the adaptee class to a target interface. This allows integrating code that weren't originally designed to work together.

- One version of the Adapter Design Pattern uses object composition to wrap an object of the adaptee class in an adapter class that implements the target interface.

- The other version of the pattern relies on multiple inheritance, where the adapter class implements the target interface and is a subclass of the adaptee class.

- The Façade Design Pattern hides the multiple interfaces of a subsystem of classes with a simpler and higher-level interface, thereby making the subsystem easier to use.

The Iterator and Visitor
Design Patterns

11

This chapter covers

- The Iterator Design Pattern
- The Visitor Design Pattern

The two design patterns in this chapter provide models for applications that must flexibly access data stored in various data structures, such as vectors, lists, and trees. The example applications continue the theme of generating sports reports.

Manning Comix

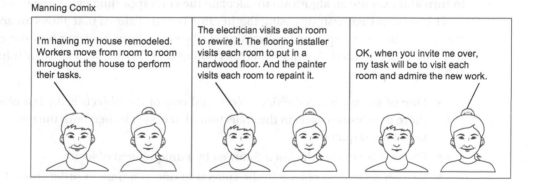

I'm having my house remodeled. Workers move from room to room throughout the house to perform their tasks.	The electrician visits each room to rewire it. The flooring installer visits each room to put in a hardwood floor. And the painter visits each room to repaint it.	OK, when you invite me over, my task will be to visit each room and admire the new work.

The Iterator Design Pattern enables a single algorithm to iterate over multiple sequential collections of objects without needing to know how the collections are implemented. Our first example application is modeled from this design pattern. The application's algorithm can generate a report about the players on several baseball teams, even though each team stores its player data in a different form of sequential collection.

The Visitor Design Pattern works with a single data collection that contains different types of data. The collection is often structured as a tree. The pattern encapsulates different algorithms, each designed to process the tree nodes. Our second example program is modeled from this design pattern. The application's algorithms can generate different reports from the same collection of intramural games data.

The Iterator Design Pattern is appropriate for applications that have a *single algorithm* that must work on *multiple sequential collections*, which are in different forms.

The Visitor Design pattern is appropriate for applications that have *multiple algorithms*, which must work on a *single data collection*.

NOTE   Be sure to read the introduction to part 4 for important information about design patterns in general and to learn how this and subsequent chapters teach each pattern.

11.1   *The Iterator Design Pattern encapsulates iterating over different sequential collections*

We often must write code that iterates over sequential collections of objects and performs an operation on each object. The objects are all the same datatype, but the collections are in different forms. For example, an application might have to work with an array, a vector, and a linked list of employee objects. No matter what form of sequential collection the objects are stored in, the application must be able to access each object in turn and execute an algorithm to calculate the corresponding employee's pay.

This section demonstrates using the Iterator Design Pattern that allows an application to iterate over sequential collections of objects without knowing how the collections are implemented. A sequential collection of objects is either empty, or it has the following properties:

- One of the objects is the first object, and one of the objects is the last object. If there is only one object in the collection, that object is then both the first and the last of the sequence.
- Each object except the last is followed by a unique next object.
- We can access the objects in the collection one at a time in order from the first one to the last one.

- We can tell when we've accessed all the objects in the sequence, that is, when we've reached the end of the collection.

Arrays, vectors, and linked lists are examples of sequential collections. We can even treat the C++ map as a sequential collection because, internally, it stores its objects sorted by their keys.

As a concrete example, suppose the athletics department wants to print lists of the players on each intramural baseball team. The department doesn't care about the particular order of the players in each list, as long as it includes every player's student id and name. An example set of printed lists for team 1, team 2, and team 3 is

```
TEAM 1
12436 Alwin, Jim
26410 Bond, Bob
14306 Charles, Ronda
61835 Dunn, Fred
30437 Edwards, Gina
76517 Fanning, Pat
98734 Galway, Leslie
14998 Hiroshi, Scott
47303 Ingles, Mary

TEAM 2
12436 Jackson, Tammy
44551 Killebrew, Wally
14306 Lamprey, Roberta
61835 Mays, Serena
30437 Norton, Donna
76517 OBrien, George
98734 Paulson, Marsha
14998 Quark, John
47303 Rogers, Jena

TEAM 3
10547 Ulster, Doug
38331 Vicks, Ron
40067 Aaron, Patricia
46841 Smith, Ken
47781 Wong, Henrietta
56712 Yonnick, Billy
61472 Xavier, Nancy
72288 Zachs, Robby
98765 Terrance, Laura
```

Also, suppose that due to lack of coordination, each team stores its list of `Player` objects as a sequential collection in a different form than other teams. Team 1 uses an array, team 2 uses a vector, and team 3 uses a map.

11.1.1 Desired design features

An application with an algorithm that must work with different forms of sequential collections of objects should have the following design features:

- *DF 1*—The application should be able to execute an algorithm that processes the objects without knowing how the sequential collections are implemented.
- *DF 2*—The collections should be independent from one another.
- *DF 3*—It should be possible to add new sequential collections without modifying the application's algorithm code.

11.1.2 Before using the Iterator Design Pattern

It is not an unreasonable architecture for the first version of our example team report application to have three `Team` subclasses to generate the player lists, one subclass per form of collection (figure 11.1), and an overloaded `print()` member function for each form.

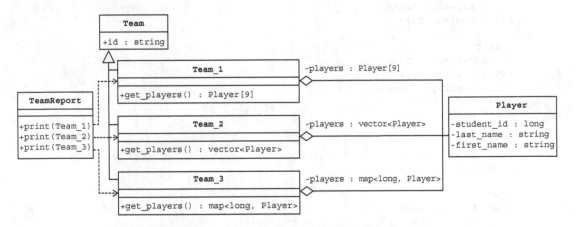

Figure 11.1   Each `Team` subclass stores its `Player` objects in a different type of sequential collection, array, vector, or map. Therefore, class `TeamReport` has three overloaded `print()` member functions, one for each type of collection.

Class `Player` has each player's student id, last name, and first name. A baseball team consists of nine players, so for simplicity, we'll hardcode the collection sizes to nine.

Listing 11.1   (Program 11.1 Players): `Player.h` (before the design pattern)

```
#include <string>

using namespace std;

class Player
{
```

```
public:
    Player(const long id, const string last, const string first)
        : student_id(id), last_name(last), first_name(first) {}

    long   get_student_id() const { return student_id; }
    string get_last_name()  const { return last_name; }
    string get_first_name() const { return first_name; }

private:
    long    student_id;
    string  last_name;
    string  first_name;
};
```

Each of the Team subclasses stores its sequential collection of Player objects in a different form of sequential collection.

Listing 11.2   (Program 11.1 Players): Team.h (before the design pattern)

```
#include <string>
#include <vector>
#include <map>
#include "Player.h"

using namespace std;

class Team
{
public:
    Team(const string id) : id(id) {}

    string get_id() const { return id; }

private:
    string id;
};

class Team_1 : public Team
{
public:
    Team_1();

    ~Team_1() { for (int i = 0; i < 9; i++) delete players[i]; }

    Player **get_players() { return players; }

private:
    Player *players[9];                      ◄────────┐  Player objects stored
};                                                    │  in an array

class Team_2 : public Team
{
public:
    Team_2();
```

```
    ~Team_2 () { for (int i = 0; i < 9; i++) delete players[i]; }

    vector<Player *> get_players() const { return players; }

private:
    vector<Player *> players;                    ◄──────┐   Player objects stored
};                                                      │   in a vector

class Team_3 : public Team
{
public:
    Team_3();

    ~Team_3 ()
    {
        for (auto it = players.begin(); it != players.end(); it++)
        {
            delete it->second;
        }
    }

    map<long, Player *> get_players() const { return players; }

private:
    map<long, Player *> players;                 ◄──────┐   Player objects stored
};                                                      │   in a map
```

Each element of a C++ map is a `pair` object whose member variable `first` is the key and member variable `second` is the corresponding value. A `map` internally stores its elements sorted by their keys.

It's unfortunate that the three sequential collections are different.

We may be dealing with legacy code, parts of which were written by different programmers at different times for different purposes.

The constructor of each `Team` subclass enters players in a way into the team's sequential collection according to the type of collection.

> **Listing 11.3   (Program 11.1 Players):** `Team.cpp` **(before the design pattern)**

```
#include "Team.h"

Team_1::Team_1() : Team("TEAM 1")          ◄────── Enter into an array.
{
    players[0] = new Player(12436, "Alwin", "Jim");
```

```
    players[1] = new Player(26410, "Bond", "Bob");
    players[2] = new Player(14306, "Charles", "Ronda");
    players[3] = new Player(61835, "Dunn", "Fred");
    players[4] = new Player(30437, "Edwards", "Gina");
    players[5] = new Player(76517, "Fanning", "Pat");
    players[6] = new Player(98734, "Galway", "Leslie");
    players[7] = new Player(14998, "Hiroshi", "Scott");
    players[8] = new Player(47303, "Ingles", "Mary");
}

Team_2::Team_2() : Team("TEAM 2")          ◄──── Enter into a vector.
{
    players.push_back(new Player(12436, "Jackson", "Tammy"));
    players.push_back(new Player(44551, "Killebrew", "Wally"));
    players.push_back(new Player(14306, "Lamprey", "Roberta"));
    players.push_back(new Player(61835, "Mays", "Serena"));
    players.push_back(new Player(30437, "Norton", "Donna"));
    players.push_back(new Player(76517, "OBrien", "George"));
    players.push_back(new Player(98734, "Paulson", "Marsha"));
    players.push_back(new Player(14998, "Quark", "John"));
    players.push_back(new Player(47303, "Rogers", "Jena"));
}

Team_3::Team_3() : Team("TEAM 3")          ◄──── Enter into a map.
{
    players[46841] = new Player(46841, "Smith", "Ken");
    players[98765] = new Player(98765, "Terrance", "Laura");
    players[10547] = new Player(10547, "Ulster", "Doug");
    players[38331] = new Player(38331, "Vicks", "Ron");
    players[47781] = new Player(47781, "Wong", "Henrietta");
    players[57974] = new Player(61472, "Xavier", "Nancy");
    players[56712] = new Player(56712, "Yonnick", "Billy");
    players[72288] = new Player(72288, "Zachs", "Robby");
    players[40067] = new Player(40067, "Aaron", "Patricia");
}
```

Because of the three different types of sequential collections of team players, class
`TeamReport` has three overloaded `print()` member functions to print the lists.

> **Listing 11.4   (Program 11.1 Players):** `TeamReport.h` (before the design pattern)

```
#include "Team.h"

using namespace std;

class TeamReport
{
public:
    void print(Team_1& team) const;
    void print(Team_2& team) const;
    void print(Team_3& team) const;
};
```

Each print() member function must iterate over its sequential collection of Player objects in a manner appropriate for an array, a vector, or a map.

Listing 11.5   (Program 11.1 Players): `TeamReport.cpp` (before the design pattern)

```cpp
#include <iostream>
#include "Player.h"
#include "TeamReport.h"
#include "Team.h"

using namespace std;

void TeamReport::print(Team_1& team) const
{
    cout << endl;
    cout << team.get_id() << endl;

    Player **players = team.get_players();

    for (int i = 0; i < 9; i++)              ◄———— Iterate over an array.
    {
        cout << players[i]->get_student_id() << " ";
        cout << players[i]->get_last_name()  << ", ";
        cout << players[i]->get_first_name() << endl;
    }
}

void TeamReport::print(Team_2& team) const
{
    cout << endl;
    cout << team.get_id() << endl;

    for (Player *player : team.get_players())          ◄———— Iterate over a vector.
    {
        cout << player->get_student_id() << " ";
        cout << player->get_last_name()  << ", ";
        cout << player->get_first_name() << endl;
    }

}

void TeamReport::print(Team_3& team) const
{
    cout << endl;
    cout << team.get_id() << endl;

    map<long, Player *> players = team.get_players();
    map<long, Player *>::iterator it;

    for (it = players.begin(); it != players.end(); it++)     ◄─────┐
    {                                                               Iterate
                                                                  over a map.
```

```
        cout << it->second->get_student_id() << " ";
        cout << it->second->get_last_name()  << ", ";
        cout << it->second->get_first_name() << endl;
    }
}
```

A test program prints the example set of lists at the beginning of this section.

```cpp
#include "TeamReport.h"
#include "Team.h"

int main()
{
    TeamReport reporter;

    Team_1 team_1;
    reporter.print(team_1);

    Team_2 team_2;
    reporter.print(team_2);

    Team_3 team_3;
    reporter.print(team_3);

    return 0;
}
```

Class **TeamReporter** must know how each of the sequential collections are implemented — as an array, a vector, or a map. It requires overloaded **print()** member functions. That violates DF 1.

Adding another report with yet another form of sequential collection, such as a linked list, would require adding another overloaded **print()** member function. That violates DF 3.

There are several design problems with this version of the list application, especially in class `TeamReport`:

- *Duplicated code*—Each overloaded `print()` member function must iterate over its sequential collection of `Player` objects in a different way depending on the form of the collection. This will become a greater problem if there are more teams and sequential collections to store players, such as linked lists or trees.

- *Classes not loosely coupled*—Each overloaded `print()` function must know how the `Player` objects are stored to properly iterate over its sequential collection. Therefore, class `TeamReport` is not loosely coupled with the `Team` subclasses.

11.1.3 *After using the Iterator Design Pattern*

This is an architecture problem that the Iterator Design Pattern can help solve. The key idea is for the client code (class `TeamReport` in our application) to delegate to iterator classes the task of iterating over the different forms of sequential collections of `Player` objects. Each iterator class knows how to iterate over a particular form of sequence, and it can provide access to the `Player` objects without exposing to the client code how the objects are stored.

> **The Iterator Design Pattern**
>
> "Provide a way to access the elements of an aggregate object sequentially without exposing its underlying representation" (GoF 257).

The Iterator Design Pattern enables class `TeamReport` to be loosely coupled from the `Team` subclasses. Each subclass no longer has a `get_players()` member function that provides direct access to its sequential collection of `Player` objects. Therefore, each subclass can hide how it implements its collection. Instead, each subclass has a `create_iterator()` member function that creates an `Iterator` object, which knows how to iterate over that subclass's collection of `Player` objects.

Class `TeamReport` lets the `Iterator` subclasses do the work of iterating over the `Player` object sequences. There is an `Iterator` subclass for each form of sequential collection. Therefore, class `TeamReport` doesn't need to know how each `Team` subclass implemented its sequential collection (figure 11.2).

The Iterator Design Pattern adds more classes, when you compare figure 11.1 to figure 11.2.

Yes, using a design pattern can make small applications appear more complex. A good designer must weigh the advantages of using a design pattern versus writing code that may be less flexible and harder to modify.

The `Iterator` superclass declares two pure virtual member functions, `next()` and `has_next()`. Each of its subclasses has a private `cursor` member variable to keep track of the current `Player` object within its sequence. The cursor is either an array index, a vector iterator, or a map iterator, according to the type of sequential collection. Each subclass constructor initializes its cursor to the beginning of its sequence. The `next()` member function returns the `Player` object at the cursor (the current element) and advances the cursor to the next element. The `has_next()` member function returns true if there are more elements and false if the cursor is past the end of the sequence (listing 11.7).

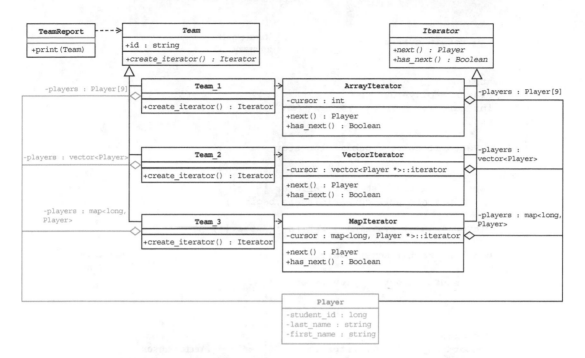

Figure 11.2 Each `Team` subclass creates an iterator that is appropriate for its sequential collection of `Player` objects. Class `TeamReport` delegates iterating over the various forms of sequential collections to the `Iterator` subclasses. Each `Iterator` subclass knows how to iterate over its form of sequential collection and has a private `cursor` member variable to keep track of the current `Player` object. Class `TeamReport` does not know how each `Team` subclass stores its sequence of `Player` objects, and therefore, it is loosely coupled from the `Team` subclasses. The grayed-out portions of the diagram haven't changed logically from figure **11.1**.

Listing 11.7   (Program **11.2** Players-IteratorDP): `Iterator.h`

```
#include "Player.h"

class Iterator
{
public:
    virtual ~Iterator() {};

    virtual Player *next() = 0;
    virtual bool has_next() const = 0;
};

class ArrayIterator : public Iterator
{
public:
    ArrayIterator(Player *ps[]) : players(ps), cursor(0) {}

    Player *next() override { return players[cursor++]; }

    bool has_next() const override
```

Iterate over
an array.

```
        {
            return cursor < 9;                          Iterate over
        }                                               an array.

private:
    Player **players;
    int cursor;                  ◄────── Array cursor
};


class VectorIterator : public Iterator
{
public:
    VectorIterator(const vector<Player *> ps)
        : players(ps), cursor(players.begin()) {}

    Player *next() override { return *(cursor++); }

    bool has_next() const override
    {                                                   Iterate over
        return cursor != players.end();                 a vector.
    }

private:
    vector<Player *> players;
    vector<Player *>::iterator it;    ◄────── Vector cursor
};

class MapIterator : public Iterator
{
public:
    MapIterator(const map<long, Player *> ps)
        : players(ps), cursor(players.begin()) {}

    Player *next() override { return (cursor++)->second; }

    bool has_next() const override
    {                                                   Iterate over
        return cursor != players.end();                 a map.
    }

private:
    map<long, Player *> players;
    map<long, Player *>::iterator cursor;   ◄────── Map cursor
};
```

Each `Team` subclass must now create and return an iterator object appropriate for its form of sequential collection.

Listing 11.8   (Program 11.2 Players-IteratorDP): `Team.h`

```
#include <string>
#include <vector>
#include <map>
#include "Player.h"
#include "Iterator.h"
```

```cpp
using namespace std;

class Team
{
public:
    Team(const string id) : id(id) {}
    virtual ~Team() {}

    string get_id() const { return id; }

    virtual Iterator *create_iterator() = 0;

private:
    string id;
};

class Team_1: public Team
{
public:
    Team_1();
    ~Team_1() { for (int i = 0; i < 9; i++) delete players[i]; }

    Iterator *create_iterator() override
    {
        return new ArrayIterator(players);        ◄───── Create and return
    }                                                    an array iterator.
private:
    Player *players[9];
};

class Team_2 : public Team
{
public:
    Team_2();
    ~Team_2 () { for (int i = 0; i < 9; i++) delete players[i]; }

    Iterator *create_iterator() override
    {
        return new VectorIterator(players);       ◄───── Create and return
    }                                                    a vector iterator.

private:
    vector<Player *> players;
};

class Team_3 : public Team
{
public:
    Team_3();

    ~Team_3 ()
    {
        for (auto it = players.begin(); it != players.end(); it++)
        {
```

```
                    delete it->second;
            }
    }

    Iterator *create_iterator() override
    {
        return new MapIterator(players);
    }
```
← Create and return a map iterator.

```
private:
    map<long, Player *> players;
};
```

We can reduce class `TeamReport` to only a single `print()` member function.

Listing 11.9   (Program 11.2 Players-IteratorDP): `TeamReport.h`

```
#include "Team.h"

class TeamReport
{
public:
    void print(Team& team);
};
```

Class `TeamReport` now delegates the task of iterating over the different sequential collections of `Player` objects to the `Iterator` subclasses. Its implementation of member function `print()` is much simpler as a result, as shown in the following listing. The call to `create_iterator()` relies on polymorphism to create and return the appropriate `Iterator` object for the team's sequential collection of `Player` objects.

Listing 11.10   (Program 11.2 Players-IteratorDP): `TeamReport.cpp`

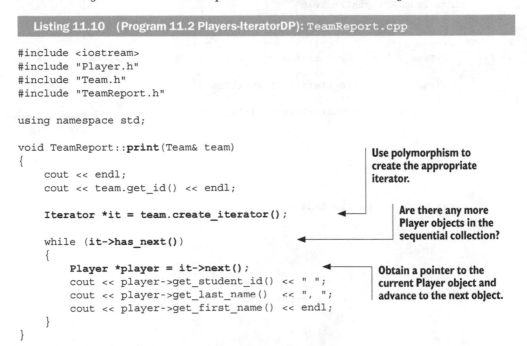

```
#include <iostream>
#include "Player.h"
#include "Team.h"
#include "TeamReport.h"

using namespace std;

void TeamReport::print(Team& team)
{
    cout << endl;
    cout << team.get_id() << endl;
```
Use polymorphism to create the appropriate iterator.
```
    Iterator *it = team.create_iterator();
```
← Are there any more Player objects in the sequential collection?
```
    while (it->has_next())
    {
        Player *player = it->next();
```
← Obtain a pointer to the current Player object and advance to the next object.
```
        cout << player->get_student_id() << " ";
        cout << player->get_last_name()  << ", ";
        cout << player->get_first_name() << endl;
    }
}
```

The same test program (listing 11.6) generates the same output.

Each **Iterator** object is a kind of adapter — one specifically designed to hide the implementation of a sequential collection.

We can add another form of sequential collection along with its **Iterator** subclass without modifying the algorithm that generates the team reports.

Using the Iterator Design Pattern provided several important benefits:

- *Delegated iterations*—Class `TeamReport` delegates iterating over the sequential collections to the `Iterator` subclasses, which is an application of the Delegation Principle (section 2.3.2).
- *Loosely coupled classes*—Class `TeamReport` no longer needs to know how each `Team` subclass implements its sequential collection, which is an application of the Principle of Least Knowledge (section 2.3.2). Therefore, class `TeamReport` is loosely coupled from the `Team` subclasses.
- *Encapsulated iteration algorithms*—The `Iterator` subclasses encapsulate the different algorithms to iterate over the various forms of sequential collections, which is an application of the Encapsulate What Varies Principle (section 2.3.2).
- *Reduced code duplication*—The iteration algorithms are not duplicated, which is an application of the Don't Repeat Yourself Principle (2.3.3).
- *Sharable iteration algorithms*—It will be easy to share the algorithms among similar sequential collections or to add new algorithms for other collections.

11.1.4 *Iterator's generic model*

Figure 11.3 shows the generic model of the Iterator Design Pattern. Recall that it is from the design pattern's generic model that we can create a custom solution to an architecture problem (section 8.1.3).

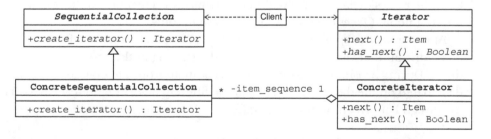

Figure 11.3 **The generic model of the Iterator Design Pattern. Compare it with figure 11.2. The client delegates iterating over the sequential collections to the** `Iterator` **subclasses, and thus the client is loosely coupled from the collections. Table 11.1 shows how the example application applies the pattern.**

Table 11.1   The Iterator Design Pattern as applied by the example application

Design pattern	Applied by the example application
Class `Client`	Class `TeamReport`
Superclass `SequentialCollection`	Superclass `Team`
Concrete sequential collections	Subclasses `Team_1`, `Team_2`, and `Team_3`
Cuperclass `Iterator`	Superclass `Iterator`
Concrete iterators	`ArrayIterator`, `VectorIterator`, and `MapIterator`
Item	`Player` object

C++ iterators

Our implementation of the Iterator Design Pattern used native C++ iterators in some of the `Iterator` subclasses (listing 11.7), namely `vector<Player *>::iterator` and `map<long, Player *>::iterator`. Native C++ iterators do not fully conform to the Iterator Design Pattern. They have no iterator superclass, so it won't be possible to use the Code to the Interface Principle and write a function that uses polymorphism to obtain an appropriate iterator at run time, like we did in member function `Team-Report::print()` (listing 11.10). If we need to take advantage of polymorphism to iterate over different sequential collections, the Iterator Design Pattern can be a good wrapper for C++ iterators.

11.2   The Visitor Design Pattern encapsulates different algorithms that operate on a data collection

The Visitor Design Pattern works with different algorithms that operate on an application's data collection. The pattern is often used to provide a model for an architecture where the data is hierarchical; therefore, the collection is a tree data structure. The objects are nodes of the tree, and they can be instantiated from different classes; therefore, the nodes' data can involve different datatypes. The node at the top of the tree is the root node. (Trees often grow upside down in software.)

At run time, the application makes multiple passes over the tree. Each pass employs an algorithm that visits (accesses) each node, starting at the root and working its way down. During a visit, the algorithm performs an appropriate operation on the node's data, based on the datatype. There can be a different algorithm for each pass. The Visitor Design Pattern encapsulates the different algorithms.

Does the Visitor Design Pattern only work with tree structures?

No, it can work with any collection of objects. But trees are quite common.

Figure 11.4 is an example of a data collection in the form of a tree structure that represents the products sold in a store. The Store node at the top is the root node. The tree nodes include three departments: Produce, Soups, and Soaps. The Produce Department has Vegetables and Fruits categories. The Soaps Department has Bar, Dish, and Laundry categories. At the bottom of the tree, the leaf nodes (shaded in gray) represent the products.

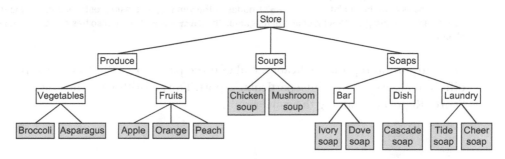

Figure 11.4   An example tree data structure of hierarchical data for a store. Store is the root node. The intermediate tree nodes are store departments Produce, Soups, and Soaps; categories Vegetables and Fruits in the Produce Department; and categories Bar, Dish, and Laundry in the Soaps Department. The leaf nodes at the bottom (shaded in gray) are the products.

The store application can make several passes over the tree and execute a different algorithm for each pass. For example, the first pass's algorithm can simply print the data hierarchically by department and category. If the product nodes contain the unit price and the number of units sold, the second pass algorithm can print how many units of each product were sold. The third pass algorithm can calculate and print the revenue each department earned from selling these products.

For a concrete example, we'll continue our theme of printing reports by the athletics department. Suppose the department wants an application that prints reports about intramural games played during a weekend. Residence halls named North, South, East, and West have teams that play baseball, football, and volleyball games. We can represent the data collection as a tree structure (figure 11.5). Each `Game` node has pointers to the leaf `Hall` nodes, which represent the winning and losing residence hall of each game. The `Game` nodes each also contain winning and losing points of its game. The `Intramural` node also has a vector of `Hall` objects to keep track of the residence halls. This vector is not part of the hierarchical tree structure.

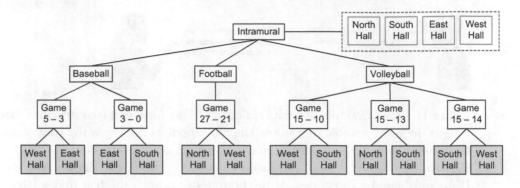

Figure 11.5   A data collection as a tree structure that represents intramural baseball, football, and volleyball intramural games played by teams from residence halls North, South, East, and West. The Games nodes each has pointers to the Hall nodes of the winning and losing residence halls, and it also contains the winning and losing points of its game. The Intramural node also has a vector of Hall objects.

Our intramural reports application makes three passes over this tree. Each pass uses a different algorithm to print a particular report. The algorithm for the first pass prints a Scores Report containing the game results:

```
SCORES REPORT

  baseball
     West Hall beat  East Hall  5 to  3
     East Hall beat South Hall  3 to  0

  football
    North Hall beat  West Hall 27 to 21

  volleyball
     West Hall beat South Hall 15 to 10
    North Hall beat South Hall 15 to 13
    South Hall beat  West Hall 15 to 14
```

The algorithm for the second pass prints an Activities Report that shows how many games of each sport were played:

```
ACTIVITIES REPORT

    baseball: 2 game(s)
    football: 1 game(s)
  volleyball: 3 game(s)
```

Finally, the algorithm for the third pass prints a Winnings Report that shows how many games each residence hall won:

```
WINNINGS REPORT

  North Hall won 2 game(s)
  South Hall won 1 game(s)
   East Hall won 1 game(s)
   West Hall won 2 game(s)
```

11.2.1 Desired design features

An application that makes multiple passes over a data collection with a different algorithm for each pass should have the following design features:

- *DF 1*—The pass algorithms should be independent from each other.
- *DF 2*—The data collection and the algorithms that operate on collection's data should be independent from each other.
- *DF 3*—Adding new passes and their algorithms should not require modifying the data collection.

11.2.2 Before using the Visitor Design Pattern

As a demonstration, the first version of the application will not use the Visitor Design Pattern, and it will have some major faults. Afterward, we'll refactor the code to be modeled after the pattern and highlight the benefits of using the pattern.

Figure 11.6 shows how we can implement this hierarchical data collection as a tree with four classes: `Intramural`, `Sport`, `Game`, and `Hall`. Each class except `Hall` (which represents the leaf nodes) aggregates the class immediately below in the hierarchy. Each class has member variables and member functions to implement the three report-generation algorithms.

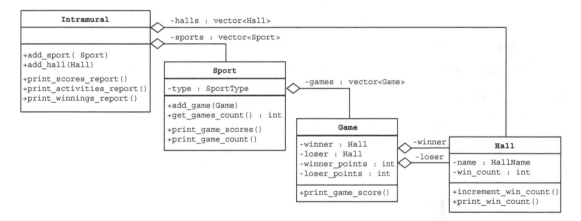

Figure 11.6 **The four major classes of the first version of the intramural sports reports' application. To implement the hierarchical tree structure, each class except `Hall` aggregates the next class below in the hierarchy. Each class has member variables and member functions to implement the algorithms that generate the reports. The `Intramural` class's vector of `Hall` objects is not part of the hierarchy.**

Class `Intramural` has private member variable `sports`, a vector of `Sport` objects at the next lower level of the tree data structure. It also has private member variable `halls`, a vector to keep track of all the residence halls. We can't simply rely on having all the `Hall` objects uniquely pointed to by the `Game` objects because a residence hall may participate in more than one (or no) games. Class `Sport` has private member `games`, a vector of the Game objects of that sport at the next lower level of the tree. Class Game has private member variables winner and loser that point to the Hall objects representing the winning and losing residence hall, respectively, at the lowest level of the tree. It also has private member variables winner_points and loser_points.

Two enumeration classes supply enumeration constants. Each class has an overloaded << output operator for report generation.

Listing 11.11   (Program 11.3 Results): Enums.h (before the design pattern)

```
#include <iostream>

using namespace std;

enum class SportType { BASEBALL, FOOTBALL, VOLLEYBALL };

inline ostream& operator <<(ostream& ostr, const SportType& type)
{
    switch (type)
    {
        case SportType::BASEBALL   : ostr << "baseball";   break;
        case SportType::FOOTBALL   : ostr << "football";   break;
        case SportType::VOLLEYBALL : ostr << "volleyball"; break;
    }

    return ostr;
}

enum class HallName { NORTH, SOUTH, EAST, WEST };

inline ostream& operator <<(ostream& ostr, const HallName& hall)
{
    switch (hall)
    {
        case HallName::NORTH : ostr << "North Hall"; break;
        case HallName::SOUTH : ostr << "South Hall"; break;
        case HallName::EAST  : ostr << "East Hall";  break;
        case HallName::WEST  : ostr << "West Hall";  break;
    }

    return ostr;
}
```

Each Hall object represents a residence hall. Its private win_count member variable records the number of times the hall won a game. The number will appear for each hall in the Winnings Report.

Listing 11.12   (Program 11.3 Results): Hall.h (before the design pattern)

```
#include "Enums.h"

using namespace std;
```

```
class Hall
{
public:
    Hall(const HallName name) : name(name), win_count(0) {}

    HallName get_name() const { return name; }

    void increment_win_count() { win_count++; }
    void print_win_count() const;

private:
    HallName name;
    int win_count;
};
```

Member function `print_win_count()` prints one line of the Winnings Report. For example, it can print

```
North Hall won 2 game(s)
```

Listing 11.13   (Program 11.3 Results): `Hall.cpp` **(before the design pattern)**

```
#include <iostream>
#include <iomanip>
#include "Hall.h"

void Hall::print_win_count() const          ◄──────  Print one line of the
{                                                     Winnings Report.
    cout << setw(12) << name << " won "
        << win_count << " game(s)" << endl;
}
```

Each `Game` object represents a single intramural game between two residence halls. Its two private member variables `winner` and `loser` point to the objects that represent the residence halls that won and lost the game, respectively. Member variables `winner_points` and `loser_points` are the game points of the winner and loser, respectively.

Listing 11.14   (Program 11.3 Results): `Game.h` **(before the design pattern)**

```
#include "Hall.h"

using namespace std;

class Game
{
public:
    Game(Hall * const winner, const int winner_points,
        Hall * const loser , const int loser_points)
        : winner(winner), loser(loser),
          winner_points(winner_points),
          loser_points(loser_points)
    {
```

```
            winner->increment_win_count();
    }

    void print_game_score() const;

private:
    Hall *winner;
    Hall *loser;

    int winner_points;
    int loser_points;
};
```

Member function `print_game_score()` prints the result of a single game as part of the Scores Report. For example, it can print

```
West Hall beat East Hall 5 to 3
```

Listing 11.15   **(Program 11.3 Results):** `Game.cpp` **(before the design pattern)**

```
#include <iostream>
#include <iomanip>
#include "Hall.h"
#include "Game.h"

using namespace std;
                                            ┌──  Print one line of the
void Game::print_game_score() const  ◄──────┘    Scores Report.
{
    cout << setw(14) << winner->get_name() << " beat "
         << setw(10) << loser->get_name()
         << setw(3)  << winner_points
         << " to "   << setw(2) << loser_points << endl;
}
```

Each `Sport` object represents a type of sport, either baseball, football, or volleyball. Its private member variable `games` is a vector of the games of that sport type that were played. Member function `append()` appends a `Game` object to the end of the vector.

Listing 11.16   **(Program 11.3 Results):** `Sport.h` **(before the design pattern)**

```
#include <vector>
#include "Game.h"

using namespace std;

class Sport
{
public:
    Sport(const SportType type) : type(type) {}
    ~Sport() { for (Game *game : games) delete game; }
```

```
        void add_game(Game *game) { games.push_back(game); }

        void print_game_scores() const;
        void print_game_count()  const;

private:
    SportType type;
    vector<Game *> games;
};
```

Vector of games of the sport that were played.

Member function print_game_scores() prints the sport type and then iterates over the games vector to print the scores of all the games of that type. This output is part of the Scores Report (listing 11.17). For example, the function can print

```
volleyball
    West Hall beat South Hall 15 to 10
    South Hall beat North Hall 15 to 13
    South Hall beat  West Hall 15 to 14
```

Member function print_game_count() prints the number of games of the sport type that were played. This count will appear in one line the Activities Report. For example,

```
baseball: 2 game(s)
```

Listing 11.17 (Program 11.3 Results): Sport.cpp (before the design pattern)

```
#include <iostream>
#include <iomanip>
#include "Game.h"
#include "Sport.h"

using namespace std;

void Sport::print_game_scores() const
{
    cout << endl << "  " << type << endl;

    for (Game *game : games) game->print_game_score();
}

void Sport::print_game_count() const
{
    cout << setw(12) << type << ": "
         << games.size() << " game(s)" << endl;
}
```

Print the game scores for this sport as part of the Scores Report.

Print one line of the Activities Report.

Class Intramural is the root of the tree. Private member variables sports and halls are vectors that keep track of the sports and residence halls, respectively. Member functions add_sport() and add_hall() append Sport and Hall objects into the vectors.

Listing 11.18   (Program 11.3 Results): `Intramural.h` **(before the design pattern)**

```cpp
#include <map>
#include "Sport.h"
#include "Hall.h"

class Intramural
{
public:
    ~Intramural()
    {
        for (Sport *sport : sports) delete sport;
        for (Hall  *hall  : halls)  delete hall;
    }

    void add_sport(Sport *sport) { sports.push_back(sport); }
    void add_hall(Hall *hall)    { halls.push_back(hall); }

    void print_scores_report() const;
    void print_activities_report() const;
    void print_winnings_report() const;

private:
    vector<Sport *> sports;
    vector< Hall *>  halls;
};
```

The public printing member functions of class `Intramural` generate the three intramural sports reports (listing 11.19):

- *Scores Report*—Member function `print_scores_report()` iterates over the `Sport` objects and calls member function `print_game_scores()` on each object.

- *Activities Report*—Member function `print_activities_report()` iterates over the `Sport` objects and calls member function `print_game_count()` on each object.

- *Winnings Report*—Member function `print_winnings_report()` iterates over the `Hall` objects and calls member function `print_win_count()` on each object.

Listing 11.19   (Program 11.3 Results): `Intramural.cpp` **(before the design pattern)**

```cpp
#include <iostream>
#include <iomanip>
#include "Sport.h"
#include "Hall.h"
#include "Intramural.h"

void Intramural::print_scores_report() const
{
```

```
    cout << endl << "SCORES REPORT" << endl;

    for (Sport *sport : sports) sport->print_game_scores();
}

void Intramural::print_activities_report() const
{
    cout << endl << "ACTIVITIES REPORT" << endl << endl;

    for (Sport *sport : sports) sport->print_game_count();
}

void Intramural::print_winnings_report() const
{
    cout << endl << "WINNINGS REPORT" << endl << endl;

    for (Hall *hall : halls) hall->print_win_count();
}
```

Generating each report requires a call chain among the member functions of the main classes (figure 11.7).

```
Scores Report
Intramural::print_scores_report()
  ➡ Sport::print_game_scores()
      ➡ Game::print_game_score()

Activities Report
Intramural::print_activities_report()
  ➡ Sport::print_game_count()

Winnings Report
Intramural::print_winnings_report()
  ➡ Hall::print_win_count()
```

Figure 11.7   **A call chain through the member functions of the main classes is necessary to generate each report.**

To generate sample data, the test program first calls function `build_tree()` that hard-codes building a tree data structure and returns a pointer to the tree root. Then, the program calls the member functions of the root `Intramural` node to print the three intramural reports.

Listing 11.20   **(Program 11.3 Results):** `tester.cpp` **(before the design pattern)**

```
#include "Enums.h"
#include "Intramural.h"
#include "Sport.h"
#include "Game.h"
#include "Hall.h"

using namespace std;
```

```
Intramural *build_tree();

int main()
{
    Intramural *intramural = build_tree();

    intramural->print_scores_report();          Print the
    intramural->print_activities_report();       reports.
    intramural->print_winnings_report();

    delete intramural;
    return 0;
}

Intramural *build_tree()
{
    Intramural *intramural = new Intramural();

    Sport *baseball   = new Sport(SportType::BASEBALL);     Create the
    Sport *football   = new Sport(SportType::FOOTBALL);      sports.
    Sport *volleyball = new Sport(SportType::VOLLEYBALL);

    intramural->add_sport(baseball);
    intramural->add_sport(football);
    intramural->add_sport(volleyball);

    Hall *north = new Hall(HallName::NORTH);
    Hall *south = new Hall(HallName::SOUTH);      Create the
    Hall *east  = new Hall(HallName::EAST);       residence halls.
    Hall *west  = new Hall(HallName::WEST);

    intramural->add_hall(north);
    intramural->add_hall(south);
    intramural->add_hall( east);
    intramural->add_hall( west);

    baseball->add_game(new Game(west, 5, east, 3));
    baseball->add_game(new Game(east, 3, south, 0));

    football->add_game(new Game(west, 21, north, 27));       Create the
                                                            games.
    volleyball->add_game(new Game(west,  15, south, 10));
    volleyball->add_game(new Game(south, 13, north, 15));
    volleyball->add_game(new Game(south, 15, west,  14));

    return intramural;
}
```

The algorithms for generating the three intramural reports are implemented in bits and pieces among the tree node classes `Intramural`, `Sport`, `Game`, and `Hall`. That violates DF 2.

 This will become a major nightmare if we need to add more reports or sport types. That violates DF 3.

The application suffers from many faults. The two most egregious ones are

- *Classes with multiple responsibilities*—Each of the classes `Intramural`, `Sport`, and `Game` has two primary responsibilities. Each class must have member variables and member functions to implement the data collection as a tree structure. But each class must also have member variables and member functions to implement the three report generation algorithms.
- *Inflexible application architecture*—If we decide to modify a report's content or add a new report, we will need to make changes throughout the classes.

11.3 After using the Visitor Design Pattern

The Visitor Design Pattern removes these faults. It models a software architecture for our example intramural reports application that separates the algorithm code for generating reports from the code that maintains the tree-structured data collection. Our application will have three `Visitor` classes, and each one encapsulates a report generation algorithm. `Visitor` is an interface, and each class that implements the interface must implement member functions that visit the different types of tree nodes to execute the class's algorithm (figure 11.8). In our example, the three `Visitor` classes are `ScoresReportVisitor`, `ActivitiesReportVisitor`, and `WinningsReportVisitor`. They implement the algorithms to generate the Scores, the Activities, and the Winnings Report, respectively. We'll be able to modify or add new `Visitor` classes and their algorithms without affecting the data collection.

The Visitor Design Pattern

"Represent an operation to be performed on the elements of an object structure. Visitor lets you define a new operation without changing the classes of the elements on which it operates" (GoF 331).

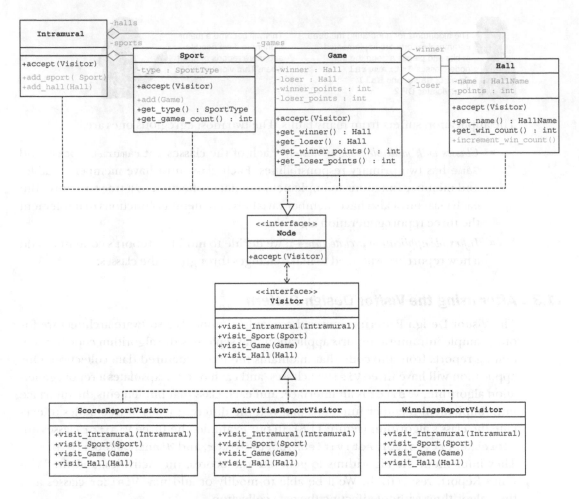

Figure 11.8   The parts that haven't changed logically from figure 11.6 are shown in gray. As in the earlier figure, the tree nodes of the data collection are objects of classes `Intramural`, `Sport`, `Game`, **and** `Hall`. **Now each tree node class implements interface** `Node` **and has member function** `accept()` **to accept a** `Visitor` **object. The three** `Visitor` **classes** `ScoresReportVisitor`, `ActivitiesReportVisitor`, **and** `WinningsReportVisitor` **each implements interface** `Visitor` **and encapsulates a report generation algorithm. Each** `Visitor` **class has member functions that visit the tree nodes, one visit function for each type of node.**

Each `Visitor` class implements the Visitor interface and encapsulates the algorithm to generate a particular report. Class `ScoresReportVisitor` implements the algorithm to generate the Scores Report. Similarly, class `ActivitiesReportVisitor` implements the algorithm to generate the Activities Report. Finally, class `WinningsReportVisitor` implements the algorithm to generate the Winnings Report.

Each `Visitor` class has member functions `visit_Intramural()`, `visit_Sport()`, `visit_Game()`, and `visit_Hall()` that visit `Intramural`, `Sport`, `Game`, and `Hall` nodes of the tree data structure, respectively.

Listing 11.21 (Program 11.4 Results-VisitorDP): `Visitor.h`

```cpp
#include <map>
#include "Enums.h"

using namespace std;

class Intramural;
class Sport;
class Game;
class Hall;

class Visitor
{
public:
    virtual ~Visitor() {}

    virtual void visit_Intramural(Intramural *node) = 0;
    virtual void visit_Sport(Sport *node) = 0;
    virtual void visit_Game(Game *node) = 0;
    virtual void visit_Hall(Hall *node) = 0;
};
```

Member functions to visit the different types of tree nodes

```cpp
class ScoresReportVisitor : public Visitor
{
public:
    void visit_Intramural(Intramural *node) override;
    void visit_Sport(Sport *node) override;
    void visit_Game(Game *node) override;
    void visit_Hall(Hall *node) override;
};

class ActivitiesReportVisitor : public Visitor
{
public:
    void visit_Intramural(Intramural *node) override;
    void visit_Sport(Sport *node) override;
    void visit_Game(Game *node) override;
    void visit_Hall(Hall *node) override;
};

class WinningsReportVisitor : public Visitor
{
public:
    void visit_Intramural(Intramural *node) override;
    void visit_Sport(Sport *node) override;
    void visit_Game(Game *node) override;
    void visit_Hall(Hall *node) override;
};
```

Why are there separate names for the **Visitor** member functions? Can't we use overloading and have only one name, like **visit(Intramural *node)**, **visit(Sport *node)**, etc.?

It's your choice! You may find that naming each **Visitor** member function after a **Node** class makes it easier to see which type of node each member function can visit.

Intramural, Sport, Game, and Hall are now each a subclass of superclass Node. Each Node class must implement the accept() member function.

```
#include "Visitor.h"

using namespace std;

class Node
{
public:
    virtual ~Node() {}

    virtual void accept(Visitor& visitor) = 0;
};
```

Each Node class must implement member function accept(), which accepts any Visitor object. To accept the visit, the node uses polymorphism to call the visitor's visit member function that's appropriate for the node type.

The accept() function enables the application to bind at run time a type of node, such as Intramural, to a type of visitor, such as ScoresReportVisitor. After an Intramural node accepts a ScoresReportVisitor visitor, the node calls the visitor's visit_Intramural() member function (listing 11.23). By passing a pointer to itself (this) to the visitor's member function, it gives the visitor access to the node's public member functions. The visitor can then use the node and its member functions to execute the algorithm to generate the Scores Report. This accept() function also iterates over the Sport and Hall objects in the tree to make each of those objects accept the visitor. The function hides the implementation of the data collection from the Visitor classes.

```
#include <vector>
#include "Node.h"
#include "Sport.h"
#include "Visitor.h"
```

```cpp
class Intramural : public Node
{
public:
    ~Intramural()
    {
        for (Sport *sport : sports) delete sport;
        for (Hall  *hall  : halls)  delete hall;
    }

    void accept(Visitor& visitor) override
    {
        visitor.visit_Intramural(this);

        for (Sport *sport : sports) sport->accept(visitor);
        for (Hall  *hall  : halls)   hall->accept(visitor);
    }
    void add_sport(Sport *sport) { sports.push_back(sport); }
    void add_hall(Hall *hall)    { halls.push_back(hall); }

private:
    vector<Sport *> sports;
    vector< Hall *> halls;
};
```

Use polymorphism to determine which Visitor class's visit_Intramural() member function to call.

Make each Sport object accept the visitor.

Make each Hall object accept the visitor

Each **Visitor** class implements the algorithm to generate a particular report. Each type of **Node** object has an **accept()** member function that accepts a **Visitor** object. The **accept()** function then calls the **Visitor** object's **visit_*()** member function that corresponds to the type of the **Node** object. At run time, polymorphism determines which **Visitor** class's **visit_*()** function is called.

Each **Visitor** class has member functions that visit **Node** objects, one function for each type of node. These functions together execute the **Visitor** class's algorithm as they visit the nodes one after another. This design pattern effectively separates the data collection from the report generation algorithms.

Similarly, Node class Sport implements member function accept(), which then uses polymorphism to determine which Visitor class's visit_Sport() member function to call (listing 11.24). It iterates over the Game objects to make each one accept the visitor.

Because the accept() function passes a pointer to the node (this) to the visitor's visit_Sport() member function, the visit function can call the node's public get_type() and get_games_count() member functions.

Listing 11.24 (Program 11.4 Results-VisitorDP): Sport.h

```cpp
#include <vector>
#include "Node.h"
#include "Game.h"
#include "Visitor.h"
```

```
using namespace std;

class Sport : public Node
{
public:
    Sport(const SportType type) : type(type) {}
    ~Sport() { for (Game *game : games) delete game; }

    void accept(Visitor& visitor) override
    {
        visitor.visit_Sport(this);

        for (Game *game : games) game->accept(visitor);
    }

    SportType get_type() const { return type; }

    void add_game(Game *game) { games.push_back(game); }
    int get_games_count() const { return games.size(); }

private:
    SportType type;
    vector<Game *> games;
};
```

> **Use polymorphism to determine which Visitor class's visit_Sport() member function to call.**

> **Make each Game object accept the visitor.**

Likewise for Node class Game. The Game node has public member functions get_winner(), get_loser(), get_winner_points(), and get_loser_points() that the visitor's visit_Game() member function can call.

Listing 11.25   (Program 11.4 Results-VisitorDP): Game.h

```
#include "Node.h"
#include "Hall.h"
#include "Visitor.h"

class Game : public Node
{
public:
    Game(Hall * const winner, const int winner_points,
         Hall * const loser , const int loser_points)
        : winner(winner), loser(loser),
          winner_points(winner_points),
          loser_points(loser_points)
    {
        winner->increment_win_count();
    }

    void accept(Visitor& visitor) override
    {
        visitor.visit_Game(this);
    }
```

> **Use polymorphism to determine which Visitor class's visit_Game() member function to call.**

```
    Hall *get_winner() const { return winner; }
    Hall *get_loser()  const { return loser;  }

    int get_winner_points() const { return winner_points; }
    int get_loser_points()  const { return  loser_points; }
private:
    Hall *winner;
    Hall *loser;

    int winner_points;
    int loser_points;
};
```

The **Node** classes had to expose some of their internal components by providing public getter member functions to allow access by the **Visitor** objects.

This is a drawback of the Visitor Design Pattern. A software designer must weigh the pros and cons of each design pattern.

As for the Node class Hall, it has public member functions get_name() and get_win_count() that the visitor's visit_Hall() member function can call.

Listing 11.26　(Program 11.4 Results-VisitorDP): Hall.h

```
#include "Enums.h"
#include "Node.h"
#include "Visitor.h"

class Hall : public Node
{
public:
    Hall(const HallName name) : name(name), win_count(0) {}

    void accept(Visitor& visitor) override
    {
        visitor.visit_Hall(this);         ◄─────   Use polymorphism to
    }                                              determine which
                                                   Visitor class's visit_
    HallName get_name() const { return name; }     Hall() member
                                                   function to call.
    int get_win_count() const { return win_count; }
    void increment_win_count() { win_count++; }

private:
    HallName name;
    int win_count;
};
```

In this version of our sports reports application, `Visitor` class `ScoresReportVisitor` encapsulates all the code to generate the reports that was scattered among the `Intramural`, `Sport`, and `Game` classes (table 11.2).

Table 11.2 `Visitor` **class** `ScoresReportVisitor` **encapsulates the algorithm to generate the Scores Report.**

First version	Version with class **ScoresReportVisitor**
`Intramural::print_scores_report()`	`visit_Intramural()`
`Sport::print_game_scores()`	`visit_Sport()`
`Game::print_game_score()`	`visit_Game()`

The visit member functions of subclass `ScoresReportVisitor` encapsulates the algorithm to produce the Scores Report (listing 11.27):

1 Member function `visit_Intramural()` prints the report title SCORES REPORT.
2 Member function `visit_Sport()` prints the name of the sport type.
3 Member function `visit_Game()` prints the results of a game.
4 Member function `visit_Hall()` does nothing.

Listing 11.27   (Program 11.4 Results-VisitorDP): `ScoresReportVisitor.cpp`

```
#include <iostream>
#include <iomanip>
#include "Enums.h"
#include "Intramural.h"
#include "Sport.h"
#include "Game.h"

using namespace std;

void ScoresReportVisitor::visit_Intramural(Intramural *intramural)
{
    cout << endl << "SCORES REPORT" << endl;
}

void ScoresReportVisitor::visit_Sport(Sport *sport)
{
    cout << endl << "  " << sport->get_type() << endl;
}

void ScoresReportVisitor::visit_Game(Game *game)
{
```

```
        Hall *winner = game->get_winner();
        Hall *loser  = game->get_loser();

        int winner_points = game->get_winner_points();
        int  loser_points = game->get_loser_points();

        cout << setw(14) << winner->get_name() << " beat "
             << setw(10) << loser->get_name()
             << setw(3)  << winner_points
             << " to "   << setw(2) << loser_points << endl;
}

void ScoresReportVisitor::visit_Hall(Hall *hall)
{
    // do nothing
}
```

Visitor class **ScoresReportVisitor** has a **visit_*()** member function for each type of tree node. As each method visits a node of the appropriate type, it generates a part of the Scores Report.

We'll be able to modify the reports, or even generate new reports by adding more **Visitor** classes, without needing to make changes to the tree data collection.

The visit member functions of the `Visitor` class `ActivitiesReportVisitor` encapsulates all the code to generate the Sports Report that formerly resided in the `Intramural` and `Sport` classes (table 11.3).

Table 11.3 `Visitor` **class** `ActivitiesReportVisitor` **encapsulates the algorithm to generate the Activities Report.**

First version	Version with class ActivitiesReportVisitor
Intramural::print_activities_report()	visit_Intramural()
Sport::print_game_count()	visit_Sport()

The visit member functions of subclass `ActivitiesReportVisitor` implement the algorithm to produce the Sports Report (listing 11.28).

1 Member function `visit_Intramural()` prints the report title ACTIVITIES REPORT.

2 Member function `visit_Sport()` prints the number of games of the sport type.

3 Member function `visit_Game()` does nothing.

4 Member function `visit_Hall()` does nothing.

Listing 11.28 (Program 11.4 Results-VisitorDP): `ActivitiesReportVisitor.cpp`

```cpp
#include <iostream>
#include <iomanip>
#include "Enums.h"
#include "Intramural.h"
#include "Sport.h"
#include "Game.h"

using namespace std;

void ActivitiesReportVisitor::visit_Intramural(Intramural *intramural)
{
    cout << endl << "ACTIVITIES REPORT" << endl << endl;
}


void ActivitiesReportVisitor::visit_Sport(Sport *sport)
{
    cout << setw(12) << sport->get_type() << ": "
        << sport->get_games_count() << " game(s)" << endl;
}

void ActivitiesReportVisitor::visit_Game(Game *game)
{
    // do nothing
}

void ActivitiesReportVisitor::visit_Hall(Hall *hall)
{
    // do nothing
}
```

The visit member functions of the `Visitor` class `WinningsReportVisitor` encapsulates all the code to generate the Winnings Report that formerly resided in the `Intramural` and `Sport` classes (table 11.4).

Table 11.4 `Visitor` **class** `WinningsReportVisitor` **encapsulates the algorithm to generate the Winnings Report.**

First version	Version with class WinningsReportVisitor
`Intramural::print_halls_report()`	`visit_Intramural()`
`Sport::print_game_count()`	`visit_Hall()`

The visit member functions of subclass `WinningsReportVisitor` implement the algorithm to produce the Residence Halls Report (listing 11.29):

1 Member function `visit_Intramural()` prints the report title WINNINGS REPORT.

2 Member function `visit_Sport()` docs nothing.

3 Member function `visit_Game()` does nothing.

4 Member function `visit_Hall()` prints a residence hall's number of wins.

Listing 11.29   (Program 11.4 Results-VisitorDP): `WinningsReportVisitor.cpp`

```cpp
#include <iostream>
#include <iomanip>
#include "Enums.h"
#include "Intramural.h"
#include "Sport.h"
#include "Game.h"

using namespace std;

void WinningsReportVisitor::visit_Intramural(Intramural *intramural)
{
    cout << endl << "WINNINGS REPORT" << endl << endl;
}

void WinningsReportVisitor::visit_Sport(Sport *sport)
{
    // do nothing
}

void WinningsReportVisitor::visit_Game(Game *game)
{
    // do nothing
}

void WinningsReportVisitor::visit_Hall(Hall *hall)
{
    cout << setw(12) << hall->get_name() << " won "
        << hall->get_win_count() << " game(s)" << endl;
}
```

Several of the `visit_*()` member functions don't do anything.

We can make **Visitor** into a superclass where the default implementation of each member function does nothing. Then, a **Visitor** subclass needs to override only the member functions that do something.

After building the example tree data structure, the test program creates the Scores-ReportVisitor, the ActivitiesReportVisitor, and the WinningsReportVisitor objects. Then, it generates each report by calling the intramural_node (the tree root) to accept each visitor object in turn.

Listing 11.30   (Program 11.4 Results-VisitorDP): `tester.cpp`

```cpp
#include "Intramural.h"
#include "Sport.h"
#include "Game.h"
#include "Hall.h"
#include "Visitor.h"

using namespace std;

Intramural *build_tree();

int main()
{
    Intramural *intramural_node = build_tree();

    ScoresReportVisitor     scores_report_visitor;
    ActivitiesReportVisitor activities_report_visitor;
    WinningsReportVisitor    winnings_report_visitor;

    intramural_node->accept(scores_report_visitor);
    intramural_node->accept(activities_report_visitor);
    intramural_node->accept(winnings_report_visitor);

    delete intramural_node;
    return 0;
}

Intramural *build_tree()
{
    Intramural *intramural_node = new Intramural();

    Sport *baseball   = new Sport(SportType::BASEBALL);
    Sport *football   = new Sport(SportType::FOOTBALL);
    Sport *volleyball = new Sport(SportType::VOLLEYBALL);

    intramural_node->add_sport(baseball);
    intramural_node->add_sport(football);
    intramural_node->add_sport(volleyball);

    Hall *north = new Hall(HallName::NORTH);
    Hall *south = new Hall(HallName::SOUTH);
    Hall *east  = new Hall(HallName::EAST);
    Hall *west  = new Hall(HallName::WEST);

    intramural_node->add_hall(north);
    intramural_node->add_hall(south);
    intramural_node->add_hall( east);
    intramural_node->add_hall( west);
```

Print the Scores Report.

Print the Activities Report.

Print the Winnings Report.

```
baseball->add_game(new Game(west, 5, east,  3));
baseball->add_game(new Game(east, 3, south, 0));

football->add_game(new Game(north, 27, west, 21));

volleyball->add_game(new Game(west,  15, south, 10));
volleyball->add_game(new Game(north, 15, south, 13));
volleyball->add_game(new Game(south, 15, west,  14));

return intramural_node;
}
```

The key benefits of using the Visitor Design Pattern to model the architecture of the second version of our intramural games reports application include:

- *Encapsulated algorithms*—The algorithms to generate and print the Games Report, the Sports Report, and the Residence Halls Report are each encapsulated in the Visitor classes ScoresReportVisitor, ActivitiesReportVisitor, and WinningsReportVisitor, respectively. This is the Encapsulate What Varies Principle (section 2.3.2). It will be possible to modify or delete a report algorithm or add new ones without affecting other classes.

- *Classes with single responsibility*—The Node classes Intramural, Sport, Game, and Hall are responsible only for maintaining the tree data structure. The Visitor classes are responsible only for report generation. This is the Single Responsibility Principle (section 2.3).

- *Loose coupling*—The tree data structure is loosely coupled with the report generation algorithms, and the algorithms are loosely coupled with each other. The Node classes do not know what the report generation algorithms are or how they're implemented by the Visitor classes. This is the Principle of Least Knowledge (section 2.3.2). We will be able to modify or delete algorithms or add new algorithms without modifying the data structure or the existing algorithms.

11.3.1 *Visitor's generic model*

Figure 11.9 shows the generic model of the Visitor Design Pattern. Recall that it is from the design pattern's generic model that we can create a custom solution to an architecture problem (section 8.1.3).

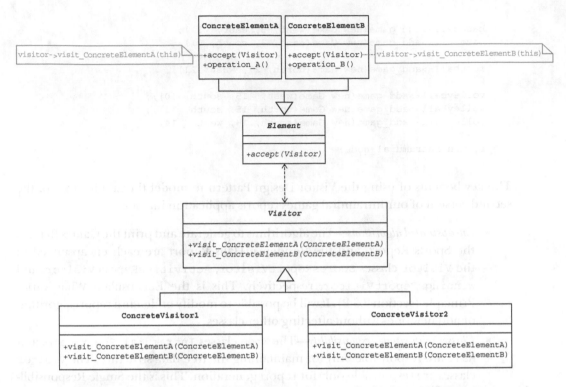

Figure 11.9 **The generic model of the Visitor Design Pattern. Compare it with figure 11.8. Each `Visitor` class encapsulates an algorithm. To execute an algorithm during a pass of the `Element` objects, each element object accepts a `Visitor` object. The `accept()` function of each concrete `Element` object calls the visit member function that corresponds to that `Element` object. The visit member functions together execute the `Visitor` class's algorithm as they visit the `Element` objects one after another.**

Table 11.5 shows how the example application applies the pattern.

Table 11.5 **The Visitor Method Design Pattern as applied by the example application**

Design pattern	Applied by the example application
Superclass `Element`	Interface `Node`
Subclasses `ConcreteElementA`, etc.	Classes `Intramural`, `Sport`, `Game`, and `Hall`
Superclass `Visitor`	Interface `Visitor`
Subclasses `ConcreteVisitor1`, etc.	Classes `ScoresReportVisitor`, `ActivitiesReport-Visitor`, and `WinningsReportVisitor`
Member functions `visit_ConcreteElementA()`, etc.	Member functions `visit_Intramural()`, `visit_Sport()`, `visit_Game()`, and `visit_Hall()`

The Iterator Design Pattern models an architecture where there are multiple types of sequential collections that all contain the same type of objects. The pattern encapsulates ways to iterate over the collections to perform an algorithm on the objects.

The Visitor Design Pattern models an architecture where there is a single collection of various types of objects. The pattern encapsulates different algorithms to perform on the objects during separate passes over the collection.

Summary

- The Iterator Design Pattern models a solution for a software architecture that has a single algorithm that processes elements one after another, which are stored in multiple sequential collections, without exposing how the collections are implemented. The client and its algorithm are loosely coupled with the collections.

- We will be able to modify or delete a data collection, or add a new sequential collection with its iterator, without modifying the algorithm or the existing collections.

- The Visitor Design Pattern models a solution for a software architecture that makes multiple passes over the objects of a single data collection. The objects can be instantiated from diverse classes. Each pass executes a different algorithm on the objects, and each algorithm has member functions to process each type of object.

- The Visitor Design Pattern encapsulates each algorithm as a visitor class, so the algorithms are loosely coupled with the data collection, and the algorithms are loosely coupled with each other. We will be able to modify or delete algorithms or add new algorithms without modifying the data collection or the existing algorithms.

The Observer
Design Pattern

12

In this chapter, we continue with the theme of sports reports generated by a college athletics department. The Observer Design Pattern supports the publisher–subscriber model, where one component creates data objects that subscriber components process individually, each in its own way. The publisher component doesn't know how the subscriber components are implemented nor does it care what the subscribers do with the data.

Our example application monitors the progress of a baseball game. It prints game statistics both while the game is in progress and after it is over.

Manning Comix

> **NOTE** Be sure to read the introduction to part 4 for important information about design patterns in general and to learn how this and subsequent chapters teach each pattern.

12.1 The Observer Design Pattern represents the publisher–subscriber model

The Observer Design Pattern represents the publisher–subscriber model. A good example of this model is an online news streaming service. People who are interested in the news stories subscribe to the service. As each news story becomes available, the streaming service notifies each subscriber by providing the story's headline. Then, each subscriber can decide independently whether to request the story by clicking on the headline. The streaming service is therefore the publisher of the stories. Different people can subscribe and unsubscribe at any time. Each subscriber can do whatever with the stories—read or ignore them, only scan the headlines, archive stories about a favorite team, perform sentiment analysis, and so forth. The streaming service doesn't care what each subscriber does with the stories. It only needs to keep track of who is currently subscribed, notify each subscriber when a story becomes available, and provide the means to obtain the story.

The publisher–subscriber model is also known as the producer–consumer model, where the publisher is the producer of content, and the consumers are the subscribers. The consumers are also called the observers of the stories.

For a concrete example, let's suppose a college athletics department wants three different reports about the performance of a team during a given baseball game. The reports are based on the team's hit events. A hit event made by a player on the team is either a hit (single, double, triple, or homer) or an out. The three reports are the following:

- The log report is a running log of the players' hits or outs as they occur during the game.
- The graph report is generated after the game. It consists of a bar chart of the types of hits and the outs made during the game.

- The table report is also generated after the game. It consists of a table that shows what hits and outs each player made during the game.

The components that generate the reports should receive each hit event as it occurs during the game. This will allow class `LogReport` to update its log report immediately after receiving each event. Classes `GraphReport` and `TableReport` must accumulate the event data as the events arrive, and each prints its report after the game is over. The publisher component produces the hit events, and the subscriber components consume the hit events and print the reports (Figure 12.1).

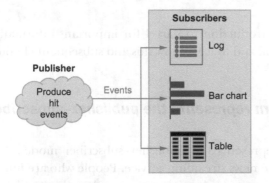

Figure 12.1   An example of the publisher–subscriber model. The publisher component produces hit events that are consumed as they occur by the subscriber components to generate the various reports.

An example of a baseball game log report generated line-by-line as each hit event occurs is

```
GAME HITS LOG

 1     Al hit a single
 2   Beth hit a double
 3   Carl hit an out
 4  Donna hit a double
 5     Ed hit a double
 6   Fran hit a single
 7 George hit an out
 8  Heidi hit an out
 9   Ivan hit a single
10     Al hit an out
...
60   Fran hit a single
61 George hit a double
62  Heidi hit an out
63   Ivan hit an out
64     Al hit an out
```

An example of a graph report that displays a bar chart of the types of hits that occurred during a completed baseball game is

```
GAME HITS GRAPH

22 singles
12 doubles
 2 triples
 1 homers

         ....5...10...15...20...25...30
Singles: SSSSSSSSSSSSSSSSSSSSSS
Doubles: DDDDDDDDDDDD
Triples: TT
 Homers: H
```

An example of a table report that shows what hits and outs each player made during a completed game is

```
GAME HITS TABLE

Player    Outs   Singles Doubles Triples Homers
------------------------------------------------
Al         2       5       1
Beth       2       2       3
Carl       3       3       1
Donna      2       2       2       1
Ed         6       1
Fran       2       4                       1
George     2       2       2       1
Heidi      5               2

Ivan       3       4
```

These reports represent three different perspectives of the same data.

Each report-generating component consumes each data event as it occurs.

12.1.1 Desired design features

Based on how the publisher–subscriber model works, here are some desired design features for a software solution:

- *DF 1*—The publisher can create content at arbitrary times.
- *DF 2*—The publisher immediately notifies all of its subscribers as soon as it has new content.
- *DF 3*—Once notified, a subscriber can choose to ask for the new content.
- *DF 4*—The publisher provides any new content to a subscriber that asks for it, but otherwise, the publisher doesn't care or have any control over what the subscriber does with the content.
- *DF 5*—A subscriber can do whatever it wants with the content.

- *DF 6*—Consumers can subscribe and unsubscribe at arbitrary times. Without any code changes, the publisher can acquire a new subscriber, or an existing subscriber can unsubscribe.
- *DF 7*—The publisher has no knowledge of how any of its subscribers are implemented, nor do the subscribers know how the publisher is implemented.

12.1.2 *Before using the Observer Design Pattern*

To test the first version of our baseball game reports application (figure 12.2), class `EventMaker` uses a random number generator to generate hit events. A hit event is content represented by an `Event` object that is created and returned by each call to member function `next_event()`. Each `Event` object consists of a player's name and a randomly generated out or a single, double, triple, or homer (integer values 0, 1, 2, 3, or 4, respectively).

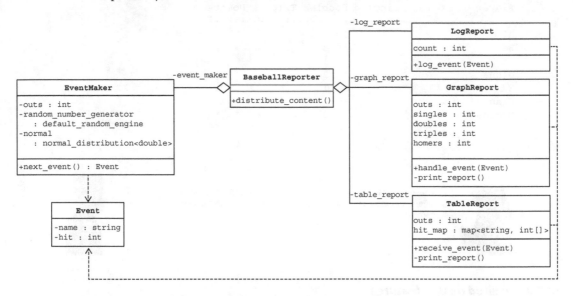

Figure 12.2   The initial architecture of the baseball game reports application. Member function `distribute_content()` **of class** `BaseballReporter` **repeatedly calls the** `next_event()` **member function of class** `EventMaker` **to obtain new** `Event` **objects one at a time. The function passes each** `Event` **object to the** `log_event()`, `handle_event()`, **and** `receive_event()` **member functions of the report classes. Each report class can process the** `Event` **object in its own way.**

While we're developing our application, class **BaseballReporter** is the publisher. It calls member function **next_event()** of class **EventMaker** to create the next random **Event** object.

A random data generator is a good way to test our publisher–subscriber model.

The `BaseballReporter` class's member function `distribute_content()` repeatedly calls `next_event()` to obtain `Event` objects as the content one at a time until the game is over after 27 outs. The function passes each `Event` object to the `log_event()` member function of class `LogReport`, the `handle_event()` member function of class `GraphReport`, and the `receive_event()` member function of class `TableReport`. (Alas, the developers of the report classes couldn't agree on the names of the member functions.) Each report class can then process the `Event` object in its own way.

Class `EventMaker` generates `Event` objects with a random number generator to generate a player's hit (single, double, triple, or homer) or an out, as shown in the following listing.

Listing 12.1 (Program 12.1 Stats): `EventMaker.h` (before the design pattern)

```cpp
#include <string>
#include <vector>
#include <random>
#include <time.h>

using namespace std;

class Event
{
public:
    Event(const string n, const int h) : name(n), hit(h) {}

    string get_name() const { return name; }
    int    get_hit()  const { return hit; }

private:
    string name;
    int hit;
};

class EventMaker
{
public:
    EventMaker()
        : name_index(-1), outs(0),
          normal(normal_distribution<double>(0.0, 1.75))
    {
        random_number_generator.seed(time(NULL));
    }

    int get_outs() const { return outs; }

    Event *next_event();                        ◄──── Obtain the next
                                                       Event object.
private:
    vector<string> names = { "Al", "Beth", "Carl", "Donna", "Ed",
                             "Fran", "George", "Heidi", "Ivan" };
    int name_index;
    int outs;
```

```
                    default_random_engine random_number_generator;    Random number
                    normal_distribution<double> normal;                generator
};
```

Each call to member function next_event() of class EventMaker returns a new
Event object containing the name of a baseball player and a random hit or out.

Listing 12.2   (Program 12.1 Stats): EventMaker.cpp **(before the design pattern)**

```
#include <random>
#include "EventMaker.h"

using namespace std;

Event *EventMaker::next_event()
{
    if (outs < 27)
    {
        double r   = normal(random_number_generator);    Randomly generate
        int    hit = static_cast<int>(abs(r));           a hit (single,
                                                         double, triple, or
        if (hit > 4) hit = 4;                            homer) or an out.
        if (hit == 0) outs++;

        name_index = (name_index + 1)%9;

        return new Event(names[name_index], hit);
    }
    else return nullptr;
}
```

Class BaseballReporter aggregates classes EventMaker, LogReport, GraphReport,
and TableReport.

Listing 12.3   (Program 12.1 Stats): BaseballReporter.h **(before the design pattern)**

```
#include "EventMaker.h"
#include "LogReport.h"
#include "GraphReport.h"
#include "TableReport.h"

class BaseballReports
{
public:
    void distribute_content();

private:
    EventMaker event_maker;

    LogReport    log_report;
    GraphReport  graph_report;
    TableReport  table_report;
};
```

Member function `distribute_content()` repeatedly acquires one new `Event` object at a time by calling the `next_event()` member function of class `EventMaker` until there are no more objects (27 outs have occurred). For each `Event` object, it passes the object to the appropriate member function of each of the report objects.

Listing 12.4 (Program 12.1 Stats): `BaseballReporter.cpp` (before the design pattern)

```cpp
#include "BaseballReporter.h"
#include "EventMaker.h"
#include "LogReport.h"
#include "GraphReport.h"
#include "TableReport.h"

void BaseballReports::distribute_content()
{
    Event *event = event_maker.next_event();          // ◄────── Get the next event.

    while (event != nullptr)
    {
        int outs = event_maker.get_outs();

        log_report.log_event(event, outs);            // Pass the event to
        graph_report.handle_event(event, outs);       // the report member
        table_report.receive_event(event, outs);      // functions.

        delete event;
        event = event_maker.next_event();
    }
}
```

There's a serious design flaw here. The publisher **BaseballReporter** must know what member function to call on each subscriber to pass it an **Event** object.

That violates DF 7.

Member function `log_event()` of class `LogReport` gets each `Event` object.

Listing 12.5 (Program 12.1 Stats): `LogReport.h` (before the design pattern)

```cpp
#include <iostream>
#include <iomanip>
#include "EventMaker.h"

using namespace std;

class LogReport
{
public:
    LogReport() : count(0)
    {
```

```
            cout << "GAME HITS LOG" << endl;
            cout << endl;
        }

        void log_event(const Event * const event, const int outs);  ◄────┐

    private:                                              Get a hit Event object.
        int count;
    };
```

Member function `log_event()` immediately updates the log report as soon as it receives each `Event` object by printing its contents.

Listing 12.6   (Program 12.1 Stats): `LogReport.cpp` **(before the design pattern)**

```cpp
#include <iostream>
#include <iomanip>
#include "LogReport.h"

using namespace std;

void LogReport::log_event(const Event * const event, const int outs)
{
    string  name = event->get_name();
    int     hit  = event->get_hit();
    string  what;

    switch (hit)
    {
        case 0: what = "an out";   break;
        case 1: what = "a single"; break;
        case 2: what = "a double"; break;
        case 3: what = "a triple"; break;
        case 4: what = "a homer";  break;

        default: what = ""; break;
    }

    count++;
    cout << setw(2) << count << setw(7) << name        Print a line
        << " hit " << what << endl;                    of the log.
}
```

Member function `handle_event()` of class `GraphReport` gets each `Event` object. It keeps track of the numbers of outs, singles, doubles, triples, and homers.

Listing 12.7   (Program 12.1 Stats): `GraphReport.h` **(before the design pattern)**

```cpp
#include "EventMaker.h"

class GraphReport
{
public:
    GraphReport()
```

```
    {
        singles = doubles = triples = homers = 0;
    }

    void handle_event(const Event * const event, const int outs);

private:
    int singles, doubles, triples, homers;

    void print_report() const;
    void print_bar(const char ch, const int count) const;
};
```

Member function handle_event() processes the events by totaling the numbers of outs, singles, doubles, triples, and homers. As soon as the game is over (27 outs have occurred), member function print_report() prints the hit counts and a bar chart.

Listing 12.8   (Program 12.1 Stats): GraphReport.cpp **(before the design pattern)**

```
#include <iostream>
#include <iomanip>
#include "GraphReport.h"

using namespace std;

void GraphReport::handle_event(const Event * const event,
                               const int outs)
{
    int hit = event->get_hit();

    switch (hit)
    {
        case 1: singles++; break;
        case 2: doubles++; break;
        case 3: triples++; break;
        case 4: homers++;  break;

        default: break;
    }

    if (outs == 27) print_report();
}

void GraphReport::print_report() const
{
    cout << endl << endl;
    cout << "GAME HITS GRAPH" << endl;
    cout << endl;

    cout << setw(2) << singles << " singles" << endl;
    cout << setw(2) << doubles << " doubles" << endl;
    cout << setw(2) << triples << " triples" << endl;
    cout << setw(2) << homers  << " homers"  << endl;
    cout << endl;
```

```
    cout << "          ....5...10...15...20...25...30" << endl;
    cout << "Singles: "; print_bar('S', singles);
    cout << "Doubles: "; print_bar('D', doubles);
    cout << "Triples: "; print_bar('T', triples);
    cout << " Homers: "; print_bar('H', homers);
}

void GraphReport::print_bar(const char ch, const int count) const
{
    for (int i = count; i > 0; i--) cout << ch;
    cout << endl;
}
```

Member function `receive_event()` of class `TableReport` gets each `Event` object. It keeps track of the numbers of outs. It uses a map to record what hits and outs each player made during the game. The map is keyed by the players' names and each value is an array of the numbers of outs, singles, doubles, triples, and homers for the corresponding player.

Listing 12.9   **(Program 12.1 Stats):** `TableReport.h` **(before the design pattern)**

```
#include <string>
#include <map>
#include "EventMaker.h"

using namespace std;

class TableReport
{
public:
    void receive_event(const Event * const event, const int outs);

private:
    map<string, int *> hit_map;

    void print_report();
};
```

The `hit_map`, keyed by the players' names, records the type and number of hits each player made during the game in an array of five integer values. These values total the number of outs, singles, doubles, triples, and homers, respectively, made by the corresponding player. As soon as the game is over (27 outs have occurred), member function `print_report()` prints a table from the map.

Listing 12.10   **(Program 12.1 Stats):** `TableReport.cpp` **(before the design pattern)**

```
#include <iostream>
#include <iomanip>
#include "TableReport.h"

using namespace std;
```

```
void TableReport::receive_event(const Event * const event,
                                const int outs)
{
    string   name = event->get_name();
    int      hit  = event->get_hit();

    if (hit_map.find(name) == hit_map.end())
    {
        hit_map[name] = new int[5] { 0, 0, 0, 0, 0 };
    }
    hit_map[name][hit]++;

    if (outs == 27) print_report();
}
```

Create a new entry for a player.

Record the number and type of hit or an out for the player.

```
void TableReport::print_report()
{
    cout << endl << endl;
    cout << "GAME HITS TABLE" << endl;
    cout << endl;

    cout << "Player      Outs    Singles Doubles Triples Homers"
         << endl;
    cout << "-------------------------------------------------"
         << endl;

    for (auto it = hit_map.begin(); it != hit_map.end(); it++)
    {
        cout << setw(6) << left << it->first;

        int *hits = it->second;
        for (int i = 0; i < 5; i++)
        {
            if (hits[i] > 0) cout << setw(8) << right << hits[i];
            else             cout << "        ";
        }
        cout << endl;
    }
}
```

Iterate over the contents of the hit map to print table rows.

Print a table row.

None of the subscribers is given the option to ask for the content represented by the **Event** objects. They always get all the content each time.

That violates DF 3. What if a particular player's fan club only wanted to request content about that player?

The test program outputs the three baseball game reports shown at the beginning of this section.

Listing 12.11   (Program 12.1 Stats): `tester.cpp` (before the design pattern)

```cpp
#include "BaseballReports.h"

int main()
{
    BaseballReporterreports;
    reports.distribute_content();

    return 0;
}
```

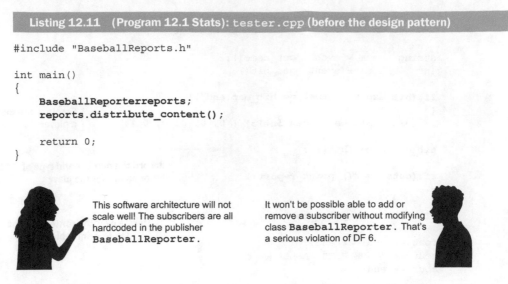

This software architecture will not scale well! The subscribers are all hardcoded in the publisher **BaseballReporter**.

It won't be possible able to add or remove a subscriber without modifying class **BaseballReporter**. That's a serious violation of DF 6.

Although it produces the correct baseball game reports, this version of the application has major architectural problems, including

- *Hardcoded subscribers*—Class `BaseballReporter` hardcodes the three reports that it generates. In the publisher–subscriber model, it should be easy to add and remove subscribers.

- *Classes not loosely coupled*—Class `BaseballReporter` must know how each subscriber is implemented. Its member function `distribute_content()` must know to call `log_event()` for the log report, `handle_event()` for the graph report, and `receive_event()` for the table report. Therefore, class `Baseball-Reporter` is not loosely coupled with the report classes.

12.1.3 *After using the Observer Design Pattern*

Let's see how the Observer Design Pattern overcomes these shortcomings. The model defines superclass `Subject` and interface `Observer`. The key idea is that the subject publishes or produces the content, and there can be multiple observers of the subject's content. Therefore, in the version of our application modeled from the pattern, the publisher of the `Event` content, class `BaseballReporter`, inherits from superclass `Subject`. Each subscriber of the content, report classes `LogReport`, `GraphReport`, and `TableReport`, implements interface `Observer` (figure 12.3).

The Observer Design Pattern

"Define a one-to-many dependency between objects so that when one object changes state, all its dependents are notified and updated automatically" (GoF 293).

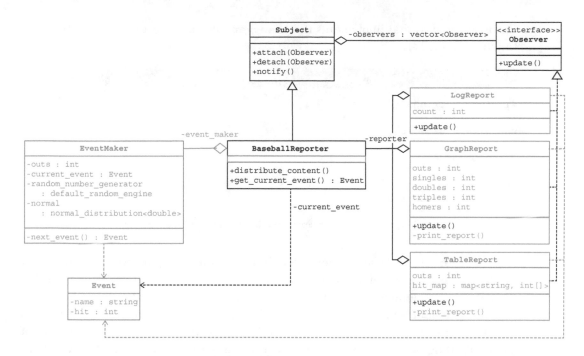

Figure 12.3 This version of the application is modeled from the Observer Design Pattern. The content publisher `BaseballReporter` is a subclass of `Subject`, and each report class implements interface `Observer`. Member variable `observers` of class `Subject` is a vector of subscribed observers. Each time `BaseballReporter` uses `EventManager` to create a new `Event` object, it points private member variable `current_event` to the object. Then it calls the `notify()` member function of superclass `Subject`, which iterates over the `observers` vector and calls the `update()` member function of each subscribed subscriber. Each subscriber can then decide whether to call member function `get_current_event()` to get the current `Event` object. The grayed-out portions of the diagram have not changed logically from figure 12.2.

Member variable `observers` of superclass `Subject` is a vector of `Observer` objects that keeps track of the current subscribers.

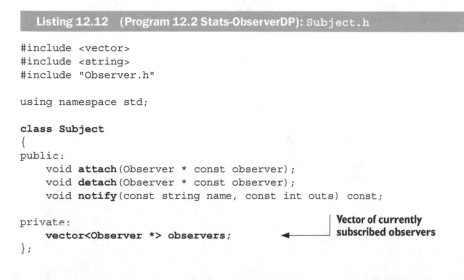

Listing 12.12 (Program 12.2 Stats-ObserverDP): `Subject.h`

```
#include <vector>
#include <string>
#include "Observer.h"

using namespace std;

class Subject
{
public:
    void attach(Observer * const observer);
    void detach(Observer * const observer);
    void notify(const string name, const int outs) const;

private:
    vector<Observer *> observers;       ◀── Vector of currently
};                                          subscribed observers
```

Each report class that implements the `Observer` interface must implement member function `update()`.

Listing 12.13   (Program 12.2 Stats-ObserverDP): `Observer.h`

```cpp
#include <string>

using namespace std;

class Observer
{
public:
    virtual ~Observer() {}

    virtual void update(const string name, const int outs) = 0;
};
```

An `Observer` object (a subscriber object in our example application) can add itself to the `observers` vector of superclass `Subject` (the publisher) by calling the latter's `attach()` member function, and it can remove itself from the vector by calling `detach()`. Whenever there is a new `Event` object, member function `notify()` iterates over the `Observer` objects in the vector and calls the `update()` member function of each one using polymorphism. Therefore, each subscriber is notified whenever there is a new `Event` object. This is a use of the Code to the Interface Principle (section 2.3.3).

Listing 12.14   (Program 12.2 Stats-ObserverDP): `Subject.cpp`

```cpp
#include <string>
#include <vector>
#include "Observer.h"
#include "Subject.h"

using namespace std;

void Subject::attach(Observer * const observer)
{
    observers.push_back(observer);
}

void Subject::detach(Observer * const observer)
{
    for (int i = 0; i < observers.size(); i++)
    {
        if (observers[i] == observer)
        {
            observers.erase(observers.begin() + i);
            return;
        }
    }
}
```

```
void Subject::notify(const string name, const int outs) const
{
    for (Observer *obs : observers) obs->update(name, outs);
}
```

Notify each Observer object (a subscriber) by calling its update() member function.

Classes Event and EventMaker have not changed from Program 12.1.

Class BaseballReporter is the publisher, and therefore, it is a subclass of Subject. After a subscribed report object is notified of a new event, if it is interested in its content, it can call the get_current_event() member function to get a pointer to the Event object, as shown in the following listing. Like before, each subscriber can process the event in its own way.

Listing 12.15 (Program 12.2 Stats-ObserverDP): BaseballReporter.h

```
#include "Subject.h"
#include "EventMaker.h"

class BaseballReporter : public Subject
{
public:
    void distribute_content();

    Event *get_current_event() const { return current_event; }

private:
    EventMaker event_maker;
    Event *current_event;
};
```

For testing purposes, as in Program 12.1, member function distribute_content() repeatedly acquires one new Event object at a time by calling the next_event() member function of class EventMaker until there are no more objects (27 outs have occurred). In this version, member variable current_event keep a pointer to the latest Event object. A call to the superclass member function notify() notifies each subscribed report object about the new content.

Listing 12.16 (Program 12.2 Stats-ObserverDP): BaseballReporter.cpp

```
#include "BaseballReporter.h"
#include "EventMaker.h"

void BaseballReporter::distribute_content()
{
    do
    {
        current_event = event_maker.next_event();

        if (current_event != nullptr)
        {
```

Create a new random hit event.

```
                notify(current_event->get_name(),
                    event_maker.get_outs());          ◀────   Notify all the subscribed
            delete current_event;                             report objects.
        }
    } while (current_event != nullptr);
}
```

Subscriber class `LogReport` implements interface `Observer`, and therefore it implements member function `update()`. The constructor initializes member variable `reporter` to point to the `BaseballReporter` object, and it registers this subscriber object with publisher `BaseballReporter`.

Listing 12.17   (Program 12.2 Stats-ObserverDP): `LogReport.h`

```
#include <iostream>
#include <iomanip>
#include <string>
#include "Observer.h"
#include "BaseballReporter.h"

using namespace std;

class LogReport : public Observer
{
public:
    LogReport(BaseballReporter * const r) : reporter(r), count(0)
    {
        r->attach(this);          ◀────   Subscribe by registering with
                                          publisher BaseballReporter.
        cout << "GAME HITS LOG" << endl;
        cout << endl;
    }

    void update(const string name, const int outs) override;

private:
    BaseballReporter *reporter;
    int count;
};
```

Whenever the subscriber `LogReport` object is notified of newly arrived content, member function `update()` calls member function `get_current_event()` of class `BaseballReporter` to get a pointer to the `Event` object. Then, like in member function `log_event()` of the previous version of the class (listing 12.6), function `update()` uses the `Event` object to print a line of the running log, as shown in the following listing.

Listing 12.18   (Program 12.2 Stats-ObserverDP): `LogReport.cpp`

```
#include <iostream>
#include <iomanip>
#include <string>
#include "EventMaker.h"
```

```
#include "BaseballReporter.h"
#include "LogReport.h"

using namespace std;

void LogReport::update(const string name, const int outs)
{
    Event   *event = reporter->get_current_event();        ◄──────  Get the newly
    string  name   = event->get_name();                            arrived Event object.
    int     hit    = event->get_hit();
    string  what;
    ...
}
```

Parameter `name` of member function `update()` is the name of the player that generated the new content. It serves as the headline the function can use to determine whether to obtain the content. Parameter `outs` is the number of outs made so far—27 outs, and the game is over.

In this example program, `update()` could easily have a parameter that's a pointer to the current `Event` object; therefore, it won't be necessary to call member function `get_current_event()` of class `BaseballReporter`. But we want to demonstrate choosing whether to obtain the content. Being able to choose can be important in an actual application if the content is a large amount of data that we don't want to obtain if it isn't wanted. A new subscriber introduced later, `FanClubReport`, takes advantage of having this choice.

Subscriber class `GraphReport` also implements interface `Observer`, and it implements member function `update()`. The constructor initializes member variable `reporter` to point to the `BaseballReporter` object, and it registers this subscriber object with publisher `BaseballReporter`.

Listing 12.19 (Program 12.2 Stats-ObserverDP): `GraphReport.h`

```
#include <string>
#include "Observer.h"
#include "BaseballReporter.h"

using namespace std;

class GraphReport : public Observer
{
public:
    GraphReport(BaseballReporter * const r) : reporter(r)
    {
        r->attach(this);                                   ◄──────  Subscribe by registering
        singles = doubles = triples = homers = 0;                  with publisher
    }                                                              BaseballReporter.

    void update(const string name, const int outs) override;

private:
    BaseballReporter *reporter;
```

```
    int singles, doubles, triples, homers;

    void print_report();
    void print_bar(const char ch, const int count);
};
```

Whenever the GraphReport object is notified of a newly arrived content, member function update() calls member function get_current_event() of class Baseball-Reporter to get a pointer to the Event object. Then, like in member function handle_event() of the previous version of the class (listing 12.8), function update() uses the Event object to total the hits, as shown in the following listing.

Listing 12.20   (Program 12.2 Stats-ObserverDP): GraphReport.cpp

```cpp
#include <iostream>
#include <iomanip>
#include "EventMaker.h"
#include "BaseballReporter.h"
#include "GraphReport.h"

using namespace std;

void GraphReport::update(const string name, const int outs)
{
    Event   *event = reporter->get_current_event();      ◄────────┐
    int      hit   = event->get_hit();                   Get the newly
    ...                                                   arrived Event object.
}
```

Finally, subscriber class TableReport is another implementor of interface Observer, and it implements member function update(). The constructor initializes member variable reporter to point to the BaseballReporter object, and it registers this subscriber object with publisher BaseballReporter.

Listing 12.21   (Program 12.2 Stats-ObserverDP): TableReport.h

```cpp
#include <string>
#include <map>
#include "Observer.h"
#include "BaseballReporter.h"

using namespace std;

class TableReport : public Observer
{
public:
    TableReport(BaseballReporter * const r) : reporter(r, outs(0)
    {
        r->attach(this);            ◄──────┐  Subscribe by registering with
    }                                          publisher BaseballReporter.

    void update(const string name, const int outs) override;
```

```
private:
    BaseballReporter *reporter;
    map<string, int *> hit_map;

    void print_report();
};
```

Member function `update()` calls member function `get_current_event()` of class `EventMaker` to get a pointer to the newly arrived `Event` object. Then, as in member function `receive_event()` of the previous version of the class (listing 12.10), function `update()` uses the `Event` object to build the hit map, as shown in the following listing.

Listing 12.22   (Program 12.2 Stats-ObserverDP): `TableReport.cpp`

```
#include <iostream>
#include <iomanip>
#include <string>
#include "EventMaker.h"
#include "BaseballReporter.h"
#include "TableReport.h"

using namespace std;

void TableReport::update(const string name, const int outs)
{
    Event   *event = reporter->get_current_event();      ◄──────┐   Get the newly
    int     hit    = event->get_hit();                          │   arrived Event object.
    ...
}
```

To demonstrate how easy it is to add a new subscriber, class `FanClubReport` prints a short report about the performance of one of the players, the club's idol.

Listing 12.23   (Program 12.2 Stats-ObserverDP): `FanClubReport.h`

```
#include <string>
#include "Observer.h"
#include "BaseballReporter.h"

using namespace std;

class FanClubReport : public Observer
{
public:
    FanClubReport(BaseballReporter * const r, const string name)
        : reporter(r), idol(name), what("")
    {
        r->attach(this);
    }

    void update(const string name, const int outs) override;
```

```
        void print_report() const;

private:
        BaseballReporter *reporter;
        string idol;
        string what;
};
```

The class's `update()` member function only obtains and processes the content of the player whose name matches the name of the club's idol. It only prints the idol's first attempt. After getting that first attempt's content, the `FanClubReport` object unsubscribes by detaching itself from the `BaseballReporter` object. Then it will no longer receive update notifications.

Listing 12.24   (Program 12.2 Stats-ObserverDP): `FanClubReport.cpp`

```
#include <iostream>
#include <iomanip>
#include <string>
#include "EventMaker.h"
#include "BaseballReporter.h"                        Only obtain and process
#include "FanClubReport.h"                              the idol's content.

using namespace std;

void FanClubReport::update(const string name, const int outs)
{
    if (name != idol) return;              ◄───────────────

    Event   *event = reporter->get_current_event();    ◄───   Obtain the
    int      hit   = event->get_hit();                        idol's content.

    switch (hit)
    {
        case 0: what = "an out";    break;
        case 1: what = "a single"; break;
        case 2: what = "a double"; break;
        case 3: what = "a triple"; break;
        case 4: what = "a homer";  break;

        default: what = ""; break;
    }

    reporter->detach(this);              ◄─────── Unsubscribe.
}

void FanClubReport::print_report() const
{
    cout << endl << endl;
    cout << "FANCLUB BULLETIN" << endl;
    cout << "The first attempt by " << idol
         << " resulted in " << what << "." << endl;
}
```

An example fan club report (for idol George) is

```
FANCLUB BULLETIN
The first attempt by George resulted in an out.
```

The test program creates a publisher `BaseballReporter` object, which it passes to each subscriber report class's constructor. Each constructor attaches the subscriber to the publisher. The program then calls member function `distribute_content()` of class `BaseballReporter` to start the stream of random `Event` objects. This will generate the three baseball game reports similar to the ones shown at the start of this section.

> **Listing 12.25** **(Program 12.2 Stats-ObserverDP):** `tester.cpp`

```cpp
#include "BaseballReporter.h"
#include "LogReport.h"
#include "GraphReport.h"
#include "TableReport.h"
#include "FanClubReport.h"

using namespace std;

int main()
{
    BaseballReporter *reporter = new BaseballReporter();

    new LogReport(reporter);
    new GraphReport(reporter);
    new TableReport(reporter);

    FanClubReport *fan_club = new FanClubReport(reporter, "George");

    reporter->distribute_content();

    fan_club->print_report();
}
```

Using the Observer Design Pattern to model the architecture of the baseball game reports application gave us several important benefits:

- *Less hardcoding*—The publisher class `BaseballReporter` no longer hardcodes the baseball game reports. We can add new subscriber report objects to the `observers` vector of class `Subject` at run time or remove existing report objects.

- *More flexible code*—It will be easy to create new `Observer` subclasses or delete ones we no longer need. This supports the Encapsulate What Varies Principle (section 2.3.2).

- *Loosely coupled classes*—Publisher class `BaseballReporter` only knows that each of its subscribers implements interface `Observer` and therefore has an `update()` member function. It does not otherwise know how each subscriber is implemented. This supports the Principle of Least Knowledge (section 2.3.2), and therefore, the publisher class `BaseballReporter` is loosely coupled from each of the report classes.

■ *Single responsibility*—Whenever a new `Event` object arrives, each subscriber report object can choose to process the object or ignore the event entirely. Each subscriber is solely responsible for generating a report in its own way. Publisher class `BaseballReporter` only responsible for generating the `Event` objects, and it doesn't know or care what the subscribers do with the events. Class `Baseball-Reporter` and the subscriber report classes support the Single Responsibility Principle (section 2.3).

The publisher knows nothing about its subscribers other than it needs to keep track of them and notify each one whenever new content becomes available.

The publisher also must allow each subscriber to obtain the new content, but otherwise, it doesn't care what the subscribers do with that content.

12.1.4 *The Observer's generic model*

Figure 12.4 shows the generic model of the Observer Design Pattern. Recall that it is from the design pattern's generic model that we can create a custom solution to an architecture problem (section 8.1.3).

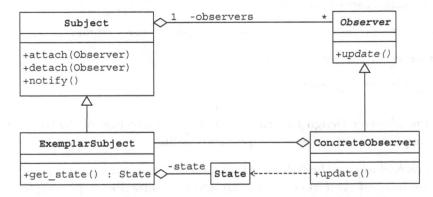

Figure 12.4   The generic model of the Observer Design Pattern. Compare it with figure 12.3. During run time, we can add subscriber `Observer` objects to or remove them from the publisher `Subject` class's collection of `Observer` objects. Whenever an `ExemplarSubject` changes state, the `Subject` class's `notify()` member function iterates over the `observers` collection and calls member function `update()` of each `ConcreteObserver` object. Each `ConcreteObject` can then choose to call the `get_state()` member function of the `ExemplarSubject` class to get the new state.

Table 12.1 shows how the example application applies the pattern.

Table 12.1 The Observer Method Design Pattern as applied by the example application

Design pattern	Applied by the example application
Subclass `ExemplarSubject`	Subclass `BaseballReporter`
`observers` collection	`vector<Observer *>` observers in class `Subject`
Class `State`	Class `Event`
Subclass `ConcreteObserver`	Classes `LogReport`, `GraphReport`, and `TableReport`

Summary

- The Observer Design Pattern implements the publisher–subscriber model by defining a one-to-many dependency between a subject object (the publisher) and a set of observer objects (the subscribers) so that when the subject object changes state, all the observer objects are notified automatically.
- The publisher is loosely coupled with the subscribers, and the publisher doesn't know or care what the subscribers do with the state changes.
- We can add or remove subscribers without changing the publisher's code.

The State Design Pattern

13

This chapter covers

- The State Design Pattern

Chapter 12 showed how the Observer Design Pattern provides a model for an application where the subject object (the publisher) plays a key role in the operation of the application by supplying content data for the observer objects (the subscribers). In this chapter, an object also plays a key role. We must monitor the runtime state changes of this object because its behavior is critical to the operation of the application.

As we saw in section 4.5, events that change the values of the object's member variables can cause an object to make a transition from one state to another. The object can behave differently according to its current state. The State Design Pattern provides a model for managing an object's states, the state transitions, and the different behaviors in each state.

NOTE Be sure to read the introduction to part 4 for important information about design patterns in general and to learn how this and subsequent chapters teach each pattern.

13.1 The State Design Pattern models state transitions

Here's an analogy. Your car is a complex object that can be in several states, but in only one state at a time. For example, it can be turned off, idling, moving, or stopped. When the car is in the off state, you can start it. When it's in the idling state, you can transition it to the moving state by stepping on the accelerator. When it's moving, you can transition it to the stopped state by stepping on the brake. Therefore, in each state, you can perform actions that correctly cause your car to make a reasonable transition to another state. Your car behaves differently, depending on the state it is in. For example, when it's in the moving state, it can be going forward.

However, your car must also handle unreasonable or useless actions. For example, if your car is stopped, stepping on the brake has no effect. If an older car is already moving forward, turning the key in the ignition will cause a horrible grinding noise.

In software, the State Design Pattern provides a model for a software application that must manage an object's runtime states and behaviors. The application must handle all the actions, reasonable or not, that can cause the object to transition from one state to another.

Recall that the state of an object during run time is uniquely determined by the set of values of its member variables. We may have an object in our application whose current state is critical to monitor, and the application's overall operation heavily depends on that object's current state and how it behaves. A useful design tactic is to explicitly name the states to make it easier to refer to each one.

For our concrete example, consider an automatic ticket machine at a sports stadium. At any moment, the machine can be in any one of several named states (figure 13.1):

- READY—The machine is ready to accept a customer's credit card.
- VALIDATING—The machine is validating a customer's credit card.
- TICKET_SOLD—The machine has sold a ticket to a customer.
- SOLD_OUT—The game is sold out, and the machine cannot sell any more tickets.

The member variables whose values determine the current state of the machine are

- count—The number of tickets left in the machine (integer)
- card_inserted—Whether or not a customer's credit card is inserted (true or false)
- card_validity—The validity of the credit card (YES, NO, or UNKNOWN)

Customer actions can change the values of the member variables and thereby cause state transitions. But sometimes, the machine itself can cause a state transition. If the ticket machine is in the READY state, a customer's action of inserting a credit card causes the machine to transition to the VALIDATING state. In that state, the machine can perform the action of checking if the credit card was validated. If the card is valid, the machine transitions to the TICKET_SOLD state where the customer can perform the action of taking the ticket. But if the card is invalid, the machine transitions back to the READY state. The customer can remove the card before it is validated, which forces the machine back to the READY state. The customer taking a sold ticket also causes the machine to transition back to the READY state. But if the customer took the last ticket, the machine transitions to the SOLD_OUT state. Upon returning to the READY state, the customer can perform the action of removing the credit card. There are no transitions out of the SOLD_OUT state.

Therefore, the possible actions by the customer and the ticket machine are

1. Insert a credit card (performed by the customer).
2. Check the credit card's validation status (performed by the ticket machine).
3. Take a purchased ticket (performed by the customer).
4. Remove the credit card (performed by the customer).

While in any state, the ticket machine has no control over the actions a customer can take, even if they are unexpected. For example, a customer may remove a credit card before the card is validated or may try to take a ticket before paying for it. Therefore, the machine must also support customer actions that we'll deem to be unreasonable. The machine must handle all possible actions in every state (figure 13.1).

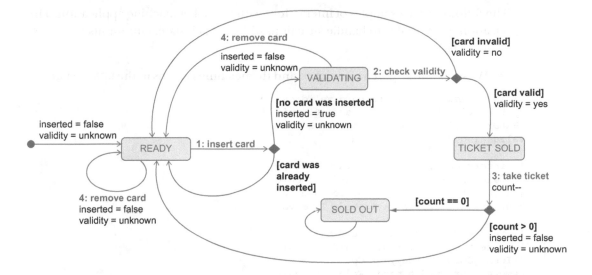

Figure 13.1   A UML state diagram showing the four states and the state transitions of an automatic ticket machine. The machine keeps track of the number of tickets it has, whether there is a credit card inserted, and the validity status of the card. Customer and machine actions (numbered; e.g., 1: insert card) or certain conditions (in square brackets; e.g., [card invalid]) can cause transitions from one state to another. This figure only shows the actions that cause transitions.

To keep it as simple as possible, the figure only shows actions that cause transitions. It does not show unreasonable actions, such as inserting a credit card into the machine while it is in the TICKET_SOLD state when a card is still in the machine. We can assume that an unreasonable action will not lead to a state transition; therefore, the machine stays in its current state.

Our example application is a simple simulation of the ticket machine. The machine will have only three tickets. To interact with the application, we trigger actions by playing the role of the customer or the machine. In response to each Command? prompt, we can enter a 1 to insert a credit card, 2 to validate the card, 3 to take a ticket, or 4 to remove our credit card. The application internally keeps track of its current state, and it must behave properly for each action according to the state. Entering 0 terminates the program.

To aid testing and debugging, the application prints, in square brackets before each command prompt, the current state of the ticket machine, the number of tickets left, whether there is a credit card inserted, and the validity of the card. For example,

```
[TICKET_SOLD 2 true yes] Command?
```

means the ticket machine is in the TICKET_SOLD state, two tickets remain, a credit card is inserted, and the card is valid.

The following are examples of interactions with the ticket machine application. The application must be able to handle all actions while in each state. Our inputs (1, 2, 3, 4, or 0) are in bold.

- We successfully purchase a ticket, and the machine returns to the READY state:

```
1: insert card, 2: check card validity
3: take ticket, 4: remove card, 0: quit
[READY 3 false unknown] Command? 1
Validating your credit card.

1: insert card, 2: check card validity
3: take ticket, 4: remove card, 0: quit
[VALIDATING 3 true unknown] Command? 2
Your credit card is validated. Take your ticket.

1: insert card, 2: check card validity
3: take ticket, 4: remove card, 0: quit
[TICKET_SOLD 3 true yes] Command? 3
Remove your credit card. Enjoy the game!

1: insert card, 2: check card validity
3: take ticket, 4: remove card, 0: quit
[READY 2 true yes] Command? 4
You've removed your credit card.

1: insert card, 2: check card validity
3: take ticket, 4: remove card, 0: quit
[READY 2 false unknown] Command? 0

Done!
```

- We attempt to purchase a ticket when the machine is sold out. The machine remains in the SOLD_OUT state:

```
1: insert card, 2: check card validity
3: take ticket, 4: remove card, 0: quit
[SOLD_OUT 0 false unknown] Command? 1
*** Game sold out. ***
Remove your credit card.

1: insert card, 2: check card validity
3: take ticket, 4: remove card, 0: quit
[SOLD_OUT 0 true unknown] Command? 4
You've removed your credit card.
```

- We change our mind and remove a card while its validity is being checked. The machine returns to the READY state:

```
1: insert card, 2: check card validity
3: take ticket, 4: remove card, 0: quit
[READY 3 false unknown] Command? 1
Validating your credit card.
```

```
1: insert card, 2: check card validity
3: take ticket, 4: remove card, 0: quit
[VALIDATING 3 true unknown] Command? 4
You removed your credit card before it was validated. No sale.

1: insert card, 2: check card validity
3: take ticket, 4: remove card, 0: quit
[READY 3 false unknown] Command?
```

- The machine fails to validate the credit card and rejects it. After we remove the credit card, the machine returns to the READY state:

```
1: insert card, 2: check card validity
3: take ticket, 4: remove card, 0: quit
[READY 2 false unknown] Command? 1
Validating your credit card.

1: insert card, 2: check card validity
3: take ticket, 4: remove card, 0: quit
[VALIDATING 2 true unknown] Command? 2
*** Credit card rejected. ***
Remove your card.

1: insert card, 2: check card validity
3: take ticket, 4: remove card, 0: quit
[READY 2 true no] Command? 4
You've removed your credit card.
```

- We try to take a ticket while the machine is still checking our credit card's validity. This is an unreasonable action, and the machine remains in its current VALIDATING state:

```
1: insert card, 2: check card validity
3: take ticket, 4: remove card, 0: quit
[READY 3 false unknown] Command? 1
Validating your credit card.

1: insert card, 2: check card validity
3: take ticket, 4: remove card, 0: quit
[VALIDATING 3 true unknown] Command? 3
Still checking your credit card's validity.

1: insert card, 2: check card validity
3: take ticket, 4: remove card, 0: quit
[VALIDATING 3 true unknown] Command?
```

As a demonstration, the first version of our example ticket machine application will not use the State Design Pattern, and then we will see its major faults. The second version will use the pattern, and we will gain its benefits.

13.1.1 Desired design features

An application that successfully implements states, behaviors, and state transitions should have the following design features:

- *DF 1*—It is always clear at runtime what is the application's current state.
- *DF 2*—The code for each state, including its behaviors and transitions, should be well encapsulated.
- *DF 3*—The code for each state should handle all the actions, whether reasonable or not for that state.
- *DF 4*—It should be possible to add, remove, or modify states with minimal code changes.
- *DF 5*—There should be minimal dependencies among the states other than the transitions.

13.1.2 Before using the State Design Pattern

For our initial version, we can design our ticket machine simulation application in a straightforward way. We'll see how many of the desired design features it has. Afterward, we'll refactor the application using a design modeled from the State Design Pattern.

Class `TicketMachine` is the heart of the first version of our application (figure 13.2).

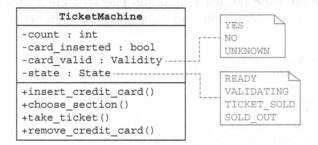

Figure 13.2   Class `TicketMachine` is the heart of the first version of our ticket machine application. Its member variables keep track of the number of tickets, whether a credit card is inserted, the validity of the credit card, and the name of the current state. The public member functions implement the customer and machine actions.

Enum classes `State` and `Validity` represent the state of the ticket machine and the validity of a credit card, respectively. Each has an overloaded output `<<` operator.

> **Listing 13.1   (Program 13.1 Tickets): `Enums.h` (before the design pattern)**

```
#include <iostream>

using namespace std;
```

```
enum class State
{
    READY, VALIDATING, TICKET_SOLD, SOLD_OUT
};

inline ostream& operator <<(ostream& ostr, const State& state)
{
    switch (state)
    {
        case State::READY:       ostr << "READY ";       break;
        case State::VALIDATING:  ostr << "VALIDATING ";  break;
        case State::TICKET_SOLD: ostr << "TICKET_SOLD "; break;
        case State::SOLD_OUT:    ostr << "SOLD_OUT ";    break;
    }

    return ostr;
}

enum class Validity
{
    YES, NO, UNKNOWN
};

inline ostream& operator <<(ostream& ostr, const Validity& valid)
{
    switch (valid)
    {
        case Validity::YES:     ostr << "yes";     break;
        case Validity::NO:      ostr << "no";      break;
        case Validity::UNKNOWN: ostr << "unknown"; break;
    }

    return ostr;
}
```

The private member variables of class `TicketMachine` keep track of the count of tickets, whether a credit card is inserted, the validity of the credit card, and the current state of the machine. Its member functions `insert_credit_card()`, `check_validity()`, `take_ticket()`, and `remove_credit_card()` implement the customer and machine actions (figure 13.1). The initial machine state is READY.

> **Listing 13.2** (Program 13.1 Tickets): `TicketMachine.h` **(before the design pattern)**

```
#include <stdio.h>
#include <stdlib.h>
#include <time.h>

#include "Enums.h"

class TicketMachine
{
public:
    TicketMachine(const int c)
        : count(c), card_inserted(false),
```

```
          card_validity(Validity::UNKNOWN), state(State::READY)      ◄──────┐
    {                                                      Initial READY state
        srand(time(NULL));
    }

    int       get_count()   const { return count; }
    bool      get_inserted() const { return card_inserted; }
    Validity  get_validity() const { return card_validity; }
    State     get()         const { return state; }

    void run();

    void insert_credit_card();   // 1
    void check_validity();       // 2     Action member
    void take_ticket();          // 3     functions
    void remove_credit_card();   // 4

private:
    int       count;
    bool      card_inserted;
    Validity  card_validity;
    State     state;         ◄────── The current machine state
};
```

Each member function must handle all four actions while the ticket machine is in any state, even if the action isn't meaningful for a particular state. The actions cause the machine to have different behaviors, depending on its current state. Some actions can cause state transitions.

Table 13.1 shows the ticket machine behaviors in each state due to action function `insert_credit_card()`. Compare the transitions indicated in this table with the transitions shown in figure 13.1.

Table 13.1   Action function 1: `insert_credit_card()`

Ticket machine state	Machine behaviors in each state
READY	If no card is already inserted,
	▪ Write "Validating your credit card."
	▪ Set `card_inserted` to true.
	▪ Set `card_validity` to unknown.
	▪ **Transition to the VALIDATING state.**
	Else if the already inserted card is invalid,
	▪ Write "Credit card rejected."
	▪ Write "Remove your card."
	Else,
	▪ Write "Remove the already-inserted card."

Table 13.1   Action function 1: `insert_credit_card()` *continued*

Ticket machine state	Machine behaviors in each state
VALIDATING	If the already inserted card is invalid, ■ Write "Credit card rejected." ■ Write "Remove your card." ■ **Transition to the READY state** Else, ■ Write "You've already inserted your card." ■ Write "Checking its validation."
TICKET_SOLD	Write "Take the ticket you've already bought." Set `card_inserted` to true. Set `card_validity` to unknown.
SOLD_OUT	Write "Game sold out." Write "Remove your card." Set `card_inserted` to true. Set `card_validity` to unknown.

Member function `insert_credit_card()` is the starting function for a ticket purchase when the customer inserts a credit card into the ticket machine while the machine is in the READY state. But the function should handle all the actions in all the states. If the machine is in the READY state, and we insert a credit card when the machine doesn't already have a card, the machine transitions to the VALIDATING state.

Listing 13.3   (Program 13.1 Tickets): `TicketMachine.cpp` **(part 1 of 5) (before DP)**

```cpp
#include <iostream>
#include "Enums.h"
#include "TicketMachine.h"

using namespace std;

void TicketMachine::insert_credit_card()  // Action 1
{
    switch (state)
    {
        case State::READY:
        {
            if (!card_inserted)
            {
                cout << "Validating your credit card. " << endl;

                card_inserted = true;
                card_validity = Validity::UNKNOWN;
                state = State::VALIDATING;
            }
            else if (card_validity == Validity::NO)
```

Transition to the
VALIDATING state.

```
                {
                    cout << "*** Credit card rejected. *** " << endl;
                    cout << "Remove your card." << endl;
                }
                else
                {
                    cout << "Remove the credit card that's "
                            << "already inserted." << endl;
                }

                break;
            }

            case State::VALIDATING:
            {
                if (card_validity == Validity::NO)
                {
                    cout << "*** Credit card rejected. *** " << endl;
                    cout << "Remove your card." << endl;
                    state = State::READY;                      ◄─────────┐
                }                                                         │ Transition to the
                else                                                      │ READY state.
                {
                    cout << "You've already inserted your credit card. "
                            << "Checking its validation." << endl;
                }

                break;
            }

            case State::TICKET_SOLD:
            {
                cout << "Take the ticket you've already bought."
                        << endl;

                card_inserted = true;
                card_validity = Validity::UNKNOWN;
                break;
            }

            case State::SOLD_OUT:
            {
                cout << "*** Game sold out. ***" << endl;
                cout << "Remove your credit card." << endl;

                card_inserted = true;
                card_validity = Validity::UNKNOWN;

                break;
            }
        }
    }
}
```

Table 13.2 shows the ticket machine behaviors in each state due to action function
check_validity(). Compare the transitions indicated in this table with the transitions shown in figure 13.1.

Table 13.2   Action function 2: `check_validity()`

Ticket machine state	Machine behaviors in each state
READY	If no card is inserted, ■ Write "First insert your credit card." Else if the card is valid, ■ Write "Remove the already-inserted credit card." Else, ■ Write "Credit card rejected." ■ Write "Remove your card."
VALIDATING	If the card's validity is unknown, ■ Randomly set `card_validity` to either yes or no. If the card is valid, ■ Write "Your credit card is validated." ■ Write "Take your ticket." ■ **Transition to the** `TICKET_SOLD` **state.** Else, ■ Write "Credit card rejected." ■ Write "Remove your card." ■ **Transition to the** `READY` **state.**
TICKET_SOLD	Write "Take the ticket you've already bought."
SOLD_OUT	Write "Game sold out." If a card is inserted ■ Write "Remove your card."

After we've inserted a credit card, and the ticket machine is in the VALIDATING state, member function check_validity() is the machine action of checking whether the machine validated the card. But the function should handle all the actions in all the states, as shown in the following listing. If the card is valid, the machine transitions to the TICKET_SOLD state; otherwise, it returns to the READY state.

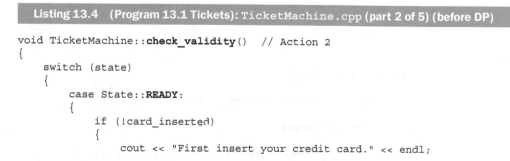

Listing 13.4   (Program 13.1 Tickets): `TicketMachine.cpp` **(part 2 of 5) (before DP)**

```cpp
void TicketMachine::check_validity()   // Action 2
{
    switch (state)
    {
        case State::READY:
        {
            if (!card_inserted)
            {
                cout << "First insert your credit card." << endl;
```

```
    }
    else if (card_validity == Validity::YES)
    {
        cout << "Remove the credit card that's "
             << "already inserted." << endl;
    }
    else
    {
        cout << "*** Credit card rejected. *** " << endl;
        cout << "Remove your card." << endl;
    }

    break;
}

case State::VALIDATING:
{
    if (card_validity == Validity::UNKNOWN)
    {
        bool valid = rand()%2 == 1;
        card_validity = valid ? Validity::YES : Validity::NO;
    }

    if (card_validity == Validity::YES)
    {
        cout << "Your credit card is validated. "
             << "Take your ticket." << endl;

        state = State::TICKET_SOLD;                    ◄────    Transition to the
    }                                                           TICKET_SOLD state.
    else
    {
        cout << "*** Credit card rejected. *** " << endl;
        cout << "Remove your card." << endl;

        state = State::READY;                          ◄────    Transition back to the
    }                                                           READY state.

    break;
}

case State::TICKET_SOLD:
{
    cout << "Take the ticket that you've already bought. "
         << endl;
    break;
}

case State::SOLD_OUT:
{
    cout << "*** Game sold out. ***" << endl;

    if (card_inserted)
    {
        cout << "Remove your credit card." << endl;
    }
```

```
            break;
        }
    }
}
```

Table 13.3 shows the ticket machine behaviors in each state due to action function `take_ticket()`. Compare the transitions indicated in this table with the transitions shown in figure 13.1.

Table 13.3   **Action function 3:** `take_ticket()`

Ticket machine state	Machine behaviors in each state
READY	If no card is inserted, ■ Write "First insert your credit card." Else if the card's validity is unknown, ■ Write "Still checking your card's validity." Else if the card is valid, ■ Write "Take the ticket you've already bought." ■ Write "Remove your credit card." Else, ■ Write "*** Credit card rejected. ***" ■ Write "Remove your credit card."
VALIDATING	If the card's validity is unknown, ■ Write "Still checking your card's validity." Else if the card is valid, ■ Write "Your card is already validated." ■ Write "Take your ticket." Else, ■ Write "*** Credit card rejected. ***" ■ Write "Remove your card."
TICKET_SOLD	Write "Remove your credit card." Write "Enjoy the game!" Decrement the ticket count. If the ticket count > 0, ■ **Transition to the READY state.** Else, ■ **Transition to the SOLD_OUT state.**
SOLD_OUT	Write "Game sold out." If a card is inserted, ■ Write "Remove your card."

Member function `take_ticket()` is the customer action of taking the newly pur-chased ticket when the machine is in the `TICKET_SOLD` state, but it should handle all the actions in all the states. If there are still tickets left, the machine transitions back to the `READY` state. Otherwise, it transitions to the `SOLD_OUT` state.

Listing 13.5   (Program 13.1 Tickets): `TicketMachine.cpp` **(part 3 of 5) (before DP)**

```cpp
void TicketMachine::take_ticket()    // Action 3
{
    switch (state)
    {
        case State::READY:
        {
            if (!card_inserted)
            {
                cout << "First insert your credit card." << endl;
            }
            else if (card_validity == Validity::UNKNOWN)
            {
                cout << "Still checking your credit card's validity."
                    << endl;
            }
            else if (card_validity == Validity::YES)
            {
                cout << "Take the ticket that you've already "
                    << "bought. Remove your card." << endl;
            }
            else
            {
                cout << "*** Credit card rejected. *** " << endl;
                cout << "Remove your card." << endl;
            }

            break;
        }

        case State::VALIDATING:
        {
            if (card_validity == Validity::UNKNOWN)
            {
                cout << "Still checking your credit card's validity."
                    << endl;
            }
            else if (card_validity == Validity::YES)
            {
                cout << "Your card is already validated. "
                    << "Take your ticket." << endl;
            }
            else
            {
                cout << "*** Credit card rejected. *** " << endl;
                cout << "Remove your card." << endl;
            }
```

```
            break;
    }

    case State::TICKET_SOLD:
    {
        cout << "Remove your credit card. "
             << "Enjoy the game!" << endl;

        count--;

        if (count > 0)
        {
            state = State::READY;         ◄────    Transition back to
        }                                           the READY state.
        else
        {
            state = State::SOLD_OUT;      ◄────    Transition to the
        }                                           SOLD_OUT state.

        break;
    }

    case State::SOLD_OUT:
    {
        cout << "*** Game sold out. ***" << endl;

        if (card_inserted)
        {
            cout << "Remove your credit card." << endl;
        }

        break;
    }
}
```

Table 13.4 shows the ticket machine behaviors in each state due to action function `remove_credit_card()`. Compare the transitions indicated in this table with the transitions shown in figure 13.1.

Table 13.4 Action function 4: `remove_credit_card()`

Ticket machine state	Machine behaviors in each state
READY	If a card is inserted,
	■ Write "You've removed your credit card."
	Else,
	■ Write "No credit card inserted."
	Set `card_inserted` to false.
	Set `card_validity` to unknown.

Table 13.4   Action function 4: `remove_credit_card()` *continued*

Ticket machine state	Machine behaviors in each state
VALIDATING	If no card is inserted,
	■ Write "No credit card inserted."
	Else if the card is invalid,
	■ Write "*** Credit card rejected. ***"
	■ Write "Remove your card."
	Else,
	■ Write "You removed your credit card. No sale."
	Set `card_inserted` to false.
	Set `card_validity` to unknown.
	Transition to the READY state.
TICKET_SOLD	Write "First take your ticket."
SOLD_OUT	If card is inserted,
	■ Write "You've removed your credit card."
	■ Set `card_inserted` to false.
	■ Set `card_validity` to unknown.
	Else,
	■ Write "No credit card inserted."

Member function `remove_credit_card()` is the action if we remove the credit card from the ticket machine when it is in the READY or the VALIDATING state. But as usual, it should handle all the actions in all the states. If we removed the card when the machine is in the VALIDATING state (the machine hasn't yet validated the card), the machine transitions back to the READY state.

Listing 13.6   (Program 13.1 Tickets): `TicketMachine.cpp` (part 4 of 5) (before DP)

```cpp
void TicketMachine::remove_credit_card()  // Action 4
{
    switch (state)
    {
        case State::READY:
        {
            if (card_inserted)
            {
                cout << "You've removed your credit card." << endl;
            }
            else
            {
                cout << "No credit card inserted." << endl;
            }

            card_inserted = false;
```

```
            card_validity = Validity::UNKNOWN;
            break;
        }

        case State::VALIDATING:
        {
            if (!card_inserted)
            {
                cout << "No credit card inserted." << endl;
            }
            else if (card_validity == Validity::NO)
            {
                cout << "*** Credit card rejected. *** " << endl;
                cout << "Remove your card." << endl;
            }
            else
            {
                cout << "You removed your credit card before it "
                     << "was validated. No sale." << endl;
            }

            card_inserted = false;
            card_validity = Validity::UNKNOWN;
            state = State::READY;        ◄─────────┐  Transition back to
            break;                                  │  the READY state.
        }

        case State::TICKET_SOLD:
        {
            cout << "First take your ticket." << endl;
            break;
        }

        case State::SOLD_OUT:
        {
            if (card_inserted)
            {
                cout << "You've removed your credit card." << endl;

                card_inserted = false;
                card_validity = Validity::UNKNOWN;
            }
            else
            {
                cout << "No credit card inserted." << endl;
            }

            break;
        }
    }
}
```

Finally, member function run() runs the simulation.

Listing 13.7   (Program 13.1 Tickets): `TicketMachine.cpp` (part 5 of 5) (before DP)

```cpp
void TicketMachine::run()
{
    int command;

    do
    {
        cout << endl;
        cout << "1: insert card, 2: check card validity" << endl;
        cout << "3: take ticket, 4: remove card, 0: quit" << endl;
        cout << "[" << state << " " << count
             << " " << boolalpha << card_inserted
             << " " << card_validity << "] ";
        cout << "Command? ";

        cin >> command;              ◀──────┐ Read 1, 2, 3, 4, or 0
                                            │ from the user.
        switch (command)
        {
            case 1: insert_credit_card(); break;
            case 2: check_validity();     break;   │ Perform customer and
            case 3: take_ticket();        break;   │ machine actions.
            case 4: remove_credit_card(); break;

            case 0: cout << endl << "Done!" << endl; break;

            default: cout << "*** Invalid command. ***" << endl;
        }

    } while (command != 0);
}
```

The test program creates a `TicketMachine` object with three tickets and calls the `run()` member function.

Listing 13.8 (Program 13.1 Tickets): `tester.cpp`

```cpp
#include <iostream>
#include "TicketMachine.h"

using namespace std;

int main()
{
    TicketMachine machine(3);
    machine.run();

    return 0;
}
```

But class `TicketMachine` is awfully complicated! Its design is focused on the actions — each action 1, 2, 3, and 4 has its own method function. The state behaviors are scattered among the action functions. Adding, removing, or modifying a state would be difficult. The design violates DF 2, DF 3, and DF 4.

The class has way too many responsibilities! The State Design Pattern will do a much better job of encapsulating the states and their behaviors.

This version of our ticket machine application works correctly. We can interact with it and see proper behaviors. But it has major faults, including the following:

- *Multiple responsibilities*—Class `TicketMachine` not only has to keep track of the machine's state but is also responsible for all the actions that occur in all the states. All the application logic is concentrated in this one class.
- *Poor encapsulation*—The states and their behaviors are not well encapsulated.
- *Inflexible code*—If we need to modify, add, or remove ticket machine states and their actions, we will need to change the `TicketMachine` class.

13.1.3 *After using the State Design Pattern*

The State Design Pattern provides a model for a software architecture that eliminates these faults (figure 13.3). Each subclass of superclass `State` represents a ticket machine state, and each `State` subclass encapsulates handling all the customer and machine actions for its state. Class `StatesBlock` privately aggregates all the `State` subclasses, and its public member function `get_initial_state()` returns the ticket machine's initial state. Class `StatesBlock` enables the `State` subclasses to be loosely coupled with each other and class `TicketMachine` to be loosely coupled with the `State` subclasses.

Member variable `state` of class `TicketMachine` points to the `State` object that represents the current state of the machine. Through polymorphism, the class defers handling each of its action member functions `insert_credit_card()`, `check_validity()`, `take_ticket()`, and `remove_credit_card()` to the corresponding action member function of the current `State` object. Each of the `State` subclass action member functions returns a `State` object that is the next state that the machine should transition to.

The State Design Pattern

"Allow an object to alter its behavior when its internal state changes. The object will appear to change its class" (GoF 305).

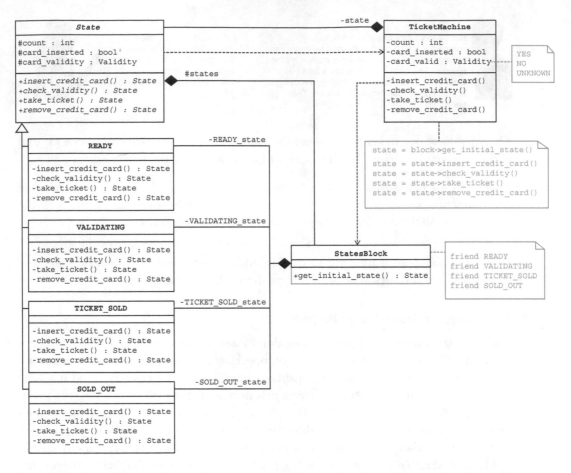

Figure 13.3   The subclasses of superclass State **encapsulate handling the customer and machine actions for each state of the ticket machine. Each action member function of the subclasses returns a** State **object that is the next state for the ticket machine to transition to. By aggregating the subclasses in class** StatesBlock, **the subclasses are loosely coupled with each other, and class** TicketMachine **is loosely coupled with the** State **subclasses. Each action member function of class** TicketMachine **defers to the corresponding member function of the current** State **object pointed to by the private** state **member variable.**

Class TicketMachine is much simpler in this version of the application because it no longer has the responsibility to manage the states and their customer and machine actions (listing 13.9). The constructor creates the StatesBlock object by passing the count, card_inserted, and card_validity member variables by reference so that the State subclasses can access and modify their values as they perform the runtime behaviors. The constructor also sets the initial value of the state member variable by calling the StatesBlock class's get_initial_state() member function.

Modeling the new version of the ticket machine application after the State Design Pattern added so many more classes!

Yes, but the added **State** classes are cohesive and loosely coupled with each other. The application has become much more flexible.

Member variable state always points to the State object representing the current machine state. Class TicketMachine defers handling each of the action member functions insert_credit_card(), check_validity(), take_ticket(), and remove_credit_card() to the current State object. Therefore, it's the current State object that dictates how the ticket machine behaves for each customer action. Each action member function returns the State object that is the next state the machine should transition to. If a customer performs an unreasonable action that requires no transition, the action function simply returns the State object for the current state.

Listing 13.9   (Program 13.2 Tickets-StateDP): `TicketMachine.h`

```
#include <time.h>

#include "Enums.h"
#include "State.h"
#include "StatesBlock.h"

class TicketMachine
{
public:
    TicketMachine(const int c)
        : count(c), card_inserted(false),
          card_validity(Validity::UNKNOWN)
    {
        srand(time(NULL));

        StatesBlock *block = new StatesBlock(count, card_inserted,
                                             card_validity);
        state = block->get_initial_state();

    }

    void run();

    void insert_credit_card()
    {
        state = state->insert_credit_card();
    }

    void check_validity()
    {
        state = state->check_validity();
    }

    void take_ticket()
```

Create the block of State objects by passing arguments by reference.

Set the initial state.

Defer actions to the current State object and get the next state.

```
    {
        state = state->take_ticket();
    }

    void remove_credit_card()
    {
        state = state->remove_credit_card();
    }
```

**Defer actions to the
current State object
and get the next state.**

```
private:
    int      count;
    bool     card_inserted;
    Validity card_validity;

    State *state;
};
```

**The current
State object**

The `run()` member function that simulates running the ticket machine requires a small change in one of the output statements (highlighted in bold):

```
cout << "[" << state->get_id() << " " << count
     << " " << boolalpha << card_inserted
     << " " << card_validity << "] ";
```

The constructor of class `StatesBlock` receives the `count`, `card_inserted`, and `card_validity` parameters from class `TicketMachine` by reference. It then passes these parameters in turn by reference to create and aggregate the `READY`, `VALIDATING`, `TICKET_SOLD`, and `SOLD_OUT` objects of the `State` subclasses.

Listing 13.10   (Program 13.2 Tickets-StateDP): `StatesBlock.h`

```
#include "State.h"

class StatesBlock
{
public:
    StatesBlock(int& count, bool& card_inserted,
                Validity& card_validity)
    {
        READY_state = new READY(*this, count,
                                card_inserted,
                                card_validity);
        VALIDATING_state = new VALIDATING(*this, count,
                                          card_inserted,
                                          card_validity);
        TICKET_SOLD_state = new TICKET_SOLD(*this, count,
                                            card_inserted,
                                            card_validity);
        SOLD_OUT_state = new SOLD_OUT(*this, count,
                                      card_inserted,
                                      card_validity);
    }

    ~StatesBlock()
```

**Receive parameters by
reference from class
TicketMachine.**

**Pass the same parameters by reference
to construct the State objects.**

```
{
    delete READY_state;
    delete VALIDATING_state;
    delete TICKET_SOLD_state;
    delete SOLD_OUT_state;
}

State *get_initial_state() const { return READY_state; }

friend READY;
friend VALIDATING;
friend TICKET_SOLD;
friend SOLD_OUT;

private:
    READY        *READY_state;
    VALIDATING   *VALIDATING_state;
    TICKET_SOLD  *TICKET_SOLD_state;
    SOLD_OUT     *SOLD_OUT_state;
};
```

The initial READY state

The aggregated
State objects

Class State is the superclass of subclasses READY, VALIDATING, TICKET_SOLD, and
SOLD_OUT (listing 13.11). Its constructor receives its parameters by reference from
the constructors of its subclasses. It stores the references into its protected reference
member variables count, card_inserted, and card_validity. Each of its subclasses
will then be able to access and modify the corresponding member variables of class
TicketMachine as they execute their respective behaviors.

The protected member variable states is a reference to class StatesBlock that
aggregates the State subclasses. By aggregating the subclasses in class StatesBlock,
the subclasses are loosely coupled with each other, and class TicketMachine is loosely
coupled with the State subclasses.

Listing 13.11   (Program 13.2 Tickets-StateDP): State.h (part 1 of 2)

```
#include <string>
#include "Enums.h"

using namespace std;

class StatesBlock;

class State
{
public:
    State(const string id, StatesBlock& states_block,
        int& count, bool& card_inserted, Validity& card_validity)
        : id(id), states(states_block),
          count(count), card_inserted(card_inserted),
          card_validity(card_validity) {}
    virtual ~State() {}

    friend class TicketMachine;
```

Reference parameters
passed by the subclasses.

```
private:
    string id;

protected:
    StatesBlock& states;

    int&      count;                          Reference variables to enable the
    bool&     card_inserted;                   subclasses to access and modify
    Validity& card_validity;                   TicketMachine member variables.

    virtual State *insert_credit_card() = 0;  // Action 1
    virtual State *check_validity()     = 0;  // Action 2     To be implemented
    virtual State *take_ticket()        = 0;  // Action 3     by each subclass
    virtual State *remove_credit_card() = 0;  // Action 4
};
```

Each `State` subclass must implement the customer action member functions `insert_credit_card()`, `check_validity()`, `take_ticket()`, and `remove_credit_card()` to perform the customer and machine action behaviors that we've defined for each state. Each member function returns a `State` object that is the next state for the ticket machine to transition to.

Listing 13.12   (Program 13.2 Tickets-StateDP): `State.h` **(part 2 of 2)**

```
class READY : public State                    Parameters passed by reference
{                                             from class TicketMachine
public:
    READY(StatesBlock& states, int& count,
          bool& card_inserted, Validity& card_validity)
        : State("READY", states, count,
                card_inserted, card_validity) {}

private:
    State *insert_credit_card() override;  // Action 1
    State *check_validity()     override;  // Action 2
    State *take_ticket()        override;  // Action 3
    State *remove_credit_card() override;  // Action 4
};

class VALIDATING : public State
{
public:
    VALIDATING(StatesBlock& states, int& count,
               bool& card_inserted, Validity& card_validity)
        : State("VALIDATING", states, count,
                card_inserted, card_validity) {}

private:
    State *insert_credit_card() override;  // Action 1
    State *check_validity()     override;  // Action 2
    State *take_ticket()        override;  // Action 3
    State *remove_credit_card() override;  // Action 4
};
```

```
class TICKET_SOLD : public State
{
public:
    TICKET_SOLD(StatesBlock& states, int& count,
                bool& card_inserted, Validity& card_validity)
        : State("TICKET_SOLD", states, count,
                card_inserted, card_validity) {}

private:
    State *insert_credit_card() override;   // Action 1
    State *check_validity()     override;   // Action 2
    State *take_ticket()        override;   // Action 3
    State *remove_credit_card() override;   // Action 4
};

class SOLD_OUT : public State
{
public:
    SOLD_OUT(StatesBlock& states, int& count,
             bool& card_inserted, Validity& card_validity)
        : State("SOLD_OUT", states, count,
                card_inserted, card_validity) {}

private:
    State *insert_credit_card() override;   // Action 1
    State *check_validity()     override;   // Action 2
    State *take_ticket()        override;   // Action 3
    State *remove_credit_card() override;   // Action 4
};
```

Parameters passed by reference from class TicketMachine

In the first version of our application, class **TicketMachine** grouped the behaviors by action first and then by ticket machine state.

By using the State Design Pattern to model the application, we now have a cohesive **State** object representing each machine state, and each **State** object encapsulates action behaviors relevant to its state.

To appreciate the change in architecture from the first version of our application to the current version, compare the following listings of the State subclass implementations to listings 13.2–13.7.

State subclass READY encapsulates all the customer and machine actions when the machine is in the READY state (listing 13.13). Each of the action member functions insert_credit_card(), check_validity(), take_ticket(), and remove_credit_card() performs the behavior of the action for the READY state and then returns the next state for the ticket machine to transition to. For example,

```
return states.VALIDATING_state;
```

If there shouldn't be a transition, the return statement is

```
return this;
```

which means to stay in the current state.

Listing 13.13   (Program 13.2 Tickets-StateDP): `READY.cpp`

```cpp
#include <iostream>
#include "Enums.h"
#include "State.h"
#include "StatesBlock.h"

using namespace std;

State *READY::insert_credit_card()  // Action 1
{
    if (!card_inserted)
    {
        cout << "Validating your credit card. " << endl;

        card_inserted = true;
        card_validity = Validity::UNKNOWN;
        return states.VALIDATING_state;
    }
    else if (card_validity == Validity::NO)
    {
        cout << "*** Credit card rejected. *** " << endl;
        cout << "Remove your card." << endl;
        return this;
    }
    else
    {
        cout << "Remove the credit card that's "
            << "already inserted." << endl;
        return this;
    }
}

State *READY::check_validity()  // Action 2
{
    if (card_inserted)
    {
        cout << "First insert your credit card." << endl;
    }
    else if (card_validity == Validity::YES)
    {
        cout << "Remove the credit card that's "
            << "already inserted." << endl;
    }
    else
    {
        cout << "*** Credit card rejected. *** " << endl;
        cout << "Remove your card." << endl;
    }

    return this;
}

State *READY::take_ticket()  // Action 3
{
```

```
    if (!card_inserted)
    {
        cout << "First insert your credit card." << endl;
    }
    else if (card_validity == Validity::UNKNOWN)
    {
        cout << "Still checking your credit card's validity."
            << endl;
    }
    else if (card_validity == Validity::YES)
    {
        cout << "Take the ticket that you've already "
            << "bought. Remove your card." << endl;
    }
    else
    {
        cout << "*** Credit card rejected. *** " << endl;
        cout << "Remove your card." << endl;
    }

    return this;
}

State *READY::remove_credit_card()  // Action 4
{
    if (card_inserted)
    {
        cout << "You've removed your credit card." << endl;
    }
    else
    {
        cout << "No credit card inserted." << endl;
    }

    card_inserted = false;
    card_validity = Validity::UNKNOWN;
    return this;
}
```

State subclass VALIDATING encapsulates all the customer and machine actions when the machine is in the VALIDATING state.

Listing 13.14 **(Program 13.2 Tickets-StateDP):** VALIDATING.cpp

```
#include <iostream>
#include "Enums.h"
#include "State.h"
#include "StatesBlock.h"

using namespace std;

State *VALIDATING::insert_credit_card()  // Action 1
{
    if (card_validity == Validity::NO)
    {
```

```cpp
            cout << "*** Credit card rejected. *** " << endl;
            cout << "Remove your card." << endl;

            return states.READY_state;
        }
        else
        {
            cout << "You've already inserted your credit card. "
                 << "Checking its validation." << endl;

            return this;
        }

    }


State *VALIDATING::check_validity()   // Action 2
{
    if (card_validity == Validity::UNKNOWN)
    {
        bool valid = rand()%2 == 1;
        card_validity = valid ? Validity::YES : Validity::NO;
    }

    if (card_validity == Validity::YES)
    {
        cout << "Your credit card is validated. "
             << "Take your ticket." << endl;

        return states.TICKET_SOLD_state;
    }
    else
    {
        cout << "*** Credit card rejected. *** " << endl;
        cout << "Remove your card." << endl;

        return states.READY_state;
    }
}


State *VALIDATING::take_ticket()   // Action 3
{
    if (card_validity == Validity::UNKNOWN)
    {
        cout << "Still checking your credit card's validity."
             << endl;
    }
    else if (card_validity == Validity::YES)
    {
        cout << "Your card is already validated. "
             << "Take your ticket." << endl;
    }
    else
    {
        cout << "*** Credit card rejected. *** " << endl;
        cout << "Remove your card." << endl;
```

```
    }

    return this;
}


State *VALIDATING::remove_credit_card()   // Action 4
{
    if (!card_inserted)
    {
        cout << "No credit card inserted." << endl;
    }
    else if (card_validity == Validity::NO)
    {
        cout << "*** Credit card rejected. *** " << endl;
        cout << "Remove your card." << endl;
    }
    else
    {
        cout << "You removed your credit card before it "
            << "was validated. No sale." << endl;
    }

    card_inserted = false;
    card_validity = Validity::UNKNOWN;
    return states.READY_state;
}
```

State subclass TICKET_SOLD encapsulates all the customer and machine actions when the machine is in the TICKET_SOLD state.

Listing 13.15   (Program 13.2 Tickets-StateDP): TICKET_SOLD.cpp

```
#include <iostream>
#include "Enums.h"
#include "State.h"
#include "StatesBlock.h"

using namespace std;

State *TICKET_SOLD::insert_credit_card()   // Action 1
{
    cout << "Take the ticket you've already bought."
        << endl;

    card_inserted = true;
    card_validity = Validity::UNKNOWN;
    return this;
}


State *TICKET_SOLD::check_validity()   // Action 2
{
    cout << "Take the ticket that you've already bought. "
        << endl;

    return this;
```

```
}

State *TICKET_SOLD::take_ticket()   // Action 3
{
    cout << "Remove your credit card. "
        << "Enjoy the game!" << endl;

    count--;

    if (count > 0)
    {
        return states.READY_state;
    }
    else
    {
        return states.SOLD_OUT_state;
    }
}

State *TICKET_SOLD::remove_credit_card()   // Action 4
{
    cout << "First take your ticket." << endl;

    return this;
}
```

State subclass SOLD_OUT encapsulates all the customer and machine actions when the machine is in the SOLD_OUT state. There are no transitions out of the SOLD_OUT state.

Listing 13.16   (Program 13.2 Tickets-StateDP): SOLD_OUT.cpp

```
#include <iostream>
#include "Enums.h"
#include "State.h"

using namespace std;

State *SOLD_OUT::insert_credit_card()   // Action 1
{
    cout << "*** Game sold out. ***" << endl;
    cout << "Remove your credit card." << endl;

    card_inserted = true;
    card_validity = Validity::UNKNOWN;
    return this;
}

State *SOLD_OUT::check_validity()   // Action 2
{
    cout << "*** Game sold out. ***" << endl;

    if (card_inserted)
    {
        cout << "Remove your credit card." << endl;
```

```
    }

    return this;
}

State *SOLD_OUT::take_ticket()   // Action 3
{
    cout << "*** Game sold out. ***" << endl;

    if (card_inserted)
    {
        cout << "Remove your credit card." << endl;
    }

    return this;
}

State *SOLD_OUT::remove_credit_card()   // Action 4
{
    if (card_inserted)
    {
        cout << "You've removed your credit card." << endl;

        card_inserted = false;
        card_validity = Validity::UNKNOWN;
    }
    else
    {
        cout << "No credit card inserted." << endl;
    }

    return this;
}
```

This version of our ticket machine application works similarly to the first version. But modeling it from the State Design Pattern has the following benefits:

- *Encapsulated customer actions*—Each `State` subclass encapsulates all the customer actions when the ticket machine is in the corresponding state. It will be possible to modify the behavior of a state or to remove or add states without changing the other `State` subclasses or class `TicketMachine`. This is the Encapsulate What Varies Principle (section 2.3.2).

- *Single responsibility classes*—Class `TicketMachine` only has the responsibility to keep track of the values of its current `state` and the other member variables. It no longer is responsible for the customer actions of each state. This is the Single Responsibility Principle (section 2.3).

- *Loosely coupled classes*—The `State` subclasses are loosely coupled with each other and class `TicketMachine` is loosely coupled with the `State` subclasses. Following the Principle of Least Knowledge (section 2.3.2), class `TicketMachine` has no dependencies on any of the `State` subclasses.

13.1.4 *State's generic model*

Figure 13.4 shows the generic model of the State Design Pattern. Recall that it is from the design pattern's generic model that we can create a custom solution to an architecture problem (section 8.1.3).

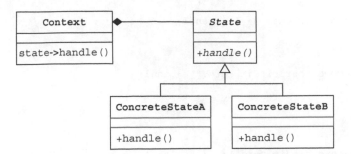

Figure 13.4   The generic model of the State Design Pattern. Compare it with figure 13.3. Instead of the Context class aggregating the State subclasses as shown above, figure 13.3 shows the State subclasses encapsulated in the StatesBlock class, which allows the State subclasses to be loosely coupled with each other and the TicketMachine class to be loosely coupled with the State subclasses. Also in figure 13.3, each of the customer action member functions returns the State object the ticket machine will transition to.

Table 13.5 shows how the example application applies the pattern.

Table 13.5   The State Method Design Pattern as applied by the example application

Design pattern	Applied by the example application
Class Context	Class TicketMachine (using class StatesBlock)
Superclass State	Superclass State
Subclasses ConcreteStateA, ConcreteStateB, etc.	Subclasses READY, VALIDATING, TICKET_SOLD, and SOLD_OUT
Member function handle()	Member functions insert_credit_card(), check_validity(), take_ticket(), and remove_credit_card()

The second version of our ticket machine application goes beyond what the State Design Pattern models, doesn't it?

Yes. By introducing class **statesBlock**, we added the extra feature of making class **TicketMachine** loosely coupled with the **State** classes.

Both the State Design Pattern and the Visitor Design Pattern share the philosophy of separating the data from operations on the data. The Visitor Design Pattern models an architecture that encapsulates different algorithms operating on the objects of a data structure according to the different datatypes of the objects. The State Design Pattern models an architecture that encapsulates different object behaviors according to the different states of the object.

Summary

- The State Design Pattern models a solution for a software architecture where it's important to monitor the runtime states of a particular object.
- A set of actions performed on the object causes it to behave according to its current state.
- Some actions cause the object to make state transitions.
- Separate state classes each encapsulates the action behaviors of the object when it is in that state.
- Each state class must implement all the action behaviors.

The Singleton, Composite, and Decorator Design Patterns

This chapter's design patterns provide models for solving architecture problems where we must manage a collection of one or more objects so that the it behaves in a unified way. Applying the right design pattern can simplify the application's code that works with the objects, and it can also make the code more flexible.

Manning Comix

The Singleton Design Pattern models the simplest case of a collection with only one object. Only one instance of its class, the singleton object, can exist during the application's run time.

The Composite Design Pattern provides a model for an application that manages objects stored in a hierarchical tree structure. The application can greatly reduce the complexity of its code if it can treat an individual object the same way it treats a composite of objects.

We may want our application to add responsibilities to an object in the form of attributes and behaviors at run time but without changing the object's code. These additional responsibilities, in the form of objects, are called "decorations" by the Decorator Design Pattern, which provides a model that handles an object's decorations in a flexible manner.

NOTE   Be sure to read the introduction to part 4 for important information about design patterns in general and to learn how this and subsequent chapters teach each pattern.

14.1   *The Singleton Design Pattern ensures a class has only one object*

Suppose your application needs to print to one or more printers. Whenever your application wants to print something, it must access a `PrintSpooler` object. Your application doesn't know whether the spooler object already exists. If the object doesn't exist, one is created without your application knowing that it happened. Each time your application wants to print, it accesses the same `PrintSpooler` object, and thus, at most one `PrintSpooler` object exists. Therefore, the object is a *singleton* object. The Singleton Design Pattern provides a model for a software architecture that supports such an object.

For our concrete example, assume that the college sports stadium has an executive suite available for use during only certain sporting events. There is only one pass that allows someone to use the suite whenever it's available. The pass is a singleton object, and there can be at most one of them.

14.1.1 Desired design features

An application that can have at most one instance of a particular class should have the following design features:

- *DF 1*—There must be a way for the application to access the singleton object.
- *DF 2*—Whenever the application needs the singleton object, it must always access the same object.
- *DF 3*—If the singleton object doesn't already exist, one must be created without any action by the application.
- *DF 4*—The singleton object doesn't need to exist if the application never accesses the object.
- *DF 5*—There can never be more than one instance of the singleton object.

14.1.2 Before using the Singleton Design Pattern

The first version of our application will not use the Singleton Design Pattern, and it will fail to have all the desired design features. Then, we'll refactor that application using the design pattern.

An obvious solution to having a singleton object is to make it the value of a global variable. In the first version of our application, class `ExecutivePass` is a straightforward implementation of the executive pass (figure 14.1).

```
        ExecutivePass
-----------------------------
-key : int
-holder : string
-----------------------------
+obtain(string)
+print()
-generate_key() : int
```

**Figure 14.1
Our first attempt
at a singleton
class**

Member function `obtain()` allows a named user to obtain and hold the pass (listing 14.1). The pass has a randomly generated four-digit `key` to identify it. Member function `print()` prints the name of the `holder` and the value of the `key`.

As we did with the `Date` class in section 6.2.2, we'll override and instrument the copy constructor and the copy assignment operator. This action will show how a singleton object can fail if it isn't designed properly.

> **Listing 14.1   (Program 14.1 ExecPass):** `ExecutivePass.h` **(before the design pattern)**

```cpp
#include <iostream>
#include <string>
#include <stdlib.h>

using namespace std;

class ExecutivePass
{
```

```
public:
    ExecutivePass() : key(generate_key()) {}              ◄─── Default constructor

    ExecutivePass(ExecutivePass& other) : key(generate_key()) {}   ◄──┐
                                                                      │  Copy
    ExecutivePass& operator =(ExecutivePass& other)   ◄──┐           │  constructor
    {                                                    │
        key = generate_key();          Copy assignment operator
        return *this;
    }

    void obtain(const string hldr) { holder = hldr; }

    void print()
    {
        cout << "Executive pass now held by " << holder
            << ", key = " << key << endl;
    }

private:
    int key;
    string holder;

    int generate_key() const { return rand()%10000 + 1000; }
};
```

In the test program, the value of the global variable pass is the ExecutivePass object.

Listing 14.2   (Program 14.1 ExecPass): tester.cpp (before using the design pattern)

```
#include <iostream>
#include "ExecutivePass.h"

ExecutivePass pass;

using namespace std;

int main()
{                                                    Ron obtains
    pass.obtain("Ron");          ◄──────────────┘    the global pass.
    cout << "obtain: "; pass.print();
                                                     Transfer the
    pass.obtain("Sal");          ◄──────────────┘    global pass to Sal.
    cout << "obtain: "; pass.print();

    ExecutivePass copy1;
    copy1 = pass;                               A local copy of the pass that is
    copy1.obtain("Bob");                        the target of an assignment
    cout << "copy 1: "; copy1.print();

    ExecutivePass copy2(pass);                  A local copy of the pass created
    copy2.obtain("Flo");                        by the copy constructor
    cout << "copy 2: "; copy2.print();

    return 0;
}
```

The program's output is

```
obtain: Executive pass now held by Ron, key = 7807
obtain: Executive pass now held by Sal, key = 7807
copy 1: Executive pass now held by Bob, key = 1073
copy 2: Executive pass now held by Flo, key = 4658
```

Obviously, this version of our application has failed. User Ron obtained the global `pass` object with its key value. The same object was successfully transferred to Sal. But we were able to create a copy of the pass, `copy1`, by assignment, which user Bob obtained. It had its own key value. Finally, we used the copy constructor to create `copy2` obtained by user Flo, and it had its own key value. We ended up with three copies of the supposedly singleton object.

Because the pass is a global object, it's automatically created when the application starts. Therefore, it exists regardless of whether it's ever accessed. That violates DF 4.

It's easy to forget about the copy constructor and the assignment operator, both of which can create copies of an object. We ended up with three copies of the singleton object. That violates DF 5.

The major faults of the first version of our application are

- *Use of a global variable*—We should not have global variables in a well-designed application. Different parts of the application can access a global variable. One part can change the variable's value unbeknownst to other parts that weren't expecting the change, resulting in unwanted surprises and possible logic errors.

- *Order of creation*—If different global objects declared in different source files depend on each other, logic errors can occur because the order in which the objects are created when the application starts is undefined.

- *Object always present*—In our example, the executive suite is not open for every sporting event. As we defined the pass globally, it is always present. This can be a problem if the singleton object is costly to construct or consumes many resources. We can't delete the global object.

- *Local copies*—We were able to create additional local copies of the singleton object.

- *Possibility to copy and assign the object*—These operations will create more instances of the supposedly singleton object.

14.1.3 *After using the Singleton Design Pattern*

We can fix the problems with class `ExecutivePass` by refactoring the code to model it after the Singleton Design Pattern.

> **The Singleton Design Pattern**
>
> "Ensure a class has only once instance, and provide a global point of access to it" (GoF 127).

We must make several significant changes (figure 14.2):

- We must make the constructor private. We cannot allow code to declare an `ExecutivePass` object or to create one dynamically with `new`. We must control the creation of a singleton pass object and should create a singleton object only when it's needed (lazy construction).
- We must disable the copy constructor and the copy assignment operator. We must not allow code to make copies of a singleton object.
- A private static `ExecutivePass` member variable must point to the one and only singleton object if it exists. Otherwise, the variable's value must be `nullptr`.
- A public static `obtain()` member function must return the pointer to the singleton object and set who's holding the pass. It must create the object if it doesn't already exist. `ExecutivePass::obtain()` is the global point of access to the singleton object.
- Deleting the singleton object must enable creating a new one later.

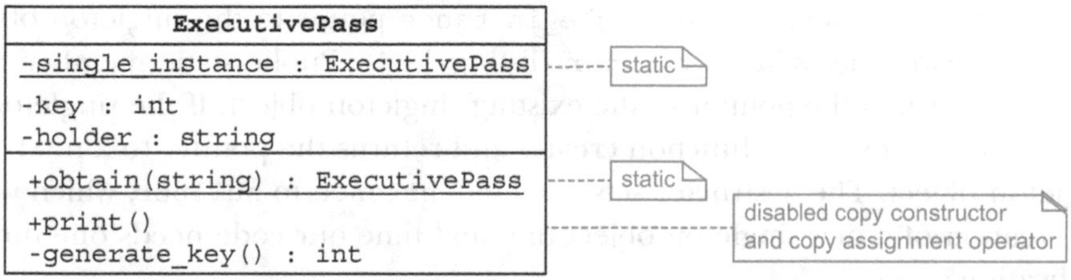

Figure 14.2   A well-designed singleton object. The constructor is private. The copy constructor and the copy assignment operator are both disabled. The static private member variable `single_instance` points to the singleton object, and the static public member function `obtain()` returns the value of the pointer.

We make the constructor private and disable the copy constructor and copy assignment operator.

Listing 14.3   (Program 14.2 ExecPass-SingletonDP): `ExecutivePass.h`

```
#include <iostream>
#include <string>
#include <stdlib.h>

using namespace std;
```

```
class ExecutivePass
{
public:
    ~ExecutivePass();

    ExecutivePass(ExecutivePass& other) = delete;
    ExecutivePass& operator =(ExecutivePass& other) = delete;

    int get_key() const { return key; }

    static ExecutivePass *obtain(const string holder);

    void print()
    {
        cout << "Executive pass now held by " << holder
            << ", key = " << key << endl;
    }

private:
    ExecutivePass() : key(generate_key()) {}

    static ExecutivePass *single_instance;

    int key;
    string holder;

    int generate_key() const { return rand()%10000 + 1000; }
};
```

Disable the copy constructor and the copy assignment operator.

Private constructor ◀——

Static pointer to the singleton object ◀——

Private static member variable `single_instance` points to the singleton object if it exists; otherwise, its value is `nullptr` (listing 14.4). Public static member function `obtain()` returns the pointer to the existing singleton object. If the singleton object doesn't already exist, the function creates and returns the pointer to a newly created singleton object. The destructor sets `single_instance` to `nullptr`, which will allow the creation of a new singleton object the next time our code needs one during the application's run.

Listing 14.4   (Program 14.2 ExecPass-SingletonDP): `ExecutivePass.cpp`

Initialize single_instance to nullptr to allow the creation of a new singleton object.

```
#include "ExecutivePass.h"

ExecutivePass *ExecutivePass::single_instance = nullptr;        ◀——

ExecutivePass::~ExecutivePass()
{
    single_instance = nullptr;        ◀——  Return the pointer to the
}                                           existing singleton object.

ExecutivePass *ExecutivePass::obtain(const string holder)        ◀——
{
    if (single_instance == nullptr)
    {
```

Create and return the pointer to a newly created singleton object if one doesn't already exist.

```
            single_instance = new ExecutivePass();
    }

    single_instance->holder = holder;
    return single_instance;
}
```

The test program demonstrates that we now have a properly behaving singleton `Exec-utivePass` object.

Listing 14.5 (Program 14.2 ExecPass-SingletonDP): `tester.cpp`

```cpp
#include <iostream>
#include "ExecutivePass.h"

using namespace std;

ExecutivePass *ExecutivePass::single_instance = nullptr;

int main()
{
    ExecutivePass *pass = ExecutivePass::obtain("Ron");
    cout << "obtain: "; pass->print();

    pass = ExecutivePass::obtain("Sal");
    cout << "obtain: "; pass->print();

    delete pass;
    cout << "delete" << endl;

    pass = ExecutivePass::obtain("Bob");
    cout << "obtain: "; pass->print();

    pass = ExecutivePass::obtain("Flo");
    cout << "obtain: "; pass->print();

    delete pass;
    return 0;
}
```

The output is

```
obtain: Executive pass now held by Ron, key = 7807
obtain: Executive pass now held by Sal, key = 7807
delete
obtain: Executive pass now held by Bob, key = 6249
obtain: Executive pass now held by Flo, key = 6249
```

Ron obtains the pass.

Transfers the pass to Sal

Transfers the pass to Flo

After deleting the old pass, Bob obtains a new pass.

14.1.4 *Singleton's generic model*

Figure 14.3 shows the generic model of the Singleton Design Pattern. Recall that it is from the design pattern's generic model that we can create a custom solution to an architecture problem (section 8.1.3).

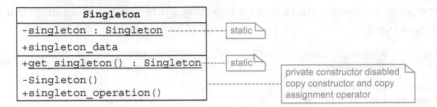

Figure 14.3   The generic model of the Composite Design Pattern. Compare with figure 14.2. The private static member variable `singleton` points to the `Singleton` object if it exists; otherwise, its value is `nullptr`. The private static member function `get_singleton()` returns a pointer to the existing `Singleton` object. If the singleton object doesn't already exist, the function creates and returns the pointer to a newly created `Singleton` object.

Table 14.1 shows how the example application applies the pattern.

Table 14.1   The Singleton Method Design Pattern as applied by the example application

Design pattern	Applied by the example application
Class `Singleton`	Class `ExecutivePass`
Static member variable `singleton`	Static member variable `single_instance`
Static member function `get_singleton()`	Static member function `obtain()`
Private constructor `Singleton()`	Private constructor `ExecutivePass()`
Member variable `singleton_data`	Member variables `key` and `holder`
Member function `singleton_operation()`	Member function `print()`

Singleton objects and multithreading

We must be extra cautious when creating singleton objects in a multithreaded program. In our example application, member function `obtain()` of class `ExecutivePass` first checks whether the singleton object already exists. If not, it creates one. But if multiple threads simultaneously execute this member function when the singleton object doesn't already exist, more than one thread can test that the value of the static member variable `single_instance` is `nullptr`, and each of those threads will create a singleton object. Member variable `single_instance` will point to the last one that was created. Chapter 15 introduces the design of multithreaded programs and how to avoid such *race conditions*.

14.2 The Composite Design Pattern treats individual and composite objects uniformly

Many applications keep the data in a tree data structure. We saw tree structures in chapter 11 and the Visitor Design Pattern. Data in tree structures often represent part-whole hierarchies. The Composite Design Pattern provides a model for a software architecture to manage such hierarchies.

An example of such a hierarchy are the objects that represent the provisions for a baseball player and the cost of each item (figure 14.4).

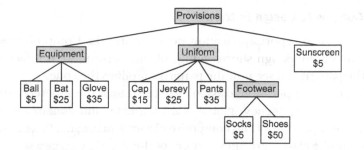

Figure 14.4   The hierarchy of objects in a tree data structure that represent the provisions for a baseball player and the cost of each item. The composite objects are shaded gray.

Suppose the athletics department wants a printout of the cost to outfit a baseball player:

```
PROVISIONS
    EQUIPMENT
            ball cost: $ 5
             bat cost: $25
           glove cost: $35
    EQUIPMENT total: $65
    UNIFORM
             cap cost: $15
          jersey cost: $25
           pants cost: $35
        FOOTWEAR
                socks cost: $ 5
                shoes cost: $50
        FOOTWEAR total: $55
    UNIFORM total: $130
    sunscreen cost: $ 5
PROVISIONS total: $200

GRAND TOTAL: $200
```

The report lists the cost of each item. It also shows the cost subtotals of the equipment, uniform, and footwear composites, and the total cost of all the items.

14.2.1 *Desired design features*

An application with data in a tree structure that represents a part-whole hierarchy should have the following features:

- *DF 1*—The application should be able to treat a composition of parts the same way as it treats an individual part.
- *DF 2*—It should be possible at run time to add new parts and compositions of parts.

14.2.2 *Before using the Composite Design Pattern*

The first version of our cost report application does not use the Composite Design Pattern. After examining the design shortcomings of that version, we'll refactor the application using the pattern and see how the pattern simplifies the code.

In the first version of our application, class `ProvisionItem` is the superclass of subclasses `Ball`, `Bat`, `Glove`, `Cap`, `Jersey`, `Pants`, `Socks`, `Shoes`, and `Sunscreen`. Class `ProvisionGroup` is the superclass of the composite classes `Equipment`, `Uniform`, and `Footwear`. Each composite class aggregates a subset of the `ProvisionItem` subclasses. Together, these classes can implement a tree-structured data hierarchy (figure 14.5).

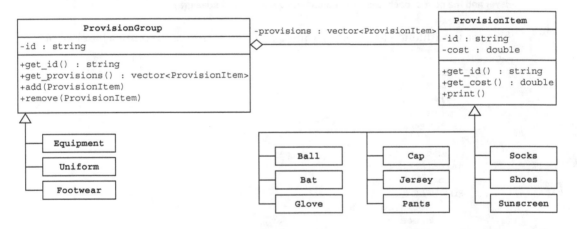

Figure 14.5 Classes `Ball`, `Bat`, `Glove`, `Cap`, `Jersey`, `Pants`, `Socks`, `Shoes`, and `Sunscreen` are subclasses of class `ProvisionItem`, and each implements the `get_cost()` member function. Composite classes `Equipment`, `Uniform`, and `Footwear` are subclasses of `ProvisionGroup`, and each aggregates a subset of the `ProvisionItem` subclasses.

Class `ProvisionItem` is the superclass of subclasses `Ball`, `Bat`, `Glove`, `Cap`, `Jersey`, `Pants`, `Socks`, `Shoes`, and `Sunscreen`. The superclass implements the common `get_id()`, `get_cost()`, and `print()` member functions and has private member variables `id` and `cost`.

Listing 14.6   (Program 14.3 CostReport): `ProvisionItem.h` **(before the design pattern)**

```cpp
#include <iostream>
#include <iomanip>
#include <string>

using namespace std;

class ProvisionItem
{
public:
    ProvisionItem(const string id, const double c)
        : id(id), cost(c) {}

    string get_id()   const { return id; }
    double get_cost() const { return cost; }

    void print()
    {
        cout << setw(6) << get_id() << " cost: $"
             << setw(2) << get_cost() << endl;
    }

private:
    string id;
    double cost;
};
```

The `ProvisionItem` subclasses `Ball`, `Bat`, and `Glove` represent equipment items. Each subclass's constructor invokes the superclass `ProvisionItem` constructor and passes its `id` and `cost`.

Listing 14.7   (Program 14.3 CostReport): `Equipment.h` **(before the design pattern)**

```cpp
#include "ProvisionItem.h"

using namespace std;

class Ball : public ProvisionItem
{
public:
    Ball(const double cost) : ProvisionItem("ball", cost ) {}
};

class Bat : public ProvisionItem
{
public:
    Bat(const double cost) : ProvisionItem("bat", cost ) {}
};

class Glove : public ProvisionItem
{
public:
    Glove(const double cost) : ProvisionItem("glove", cost ) {}
};
```

Subclasses `Cap`, `Jersey`, and `Pants` each represents a uniform item.

Listing 14.8   (Program 14.3 CostReport): `Uniform.h` **(before the design pattern)**

```
#include "ProvisionItem.h"

using namespace std;

class Cap : public ProvisionItem
{
public:
    Cap(const double cost) : ProvisionItem("cap", cost ) {}
};

class Jersey : public ProvisionItem
{
public:
    Jersey(const double cost) : ProvisionItem("jersey", cost ) {}
};

class Pants : public ProvisionItem
{
public:
    Pants(const double cost) : ProvisionItem("pants", cost ) {}
};
```

Subclasses `Socks` and `Shoes` each represents a footwear item.

Listing 14.9   (Program 14.3 CostReport): `Footwear.h` **(before the design pattern)**

```
#include "ProvisionItem.h"

using namespace std;

class Socks : public ProvisionItem
{
public:
    Socks(const double cost) : ProvisionItem("socks", cost) {}
};

class Shoes : public ProvisionItem
{
public:
    Shoes(const double cost) : ProvisionItem("shoes", cost ) {}
};
```

And subclass Sunscreen represents a sunscreen item.

Listing 14.10 (Program 14.3 CostReport): `Sunscreen.h` **(before the design pattern)**

```
#include "ProvisionItem.h"

using namespace std;

class Sunscreen : public ProvisionItem
```

```
{
public:
    Sunscreen(const double cost)
        : ProvisionItem("sunscreen", cost) {}
};
```

Classes `Equipment`, `Uniform`, and `Footwear` are subclasses of superclass `Provision-Group`. The superclass provides the common member variable `provisions`, which is a vector of `ProvisionItem` objects. The `add()` member function appends a `Provision-Item` object to the vector, and the `remove()` member function removes a `Provision-Item` object from the vector.

Listing 14.11   (Program 14.3 CostReport): `ProvisionGroup.h` **(before the DP)**

```cpp
#include <vector>
#include <algorithm>
#include "ProvisionItem.h"

using namespace std;

class ProvisionGroup
{
public:
    ProvisionGroup(string id) : id(id) {}

    ~ProvisionGroup()
    {
        for (ProvisionItem *item : provisions) { delete pi; };
    }

    string get_id() const { return id; }

    vector<ProvisionItem *> get_provisions() const
    {
        return provisions;
    }

    void add(ProvisionItem *item) { provisions.push_back(item); }

    void remove(ProvisionItem *item)
    {
        auto pos = find(provisions.begin(), provisions.end(), item);
        if (pos != provisions.end()) provisions.erase(pos);
    }

private:
    vector<ProvisionItem *> provisions;
};

class Equipment : public ProvisionGroup
{
public:
    Equipment() : ProvisionGroup("EQUIPMENT") {}
```

Subclasses of superclass ProvisionGroup

```
};

class Uniform : public ProvisionGroup
{
public:
    Uniform() : ProvisionGroup("UNIFORM") {}
};

class Footwear : public ProvisionGroup
{
public:
    Footwear() : ProvisionGroup("FOOTWEAR") {}
};
```

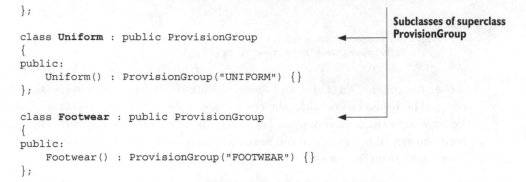

**Subclasses of superclass
ProvisionGroup**

Class `CostReport` creates the data and generates the report.

Listing 14.12   (Program 14.3 CostReport): `CostReport.h` **(before the design pattern)**

```
#include "ProvisionGroups.h"
#include "Sunscreen.h"

class CostReport
{
public:
    CostReport();
    ~CostReport();

    void generate_report();

private:
    Equipment *equipment;
    Uniform    *uniform;
    Footwear   *footwear;
    Sunscreen *sunscreen;
};
```

The constructor builds the data hierarchy. It creates the `ProvisionItem` objects and adds them to the appropriate `Equipment`, `Uniform`, and `Footwear` objects. It also creates the standalone `Sunscreen` object.

Listing 14.13   (Program 14.3 CostReport): `CostReport.cpp` **(before the design pattern)**

```
#include <iostream>
#include <iomanip>
#include "ProvisionItem.h"
#include "ProvisionGroups.h"
#include "Equipment.h"
#include "Uniform.h"
#include "Footwear.h"
#include "Sunscreen.h"
#include "CostReport.h"

using namespace std;
```

```
CostReport::CostReport()
    : equipment(new Equipment()), uniform(new Uniform()),
      footwear(new Footwear()), sunscreen(new Sunscreen(5))
{
    equipment->add(new Ball(5));
    equipment->add(new Bat(25));
    equipment->add(new Glove(35));

    uniform->add(new Cap(15));
    uniform->add(new Jersey(25));
    uniform->add(new Pants(35));

    footwear->add(new Socks(5));
    footwear->add(new Shoes(50));
}

CostReport::~CostReport()
{
    delete equipment;
    delete uniform;
    delete footwear;
    delete sunscreen;
}
```

...

Member function `generate_report()` generates the cost report. It first computes the total costs of the equipment, uniform, and footwear items, and then it computes the overall total cost.

Listing 14.14 (Program 14.3 CostReport): `CostReport.cpp` (before the design pattern)

...

```
void CostReport::generate_report()
{
    double equipment_cost = 0;
    for (ProvisionItem *pi : equipment->get_provisions())
    {
        equipment_cost += pi->get_cost();
    }

    double uniform_cost = 0;
    for (ProvisionItem *pi : uniform->get_provisions())
    {
        uniform_cost += pi->get_cost();
    }

    double footwear_cost = 0;
    for (ProvisionItem *pi : footwear->get_provisions())
    {
        Footwear_cost += pi->get_cost();
    }

    uniform_cost += footwear_cost;
```

Compute the cost of each composite ProvisionGroup.

```
cout << "PROVISIONS" << endl;
```
Print the cost of the individual ProvisionItem objects.
```
cout << "    " << equipment->get_id() << endl;
for (ProvisionItem *pi : equipment->get_provisions())
{
    cout << "        ";
    pi->print();
}
cout << "    " << equipment->get_id() << " total: $"
    << setw(2) << equipment_cost << endl;

cout << "    " << uniform->get_id() << endl;
for (ProvisionItem *pi : uniform->get_provisions())
{
    cout << "        ";
    pi->print();
}

cout << "        " << footwear->get_id() << endl;
for (ProvisionItem *pi : footwear->get_provisions())
{
    cout << "            ";
    pi->print();
}
cout << "        " << footwear->get_id() << " total: $"
    << setw(2) << footwear_cost << endl;

cout << "    " << uniform->get_id() << " total: $"
    << setw(2) << uniform_cost << endl;

cout << "    ";
sunscreen->print();

double provisions_total = equipment_cost
                        + uniform_cost
                        + sunscreen->get_cost();
```
Compute the overall cost.
```
cout << "PROVISIONS total: $" << provisions_total << endl;

cout << endl;
cout << "GRAND TOTAL: $" << provisions_total << endl;
}
```

The test program generates the desired cost report.

Listing 14.15   (Program 14.3 CostReport): `tester.cpp`

```
#include "CostReport.h"

int main()
{
    CostReport report;
    report.generate_report();

    return 0;
}
```

The application does produce the desired report. But member function `generate_report()` treats `ProvisionGroup` and `ProvisionItem` objects differently. That violates DF 1.

Member function `generate_report()` is hardcoded to handle only these particular `ProvisionGroup` and `ProvisionItem` objects. It won't be easy to add new items or groups. That violates DF 2.

Indeed, problems with this version of the application include

- *Complicated report generator*—Member function `generate_report()` of class `CostReport` is complicated. It will be hard to change if we change the organization of the data.

- *Individual and composite objects treated differently*—We want objects at all levels of the tree, individual or composite, to be treated the same. Member function `generate_report()` treats them differently.

- *Hardcoded report generator*—Member function `generate_report()` is hardcoded to print only the one report.

- *Incomplete tree*—We did not build the complete tree data structure. For example, footwear wasn't made a part of the uniform. An incomplete tree isn't a problem for generating the cost report in this application, but other applications may need the complete tree.

14.2.3 *After using the Composite Design Pattern*

We can refactor the first version of our cost report application to an architecture modeled from the Composite Design Pattern. The goal of the Composite Design Pattern is to treat individual objects the same way as compositions of objects in a tree data structure. We want all the leaf classes of the data tree, `Ball`, `Bat`, `Glove`, `Cap`, `Jersey`, `Pants`, `Socks`, `Shoes`, and `Sunscreen`, and the composition classes `Equipment`, `Uniform`, and `Footwear` to present the same interface.

> **The Composite Design Pattern**
>
> "Compose objects into tree structures to represent part-whole hierarchies. Composite lets its clients treat individual objects and compositions of objects uniformly" (GoF 163).

To use this model, we also make class `ProvisionItem` the superclass of class `ProvisionGroup`. Doing so ultimately makes the composite classes `Equipment`, `Uniform`, and `Footwear` subclasses of `ProvisionItem`. Classes `Ball`, `Bat`, `Glove`, `Cap`, `Jersey`, `Pants`, `Socks`, `Shoes`, and `Sunscreen` remain subclasses of `ProvisionItem`, and class `ProvisionGroup` maintains a vector of `ProvisionItem` objects (figure 14.6).

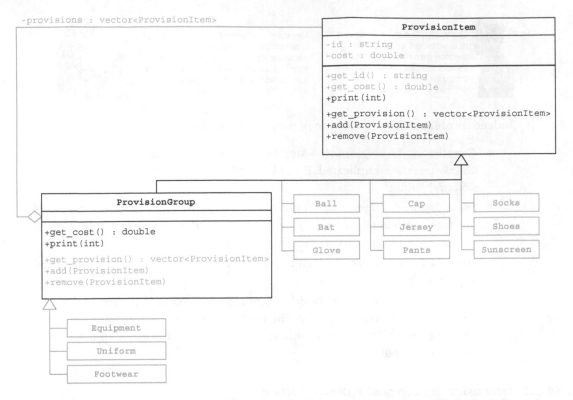

Figure 14.6   In the second version of our cost report application modeled by the Composite Design Pattern, class `ProvisionGroup` **is itself a subclass of class** `ProvisionItem`**. That makes classes** `Equipment`, `Uniform`, **and** `Footwear` **ultimately the subclasses of** `ProvisionItem`**. The grayed-out portions of the diagram haven't changed logically from figure 14.5.**

Classes `ProvisionItem` and `ProvisionGroup` will have the same member functions. Therefore, class `ProvisionItem` gains member functions `get_provisions()`, `add()`, and `remove()`. Class `ProvisionGroup` inherits member functions `get_cost()` and `print()`. Class `ProvisionItem` provides default implementations of all of its member functions (listing 14.16). Member functions `get_id()` and `get_cost()` of superclass `ProvisionItem` haven't changed—we want subclasses `Ball`, `Bat`, `Glove`, `Cap`, `Jersey`, `Pants`, `Socks`, `Shoes`, and `Sunscreen` to continue inheriting and using these functions. Member function `print()` will take an integer parameter that determines how many spaces, if any, to indent at the beginning of a print line.

Because member functions `get_provisions()`, `add()`, and `remove()` don't make sense for the individual objects, each function's default implementation throws an `InvalidOperation` exception. The composite classes `Equipment`, `Uniform`, and `Footwear` will override these member functions to have useful behaviors, and therefore, they are virtual.

Listing 14.16 (Program 14.4 CostReport-CompositeDP): `ProvisionItem.h`

```cpp
#include <iostream>
#include <iomanip>
#include <string>
#include <vector>

using namespace std;

class InvalidOperation {};

class ProvisionItem
{
public:
    ProvisionItem(const string id) : id(id), cost(0) {}

    ProvisionItem(const string id, const double c)
        : id(id), cost(c) {}

    virtual ~ProvisionItem() {}

    string get_id() const { return id; }

    virtual double get_cost() const { return cost; }

    virtual void print(const int indentation)
    {
        for (int i = 0; i < indentation; i++) cout << "    ";

        cout << setw(6) << get_id() << " cost: $"
             << setw(2) << get_cost() << endl;
    }

    virtual vector<ProvisionItem *> get_provisions() const
    {
        throw new InvalidOperation();
    }

    virtual void add(ProvisionItem *item)
    {
        throw new InvalidOperation();
    }

    virtual void remove(ProvisionItem *item)
    {
        throw new InvalidOperation();
    }

private:
    string id;
    double cost;
};
```

Indent before printing. ◄

Default behavior for the individual objects ◄

Superclass `ProvisionItem` now has two responsibilities! It has member functions for the individual objects and for the composite objects.

The Composite Design Pattern makes a tradeoff. It eases up on the Single Responsibility Principle in favor of uniformity and simplicity.

Uniformity enables our application modeled after the Composite Design Pattern to treat individual objects such as a `Ball` object the same as it treats a composite object such as a `Footwear` object. The report generation code will be simpler—it does not need to know whether it is dealing with an individual object or a composite object.

The public and protected constructors of class `ProvisionGroup` each invokes the constructor of its superclass `ProvisionItem`. This composite class overrides member functions `get_cost()`, `print()`, `get_provisions()`, `get_provisions()`, `add()`, and `remove()` to implement behaviors appropriate for composite objects, as shown in the following listing. Member functions `get_cost()` and `print()` each iterates over the `ProvisionItem` objects in the `provisions` vector and calls `get_cost()` and `print()`, respectively, on each object.

Listing 14.17   (Program 14.4 CostReport-CompositeDP): `ProvisionGroup.h` (pt 1 of 2)

```cpp
#include <iostream>
#include <iomanip>
#include <string>
#include <vector>
#include <algorithm>
#include "ProvisionItem.h"

using namespace std;

class ProvisionGroup : public ProvisionItem
{
public:
    ProvisionGroup() : ProvisionItem("PROVISIONS", 0) {}

    ~ProvisionGroup()
    {
        for (ProvisionItem *item : provisions) { delete item; };
    }

    double get_cost() const override
    {
        double cost = 0;
        for (ProvisionItem *item : provisions)
        {
            cost += item->get_cost();
        }

        return cost;
    }
```

Iterate over the ProvisionItem objects to compute the total cost of the items.

```
    void print(const int indentation) override
    {
        for (int i = 0; i < indentation; i++) cout << "    ";
        cout << get_id() << endl;

        for (ProvisionItem *item : provisions)
        {
            item->print(indentation + 1);
        }

        for (int i = 0; i < indentation; i++) cout << "    ";
        cout << get_id() << " total: $" << get_cost() << endl;
    }

    vector<ProvisionItem *> get_provisions() const override
    {
        return provisions;
    }

    void add(ProvisionItem *item) override
    {
        provisions.push_back(item);
    }

    void remove(ProvisionItem *item) override
    {
        auto pos = find(provisions.begin(), provisions.end(), item);
        if (pos != provisions.end()) provisions.erase(pos);
    }

protected:
    ProvisionGroup(const string id) : ProvisionItem(id) {}

private:
    vector<ProvisionItem *> provisions;
};
```

Annotations:
- **Iterate over the ProvisionItem objects to print each object.** (points to `item->print(indentation + 1);`)
- **Overridden member functions for ProvisionGroup objects** (points to `get_provisions`, `add`, and `remove`)

...

Each constructor of the composite subclasses `Equipment`, `Uniform`, and `Footwear` invokes the protected constructor of superclass `ProvisionGroup`.

Listing 14.18 **(Program 14.4 CostReport-CompositeDP):** `ProvisionGroup.h` (pt 2 of 2)

...

```
class Equipment : public ProvisionGroup
{
public:
    Equipment() : ProvisionGroup("EQUIPMENT") {}
};

class Uniform : public ProvisionGroup
```

```
{
public:
    Uniform() : ProvisionGroup("UNIFORM") {}
};

class Footwear : public ProvisionGroup
{
public:
    Footwear() : ProvisionGroup("FOOTWEAR") {}
};
```

Class `CostReport` gains an added member variable `provisions`.

Listing 14.19   (Program 14.4 CostReport-CompositeDP): `CostReport.h` (pt 2 of 2)

```
#include "ProvisionGroup.h"
#include "Sunscreen.h"

class CostReport
{
public:
    CostReport();
    ~CostReport();

    void generate_report();

private:
    ProvisionGroup provisions;

    Equipment *equipment;
    Uniform   *uniform;
    Footwear  *footwear;
    Sunscreen *sunscreen;
};
```

The constructor of class `CostReport` builds the entire data tree of figure 14.4. Class `Footwear` becomes a subcollection under class `Uniform`.

Listing 14.20   (Program 14.4 CostReport-CompositeDP): `CostReport.cpp`

```
#include <iostream>
#include <iomanip>
#include "ProvisionItem.h"
#include "ProvisionGroup.h"
#include "Equipment.h"
#include "Uniform.h"
#include "Footwear.h"
#include "Sunscreen.h"
#include "CostReport.h"

using namespace std;

CostReport::CostReport()
```

```
        : equipment(new Equipment()), uniform(new Uniform()),
          footwear(new Footwear()), sunscreen(new Sunscreen)
{
    equipment->add(new Ball(5));
    equipment->add(new Bat(25));
    equipment->add(new Glove(35));

    uniform->add(new Cap(15));
    uniform->add(new Jersey(25));
    uniform->add(new Pants(35));

    footwear->add(new Socks(5));
    footwear->add(new Shoes(50));

    uniform->add(footwear);              ◄───────  Make Footwear a
                                                   subcollection of Uniform.
    provisions.add(equipment);
    provisions.add(uniform);
    provisions.add(sunscreen);
}

CostReport::~CostReport()
{
    delete equipment;
    delete uniform;
    delete footwear;
    delete sunscreen;
}

void CostReport::generate_report()
{
    provisions.print(0);

    cout << endl;
    cout << "GRAND TOTAL: $" << setw(3) << provisions.get_cost()
         << endl;
}
```

ProvisionItem subclasses Ball, Bat, Glove, Cap, Jersey, Pants, Socks, Shoes, and Sunscreen have not changed in this version of the application, nor has the test program. The output is the same.

The primary benefits we've gained from using the Composite Design Pattern are

- *Uniformity*—The class for individual objects and the class for composite objects share an interface. Therefore, our code can treat individual objects the same as it treats composite objects.
- *Simplicity*—Code that performs operations on the components of the tree, such as computing costs and printing, is simpler.
- *Flexibility*—It won't be hard to add new ProvisionItem and ProvisionGroup objects or remove existing ones.

14.2.4 Composite's generic model

Figure 14.7 shows the generic model of the Composite Design Pattern. Recall that it is from the design pattern's generic model that we can create a custom solution to an architecture problem (section 8.1.3)...

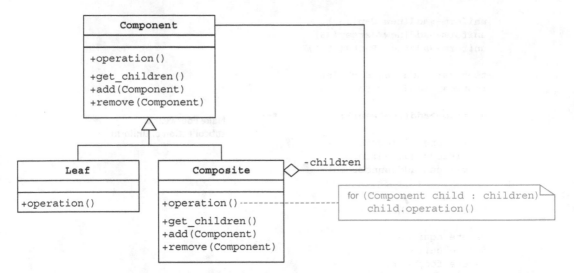

Figure 14.7   The generic model of the Composite Design Pattern. Compare it with figure 14.6. Both the individual Leaf class and the Composite class inherit from the Component superclass.

Table 14.2 shows how the example application applies the pattern.

Table 14.2   The Composite Design Pattern as applied by the example application

Design pattern	Applied by the example application
Superclass Component	Superclass ProvisionItem
Class Composite	Class ProvisionGroup
Class Leaf	Classes Ball, Bat, Glove, Cap, Jersey, Pants, Socks, Shoes, and Sunscreen

Manning Comix

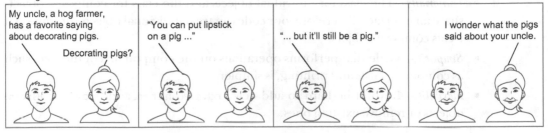

14.3　The Decorator Design Pattern dynamically adds object responsibilities

Classes have member variables whose runtime values are the attributes of its objects. As chapter 2 emphasized, managing object attributes is an important aspect of application design. Classes also have member functions that control their objects' runtime behaviors. Member variables and member functions implement the responsibilities of a class, and good design assigns a primary responsibility to each class. But what if we need the flexibility to dynamically add more responsibilities to a class's objects? The Decorator Design Pattern provides a model for an application architecture that flexibly manages object responsibilities.

As an example of such an application, suppose that besides the base tickets sold out of a ticket machine, the athletics department has online sales of special enhanced tickets. Ticket enhancements can include an invitation to a pregame party, VIP seating, and drink coupons. We can implement these enhancements as attributes of a ticket, and each enhancement requires the behavior of adding its cost to the base price of a ticket. We can consider each ticket enhancement to be an additional responsibility for the ticket.

14.3.1　Desired design features

An application should have the following features to be able to dynamically add additional responsibilities to an existing class:

- *DF1*—We should not need to modify the class to which we add new responsibilities.
- *DF 2*—We should be able to dynamically add any number of responsibilities in any order and combination during run time.
- *DF 3*—The class should not have dependencies on the implementations of the responsibilities.
- *DF 4*—It should be possible to add, delete, or modify responsibilities without modifying the classes that has them.
- *DF 5*—Code that uses an object that can acquire additional responsibilities should not treat the object any differently based on the number (including none), order, or combination of additional responsibilities.

14.3.2　Before using the Decorator Design Pattern

We'll develop two versions of our enhanced ticket application. The first version implements the ticket attributes and behaviors in an obvious way, as member variables and member functions of the `Ticket` class. But that implementation will have some major shortcomings. Then we'll model the design of the second version of our application from the Decorator Design Pattern, which will greatly increase the flexibility of managing the additional ticket behaviors.

The first version of our ticket application simply makes each ticket enhancement and cost an attribute of the `Ticket` class (figure 14.8).

```
                        Ticket

-BASE_PRICE    :        double = 30
-PARTY_PRICE   :        double = 25
-VIP_PRICE     :        double = 20
-COUPON_PRICE  :        double =  5

-pregame_party : bool
-vip_seating   : bool
-drink_coupons : int

+get_cost() : double
```

Figure 14.8   **We implement the enhancements to a base ticket as member variables of the `Ticket` class. Each enhancement has a cost.**

The member variables of class `Ticket` implement the ticket enhancements and their costs. Member function `get_cost()` calculates and returns the total cost of a ticket, as shown in the following listing. The responsibility of a `Ticket` object is to manage a ticket's enhancements and compute its total cost.

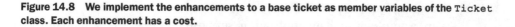

Listing 14.21   (Program 14.5 Enhanced): `Ticket.h` (before the design pattern)

```cpp
#include <iostream>
#include <iomanip>

using namespace std;

class Ticket
{
public:
    Ticket(const bool party, const bool vip, const int coupons)
        : pregame_party(party), vip_seating(vip),
          drink_coupons(coupons) {}

    double get_cost() const
    {
        double total = BASE_PRICE;

        if (pregame_party) total += PARTY_PRICE;
        if (vip_seating)   total += VIP_PRICE;

        return total + drink_coupons*COUPON_PRICE;
    }

    friend ostream& operator <<(ostream& ostr, const Ticket& ticket);

private:
    bool pregame_party;
    bool vip_seating;          │  Enhancements
    int  drink_coupons;

    double const BASE_PRICE   = 30;
    double const PARTY_PRICE  = 25;   │  Costs
```

```cpp
    double const VIP_PRICE    = 20;                  | Costs
    double const COUPON_PRICE =  5;                  |
};

inline ostream& operator <<(ostream& ostr, const Ticket& ticket)
{
    ostr << setw(24) << "base ticket price: $"
         << setw(2)  << ticket.BASE_PRICE << endl;

    if (ticket.pregame_party)
    {
        ostr << setw(24) << "pregame party price: $"
             << setw(2) << ticket.PARTY_PRICE << endl;
    }

    if (ticket.vip_seating)
    {
        ostr << setw(24) << "VIP seating price: $"
             << setw(2)  << ticket.VIP_PRICE << endl;
    }

    int count = ticket.drink_coupons;

    if (count > 0)
    {
        ostr << setw(24) << "drink coupon price: $"
             << setw(2)  << count*ticket.COUPON_PRICE
             << " = " << count << " x $"
             << ticket.COUPON_PRICE << endl;
    }

    return ostr;
}
```

A test program creates and prints some sample tickets with enhancements.

Listing 14.22   (Program 14.5 Enhanced): `tester.cpp` (before the design pattern)

```cpp
#include <iostream>
#include <string>
#include "Ticket.h"

using namespace std;

void print(const string& name, const Ticket& ticket);

int main()
{
    Ticket ticket1(true, true, 2);
    print("John", ticket1);

    Ticket ticket2(true, false, 3);
    print("Mary", ticket2);

    Ticket ticket3(false, false, 0);
```

```
    print("Leslie", ticket3);

    Ticket ticket4(false, true, 1);
    print("Sidney", ticket4);

    return 0;
}

void print(const string& name, const Ticket& ticket)
{
    cout << endl;
    cout << name << "'s ticket:" << endl;
    cout << ticket;
    cout << "TOTAL COST: $" << ticket.get_cost() << endl;
}
```

The output is

```
John's ticket:
    base ticket price: $30
 pregame party price: $25
   VIP seating price: $20
   drink coupon price: $10 = 2 x $5
TOTAL COST: $85

Mary's ticket:
    base ticket price: $30
 pregame party price: $25
   drink coupon price: $15 = 3 x $5
TOTAL COST: $70

Leslie's ticket:
    base ticket price: $30
TOTAL COST: $30

Sidney's ticket:
    base ticket price: $30
   VIP seating price: $20
   drink coupon price: $ 5 = 1 x $5
TOTAL COST: $55
```

Class **Ticket** implements all the ticket enhancements by itself! That violates DF 1, DF 2, DF 3, and DF 4.

The way it calculates the cost of a ticket depends on how many enhancements the ticket has. That violates DF 5.

Indeed, inflexibility is the major fault of this design:

- *Inflexible code*—By hardcoding the kinds of ticket enhancements, it won't be possible to add, remove, or modify enhancements without needing to modify the Ticket class.

- *Enhancement implementations not hidden*—Class `Ticket` has intimate knowledge of how the ticket enhancements are implemented and treats tickets (i.e., compute their costs) differently depending on the enhancements.

14.3.3 *After using the Decorator Design Pattern*

The Decorator Design Pattern treats each ticket enhancement as a decoration that conceptually wraps the base ticket and any prior enhancements (figure 14.9).

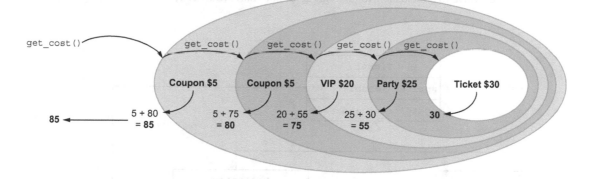

Figure 14.9 **An enhanced ticket is conceptually wrapped by any number of pregame party, VIP seating, and drink coupon decorators. Each decorator wraps the base ticket and any prior wrappers. To calculate the cost of an enhanced ticket, each decorator calls the** `get_cost()` **member function of whatever it wraps (either another decorator or the base ticket). Each return value is the cost of the decorator plus the total cost of whatever it wraps.**

The figure shows a base ticket decorated with a pregame party enhancement, and they are further decorated by a VIP seating enhancement and two drink coupons. Each decorator adds the responsibility to the ticket to include the decorator cost to the total ticket price. Each decorator and the ticket has a `get_cost()` function. Each decorator's function returns the cost of the decorator plus the total cost of whatever it wraps.

To implement this nested wrapping architecture, we make each decorator an object, and we link the decorator objects together in the order that they wrap each other. The last decorator in the chain links with the base ticket object (figure 14.10). Therefore, the ticket itself is wrapped the most deeply.

Figure 14.10 **Each decorator object except the last on in the chain points to the decorator object that it wraps. The last decorator object in the chain points to the ticket object.**

An additional requirement: No matter how many additional responsibilities a ticket has from its decorations, it's still a ticket. Our application code should treat a decorated ticket no differently than an undecorated base ticket. To meet this requirement, we need the base ticket class and the decorator classes all to be subclasses of a `Ticket` superclass (figure 14.11). We can also design a `Decorator` superclass whose subclasses are the decorator classes. Its member variables will include the link to the next `Decorator` wrapper object or to the `Ticket` object. `Decorator` will itself a subclass of `Ticket`.

> ## The Decorator Design Pattern
> "Attach additional responsibilities to an object dynamically. Decorators provide a flexible alternative to subclassing for extending functionality" (GoF 175).

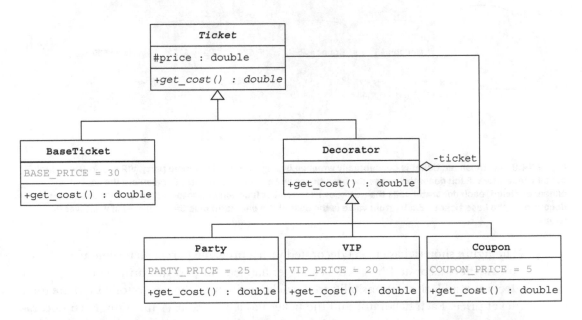

Figure 14.11 Abstract superclass `Ticket` has subclasses that represent either a base ticket or a ticket wrapped by one or more decorators. The `Decorator` superclass has a `ticket` link to the next `Decorator` object or to the `BaseTicket` object. `Party`, `VIP`, and `Coupon` are decorators. One or more of their objects can wrap a `BaseTicket` object. Each `Decorator` object adds the responsibility to include its cost to the total ticket cost.

Abstract class `Ticket` is the superclass of class `BaseTicket` and superclass `Decorator`.

Listing 14.23   (Program 14.6 Enhanced-DecoratorDP): `Ticket.h`

```
#include <iostream>
#include <iomanip>
#include <string>

using namespace std;

class Ticket
{
```

```
public:
    Ticket(const string desc, const double pr)
        : description(desc), price(pr)
    {
        cout << setw(17) << description
            << " price: $" << setw(2) << price << endl;
    }

    virtual ~Ticket() {}

    virtual double get_cost() const = 0;

    string get_description() const { return description; }

protected:
    string description;
    double price;
};
```

Print a Ticket object when it's created.

Each object of class `BaseTicket` represents a ticket before any decorations. Its cost is simply the `BASE_PRICE`.

Listing 14.24 (Program 14.6 Enhanced-DecoratorDP): `BaseTicket.h`

```
#include "Ticket.h"

const double BASE_PRICE = 30;

class BaseTicket : public Ticket
{
public:
    BaseTicket() : Ticket("base ticket", BASE_PRICE) {}

    double get_cost() const override { return BASE_PRICE; }
};
```

Superclass `Decorator` represents the ticket decorations. Each decorator object adds the responsibility to include its cost to the total ticket cost. Member function `get_cost()` returns its own price plus the cost of whatever it wraps. Member variable `ticket` points to the next `Ticket` object in the chain, whether it's a `BaseTicket` object or another `Decorator` object.

Listing 14.25 (Program 14.6 Enhanced-DecoratorDP): `Decorator.h`

```
#include <string>
#include "Ticket.h"

using namespace std;

class Decorator : public Ticket
{
public:
    Decorator(const string description, const double price,
```

```
                    Ticket *tckt)
           : Ticket(description, price), ticket(tckt) {}

    virtual ~Decorator() { delete ticket; }

    double get_cost() const override
    {
        return price + ticket->get_cost();
    }

private:
    Ticket *ticket;
};
```

Return this Ticket object's price plus the cost of whatever it wraps.

The Ticket object that this object wraps

Class `Party` is the pregame party decoration for a ticket.

Listing 14.26   (Program 14.6 Enhanced-DecoratorDP): `Party.h`

```
#include "Decorator.h"

const double PARTY_PRICE = 25;

class Party : public Decorator
{
public:
    Party(Ticket *ticket)
        : Decorator("pregame party", PARTY_PRICE, ticket) {}
};
```

Class `VIP` is the VIP seating decoration for a ticket.

Listing 14.27   (Program 14.6 Enhanced-DecoratorDP): `VIP.h`

```
#include "Decorator.h"

const double VIP_PRICE = 20;

class VIP : public Decorator
{
public:
    VIP(Ticket *ticket)
        : Decorator("VIP seating", VIP_PRICE, ticket) {}
};
```

Finally, class `Coupon` is the drink coupon decoration for a ticket.

Listing 14.28   (Program 14.6 Enhanced-DecoratorDP): `Coupon.h`

```
#include "Decorator.h"

const double COUPON_PRICE = 5;

class Coupon : public Decorator
{
```

```
public:
    Coupon(Ticket *ticket)
        : Decorator("drink coupon", COUPON_PRICE, ticket) {}
};
```

The test program creates BaseTicket objects and decorates each one by wrapping it with any number and combination of Decorator objects in any order. If a ticket includes multiple drink coupons, we decorate the ticket by wrapping it with multiple Coupon objects.

Listing 14.29   (Program 14.6 Enhanced-DecoratorDP): `tester.cpp`

```cpp
#include "BaseTicket.h"
#include "Party.h"
#include "VIP.h"
#include "Coupon.h"

using namespace std;

void print(const string name, const Ticket * const ticket);

int main()
{
    Ticket *ticket = new BaseTicket();
    ticket = new Party(ticket);
    ticket = new VIP(ticket);
    ticket = new Coupon(ticket);       │ Multiple drink
    ticket = new Coupon(ticket);       │ coupons

    print("John", ticket);
    delete ticket;

    ticket = new BaseTicket();
    ticket = new Coupon(ticket);
    ticket = new Coupon(ticket);
    ticket = new Party(ticket);
    ticket = new Coupon(ticket);

    print("Mary", ticket);
    delete ticket;

    ticket = new BaseTicket();

    print("Leslie", ticket);
    delete ticket;

    ticket = new BaseTicket();
    ticket = new Coupon(ticket);
    ticket = new VIP(ticket);

    print("Sidney", ticket);
    delete ticket;

    return 0;
```

```
}

void print(const string name, const Ticket * const ticket)
{
    cout << endl;
    cout << setw(26) << name + "'s ticket TOTAL: $"
         << ticket->get_cost() << endl;
    cout << "--------------------------" << endl;
}
```

The results are the same as in the first version of our application, although formatted differently:

```
        base ticket price: $30
    pregame party price: $25
      VIP seating price: $20
      drink coupon price: $ 5
      drink coupon price: $ 5

    John's ticket TOTAL: $85
--------------------------
        base ticket price: $30
      drink coupon price: $ 5
      drink coupon price: $ 5
    pregame party price: $25
      drink coupon price: $ 5

    Mary's ticket TOTAL: $70
--------------------------
        base ticket price: $30

  Leslie's ticket TOTAL: $30
--------------------------
        base ticket price: $30
      drink coupon price: $ 5
      VIP seating price: $20

   Sidney's ticket TOTAL: $55
--------------------------
```

As usual, modeling the application after a design pattern added more classes. But these classes appear to be cohesive and loosely coupled.

The Decorator Design Pattern made our application much more flexible. We can add, remove, or modify ticket enhancements without modify any existing classes.

The benefits of modeling our ticket application after the Decorator Design Pattern include

- *Dynamically enhanced objects*—This is done during run time by adding responsibilities.

- *No hardcoded enhancements*—It won't be hard to create new ticket enhancements, such as a reserved parking space. We would add another `Decorator` subclass, say `Parking`. It will also be easy to remove any decorators we no longer want.

- *Loosely coupled and cohesive classes*—The ticket decorations are loosely coupled with each other. Each one has the sole responsibility for its decoration. The `Ticket` class and the `Decorator` classes are loosely coupled from each other. A ticket does not need to know how it is enhanced, if at all.

- *Uniform treatment of base ticket and decorated ticket objects*—We don't have to write special code for each.

14.3.4 *Decorator's generic model*

Figure 14.12 shows the generic model of the Decorator Design Pattern. Recall that it is from the design pattern's generic model that we can create a custom solution to an architecture problem (section 8.1.3).

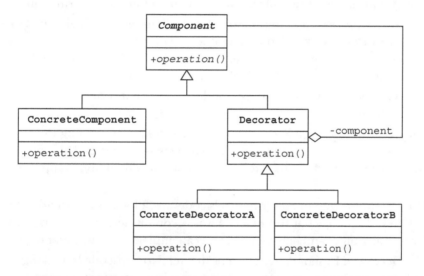

Figure 14.12   The generic model of the Decorator Design Pattern. Compare it with figure 14.11. A `ConcreteComponent` **object by itself is a** `Component`. **A** `ConcreteComponent` **wrapped by Decorator objects is also a** `Component`. **The component member variable of superclass** `Decorator` **points either to a** `ConcreteComponent` **object or to a** `Decorator` **object. This chain implements the nested wrapping of the** `Decorator` **objects.**

Table 14.3 shows how the example application applies the pattern.

Table 14.3   The Decorator Design Pattern as applied by the example application

Design pattern	Applied by the example application
Superclass `Component`	Superclass `Ticket`
Class `ConcreteComponent`	Class `BaseTicket`
Superclass `Decorator`	Superclass `Decorator`
Subclasses `ConcreteDecoratorA`, `ConcreteDecoratorB`, etc.	Classes `Party`, `VIP`, and `Coupon`
Member function `operation()`	Member function `get_cost()`

Summary

- The Singleton Design Pattern models code that must ensure that at most one object of a given class can exist during the run time of an application. We control the creation of the object by making the constructor of the singleton class private. A static member variable points to the singleton object at run time.

- The Singleton Design Pattern also requires disabling the singleton class's copy constructor and copy assignment operator. This prevents making copies of the singleton object during run time. We must be cautious that a multithreaded application does not create multiple singleton objects.

- The Composite Design Pattern models code that works with hierarchical tree-structured data.

- The Composite Design Pattern simplifies the code by providing the same interface for classes that represent individual objects as for classes that represent composite objects. That allows our code to treat individual and composite objects uniformly.

- The Decorator Design Pattern models code that allows us to extend the responsibilities of an object at run time. This is accomplished with decorations in the form of attributes and behaviors that we can implement as wrapper objects.

- The Decorator Design Pattern lessens the need to hardcode by making it easy to add new decorations or modify or remove existing ones without modifying any other classes.

Part 5

Additional Design Techniques

Recursion is a powerful technique supported by modern programming languages. Well-designed recursive programs can be simpler and more elegantly designed than their iterative counterparts. But recursive thinking is required to know when to use recursion and how to do it appropriately. Recursion combined with backtracking can exploit a computer's ability to try many solution paths rapidly and exhaustively. The example programs in chapter 15 introduce recursive thinking, and they demonstrate recursion and recursion with backtracking.

Multithreading is a technique that enables a program to run multiple execution paths simultaneously. Well-designed multithreaded programs can perform better than their single-threaded versions, especially on multicore machines. Chapter 16 briefly introduces the topic of multithreading through several classic example applications.

Designing solutions with recursion and backtracking

This chapter covers

- Recursion for designing solutions to programming problems
- Dynamic backtracking to try different solution paths during run time

Recursion is a software design technique used to create solutions to certain programming problems. It involves a function that calls itself, and nearly all modern programming languages support this important technique. If we use recursion properly with certain classes of programming problems, we can design solutions that are simple, elegant, and as some might claim, magical. With recursion, we can design solutions that may be difficult to solve otherwise.

Manning Comix

Recursion requires a different way of thinking about how to design a programming solution to a problem. Unfortunately, for some programmers, it is too mysterious and forbidding to use. This chapter clears away the mystery and demonstrates how combining recursion with dynamic backtracking gives us even more powerful design tools. However, we'll also see how misusing recursion can lead to surprising performance disasters. With experience, we can learn when it is appropriate to design with recursion.

15.1   *Recursion compared to the for loop*

We can remove some of the mystery behind recursion by comparing it to the familiar `for` loop. The key idea behind recursion is that we solve a programming problem by dividing it into a smaller but similar problem that we can solve the same way. Solving the smaller problem leads to the solution of the larger problem. We keep dividing a problem into smaller similar problems until the problem is so small that its solution is obvious and immediate. That solution becomes part of the solution to the next-to-the-smallest problem, which in turn becomes part of the solution to the next larger problem. As we unwind from the recursion and get back to the largest problem, the solutions to the smaller problems become part of the solution to the original problem.

We write a recursive function to solve a programming problem, and the function calls itself to solve a smaller but similar problem. A function makes a recursive call when it calls itself, which is often termed a *nested* call. The recursive calls repeat and nest deeper to solve increasingly smaller problems until the problem is small enough for the function to return immediately with its result without making another recursive call, thereby preventing infinite recursion. This smallest problem is called a *base case* of the recursion. The result from a base case enables the second-to-the-last recursive call to return with a result, with return results one by one from all the recursive calls back up the chain to the original call. The return from the original function call solves the programming problem. The recursive calls and the results from unwinding the calls are what make such solutions simple and elegant.

One way to understand recursion is to compare it to a basic counting `for` loop, such as

```
for (int i = INITIAL_VALUE; i < LIMIT_VALUE; i++) ...
```

Table 15.1 shows the comparison.

Table 15.1   Comparing a `for` loop to recursion

	`for` loop	Recursion
Initial condition	`i = INITIAL_VALUE`	The original problem
Repeated updating	`i++`	Repeatedly divide the problem into smaller but similar problems.
Terminating condition	`i >= LIMIT_VALUE`	The problem is so small that its solution is immediate and obvious (a base case).

It is vitally important for the `for` loop to eventually complete. Therefore, each iteration of the loop must update the control variable so that the variable's value approaches the terminating condition. Similarly, for the recursion to eventually end, the problem must become smaller and smaller and approach a base case, where the problem is so small that its solution is immediate and obvious, and there are no further recursive calls.

The two example programs in sections 15.2 and 15.3 demonstrate recursion. Neither of the problems that these programs solve ought to be done with recursion—they are much more efficiently solved with conventional iteration such as `for` or `while` loops. But we'll use them to show how recursion works.

15.2   *Finding the largest value by recursion*

Our first example program uses recursion to find the largest value in a vector of integer values. To design the recursive solution, we must determine the entries of the last column of table 15.1:

- *Initial condition*—The original vector of values.
- *Update*—A smaller but similar problem of finding the largest value in a shorter vector.
- *Terminating condition*—The base case of a vector consisting of a single element (or no elements at all).

Figure 15.1 shows how the recursion works. We start by passing the original vector of values to recursive function `largest()`. The function records the value of the vector's first element in variable `first_value`, and then it removes the first element, producing a shorter vector that is the rest of the vector. The function compares `first_value` to the largest value in the rest of the vector, and the larger of the two is the solution to the original problem.

But how does function `largest()` know what the largest value is in the rest of the vector? That's the result of a recursive call to the function with the shorter vector. Each recursive call receives a vector argument that is one element shorter, so the calls approach the base case. Each recursive call returns the solution to its problem. The last call receives a vector argument that consists of only one element, which is the call's immediate and obvious return value. The last call does not make another recursive call, thereby stopping the chain of recursive calls. The immediate return value enables the caller of the base case to complete its comparison and return a value. As the recursion unwinds, the return value from each recursive call enables the caller to complete its comparison and return a result, until the original call returns with the largest value of the entire vector.

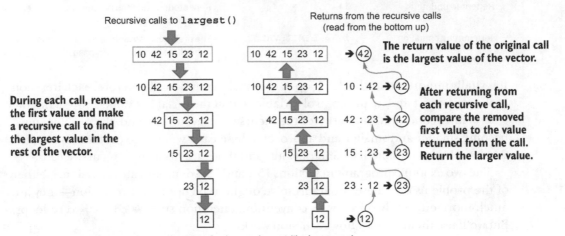

A vector of only one element (the base case) immediately returns its value and stops the recursive calls.

Figure 15.1   How the recursive function `largest()` finds the largest value in a vector. The boxed values are the ever-shortening vector arguments of the calls. The return value of each recursive call enables the caller to return its value.

Recursive function `largest()` works as suggested by figure 15.1.

Listing 15.1   (Program 15.1 Largest): `largest.cpp` (recursion demonstration only)

```cpp
#include <iostream>
#include <iomanip>
#include <vector>
#include <stdlib.h>
#include <time.h>

using namespace std;

const int SIZE = 12;

int largest(vector<int> v);

int main()
{
    vector<int> data;

    srand(time(0));
    for (int i = 0; i < SIZE; i++) data.push_back(rand()%100);

    cout << "Largest of";
    for (int d : data) cout << setw(3) << d;
```

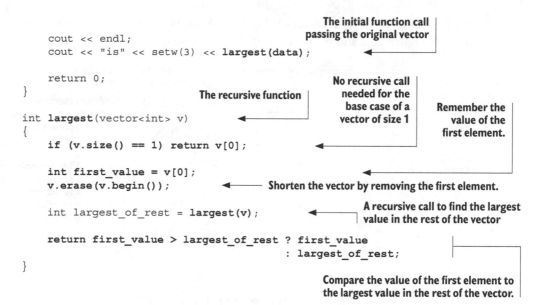

```
        cout << endl;
        cout << "is" << setw(3) << largest(data);

        return 0;
}

int largest(vector<int> v)
{
        if (v.size() == 1) return v[0];

        int first_value = v[0];
        v.erase(v.begin());

        int largest_of_rest = largest(v);

        return first_value > largest_of_rest ? first_value
                                             : largest_of_rest;
}
```

The initial function call passing the original vector

The recursive function

No recursive call needed for the base case of a vector of size 1

Remember the value of the first element.

Shorten the vector by removing the first element.

A recursive call to find the largest value in the rest of the vector

Compare the value of the first element to the largest value in the rest of the vector.

Here is the example output with a vector of randomly generated values:

```
Largest of 84 87 60 50 81 15 68 82 92  1 59 31
is 92
```

Well, that program works, but it's inefficient. That is not how I would write a function to find the largest value in a vector.

Of course not. We used a simple example to show *how* recursion works.

15.3 *Reversing a vector by recursion*

Here's another example program that shows how recursion works. We will write a recursive function reverse() that reverses the contents of a vector. As with the previous example, this is not the best way to solve this problem, but it's another good way to show how recursion works.

We first pass the original vector containing, for example, integer values 10, 20, 30, 40, and 50 to recursive function reverse(). The function removes the first element of the vector, recursively reverses the rest of the vector, which is shorter (shown below inside the square brackets), and then appends the removed first element to the end of the vector:

```
10 [ 20 30 40 50 ]
   [ 50 40 30 20 ] 10
```

We reverse the shorter vector by passing it to a recursive call to reverse(). Each recursive call gets a shorter vector. The recursion ends when the vector eventually reaches

CHAPTER 15 *Designing solutions with recursion and backtracking*

the base case of only one element. The final result is a vector containing 50, 40, 30, 20, and 10. Figure 15.2 shows how to recursively reverse the vector contents.

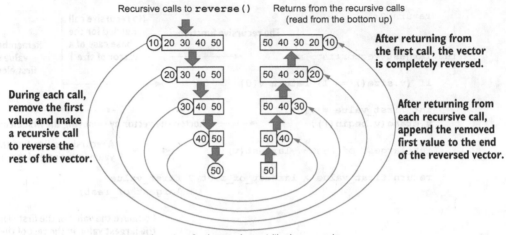

Figure 15.2   The contents of a vector reversed by the recursive function `reverse()`. Each call removes the first value, recursively reverses the rest of the vector, and then appends the removed first value to the end.

Recursive function `reverse()` works as suggested by figure 15.2.

Listing 15.2   (Program 15.2 Reverse): `reverse.cpp` (recursion demonstration only)

```cpp
#include <iostream>
#include <iomanip>
#include <vector>

using namespace std;

const int SIZE = 5;

void reverse(vector<int>& v);

int main()
{
    vector<int> data;

    for (int i = 1; i <= SIZE; i++) data.push_back(10*i);

    cout << "Reverse of";
    for (int d : data) cout << setw(3) << d;
    cout << endl;

    reverse(data);                    The initial
                                      function call
    cout << "            is";
```

```
    for (int d : data) cout << setw(3) << d;
    cout << endl;

    return 0;
}

void reverse(vector<int>& v)
{
    if (v.size() == 1) return;

    int first_value = v[0];
    v.erase(v.begin());

    reverse(v);
    v.push_back(first_value);
}
```

The recursive function

No recursive call needed for the base case of a vector of size 1

Remember the value of the first element.

Shorten the vector by removing the first element.

A recursive call to reverse the contents of the rest of the vector

Append the first element to the end of the reversed vector.

Example output is

```
Reverse of 10 20 30 40 50
       is 50 40 30 20 10
```

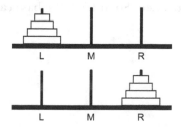

That last example may be a good aid to learning about recursion. But I wouldn't solve a vector reversal problem that way.

The remaining example programs in this chapter demonstrate *appropriate* uses of recursion.

15.4   Solve the Towers of Hanoi puzzle by recursion

The Towers of Hanoi puzzle provides an excellent opportunity to demonstrate an appropriate use of recursion. This is a problem that has a very elegant recursive solution but is difficult to solve without using recursion. We need to apply recursive thinking.

Figure 15.3 shows the starting and ending positions of the puzzle with four disks. Each disk has a hole in its center, and they are stacked in size order on one of three pins with the smallest disk on top. The goal is to move all the disks from the source pin to the destination pin, where they are again stacked in size order. We've labeled the pins L, M, and R (for left, middle, and right, respectively).

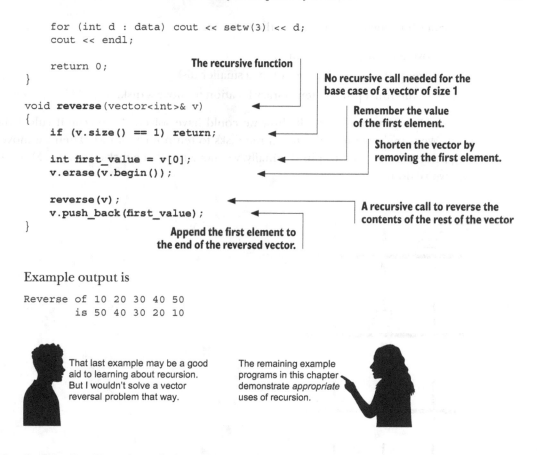

Figure 15.3   The starting and ending positions of four disks in the Towers of Hanoi puzzle. We moved the disks from source pin L to destination pin R.

The rules for moving the disks are the following:

1 Move only one disk at a time.
2 Never put a larger disk on top of a smaller disk.
3 Use the third pin as a temporary location to move a disk.

Figure 15.4 shows conceptually how we could have solved the puzzle if rule 1 didn't exist. We somehow move the top three disks to temporary pin M. Then we move the largest disk from pin L to pin R. Finally, we move the three disks from pin M to pin R, and we're done.

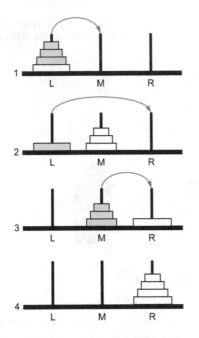

Figure 15.4   A conceptual solution with four disks that uses pin M as the temporary pin.

But how do we move three disks without violating the rule about moving only one disk at a time? Moving three disks is a smaller problem than moving four disks. This is a problem that suggests a recursive solution.

To convince ourselves that a recursive solution is possible, let's start with the base case. Figure 15.5 shows that moving a single disk from the source pin L to its destination pin R is an immediate operation—no recursion needed. So indeed, the base case will stop further recursion.

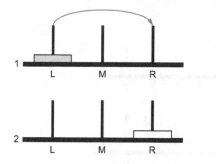

Figure 15.5 The base case of moving a single disk from pin L to pin R. No recursion is needed.

Figure 15.6 shows the sequence of moves to get two disks from source pin L to destination pin R. It requires using pin M as the temporary pin. There are three single-disk moves, first from pin L to pin M (L is the source, and M is the destination of this move), then from pin L to pin R (L is the source, and R is the destination of this move), and finally, from pin M to pin R (M is the source, and R is the destination of this move). Note that the pins can change roles—in step 1, M was the destination, and in step 3, M was the source. We used recursion with a smaller number of disks (only one) to solve the single-disk moves.

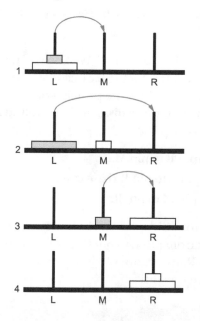

Figure 15.6 The sequence of moves to get two disks from pin L to pin R using pin M as the temporary pin

We can solve the puzzle for three disks. To demonstrate more clearly that we're using recursion, figure 15.7 solves the puzzle, moving them from pin L to pin R.

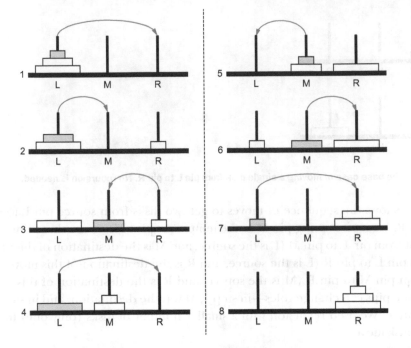

Figure 15.7   The sequence of moves to get three disks from pin L to pin R. During the steps, the pins change source, destination, and temporary pin roles.

Steps 1, 2, and 3 moves the top two disks from pin L to pin M. We know that we can recursively solve the problem of moving two disks. Step 4 is the base case of moving one disk from pin L to pin R. Steps 5, 6, and 7 recursively solve the problem of moving two disks from pin M to pin R. That solves the puzzle for three disks, which involved recursively solving moves of one and two disks:

- Recursively solve moving two disks from pin L to pin M.
- Recursively solve moving one disk from pin L to pin R (base case).
- Recursively solve moving two disks from pin M to pin R.

Now we know that we can solve the puzzle for four disks—recursively move three disks from pin L to pin M, recursively move one disk from pin L to pin R (the base case), and recursively move three disks from pin M to pin R. In fact, to solve the puzzle for N disks, we recursively use the solution for N-1 disks and one disk.

Listing 15.3   (Program 15.3 Towers): `towers.cpp`

```cpp
#include <iostream>
#include <iomanip>
#include <vector>

using namespace std;
```

```cpp
const int N = 3;

void solve(const int  n,
           const char source,
           const char temporary,
           const char destination )

int main()
{
    solve(N, 'L', 'M', 'R');          ◄────  Initial call with N disks
                                              with pin names and roles
    return 0;
}

void solve(const int  n,          ◄────  Recursive function
           const char source,
           const char temporary,
           const char destination )
{
    if (n == 1)
    {
        cout << «Move « << source << « ==> « << destination << endl;    Base
    }                                                                   case
    else
    {
        solve(n - 1, source,    destination, temporary);
        solve(1,     source,    temporary,   destination);    Recursive calls
        solve(n - 1, temporary, source,      destination);    with fewer disks
    }
}
```

Here is output from the solution for N = 3 disks:

```
Move L ==> R
Move L ==> M
Move R ==> M
Move L ==> R
Move M ==> L
Move M ==> R
Move L ==> R
```

It's impressive how those three calls to recursive function **solve()** can solve the puzzle for any number of disks.

It would be very challenging to write a program to solve the Towers of Hanoi puzzle without using recursion.

15.5 *Recursive algorithms for a binary search tree*

Recursive algorithms can be ideal for data structures that are recursively defined. One such recursive data structure is the binary tree, and we'll see how to design recursive functions to operate on the tree nodes.

A *binary tree* is a tree structure where each nonempty node has zero, one, or two children. Therefore, the node has two links: the left child link and the right child link. Each link is either `nullptr` or points to a child node that is the root of a subtree (figure 15.8). Each subtree is itself a binary tree, and therefore a binary tree is recursively defined. The root represents the entire tree. We can consider a `nullptr` link to be a pointer to an empty node, which represents an empty tree. The subtrees get smaller as we move down, until we reach a base case of an empty tree.

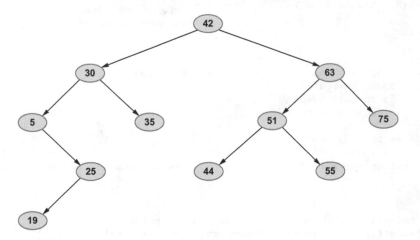

Figure 15.8   A binary tree, where each nonempty node has zero, one, or two child nodes that are roots of subtrees. Each subtree is itself a binary tree, so a binary tree is recursively defined. This binary tree is also a binary search tree (BST), where at each nonempty parent node, values in the left child subtree are less than or equal to the parent node's value, and values in the right subtree are greater. Each subtree is itself a BST, so a BST is recursively defined.

A binary tree is a *binary search tree* (BST) if it further meets the following conditions:

- Each nonempty node has a value.
- The left child (if it exists) of any nonempty parent node is a subtree whose node values are all less than or equal to the value of the parent node.
- The right child (if it exists) of any nonempty parent node is a subtree whose node values are all greater than the value of the parent node.

A BST is recursively defined because each node is the root of a subtree that is itself a BST.

Listing 15.4   (Program 15.4-BST): `Node.h`

```
#include "BST.h"

class Node
{
public:
    Node(const int v) : value(v), left(nullptr), right(nullptr) {}
```

```
    friend class BST;

public:
    int value;
    Node *left;
    Node *right;
};
```

|| Pointers to the left and right child nodes, each the root of a BST

15.5.1 *Inserting into a BST with recursion*

We'll define three recursive operations for a BST: inserting a node, printing all the nodes, and removing all the nodes. The two public member functions `insert()` and `print()` start at the root of the tree by calling the corresponding private member functions.

Listing 15.5 (Program 15.4-BST): `BST.h`

```
#include "Node.h"

class BST
{
public:
    BST() : root(nullptr) {}

    virtual ~BST() { remove(root); }

    void insert(const int value) { insert(value, root); }
    void print() const           { print(root); }

private:
    Node *root;

    void insert(const int value, Node*& link);
    void print (const Node * const link) const;
    void remove(const Node * const link) const;
};
```

Remove starting at the root.

Insert starting at the root.

Print starting at the root.

|| Recursive member functions

We pass a pointer to a node to each of the private member functions `insert()`, `print()`, and `remove()`. The pointer can be `nullptr`. We pass the pointer by reference to member function `insert()` to allow the function to set the pointer. We also pass the value to insert into the tree. Private member functions `insert()`, `print()`, and `remove()` each works recursively.

Listing 15.6 (Program 15.4-BST): `BST.cpp` (part 1 of 3)

```
#include <iostream>
#include <iomanip>
#include "BST.h"

using namespace std;

void BST::insert(const int value, Node*& link)
```

Create the new node and insert it here.

Otherwise, insert either somewhere in the left subtree.

```
{
    if       (link == nullptr)       link = new Node(value);
    else if (value <= link->value) insert(value, link->left);
    else                            insert(value, link->right);
}
...
```

Or, insert somewhere in the right substree.

We pass to private member function `insert()` a new value to be inserted into the tree and, by reference, a pointer to a node. The function first checks whether the pointer is `nullptr`, the base case of an empty subtree. If so, the function creates a new node with the value and sets the pointer to a new node, thereby replacing the empty subtree and inserting the new value.

Otherwise, if the pointer we pass points to an existing node, the private `insert()` member function recursively calls itself to insert the new value into either the node's left child subtree or right child subtree, depending on the comparison between the new value and the node's value. Each call works on a smaller subtree, closer to a base case of an empty subtree. At a base case, a new node containing the new value replaces the empty subtree, thereby inserting it into the tree at its proper place (figure 15.9). Because the public `insert()` member function passes the pointer to the root of the tree (listing 15.5), when the tree is initially empty, the private `insert()` member function sets the root pointer to a new node containing the very first value.

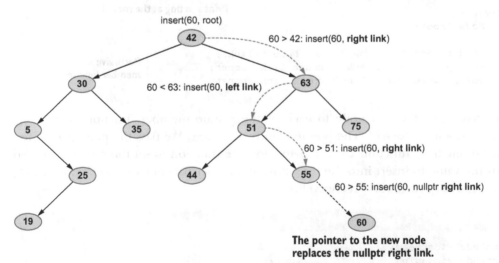

Figure 15.9 **The values were inserted into this BST in the order 42, 30, 5, 35, 63, 75, 25, 51, 44, 19, and 55. To insert the new value 60 into the tree, private function `insert()` is called recursively until it reaches a base case of an empty subtree. The new node replaces the empty subtree, and the value is thereby inserted into the tree at its proper place.**

15.5.2 *Printing a BST with recursion*

Private member function `print()` recursively prints the values of the BST nodes in sorted order (figure 15.10).

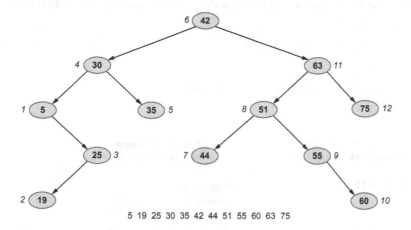

5 19 25 30 35 42 44 51 55 60 63 75

Figure 15.10   Recursively printing the values of a BST in sorted order. At each parent node, first print the values in its left child subtree. Next, print the parent node's value, and then print the values in the parent node's right child subtree. The small numbers next to each node indicate the order that the nodes are printed.

We pass a pointer to a node to print to the private member function `print()` (listing 15.7). The public `print()` function starts the printing by passing the root pointer to the private function (listing 15.5):

1 The function first calls itself recursively, passing the parent node's left child link to print the values less than or equal to the parent node's value.
2 Next, the function prints the parent node's value.
3 Then, the function calls itself recursively again, this time passing the parent node's right child link to print the values greater than the parent node's value.

Listing 15.7   (Program 15.4-BST): BST.cpp (part 2 of 3)

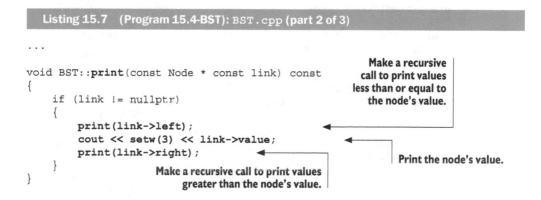

```
...

void BST::print(const Node * const link) const
{
    if (link != nullptr)
    {
        print(link->left);
        cout << setw(3) << link->value;
        print(link->right);
    }
}

...
```

Make a recursive call to print values less than or equal to the node's value.

Print the node's value.

Make a recursive call to print values greater than the node's value.

15.5.3 *Removing all the nodes of a BST with recursion*

Removing nodes recursively is similar to printing them, except that the private `remove()` member function called by the destructor function (listing 15.5) first recursively removes the two child subtrees of a node before removing the node itself.

Listing 15.8   (Program 15.4-BST): `BST.cpp` (part 3 of 3)

```
...

void BST::remove(const Node * const link) const
{
    if (link != nullptr)
    {
        remove(link->left);              Recursively remove
        remove(link->right);             both child subtrees.

        delete link;      ◄──────────    Remove the
    }                                     node itself
}
```

The test program generates random integer values, inserts them into the BST, and prints the tree's values in sorted order.

Listing 15.9   (Program 15.4-BST): `tester.cpp`

```cpp
#include <iostream>
#include <iomanip>
#include <stdlib.h>
#include <time.h>
#include "BST.h"

using namespace std;

int main()
{
    const int TREE_SIZE = 20;

    BST tree;
    srand(time(0));

    cout << "Inserting:";
    for (int i = 0; i < TREE_SIZE; i++)
    {
        int value = rand()%100;
        tree.insert(value);
        cout << setw(3) << value;
    }

    cout << endl << " Printing:";
    tree.print();
}
```

Here is example program output:

```
Inserting: 75 56 60 38 22  9 98 58 10 98 30 55 27 58 95 42 71 80 29 52
 Printing:  9 10 22 27 29 30 38 42 52 55 56 58 58 60 71 75 80 95 98 98
```

> **Tree traversals**
>
> Recursive function `print()` performs an *inorder* tree traversal—the function visits the node (to print the node's value) *in between* visiting the node's left child subtree and right child subtree. Recursive function `remove()` performs a *postorder* tree traversal—the function visits the node (to delete the node) *after* visiting the node's left child subtree and right child subtree.

Why is it called a binary *search* tree?

The way the values are stored in a BST makes it easy to write a fast and efficient algorithm to search the tree for a particular value.

15.6 *Quicksort an array with recursion*

Quicksort is an algorithm for rapidly sorting an array of values. It is another excellent example use of recursion.

Quicksort relies on a procedure to partition an array into two subarrays. For example, to quicksort the array

76 34 61 21 51 ⑯ 26 61 6 32 15

we first choose an element at or near the center of the array as the *pivot element*: 16 (circled above). In a procedure explained in the following, we rearrange the elements so that all the values less than or equal to the pivot value are to the left of the pivot, and all the values greater than the pivot value are to the right of the pivot:

| 6 15 | 16 | 21 51 34 26 61 76 32 61 |

Now we have two independent subarrays on both sides of the pivot (boxed above). Neither subarray is necessarily sorted, and we will recursively quicksort each one.

The quicksort algorithm:

1 Choose a pivot element. (In this example, we'll choose the element at or near the middle of the array.)

2 Partition the array to be sorted into two subarrays on either side of the pivot.

   a Base case 1: If the subarray size is 0 or 1, do nothing because it is already sorted.

    b Base case 2: If the subarray size is 2, swap the two elements if necessary.

    c Otherwise, recursively quicksort the two subarrays.

Some key facts about the algorithm are the following:

- After we've chosen the pivot element and performed the partitioning, the pivot element is already in its proper place in the final sorted array.
- Elements in partitions that meet either base case (after swapping if necessary in base case 2) are already in their proper places in the final sorted array.

15.6.1 Quicksort in action

Figure 15.11 shows the quicksort algorithm in action as it sorts an array. Line A is the original array, and Line L is the sorted array. As the sort progresses, the circled value is the pivot value of each step, and the bold values are those that are already in their proper places in the final sorted array. The subarrays to be recursively quicksorted are boxed, and the subarray being quicksorted in each step is shaded.

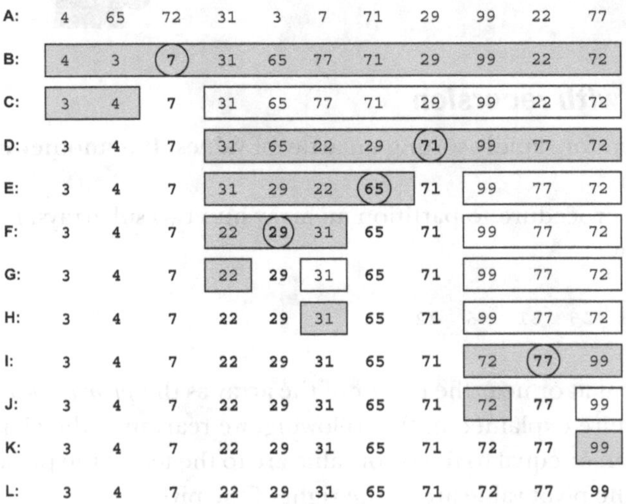

Figure 15.11 The quicksort algorithm in action as it sorts an array. The circled values are the chosen pivot elements that create the subarrays on both sides after partitioning. The rectangles enclose the subarrays to be quicksorted recursively. In each line, the shaded subarray is the one actively being sorted. The values in bold are already in their correct places in the final sorted array. Note that the chosen pivot elements are always already in their correct places after partitioning.

Line B shows that we start sorting the entire array. We partitioned the array with pivot element 7 into two subarrays (line C). We recursively sort the first subarray consisting of the two values 4 and 3, which we swap. This is base case 2.

    Next (line D), we recursively sort the other subarray by first picking 71 as the pivot element. This results in two more subarrays (line E). We recursively sort the left subarray where we pick 65 as the pivot element (line E). As the pivot value ended up at the right end of the subarray after partitioning, the resulting subarray to the right of 65 is empty (base case 1).

Lines G, H, J, and K show partitions that each contains only one element (base case 1). Their values are already in their proper places.

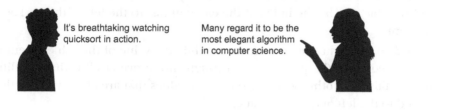

It's breathtaking watching quicksort in action.

Many regard it to be the most elegant algorithm in computer science.

15.6.2 *Partitioning an array into subarrays*

The key procedure in the quicksort algorithm is partitioning an array into two subarrays. Figure 15.12 shows how to do it with pivot value 52 (circled). Variables i and j are array indexes. When the partitioning is done, all values to the left of 52 are less, and all values to the right of 52 are greater. The two subarrays (boxed) are now ready to be recursively quicksorted.

A:	60	16	49	63	6	(52)	23	31	72	74	1	pivot 52
B:	60 i	16	49	63	6	1	23	31	72	74 j	(52)	1⟷52
C:	60 i	16	49	63	6	1	23	31 j	72	74	(52)	moved j
D:	31 i	16	49	63	6	1	23	60 j	72	74	(52)	31⟷60
E:	31	16	49	63 i	6	1	23	60 j	72	74	(52)	moved i
F:	31	16	49	63 i	6	1	23 j	60	72	74	(52)	moved j
G:	31	16	49	23 i	6	1	63 j	60	72	74	(52)	23⟷63
H:	31	16	49	23	6	1	63 ij	60	72	74	(52)	moved i
I:	31	16	49	23	6	1 j	63 i	60	72	74	(52)	moved j
J;	31	16	49	23	6	1	52	60	72	74	63	52⟷63

Figure 15.12 Choosing 52 (circled) to be the pivot value and then partitioning the array into two subarrays Variables i and j are array indexes. After partitioning, all values to the left of 52 are less or equal, and all values to the right of 52 are greater. The two boxed subarrays on either side of the pivot are now ready to be recursively quicksorted.

The steps to partition an array are the following:

1 Choose one element of the array to be the pivot element. In our examples, we'll choose the element at or near the middle (line A).

2 Park the pivot element out of the way by swapping it with the rightmost element of the array (line B). Set variable i to the element index of the leftmost element and variable j to be the index of the element just to the left of the parked pivot element.

3 Move i to the right (i.e., increment i) while the value of the ith element is less than or equal to the pivot value. (It might not move at all if that condition is already false.) In other words, i skips over values that are already correctly positioned to the left of the pivot value.

4 Move j to the left (i.e., decrement j) while the value of the jth element is greater than the pivot value (line C). (It might not move at all if that condition is already false.) In other words, j skips over values that are already correctly positioned to the right of the pivot value.

5 After i and j have both stopped moving, if i < j, swap the ith and jth element values (line D).

6 Repeat steps 3, 4, and 5 (lines E through I) until j crosses i (line I). Swap the value of the ith element with the pivot element that we had parked earlier at the right (line J). The array is now partitioned into two subarrays on both sides of the pivot element.

Here is a complete quicksort with all the details. Each pivot value is shown parenthesized, and the subarray currently being recursively quicksorted is enclosed in square brackets:

```
 86   95   51   95   28   33    9   15   84   86   67
-----------------------------------------------------
[86   95   51   95   28  (33)   9   15   84   86   67]  pivot (33)
[86   95   51   95   28   67    9   15   84   86   33]  67 <=> 33
  i                                          j
[86   95   51   95   28   67    9   15   84   86   33]  moved j
  i                                     j
[15   95   51   95   28   67    9   86   84   86   33]  15 <=> 86
  i                                     j
[15   95   51   95   28   67    9   86   84   86   33]  moved i
       i                                j
[15   95   51   95   28   67    9   86   84   86   33]  moved j
       i                           j
[15    9   51   95   28   67   95   86   84   86   33]  9 <=> 95
       i                           j
[15    9   51   95   28   67   95   86   84   86   33]  moved i
            i                      j
[15    9   51   95   28   67   95   86   84   86   33]  moved j
            i              j
```

```
[15    9   28   95   51   67   95   86   84   86   33]   28 <=> 51
           i        j
[15    9   28   95   51   67   95   86   84   86   33]   moved i
            i   j
[15    9   28   95   51   67   95   86   84   86   33]   moved j
        j   i
[15    9   28  (33)  51   67   95   86   84   86   95]   33 <=> 95
-----------------------------------------------------
[15  ( 9)  28]  33   51   67   95   86   84   86   95    pivot (9)
[15   28    9]  33   51   67   95   86   84   86   95    28 <=> 9
 i     j
[15   28    9]  33   51   67   95   86   84   86   95    moved j
 i
[ 9)  28   15]  33   51   67   95   86   84   86   95     9 <=> 15
-----------------------------------------------------
  9  [28   15]  33   51   67   95   86   84   86   95
  9  [15   28]  33   51   67   95   86   84   86   95    15 <=> 28
-----------------------------------------------------
  9   15   28   33  [51   67   95  (86)  84   86   95]   pivot (86)
  9   15   28   33  [51   67   95   95   84   86   86]   95 <=> 86
                     i                    j
  9   15   28   33  [51   67   95   95   84   86   86]   moved i
                          i                    j
  9   15   28   33  [51   67   86   95   84   95   86]   86 <=> 95
                          i                    j
  9   15   28   33  [51   67   86   95   84   95   86]   moved i
                               i               j
  9   15   28   33  [51   67   86   95   84   95   86]   moved j
                               i    j
  9   15   28   33  [51   67   86   84   95   95   86]   84 <=> 95
                               i    j
  9   15   28   33  [51   67   86   84   95   95   86]   moved i
                                    ji
  9   15   28   33  [51   67   86   84   95   95   86]   moved j
                                    j    i
  9   15   28   33  [51   67   86   84  (86)  95   95]   86 <=> 95
-----------------------------------------------------
  9   15   28   33  [51  (67)  86   84]  86   95   95    pivot (67)
  9   15   28   33  [51   84   86   67]  86   95   95    84 <=> 67
                          i         j
  9   15   28   33  [51   84   86   67]  86   95   95    moved i
                               i    j
  9   15   28   33  [51   84   86   67]  86   95   95    moved j
                          j    i
  9   15   28   33  [51  (67)  86   84]  86   95   95    67 <=> 84
-----------------------------------------------------
  9   15   28   33  [51]  67   86   84   86   95   95
-----------------------------------------------------
  9   15   28   33   51   67  [86   84]  86   95   95
  9   15   28   33   51   67  [84   86]  86   95   95    84 <=> 86
-----------------------------------------------------
  9   15   28   33   51   67   84   86   86  [95   95]
```

15.6.3 *Quicksort implementation*

Class `Quicksort` implements the quicksort algorithm, as shown in the following listing. Important member functions are the recursive `sort()` function and the `partition()` and `swap_values()` functions.

Listing 15.10 (Program 15.5 Quicksort): `Quicksort.h`

```
#include <iostream>
#include <iomanip>

using namespace std;

class Quicksort
{
public:
    Quicksort(int * const d, const int s) : data(d), size(s) {};

    void sort() { sort(0, size-1); }

    bool verify_sorted();

private:
    int *data;                              ◄──── The data to be sorted
    int size;

    void sort(const int left_index, const int right_index);    ◄── The recursive sorting function
    int partition(const int left_index, const int right_index);
    void swap_values_at(const int index1, const int index2);

    friend ostream& operator <<(ostream& ostr, const Quicksort& q);
};
```

Member function `sort()` implements the base cases and the recursive calls on the two subarrays after partitioning. The leftmost and rightmost element indices of the subarray to be sorted are `left_index` and `right_index`, respectively.

Listing 15.11 (Program 15.5 Quicksort): `Quicksort.cpp` (part 1 of 3)

```
#include <iostream>
#include <iomanip>
#include "Quicksort.h"

using namespace std;

void Quicksort::sort(const int left_index, const int right_index)
{
    int partition_size = right_index - left_index + 1;

    if (partition_size < 2) return;      ◄── Base case 1: return immediately.

    if (partition_size == 2)             ◄── Base case 2: swap values if necessary.
    {
        if (data[left_index] > data[right_index])
```

```
        {
            swap_values_at(left_index, right_index);
        }
    }
    else                                                    Get the index of
    {                                                       the pivot element.
        int pivot_index = partition(left_index, right_index);  ◄

        sort(left_index, pivot_index - 1);
        sort(pivot_index + 1, right_index);
    }
}
```

Recursively sort the two subarrays on both sides of the pivot element.

...

Member function partition() implements the steps to partition a subarray whose left-most and rightmost element indexes are left_index and right_index, respectively.

Listing 15.12   (Program 15.5 Quicksort): Quicksort.cpp **(part 2 of 3)**

Choose a pivot element near the middle of the subarray.

```
...

int Quicksort::partition(const int left_index, const int right_index)
{
    int middle_index = (left_index + right_index)/2;
    int pivot_value  = data[middle_index];

    swap_values_at(middle_index, right_index);          ◄

    int i = left_index - 1;                       Park the pivot element at the
    int j = right_index;                          right end of the subarray.

    while (i < j)
    {
        do
        {                           Move i to the right.
            i++;                ◄
        } while ((i < right_index) && (data[i] < pivot_value));

        do
        {                           Move j to the left.
            j--;                ◄
        } while ((j >= left_index) && (data[j] > pivot_value));

        if (i < j) swap_values_at(i, j);        ◄        Swap the values of the
    }                                                    ith and jth elements.

    swap_values_at(i, right_index);        ◄
    return i;
}                                      Move the parked pivot
                                       element to its proper place.

...
```

The remaining member functions swap values and verify that the array is properly sorted. The overloaded output operator << prints the array.

Listing 15.13   (Program 15.5 Quicksort): `Quicksort.cpp` **(part 3 of 3)**

```
...

void Quicksort::swap_values_at(const int index1, const int index2)
{
    int temp = data[index1];
    data[index1] = data[index2];
    data[index2] = temp;
}

bool Quicksort::verify_sorted()
{
    for (int i = 0; i < size - 1; i++)
    {
        if (data[i] > data[i+1]) return false;
    }

    return true;
}

ostream& operator <<(ostream& ostr, const Quicksort& q)
{
    for (int i = 0; i < q.size; i++) ostr << setw(3) << q.data[i];

    return ostr;
}
```

The test program generates an array of random values to quicksort.

Listing 15.14   (Program 15.5 Quicksort): `tester.cpp`

```
#include <iostream>
#include <stdlib.h>
#include <time.h>

#include "Quicksort.h"

using namespace std;

int main()
{
    const int SIZE = 20;
    int data[SIZE];

    srand(time(0));
    for (int i = 0; i < SIZE; i++) data[i] = rand()%100;

    Quicksort qsorter(data, SIZE);
    cout << "Before:" << qsorter << endl;
    qsorter.sort();
```

```
        cout << " After:" << qsorter << endl;

        cout << (qsorter.verify_sorted() ? "SORTED" : "ERROR") << endl;
        return 0;
}
```

Example output is

```
Before: 69 38 40  5 17 69 60 26 53 36 24 10 67 64 80 83 18 10 68 97
 After:  5 10 10 17 18 24 26 36 38 40 53 60 64 67 68 69 69 80 83 97
SORTED
```

How many recursive calls does the quicksort program make to sort *N* values? Each partitioning operation places one pivot value in its correct position. After pivoting, there can be two recursive calls. So, there can be up to 2*N* recursive calls. Fortunately, the bases cases, which correctly position values without making recursive calls, significantly reduce the total number of calls.

15.7   *The Fibonacci sequence and a recursion disaster*

Recursion is a very powerful tool, but like with all power tools, we must use it carefully. A classic example of what can go wrong when improperly designing with recursion is the Fibonacci sequence 0, 1, 2, 3, 5, 8, 13, 21,... where, starting with 0 and 1, each subsequent term is the sum of the two previous terms. The mathematical definition of the sequence ise.

$$f_n = \begin{cases} 0 & if\ n = 0 \\ 1 & if\ n = 1 \\ f_{n-2} + f_{n-1} & if\ n > 1 \end{cases}$$

We might be tempted to follow this recursive mathematical definition and write a recursive function `f()`.

Listing 15.15   (Program 15.6 Fibonacci): `fibrecursive.cpp` **(recursion disaster)**

```cpp
#include <iostream>
#include <iomanip>

long f(const int n);

using namespace std;

int main()
{
    cout << «   n          f[n]» << endl;
    cout << «--------------» << endl;

    for (int n = 0; n < 50; n++)
    {
        cout << setw(3) << n << setw(12) << f(n) << endl;
    }
```

```
        return 0;
}

long f(const int n)
{
    if       (n == 0) return 0;
    else if (n == 1) return 1;
    else             return f(n-2) + f(n-1);
}
```

The output starts

```
 n        f[n]
-------------------
  0           0
  1           1
  2           1
  3           2
  4           3
  5           5
  6           8
  7          13
  8          21
  9          34
 10          55
 11          89
 12         144
 13         233
 14         377
 15         610
 16         987
 17        1597
 18        2584
 19        4181
 20        6765
 21       10946
 22       17711
 23       28657
 24       46368
 25       75025
 26      121393
 27      196418
 28      317811
 29      514229
 30      832040
 31     1346269
 32     2178309
 33     3524578
 34     5702887
 35     9227465
 36    14930352
 37    24157817
 38    39088169
 39    63245986
 40   102334155
...
```

but becomes increasingly slow. Figure 15.13 shows the reason.

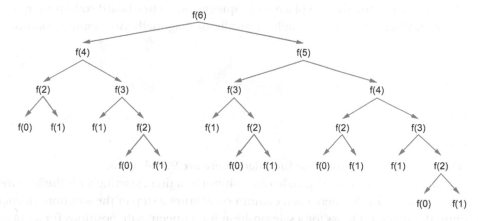

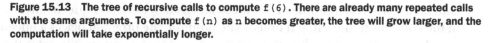

Figure 15.13 The tree of recursive calls to compute `f(6)`. There are already many repeated calls with the same arguments. To compute `f(n)` as n becomes greater, the tree will grow larger, and the computation will take exponentially longer.

A recursive solution may appear simple and elegant, but if we don't understand how the recursive calls are made, or how many calls there are, we can suffer a very nasty performance surprise. All function calls, recursive or otherwise, incur a runtime and memory cost.

15.8 *Dynamic backtracking increases the power of recursion*

The combination of recursion and dynamic backtracking is an extremely powerful design tool we can employ to solve a programming problem that involves multiple steps, and each step has several possible solution paths. From the starting step, our program uses recursion to explore each solution path successively—each recursive call takes the code down a path with a smaller problem. The base case is when the problem is small enough that it's immediately obvious whether a solution was found, and the recursive call returns true or false, respectively.

At each step, if a recursive call returns false, meaning that the solution path it was exploring was a dead-end failure, the code backtracks and recursively explores the next solution path. After exploring all the paths at a step, the program backtracks further to the previous step, where it can continue to recursively explore other solution paths. The program completes when it backtracks all the way to the starting step and has explored all the solution paths at that step. Recursion with dynamic backtracking often constitutes a brute force solution to the problem. We exploit the speed of the computer to try many solution paths.

Our first example program uses recursion with backtracking to solve the eight queens puzzle. The second example program solves Sudoku puzzles.

15.9 *Solving the eight queens puzzle with recursion and backtracking*

The goal of the puzzle is to place eight queens on a chessboard so that no queen can attack another, either horizontally, vertically, or diagonally. An example solution is

```
Q . . . . . . .
. . . . . . Q .
. . . . Q . . .
. . . . . . . Q
. Q . . . . . .
. . . Q . . . .
. . . . . Q . .
. . Q . . . . .
```

With reflections and rotations included, there are 92 solutions.

Class `Queens` solves the puzzle one column at a time, starting with the leftmost column (listing 15.16), where each column constitutes a step of the solution. In each column, the program looks for a safe position for a queen. Safe positions for a queen in a column are wherever the queen cannot be attacked by any other queens already placed in the columns to the left. If it finds a safe position, the program places a queen there, and then it calls member function `find_solutions()` to attempt to solve the puzzle by recursively testing the next column. The subproblem is smaller because there is one fewer remaining column to consider, and we're closer to the base case of the single last column.

The recursive search for a solution from the queen's position in a column will ultimately either succeed or fail. If a solution is found, the program prints it. In either case, the program moves the queen down in its column to the next safe position. Moving the queen is the dynamic backtracking that sets up a recursive search for another solution from the new position. If there are no more safe positions in a column, the program backtracks to the previous column—it goes back a step—and moves the queen to the next safe position in that column.

The base case is the attempt to place a queen in a safe position in the last column, which can succeed or fail. The program ends when it has backtracked to the first column, and it has tried each position of that column. Private Boolean matrix `occupied` records the positions of the queens.

> **Listing 15.16   (Program 15.7 Queens):** `Queens.h`

```
const int SIZE = 8;

class Queens
{
public:
    Queens() : count(0)
    {
        for (int row = 0; row < SIZE; row ++)
        {
            for (int col = 0; col < SIZE; col ++)
            {
```

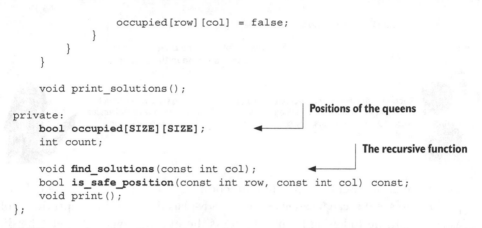

```
                    occupied[row][col] = false;
                }
            }
        }

        void print_solutions();
    private:                                          Positions of the queens
        bool occupied[SIZE][SIZE];
        int count;
                                                      The recursive function
        void find_solutions(const int col);
        bool is_safe_position(const int row, const int col) const;
        void print();
};
```

Public member function `print_solutions()` calls private recursive member function `find_solutions()` for the starting column 0 (listing 15.17). The function checks each position of a column for a safe position. If it finds a safe position for a queen in the column, it recursively calls itself to advance to the next step of the solution path by testing the next column.

After recursively checking each safe position in a column, the function backtracks by moving the queen to the next safe position in the column to continue trying new solution paths from there. If the column has no more safe positions, `find_solutions()` returns, and the solution search backtracks to the previous column to continue trying solution paths from there. The last column is the base case—there are no recursive calls from that column.

Listing 15.17   (Program 15.7 Queens): `Queens.cpp` **(part 1 of 2)**

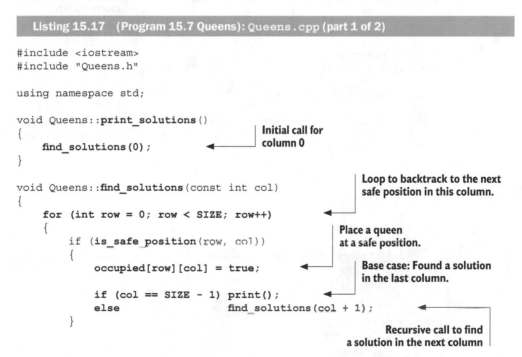

```
#include <iostream>
#include "Queens.h"

using namespace std;

void Queens::print_solutions()
{                                             Initial call for
    find_solutions(0);                        column 0
}

void Queens::find_solutions(const int col)
{                                                    Loop to backtrack to the next
                                                     safe position in this column.
    for (int row = 0; row < SIZE; row++)
    {                                                Place a queen
        if (is_safe_position(row, col))              at a safe position.
        {
            occupied[row][col] = true;               Base case: Found a solution
                                                     in the last column.
            if (col == SIZE - 1) print();
            else                 find_solutions(col + 1);
        }
                                                     Recursive call to find
                                                     a solution in the next column
```

```
        occupied[row][col] = false;
    }
}
```

Backtrack: Remove the queen and try
the next safe position in the column.

Recursive function **find_solutions()**
is simple, and yet it handles taking steps,
backtracking, and recursively checks
solution paths.

It would be a very instructive
challenge to write the function
without using recursion.

Private member Boolean member function is_safe_position() checks a board position to see if it can be attacked by already-placed queens in the previous columns, as shown in the following listing. It checks the queen's row to the left, the diagonal from the queen to the upper left, and the diagonal from the queen to the lower left. As there is only one queen per column, there can be no attacks from another queen in the same column. Private member function print() prints a solution.

Listing 15.18   (Program 15.7 Queens): `Queens.cpp` (part 2 of 2)

```
bool Queens::is_safe_position(const int row, const int col) const
{
    int c = col - 1;

    while (c >= 0)
    {
        if (occupied[row][c]) return false;
        c--;
    }

    int r = row - 1;
    c = col - 1;

    while ((r >= 0) && (c >= 0))
    {
        if (occupied[r][c]) return false;
        r--;
        c--;
    }

    r = row + 1;
    c = col - 1;

    while ((r < SIZE) && (c >= 0))
    {    #C
        if (occupied[r][c]) return false;
        r++;
        c--;
    }

    return true;
}
```

Check the queen's
row to the left.

Check the diagonal from
the queen to the upper left.

Check the diagonal from
the queen to the lower left.

```
void Queens::print()
{
    count++;

    cout << endl << "Solution #" << count << endl << endl;

    for (int row = 0; row < SIZE; row++)
    {
        for (int col = 0; col < SIZE; col++)
        {
            cout << (occupied[row][col] ? "Q " : ". ");
        }
        cout << endl;
    }
}
```

The test program prints the solutions.

Listing 15.19   (Program 15.7 Queens): `tester.cpp`

```
#include <iostream>
#include "Queens.h"

using namespace std;

int main()
{
    Queens q;
    q.print_solutions();

    cout << endl << "Done!" << endl;
    return 0;
}
```

The output includes all 92 solutions:

```
Solution #1

Q . . . . . . .
. . . . . . Q .
. . . . Q . . .
. . . . . . . Q
. Q . . . . . .
. . . Q . . . .
. . . . . Q . .
. . Q . . . . .


Solution #2

Q . . . . . . .
. . . . . . Q .
. . . Q . . . .
. . . . . Q . .
. . . . . . . Q
. Q . . . . . .
. . . . Q . . .
. . Q . . . . .
```

```
Solution #3

Q . . . . . . .
. . . . . Q . .
. . . . . . . Q
. . Q . . . . .
. . . . . Q . .
. . . Q . . . .
. Q . . . . . .
. . . . Q . . .


...


Solution #92

. . Q . . . . .
. . . . . Q . .
. . . Q . . . .
. Q . . . . . .
. . . . . . . Q
. . . . Q . . .
. . . . . . Q .
Q . . . . . . .

Done!
```

15.10 Solving Sudoku puzzles with recursion and backtracking

We can design a program that solves Sudoku puzzles using the same strategy of recursion with backtracking. For example, here is an input file containing the given cell values and zeros elsewhere:

```
0 0 0    0 0 0    0 2 0
3 0 0    0 0 6    0 0 0
0 0 0    0 8 0    4 7 0

2 0 0    3 0 0    0 0 0
0 1 0    0 4 0    0 8 0
0 0 0    0 0 5    0 0 6

0 8 7    0 1 0    0 0 0
0 0 0    9 0 0    0 0 5
0 4 0    0 0 0    0 0 0
```

The program produces the following output:

```
Input:

. . . | . . . | . 2 .
3 . . | . . 6 | . . .
. . . | . 8 . | 4 7 .
------+-------+-------
2 . . | 3 . . | . . .
. 1 . | . 4 . | . 8 .
. . . | . . 5 | . . 6
------+-------+-------
```

```
. 8 7 | . 1 . | . . .
. . . | 9 . . | . . 5
. 4 . | . . . | . . .

Solution:

8 5 9 | 7 3 4 | 6 2 1
3 7 4 | 1 2 6 | 5 9 8
6 2 1 | 5 8 9 | 4 7 3
------+-------+-------
2 6 8 | 3 9 1 | 7 5 4
7 1 5 | 6 4 2 | 3 8 9
4 9 3 | 8 7 5 | 2 1 6
------+-------+-------
5 8 7 | 4 1 3 | 9 6 2
1 3 2 | 9 6 7 | 8 4 5
9 4 6 | 2 5 8 | 1 3 7
```

To solve a Sudoku puzzle, the program starts at the top left corner and moves cell by cell, left to right, and down to the bottom right corner. Each cell is a step of the solution. The puzzle starts with cells filled-in with the numbers that are given. At each unfilled cell, the program first tries number 1 and recursively attempts to fill in the rest of the cells starting with next unfilled cell. The recursive attempts either all succeed at filling in the remaining cells and therefore the solution was found, or an attempt along the way fails. Making a recursive attempt on the next cell is a smaller problem because there is one fewer remaining cell. The base case is the last cell in the lower right corner.

If a number at any cell fails, the program backtracks by trying the next number for that cell. If all nine numbers failed at a cell, the program backtracks further by taking a step back to the previous cell and tries the next number for that cell.

Class `Sudoku` has private recursive member function `solution_found()`, which returns either true or false to indicate whether a solution was found after entering a number in a cell. Private Boolean function `is_number_ok()` tests whether a number is allowed in a cell.

Listing 15.20   (Program 15.8 Sudoku): `Sudoku.h`

```cpp
class Sudoku
{
public:
    Sudoku(const char *file_name);

    bool solve() { return has_solution(0, 0); }

    void print() const;

private:
    static const int BLOCK_SIZE = 3;
    static const int GRID_SIZE  = BLOCK_SIZE*BLOCK_SIZE;

    int grid[GRID_SIZE][GRID_SIZE];        ◄──────── Puzzle grid
```

Recursive function

```cpp
    bool has_solution(int row, int col);   ←
    bool is_number_ok(int row, int col, int number) const;
};
```

The constructor reads the input file and initializes the grid with the given values and
zeros elsewhere.

Listing 15.21   (Program 15.8 Sudoku): `Sudoku.cpp` **(part 1 of 3)**

```cpp
#include <iostream>
#include <fstream>
#include "Sudoku.h"

using namespace std;

Sudoku::Sudoku(const char *file_name)
{
    try
    {
        ifstream grid_file(file_name);
        grid_file.exceptions(ifstream::failbit | ifstream::badbit);

        for (int row = 0; row < GRID_SIZE; row++)
        {
            for (int col = 0; col < GRID_SIZE; col++)
            {
                grid_file >> grid[row][col];
            }
        }
    }
    catch (ifstream::failure& ex)
    {
        cerr << "Input file error: " << file_name << endl;
        exit(-1);
    }
}

...
```

After entering a number into a grid cell with the given `row` and `col`, Boolean member
function `solution_found()` recursively tests subsequent cells to check if the solution
was found. The `for` loop controls the backtracking. If the number it entered won't
yield the solution, the loop tries the next number.

Listing 15.22   (Program 15.8 Sudoku): `Sudoku.cpp` **(part 2 of 3)**

Base case: Reached the last cell and found the solution

```cpp
...

bool Sudoku::solution_found(int row, int col)
{
    if ((row == GRID_SIZE-1) && (col == GRID_SIZE)) return true;   ←
```

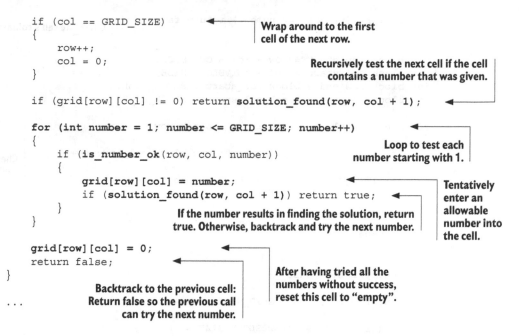

```
if (col == GRID_SIZE)          ◄——  Wrap around to the first
{                                    cell of the next row.
    row++;
    col = 0;                                    Recursively test the next cell if the cell
}                                               contains a number that was given.

if (grid[row][col] != 0) return solution_found(row, col + 1);   ◄——

for (int number = 1; number <= GRID_SIZE; number++)   ◄——
{                                                     Loop to test each
    if (is_number_ok(row, col, number))               number starting with 1.
    {
        grid[row][col] = number;                                    Tentatively
        if (solution_found(row, col + 1)) return true;  ◄——         enter an
    }                                                               allowable
}               If the number results in finding the solution, return number into
                true. Otherwise, backtrack and try the next number.  the cell.
grid[row][col] = 0;   ◄——
return false;   ◄——
}
              Backtrack to the previous cell:      After having tried all the
...           Return false so the previous call    numbers without success,
              can try the next number.             reset this cell to "empty".
```

There are two recursive calls. The first one recursively tries the next cell if the current cell contains a number that was given. In the `for` loop, after an allowable number is assigned to a cell, the second recursive call checks the next cell to see if there's a solution from there. The function call returns true if there's a solution. Otherwise, the loop tries the next number. After unsuccessfully trying all the numbers, the function resets the cell to zero ("empty") and returns false. This causes the caller to `solution_found()` to backtrack to the next allowable number for the previous cell.

The base case that stops the recursion is having an allowable number in the last cell at the bottom right corner. Backtracking to the previous cell occurs after having tried all the numbers unsuccessfully in a cell. After all the recursive calls unwind back to the first cell, the program either found a solution, or the puzzle is unsolvable.

Boolean member function `is_number_ok()` checks whether a number is allowed in a cell. It checks whether that number already appears in the cells' row, column, or block. Member function `print()` prints the solution.

Listing 15.23 (Program 15.8 Sudoku): Sudoku.cpp (part 3 of 3)

```
bool Sudoku::is_number_ok(int row, int col, int number) const
{
    for (int c = 0; c < GRID_SIZE; c++)
    {
        if (grid[row][c] == number) return false;      Check the cell's row.
    }

    for (int r = 0; r < GRID_SIZE; r++)                 Check the cell's column.
    {
```

```
            if (grid[r][col] == number) return false;
        }
```
Check the cell's column.

```
    int block_row_start = row - row%BLOCK_SIZE;
    int block_col_start = col - col%BLOCK_SIZE;
    int block_row_end = block_row_start + BLOCK_SIZE;
    int block_col_end = block_col_start + BLOCK_SIZE;

    for (int r = block_row_start; r < block_row_end; r++)
    {
        for (int c = block_col_start; c < block_col_end; c++)
        {
            if (grid[r][c] == number) return false;
        }
    }
```
Check the cell's block.

```
    return true;
}

void Sudoku::print() const
{
    for (int row = 0; row < GRID_SIZE; row++)
    {
        if ((row > 0) && (row%BLOCK_SIZE == 0))
        {
            cout << "------+-------+-------" << endl;
        }

        for (int col = 0; col < GRID_SIZE; col++)
        {
            if ((col > 0) && (col%BLOCK_SIZE == 0)) cout << "| ";

            int g = grid[row][col];
            if (g > 0) cout << g << " ";
            else       cout << ". ";
        }

        cout << endl;
    }
}
```

The test program prints the initial grid with the given numbers, calls the solve()
member function of class Sudoku, and prints the solution grid if there is a solution.

Listing 15.24 **(Program 15.8 Sudoku):** `tester.cpp`

```
#include <iostream>
#include "Sudoku.h"

using namespace std;

int main(int argc, char *argv[])
{
    Sudoku sudoku(argv[1]);
```

```
cout << "Input:" << endl << endl;
sudoku.print();

bool solved = sudoku.solve();          ←——┐  Initial call to recursive
                                            function solve()
if (solved)
{
    cout << endl << «Solution:» << endl << endl;
    sudoku.print();
}
else
{
    cout << endl << "No solution" << endl;
}

return 0;
}
```

This is a brute-force solution that doesn't use any Sudoku strategies — only recursion and backtracking.

It relies on a computer's speed to work effectively.

Summary

- Recursion is a software design technique that solves a problem by dividing it into a smaller but similar subproblem. We recursively solve each subproblem the same way.

- The recursion stops at a base case where the problem is so small that it has an obvious and immediate solution. Then, the original problem is solved as the recursion unwinds.

- When designed properly, a recursive programming solution can be simple and elegant. However, improper use can lead to serious performance problems.

- The combination of recursion and dynamic backtracking is a potent design tool for programs that explore multiple solution paths.

- Each step can have multiple solution paths that are explored using recursion. After trying a path, backtrack and try the next path.

- When all the solution paths at a step have been tried, backtrack to the previous step, and continue trying the previous step's paths.

Designing multithreaded programs

16

This chapter covers

- Multiple threads of execution
- Protecting shared resources
- Synchronizing multiple threads of execution

Knowing how to design and develop multithreaded applications allows us to take advantage of a computer's ability to handle multiple *threads* of execution. A thread is a path the computer takes through the code as it executes your program. Multi-threading means the computer is running multiple paths at the same time.

If we design multithreaded applications properly, they can take better advantage of today's multicore computers (i.e., computers with multiple CPUs). Some applications inherently require simultaneous operations, and we can only design them to be multithreaded.

456

Manning Comix

This chapter introduces designing multithreaded applications. We'll start with a simple printing example that demonstrates the need to use *mutexes*, which are software objects that use *mutual exclusion* to protect data shared by allowing only one thread at a time to modify the data. We'll progress to using mutexes in different ways to solve an example of the classic reader–writer problem. Then, we'll solve an example of the classic producer–consumer problem with other software objects called *condition variables* to more finely synchronize the execution of multiple threads.

16.1   *How do things happen simultaneously?*

Early computers each had only one central processing unit (CPU), and it was single threaded—it could only run one path through a program at a time. Later computers with sophisticated operating system support enabled *concurrent execution*, where the single CPU switches rapidly among multiple threads (hence the term *multithreading*). Switching among multiple threads is called *context switching*. The computer gave the appearance of executing multiple threads simultaneously.

Modern computers are multicore. *Parallel execution* is possible, where different cores (CPUs) are each simultaneously executing one or more threads. Therefore, a computer can simultaneously execute more threads than it has CPUs. Whenever a program starts, it runs in its main thread. Any thread can *spawn* (create and start) child threads.

Concurrency vs. parallelism

A good analogy of the difference between *concurrency* and *parallelism* involves planning a dinner party. You can do all the work yourself, cleaning the house, cooking the meal, setting the table, and so forth. When you switch among various tasks (rapidly or otherwise) during the day, you are doing them concurrently. You must plan your work carefully to get all the tasks done on time.

But if you have friends come over to help, and each friend takes care of a task, then the work can be done simultaneously in parallel. If each friend multitasks, even more work can be done at the same time. You must manage your friends to keep their work synchronized. You can't have them multitasking too much, or they will become less efficient.

(continued)

Whether you do all the work yourself or have friends help, you must protect shared resources, such as the cleaning supplies, cooking utensils, the food being prepared, and similar. You certainly don't want friends arguing over who can use the mop or trying to cook different parts of the meal at the same time using the same pan. You enforce mutual exclusion on the frying pan, for example, when you allow only one friend to use the pan at a time, while excluding others from using it.

When you design a multithreaded application, your code must manage and synchronize the threads, whether they execute concurrently or in parallel, and your code must protect any shared resources such as data in memory or external files.

Whether simultaneous execution happens concurrently, in parallel, or both, a multithreaded program must protect shared resources. If multiple threads attempt to access a shared resource (some data in memory, a file, a printer, etc.), they must share the resource properly and not step on each other. For example, if multiple threads modify the value of a shared variable simultaneously, what is the final value of that variable? This is known as a *race condition*, where the value of a variable depends on which thread happened to modify it last. Race conditions are a major debugging nightmare of multithreaded applications.

For most of our applications, we don't worry about multithreading but instead allow the runtime system (such as the computer's operating system) to manage the threads. For example, when one thread is suspended to wait for an I/O operation to complete, the runtime system automatically performs a context switch to another thread. But we can design programs that explicitly perform multithreading and protect any shared resources. As we'll see, some applications inherently require simultaneous operations and therefore must be designed to be multithreaded. In this chapter, we'll use the C++ multithreading library.

Figure 16.1 shows that when we design and write a multithreaded application, we must be aware that the application's threads all share its internal resources of the code and data in memory and external resources such as printers and files. Therefore, a major design concern is how to properly manage the sharing. The runtime system will give each thread its own runtime stack and the appearance of having its own set of machine registers. Depending on the machine hardware, the latter can be achieved by saving and restoring the register contents during context switching, or by having multiple banks of registers.

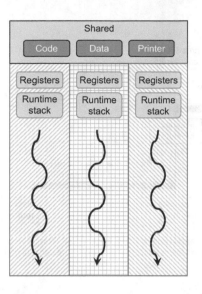

Figure 16.1   A multithreaded application with three threads. The threads share the application's internal resources of code and data in memory and external resources such as printers and files. The runtime system gives each thread its own runtime stack and the appearance of having its own set of machine registers.

16.2   *A mutex enforces mutual exclusion*

Whenever we have a shared resource in a multithreaded program, there could be statements executing in different threads that access that shared resource. Such statements constitute the *critical region* (also called a *critical section*) associated with that resource. The threads can use the same critical region code (remember that a program's code is shared by the threads), or they can have different statements in their own critical regions. Whether multiple threads use the same critical region, or each thread has its own unique critical region, each critical region contains statements that access the shared resource.

A multithreaded program must protect a shared resource. For example, if a thread is modifying the resource, it must prevent other threads from entering their critical regions to read or write that resource. This is called *mutual exclusion.*

 I'm confused. Is a critical region the same as a shared resource?

No. A critical region is the *code* in each thread that accesses a particular shared resource. It can be one critical region that all the threads use, or each thread can have its own critical region.

In figure 16.2, threads A and B both can access a variable X, the shared resource. Therefore, each thread has a critical region containing statements that reference X. When thread A enters its critical region to modify the value of X, we must prevent thread B from entering its critical region to modify the value of X. Only after thread A leaves its critical region can thread B enter its critical region. An object from the multithreading library called a *mutex* (for *mutual exclusion*) enforces this mutual exclusion. The threads lock and unlock the mutex.

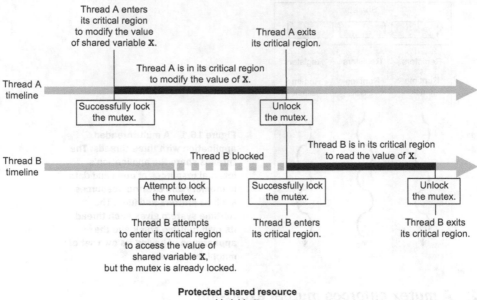

Figure 16.2   The critical regions of threads A and B modify the same shared resource, variable x. A mutex object guards the critical regions. A thread that successfully locks the mutex can enter its critical region. Attempting to lock a mutex that's already locked causes the thread to block. The thread that's exiting its critical region must unlock the mutex to allow another thread to lock it.

If more than one thread at the same time wants to enter its critical region, and the mutex is unlocked, the runtime system can determine which thread can lock the mutex and enter, or our program can explicitly choose the thread. Because we cannot always predict which thread the runtime system chooses, each run of a multithreaded program can behave differently. Unfortunately, this randomness can make multithreaded programs notoriously difficult to debug when things go wrong.

Figure 16.3 illustrates how a mutex works to guard a critical region within a thread.

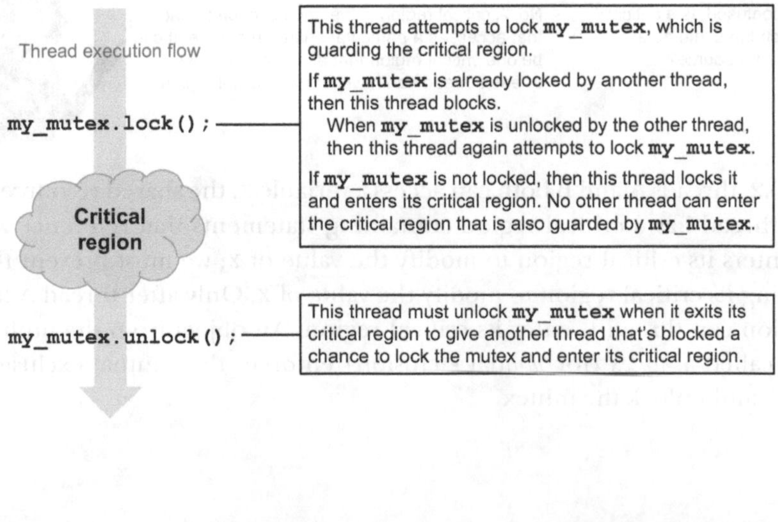

Thread execution flow

```
my_mutex.lock();
```

Critical region

This thread attempts to lock **my_mutex**, which is guarding the critical region.

If **my_mutex** is already locked by another thread, then this thread blocks.
    When **my_mutex** is unlocked by the other thread, then this thread again attempts to lock **my_mutex**.

If **my_mutex** is not locked, then this thread locks it and enters its critical region. No other thread can enter the critical region that is also guarded by **my_mutex**.

```
my_mutex.unlock();
```

This thread must unlock **my_mutex** when it exits its critical region to give another thread that's blocked a chance to lock the mutex and enter its critical region.

**Figure 16.3
Mutex guarding
a critical region.
It only allows
one thread at a
time to be in its
critical region.**

Whether different threads have the same critical region code for a particular shared resource, or each thread has its own critical region code for that resource, we use the same mutex to guard each critical region for that shared resource. During run time, if thread B wants to enter its critical region (figure 16.2), it first attempts to lock the mutex. If the mutex is already locked by thread A, then thread B blocks (suspends execution). As soon as thread A unlocks the mutex, thread B can again attempt to lock it. (There may be other threads blocked on the same mutex.) If thread B successfully locks the mutex, it enters its critical region. When thread B is done executing in its critical region, it must unlock the mutex to give another thread a chance to lock it and enter its critical region. A mutex guards critical regions to enforce mutual exclusion and thereby protects the shared resource.

The underlying pthread library

The C++ multithreading library is built upon the old `pthread` (Posix thread) library inherited from the C language. To compile multithreaded programs on the Linux platform, you must specify the `pthread` library on the command line, for example, to compile the example printing program:

```
g++ -std=c++0x *.cpp -o printing -lpthread
```

This is not required on the macOS platform:

```
g++ -std=c++0x *.cpp -o printing
```

Also, it is not required on the Windows platform:

```
cl /EHsc *.cpp /link /out:printing
```

16.2.1 *Protect the integrity of a shared resource*

With a simple printing example, we can demonstrate multithreading, a shared resource, a critical region, and a mutex that enforces mutual exclusion. The first version of our example creates three threads (figure 16.4) assigned to thread variables `hello_thread`, `use_thread`, and `go_thread`. Each thread executes function `print()`, but each thread also passes a different string argument to the function.

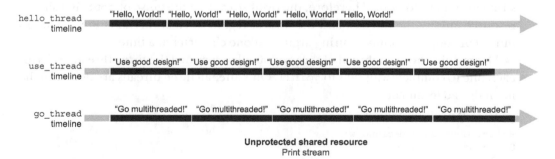

Figure 16.4 Three threads simultaneously print to the shared print stream, the unprotected shared resource.

Function print() writes to the print stream one character at a time. The print stream is therefore a resource shared by the three threads, but it is unprotected in this version of the example.

Listing 16.1   (Program 16.1 Printing-Unprotected) `printing-unprotected.cpp`

```cpp
#include <iostream>
#include <string>
#include <thread>

using namespace std;

const int COUNT = 5;

void print(string text);

int main(void)
{
    thread hello_thread(print, "Hello, world!\n");          // Spawn (create and
    thread use_thread(print, "Use good design!\n");         // start) each thread.
    thread go_thread(print, "Go multithreaded\n");

    hello_thread.join();                                    // Wait for each
    use_thread.join();                                      // thread to complete.
    go_thread.join();

    cout << endl << "Program done." << endl;
    return 0;
}

void print(string text)                                     // The function executed
{                                                           // by each thread
    for (int i = 0; i < COUNT; i++)
    {
        for (const char &ch : text) cout << ch;             // Critical region: Print the
    }                                                       // argument string one
}                                                           // character at a time.
```

As soon as the program creates each thread, it starts to execute function print(). The function executes simultaneously in three threads, each thread with a different string argument to print. Therefore, the print stream, in the guise of cout, is a shared resource among the threads, and the critical region of each thread is the function's inner for loop that prints its string argument one character at a time.

Meanwhile, the main thread of the program that spawned the three threads waits for each one to complete with calls to join(). Only after all three threads are done can the main thread terminate.

Here is a sample output:

```
Hello, GUse good designo w!
Use good designorld!
Hello, !
Use goowmorlddultithreaded
```

```
Go mu !
Helltithlo, world!
design!Hreade
Usllo, ee good
Go multithreaded
d Go mworld!
design!
ultithreaUsedHello, world!
ed
Go multithread good design!
ed


Program done.
```

Quite a mess! We did not protect the shared resource. Each of the threads is free to execute in its critical region, and with all three threads doing so simultaneously, we get intermixed output. We'll get different results each time we run the program because the program doesn't control the order that the threads start or the order they write to cout. The runtime system determines both orders.

In the second version of our multithreaded printing example, we can fix its problems by introducing a mutex to guard the critical region and thereby protect the shared print stream resource (figure 16.5). The mutex starts out unlocked. Each thread attempts to lock the mutex before entering the critical region. If the mutex is already locked by another thread, the thread blocks. When the thread that locked the mutex unlocks it, the blocked threads again attempts to lock the mutex. One thread will successfully lock the mutex, unblock, and enter the critical region to print its string. That thread must unlock the mutex when it's done printing and is ready to exit the critical region. Therefore, only one thread at a time can be inside the critical region to print its string.

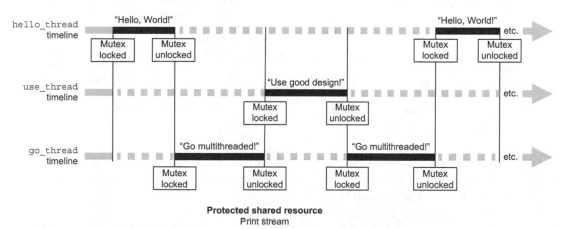

Figure 16.5 With a mutex guarding the critical regions of the threads, only one thread at a time can print to the print stream, which is the shared resource. When a thread wants to enter its critical region, it attempts to lock the mutex. If it succeeds, it can enter its critical region and print. If it doesn't, it blocks until another thread unlocks the mutex. Then, the thread can attempt to lock the mutex again. A thread must unlock the mutex before it exits its critical region. When the mutex is unlocked, the runtime system determines which blocked thread can unlock it.

In our next example program, the mutex is `print_mutex`.

Listing 16.2   (Program 16.2 Printing-MT): `printing-mt.cpp`

```cpp
#include <iostream>
#include <string>
#include <thread>
#include <mutex>

using namespace std;

const int COUNT = 5;

mutex print_mutex;                    ◄────────  The print mutex

void print(string text);

int main(void)
{
    thread hello_thread(print, "Hello, world!\n");
    thread use_thread(print, "Use good design!\n");
    thread go_thread(print, "Go multithreaded!\n");

    hello_thread.join();
    use_thread.join();
    go_thread.join();

    cout << endl << "Program done." << endl;
    return 0;
}

void print(string text)
{
    for (int i = 0; i < COUNT; i++)
    {
        print_mutex.lock();        ◄────┘ region.     Attempt to lock
        {                                              the print mutex
                                                       before entering
                                                       the critical
                                                       region.
            for (const char &ch : text) cout << ch;   ◄──  The critical region
        }                                                  accesses the shared
        print_mutex.unlock();      ◄──── Unlock the print mutex.   resource cout.
    }
}
```

We purposely surrounded the code between `print_mutex.lock()` and `print_mutex.unlock()` with braces and indented it to emphasize that the code is the critical region guarded by the mutex.

Now, the output is much more reasonable:

```
Hello, world!
Go multithreaded!
Go multithreaded!
Go multithreaded!
Go multithreaded!
```

```
Use good design!
Use good design!
Go multithreaded!
Use good design!
Use good design!
Use good design!
Hello, world!
Hello, world!
Hello, world!
Hello, world!

Program done.
```

Like before, the runtime system determines the order in which threads start and the order in which they write to cout. But with the mutex, only one thread can be in its critical region at a time. Therefore, a thread is allowed to write out its entire string argument each time without another thread jumping in with its output.

16.2.2 *The classic reader–writer problem*

A more realistic example of a multithreaded application is the classic reader–writer problem. Our next example simulates a meter that can be set to different values. Multiple technicians (the writers) each makes several attempts to set the meter's value. Meanwhile, several loggers (the readers) attempt to read and log the meter's current setting. Therefore, the meter is a shared resource (figure 16.6).

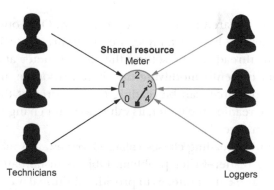

Figure 16.6 **Three technicians simultaneously attempt to set the meter's value; meanwhile, three loggers attempt to read and log the meter's current setting. Therefore, the meter is the shared resource. Only one technician should be setting the meter at a time, and no logger should read the meter while a technician is setting it. However, unless a technician is setting the meter, multiple loggers can be reading it at the same time.**

The meter is a shared resource among the technician and logger threads, and so we'll use a mutex named meter_mutex to protect the meter. Figure 16.7 shows this in a simplified fashion.

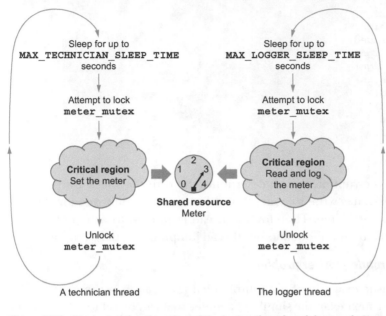

Figure 16.7   The technician threads and the logger thread each loop and attempt to enter their critical regions to access the meter, which is the shared resource. The mutex prevents more than one technician thread at a time from setting the meter. The same mutex prevents a logger from reading and logging the meter's value while a technician thread is setting the meter.

A reader-writer problem protects its shared resource is a special way. Only one writer can be modifying the resource at a time. In our example, the writers are the technician threads, and only one technician thread can be setting the shared meter at a time. However, as long as a writer isn't currently modifying the shared resource, multiple readers, which don't modify the resource, can be reading the resource at the same time. This is allowed because while reading the meter, its value does not change. In our example, the loggers are the reader threads.

C++ includes another three multithreading classes (`shared_mutex`, `unique_lock`, and `shared_lock`) to handle the reader–writer problem. Objects instantiated from classes `unique_lock` and `shared_lock` use mutexes to provide additional ways to lock them.

When a `shared_mutex` object is locked using a `unique_lock` object, no other thread can lock the same mutex using either a `unique_lock` or a `shared_lock` object. However, when a `shared_mutex` object is locked using a `shared_lock` object, other threads can also lock the same mutex using a `shared_lock` object, but no other thread can lock the mutex using a `unique_lock` object. To summarize

- `unique_lock`—Only one thread can hold a unique lock at a time on a `shared_mutex` object. No other thread can lock that mutex. This feature prevents other threads from reading or writing the shared resource while a thread is modifying it.

- `shared_lock`—Multiple threads can simultaneously hold a shared lock on a `shared_mutex` object. This allows multiple threads to read the shared resource that presumably isn't changing. However, as long as any reader thread is holding a shared lock on a `shared_mutex` object, no other thread can have a unique lock on that mutex in an attempt to modify the resource.

Our application simulates each technician with a thread, and each thread has a critical region that accesses the meter. Each technician thread can set the meter randomly to level 1, 2, 3, or 4. Setting the meter requires one second per level—for example, it takes 3 seconds to set the meter to level 3. The application simulates this by having the thread sleep for 1 second per level. After setting the meter, the thread sleeps (i.e., suspends execution) for a random number of seconds, 10 through 20, to simulate the technician resting.

The application simulates each logger with a thread, and each thread also has a critical region that accesses the meter. Each logger thread takes 3 seconds to read and log the meter's current setting, which the application simulates by having the thread sleep for 3 seconds after reading the meter. After logging the meter, the thread sleeps for random number of seconds, 1 through 15, to simulate the logger resting.

A timer keeps track of the number of elapsed seconds as the program runs in real time. When a technician thread sets the meter, the output shows the thread's id (e.g., `TECH #2`), the second when it starts to make the setting (e.g., `@15`), and a count of the seconds to make the setting (e.g., `1 2 3` for level 3). When a logger thread reads the meter, the output shows the thread's id (e.g., `LOGGER #3`), the second it starts the reading, and the meter setting it read.

Because of the randomness, each run of the application can generate different output. Example output:

```
TECH #1 @00: 1 2 3
TECH #2 @03: 1 2
TECH #3 @05: 1
                        LOGGER #1 @06: logging 1
                        LOGGER #3 @06: logging 1
                        LOGGER #2 @06: logging 1
TECH #1 @15: 1 2 3
                        LOGGER #1 @18: logging 3
TECH #2 @21: 1
                        LOGGER #2 @22: logging 1
                        LOGGER #3 @23: logging 1
TECH #3 @26: 1 2 3 4
                        LOGGER #1 @30: logging 4
                        LOGGER #2 @30. logging 4
                        LOGGER #3 @30: logging 4
TECH #1 @36: 1 2 3
TECH #1 @39: done!
                        LOGGER #2 @40: logging 3
TECH #2 @43: 1 2 3
TECH #2 @46: done!
                        LOGGER #3 @46: logging 3
```

```
                                       LOGGER #1 @46: logging 3
TECH #3 @49: 1 2 3
TECH #3 @52: done!
                                       LOGGER #2 @52: logging 3
                                       LOGGER #1 @52: logging 3
                                       LOGGER #3 @63: logging 3

Program done!
```

From examining the output, we can see that while a technician thread is setting the meter, no other thread, neither technician nor logger, can run. However, multiple logger threads can start simultaneously (e.g., at time @06) or overlap their runs (e.g., at times @22 and @23). Whenever any logger thread is running, no technician thread can run.

 I'm confused again. A program can have multiple objects and multiple threads during its run time?

 A single object can spawn multiple threads. These threads share the data stored in the object's member variables. The object's member functions can include a set of critical regions containing code that access the shared data. Therefore, the object also needs a mutex to guard the critical regions.

Class `Meter` has two private member functions, `set_meter()`, which each technician thread will execute, and `log_meter()`, which each logger thread will execute, as shown in the following listing. The value of private member variable `setting` is the meter's current setting. Mutexes `meter_mutex` and `print_mutex` protect the shared meter object and the print stream, respectively, by guarding their critical regions. Member function `elapsed_seconds()` computes and returns the elapsed time in seconds.

Listing 16.3   (Program 16.3 Reader-Writer): `Meter.h`

```cpp
#include <thread>
#include <shared_mutex>
#include <time.h>

using namespace std;
using namespace std::chrono;

class Meter
{
public:
    Meter()
        : setting(0), active_technicians_count(TECHNICIANS_COUNT)
    {
        srand(time(0));
        start_time = steady_clock::now();
    }

    void run();
```

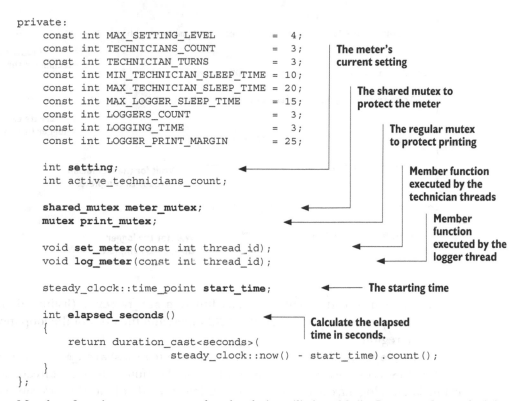

```
private:
    const int MAX_SETTING_LEVEL         =  4;
    const int TECHNICIANS_COUNT         =  3;
    const int TECHNICIAN_TURNS          =  3;
    const int MIN_TECHNICIAN_SLEEP_TIME = 10;
    const int MAX_TECHNICIAN_SLEEP_TIME = 20;
    const int MAX_LOGGER_SLEEP_TIME     = 15;
    const int LOGGERS_COUNT             =  3;
    const int LOGGING_TIME              =  3;
    const int LOGGER_PRINT_MARGIN       = 25;

    int setting;
    int active_technicians_count;

    shared_mutex meter_mutex;
    mutex print_mutex;

    void set_meter(const int thread_id);
    void log_meter(const int thread_id);

    steady_clock::time_point start_time;

    int elapsed_seconds()
    {
        return duration_cast<seconds>(
                    steady_clock::now() - start_time).count();
    }
};
```

The meter's current setting

The shared mutex to protect the meter

The regular mutex to protect printing

Member function executed by the technician threads

Member function executed by the logger thread

The starting time

Calculate the elapsed time in seconds.

Member function `run()` runs the simulation (listing 16.4). It starts the technician threads and the logger threads. Then it waits for the threads to complete.

As soon as each technician thread is created, it starts to execute member function `set_meter()`. Because it is a member function, we must fully qualify it and specify its address: `&Meter::set_meter`. The second argument `this` is the object that the function will operate on, and the value of the third argument `i + 1` is the thread's id. Similarly, as soon as each logger thread is created, it starts to execute member function `log_meter()`. After creating the threads, function `run()` waits for them to complete.

Listing 16.4 (Program 16.3 Reader–Writer) `Meter.cpp` (part 1 of 4)

```
#include <iostream>
#include <chrono>
#include <thread>
#include <shared_mutex>

using namespace std;

void Meter::run()
{
    thread technicians[TECHNICIANS_COUNT];
    thread loggers[LOGGERS_COUNT];

    for (int i = 0; i < TECHNICIANS_COUNT; i++)
```

```
    {
        technicians[i] = thread(&Meter::set_meter, this, i + 1);
    }
    for (int i = 0; i < LOGGERS_COUNT; i++)
    {
        loggers[i] = thread(&Meter::log_meter, this, i + 1);
    }
    for (int i = 0; i < TECHNICIANS_COUNT; i++)
    {
        technicians[i].join();
    }
    for (int i = 0; i < LOGGERS_COUNT; i++)
    {
        loggers[i].join();
    }
}
```

Create each technician thread.

Create each logger thread.

Wait for the technician threads to complete.

Wait for the logger threads to complete.

...

Each technician thread executes member function set_meter() (listing 16.5). The outer for loop executes TECHNICIAN_TURNS times, and the body of the loop includes the critical region.

The unique_lock object writing_lock attempts to lock shared_mutex. If a technician thread successfully acquires a unique lock on the mutex, no other thread, neither technician nor logger, can lock the mutex, and the thread holding the lock can enter its critical region. After setting the meter, a technician thread sleeps for a random number of seconds.

When object writing_lock goes out of scope, it automatically unlocks meter_mutex. Therefore, we put it in its own block, so when the program exists the block, the shared mutex is unlocked:

```
{
    unique_lock writing_lock(meter_mutex);
    {
        // critical region for setting the meter
    }
}
```

We should always make a critical region as short as possible to allow multithreading to be as efficient as possible.

Each thread should block others for as little time as possible.

Listing 16.5   (Program 16.3 Reader–Writer): `Meter.cpp` (part 2 of 4)

```
...

void Meter::set_meter(const int thread_id)
{
    for (int turn = 1; turn <= TECHNICIAN_TURNS; turn++)
    {
        {
            unique_lock<shared_mutex> writing_lock(meter_mutex);
            {
                printf("TECH #%d @%02d:", thread_id,
                                        elapsed_seconds());

                int level = rand()%MAX_SETTING_LEVEL + 1;
                setting = level;

                for (int n = 1; n <= level; n++)
                {
                    this_thread::sleep_for(chrono::seconds(1));

                    cout << setw(2) << n;
                    cout.flush();
                }
                cout << endl;

                if (turn == TECHNICIAN_TURNS)
                {
                    printf("TECH #%d @%02d: done!\n",
                        thread_id, elapsed_seconds());

                    active_technicians_count--;
                }
            }
        }

        if (turn < TECHNICIAN_TURNS)
        {
            int sleep_time =
                rand()%(  MAX_TECHNICIAN_SLEEP_TIME
                    - MIN_TECHNICIAN_SLEEP_TIME + 1)
                + MIN_TECHNICIAN_SLEEP_TIME;
            this_thread::sleep_for(chrono::seconds(sleep_time));
        }
    }
}

...
```

Annotations (right side):
- Attempt to acquire a unique lock on meter_mutex.
- Randomly choose a setting level.
- Sleep 1 second per level.
- Is this technician thread done?
- Unlock meter_mutex upon exiting the block.
- Sleep for a random number of seconds.

A logger thread executes member function `log_meter()` (listing 16.6). The `while` loop contains the critical region to log and read the meter, and it loops until all the technician threads are done. After reading and logging the meter, a logger thread sleeps for a random number of seconds.

The `shared_lock` object `reading_lock` locks `meter_mutex` as a shared lock. Multiple logger threads can lock a shared mutex at the same time, but only if a technician thread had not already locked it uniquely.

Because multiple logger threads will attempt to print, we need `print_mutex` to protect the shared print resource, like in the previous example. This time, we use a `lock_guard` object `printing_lock`. The advantage of

```
{
    lock_guard<mutex> printing_lock(print_mutex);
    {
        // critical region for printing
    }
}
```

over

```
print_mutex.lock();
{
    // critical region for printing
}
print_mutex.unlock();
```

is that the `lock_guard` object, when it goes out of scope, automatically unlocks the `print_mutex`.

Listing 16.6   (Program 16.3 Reader–Writer): `Meter.cpp` (part 3 of 4)

```
...

void Meter::log_meter(const int thread_id)
{
    while (true)                              ◄──── Loop until all the technician
    {                                               threads are done.
        int setting_read;
        int time_started;                                        Attempt to lock
                                                            meter_mutex for sharing.
        {
            shared_lock<shared_mutex> reading_lock(meter_mutex);   ◄───┘
            {
                setting_read = setting;          ◄──── Read the meter's setting.
                time_started = elapsed_seconds();

                this_thread::sleep_for(                      Sleep for
                            chrono::seconds(LOGGING_TIME));  LOGGING_TIME
                                                             seconds.
                {
                    lock_guard<mutex> printing_lock(print_mutex);  ◄───┐
                    {
                        printf("%*sLOGGER #%d @%02d: logging %d\n",
                            LOGGER_PRINT_MARGIN, " ",
                            thread_id, time_started,
                            setting_read);
                    }
                                                    Attempt to lock print_mutex.
```

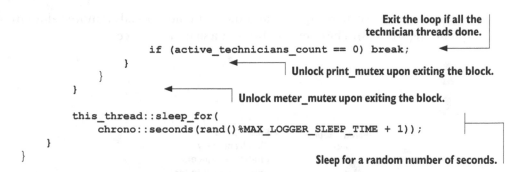

Exit the loop if all the technician threads done.

```
            if (active_technicians_count == 0) break;
        }
    }
```

Unlock print_mutex upon exiting the block.

```
}
```

Unlock meter_mutex upon exiting the block.

```
        this_thread::sleep_for(
            chrono::seconds(rand()%MAX_LOGGER_SLEEP_TIME + 1));
    }
}
```

Sleep for a random number of seconds.

...

Each technician threads modifies variable `active_technicians_count`, and each logger thread tests that variable. Therefore, `active_technicians_count` is also a shared resource. Each technician thread modifies the variable inside its critical region, and the logger thread tests the variable inside its critical region. We don't want a logger thread to test the variable's value at the same time a technician thread is modifying it. The test program simply creates the `Meter` object and calls its `run()` member function.

Listing 16.7   (Program 16.3 Reader–Writer): `tester.cpp`

```cpp
#include <iostream>
#include "Meter.h"

using namespace std;

int main()
{
    Meter meter;
    meter.run();

    cout << endl << "Program done!" << endl;
    return 0;
}
```

Why is the critical region for printing inside the critical region for reading the meter?

We don't want a technician thread to start printing before a logger thread finishes printing.

16.3 *Condition variables synchronize threads*

Some multithreaded applications require greater synchronization among their threads. Mutexes and locks alone may not be sufficient.

The classic multithreading producer–consumer application has multiple producer threads and consumer threads. Simultaneously, the producer threads enter values into a data container such as a queue, and the consumer threads remove values from the queue (figure 16.8). The queue is obviously a shared resource.

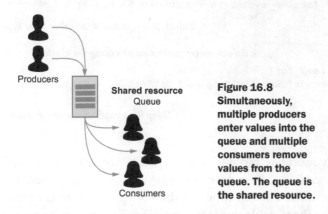

Figure 16.8
Simultaneously, multiple producers enter values into the queue and multiple consumers remove values from the queue. The queue is the shared resource.

The critical region of the producer threads is the code that enters values into the queue, and the critical region of the consumer threads is the code that removes values from the queue. We need a mutex to guard these critical regions and protect the shared queue.

However, this application requires better synchronization among the threads. Assume that function `data.size()` returns the number of values currently in the shared queue and that constant `CAPACITY` is the limited capacity of the queue:

- `data.size() == CAPACITY`—If the queue is currently full, the producer threads must wait until the queue is no longer full before entering values.
- `data.size() == 0`—If the queue is currently empty, the consumer threads must wait until the queue is no longer empty before removing values.
- data.size() == 1—If the queue just became not empty, that is, a producer thread entered a value into the queue that was empty, that producer thread must notify all the consumer threads that were waiting for the queue to become not empty.
- `data.size() == CAPACITY-1`—If the queue just became not full, that is, a consumer thread removed a value from the queue that was full, that consumer thread must notify all the producer threads that were waiting for the queue to become not full.

16.3.1 *How condition variables synchronize threads*

The C++ multithreading library provides *condition variables*, objects that we can use to synchronize the producer and consumer threads to a greater degree than we can with mutexes and locks alone. Figure 16.9 shows that each thread creates a local unique lock object `queue_lock` from `queue_mutex`, the mutex that protects the shared queue, to guard its critical region. Two condition variables, `producer_cv` and `consumer_cv`, work together to synchronize the threads. The producer and consumer threads loop to enter values into or to remove items from the shared queue, respectively.

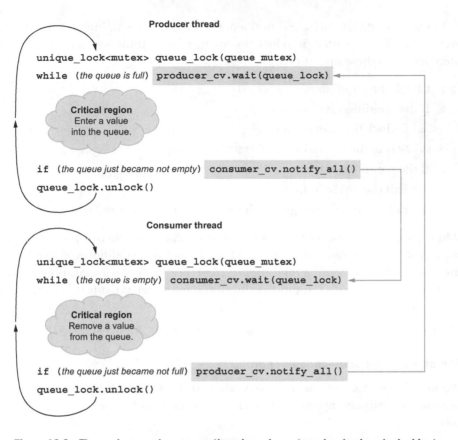

Figure 16.9 **The producer and consumer threads each creates a local unique lock object** `queue_`
`lock` **from** `queue_mutex` **to guard its critical region. The two condition variables,** `producer_cv` **and**
`consumer_cv`, **work together to synchronize the producer and consumer threads. The producer threads**
loop to enter values into the shared queue, and the consumer threads loop to remove values from the
shared queue. A producer thread cannot enter a value into the queue when the queue is full. A consumer
thread cannot remove a value from an empty queue.

Each thread first creates a local unique lock object `queue_lock` from the shared
queue's mutex:

```
unique_lock<mutex> queue_lock(shared_queue.get_mutex());
```

A lock object adds behaviors to the mutex to work with a condition variable.

After creating the lock object, each thread has a `while` loop that controls waiting on
a condition variable. For example, as long as the *condition* is true that the queue is full,
a producer thread must wait on condition variable `producer_cv` before entering an
item:

```
while (shared_queue.is_full()) producer_cv.wait(queue_lock);
```

The `wait()` call on the condition variable, passing the lock object, suspends the
thread. The thread remains suspended until the condition variable is *notified* (called to
wake up to allow rechecking the condition) by another thread.

When a condition variable is notified, the thread that's waiting on it wakes up and uses `queue_lock` to attempt to lock the queue mutex. If the lock succeeds, the thread then performs these operations:

1 Check the condition.
2 If the condition is still true,
   a Unlock the queue mutex.
   b Stay in the `while` loop and resume waiting.
3 If the condition is false,
   a Exit the `while` loop.
   b Enter the critical region with the queue mutex still locked.

When `queue_lock` goes out of scope, it automatically unlocks the queue mutex. When appropriate, it can also call `notify_all()` on another condition variable to notify all the threads that are waiting on it (figure 16.9). For example, if a consumer thread just made the queue not full, it must notify all the producer threads that were waiting on `producer_cv`:

```
if (shared_queue.just_became_not_full()) producer_cv.notify_all();
```

16.3.2 *The classic producer–consumer problem*

We now have some of the necessary tools to implement the classic multithreaded producer–consumer application. Example output with two producers and three consumers:

```
Producer #1    Producer #2    Consumer #1    Consumer #2    Consumer #3
      1 (1)
                     2 (1)
                                   -1 (0)
                                   -2 (0)
      3 (1)
                     4 (1)
                                                 -3 (0)
                                                               -4 (0)
      5 (1)
                                                               -5 (0)
                     6 (1)
                     7 (2)
                                   -6 (1)
                     8 (2)
                     Done!
                                                               -7 (1)
                                   -8 (0)
      9 (1)
     10 (2)
     Done!
                                                 -9 (1)
                                                               -10 (0)
                                                 Done!
                                                               Done!
                                   Done!
```

The runtime system controls the order that the threads start or when they execute. Each line shows the value a producer thread entered into the shared queue or the value a consumer thread removed from the queue. The numbers in parentheses indicate the number of items in the queue after the thread has entered or removed a value. The output shows the values that the consumer threads removed as negative values to help distinguish them from the values that the producer threads inserted. Each producer thread inserts five values before terminating. The consumer threads terminate after all the producer threads are done and there are no more values in the queue. A SharedQueue object is the shared resource, as shown in the following listing.

Listing 16.8 (Program 16.4 ProducerConsumer): SharedQueue.h

```
#include <queue>
#include <mutex>

using namespace std;

class SharedQueue
{
public:
    SharedQueue(const int cap) : capacity(cap) {}

    mutex& get_mutex() { return queue_mutex; }

    void enter(const int value) { data.push(value); }

    int remove()
    {
        int value = data.front();
        data.pop();
        return value;
    }

    int size() const { return data.size(); }

    bool is_empty() const { return data.size() == 0; }
    bool is_full()  const { return data.size() == capacity; }

    bool just_became_not_empty() const
    {
        return data.size() == 1;
    }

    bool just_became_not_full() const
    {
        return data.size() == capacity - 1;
    }

private:
    size_t capacity;
    queue<int> data;          ◄——— The shared queue of values

    mutex queue_mutex;        ◄——— The queue mutex
};
```

Interface `ProducerConsumer` specifies some common behaviors of the `Producer` and `Consumer` objects. Member function `get_count()` returns the number of threads that an object spawns, and member function `get_active_count()` returns how many of those threads are still active. Getter function `get_cv()` returns a reference to the condition variable that the object uses for its threads. Member function `start()` spawns the threads.

Listing 16.9   (Program 16.4 ProducerConsumer): `ProducerConsumer.h`

```cpp
#include <condition_variable>

using namespace std;

class ProducerConsumer
{
public:
    virtual ~ProducerConsumer() {}

    virtual int get_count()           const = 0;
    virtual int get_active_count() const = 0;
    virtual condition_variable& get_cv() = 0;

    virtual void start() = 0;
};
```

Class `Producer` implements interface `ProducerConsumer`, and therefore it must implement member functions `get_count()`, `get_active_count()`, `get_cv()`, and `start()` (listing 16.10). Each producer thread spawned by the `Producer` object executes member function `produce()`. Values passed to the constructor include `producer_count` for the number of producer threads, `producer_times` for the number of times each thread will produce a value to enter into the queue, and `producer_rate` for how often a thread produces values. The constructor also receives a reference to the `SharedQueue` object. The setter function `set_consumer()` allows the `Producer` object to set a pointer to the `Consumer` object.

Listing 16.10   (Program 16.4 ProducerConsumer): `Producer.h`

```cpp
#include <queue>
#include <thread>
#include <mutex>
#include <condition_variable>
#include <atomic>

#include "ProducerConsumer.h"
#include "SharedQueue.h"

using namespace std;

class Consumer;

class Producer : public ProducerConsumer
```

```
{
public:
    Producer(const int producer_count, int producer_times,
             int producer_rate, SharedQueue& sq);
    ~Producer();

    int get_count() const override { return producer_count; }

    int get_active_count() const override
    {
        return active_producers_count.load();
    }

    condition_variable& get_cv() override { return producer_cv; }

    void set_consumer(Consumer * const cons)
    {
        consumer = cons;
    }

    void start() override;

    void produce(const int thread_id);

private:
    int producer_count;
    int producer_times;
    int producer_rate;

    SharedQueue& shared_queue;
    Consumer *consumer;

    thread *threads;
    condition_variable producer_cv;

    atomic<int> data_value;
    atomic<int> active_producers_count;

    void print_spaces(const int thread_id) const;
};
```

Executed by each producer thread

Reference to the shared queue

Pointer to the Consumer object

Pointer to the array of producer threads

The producer's condition variable

Member variables data_value and active_producers_count are each an atomic integer. An atomic object wraps an integer value so that multiple threads can simultaneously perform certain primitive operations on the value without danger of any corruption or race conditions. Our application will perform autoincrement data_value++ and autodecrement active_producers_count--.

To access the current value of an atomic integer, we must call its load() member function. We see this in the getter function get_active_count():

```
return active_producers_count.load();
```

Member function print_spaces() helps to format the output.

Likewise, class Consumer implements the ProducerConsumer interface, as shown in the following listing. Values passed to the constructor include consumer_count for the number of consumer threads, `consumer_rate` for how often a thread consumes values, and a reference to the `SharedQueue` object. Each consumer thread spawned by the `Consumer` object executes member function `consume()`.

Listing 16.11 (Program 16.4 ProducerConsumer): `Consumer.h`

```cpp
#include <queue>
#include <thread>
#include <mutex>
#include <condition_variable>
#include <atomic>

#include "ProducerConsumer.h"
#include "SharedQueue.h"

using namespace std;

class Producer;

class Consumer : public ProducerConsumer
{
public:
    Consumer(const int consumers_count, const int consumer_rate,
            SharedQueue& sq);
    ~Consumer();

    int get_count() const override { return consumer_count; }

    int get_active_count() const override
    {
        return active_consumers_count.load();
    }

    condition_variable& get_cv() override { return consumer_cv; }

    void set_producer(Producer * const prod)
    {
        producer = prod;
    }

    void start() override;

    void consume(const int thread_id);         // Executed by each
                                               // consumer thread

private:
    int consumer_count;
    int consumer_rate;                         // Reference to
                                               // the shared queue

    SharedQueue& shared_queue;                 // Pointer to the
    Producer *producer;                        // Producer object

    thread *threads;                           // Pointer to the array
    condition_variable consumer_cv;            // of consumer threads
                                               // The consumer's
                                               // condition variable
```

```
    atomic<int> active_consumers_count;

    void print_spaces(const int thread_id) const;
};
```

The constructor of class `Producer` creates the `threads` array and initializes the underlying integer values of the atomic integer objects `active_producers_count` and `data_value` by calling `store()` on those objects. The destructor waits for all the threads to complete and then deletes the `threads` array.

Listing 16.12   (Program 16.4 ProducerConsumer): `Producer.cpp` (part 1 of 2)

```cpp
#include <iostream>
#include <thread>
#include <shared_mutex>
#include <condition_variable>

#include "Producer.h"
#include "Consumer.h"

using namespace std;

Producer::Producer(const int pc, int times, int rate,
                   SharedQueue& sq)
    : producer_count(pc), producer_times(times), producer_rate(rate),
      shared_queue(sq), consumer(nullptr),
      queue_mutex(sq.get_mutex())
{
    threads = new thread[producer_count];

    active_producers_count.store(producer_count);
}

Producer::~Producer()
{
    for (int i = 0; i < producer_count; i++)
    {
        threads[i].join();
    }

    delete[] threads;
}

void Producer::print_spaces(const int thread_id) const
{
    for (int i = 1; i < thread_id; i++) cout << "              ";
}
```

...

Member function `start()` spawns the producer threads (listing 16.13)

Each producer thread executes member function `produce()`. At the start of each loop, the thread sleeps for a random number of seconds. It creates `queue_lock` using `queue_mutex`. The `while` loop tests the condition. As long as the condition that the shared queue is full is true, the thread waits on condition variable `producer_cv`. Each time the condition variable is notified, the thread attempts to lock `queue_lock`. If the lock succeeds, the `while` loop can test the condition again. If the condition is still true (another producer thread made the queue full again), the thread unlocks `queue_lock` and stays in the `while` loop.

If the condition is false, the producer thread exits the `while` loop and enters its critical region, where it enters a new value into the queue. Calling `load()` on the atomic variable `data_value` retrieves its underlying integer value. If the queue just became not empty, the producer thread notifies all the consumer threads that are waiting on the condition variable `consumer_cv`. The thread must unlock `queue_lock` before leaving its critical region. The final producer thread that completes also notifies any waiting consumer threads.

Listing 16.13   (Program 16.4 ProducerConsumer): `Producer.cpp` **(part 2 of 2)**

```
...

void Producer::start()
{                                              Spawn producer threads.
    for (int i = 0; i < producer_count; i++)
    {
        threads[i] = thread(&Producer::produce, this, i + 1);
    }
}
                                               The consumer's
                                               control variable.
void Producer::produce(const int thread_id)
{
    condition_variable& consumer_cv = consumer->get_cv();

    for (int i = 0; i < producer_times; i++)   Sleep for a random
    {                                          number of seconds.
        this_thread::sleep_for(
                        chrono::seconds(rand()%producer_rate));

        {                      Create the unique lock queue_lock from the queue mutex.
            unique_lock<mutex> queue_lock(shared_queue.get_mutex());
            {
                while (shared_queue.is_full())
                {                                  Wait on condition variable
                    producer_cv.wait(queue_lock);  producer_cv while the
                }                                  queue is still full.

                data_value++;
                shared_queue.enter(data_value.load());

                print_spaces(thread_id);           Enter a new value
                printf("%4d (%1d)    \n",          into the shared queue.
                        data_value.load(), shared_queue.size());

                if (shared_queue.just_became_not_empty())
                {
```

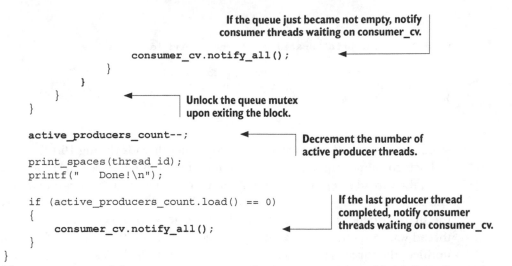

If the queue just became not empty, notify consumer threads waiting on consumer_cv.

```
            consumer_cv.notify_all();
        }
      }
    }
  }

active_producers_count--;
```

Unlock the queue mutex upon exiting the block.

Decrement the number of active producer threads.

```
print_spaces(thread_id);
printf("   Done!\n");

if (active_producers_count.load() == 0)
{
    consumer_cv.notify_all();
}
}
```

If the last producer thread completed, notify consumer threads waiting on consumer_cv.

The constructor of class Consumer creates the threads array and initializes the underlying integer value of the atomic integer objects active_consumers_count. The destructor waits for all the threads to complete and then deletes the threads array. Member function print_spaces() helps to format the output.

Listing 16.14   **(Program 16.4 ProducerConsumer):** Consumer.cpp **(part 1 of 2)**

```cpp
#include <iostream>
#include <thread>
#include <shared_mutex>
#include <condition_variable>

#include "Producer.h"
#include "Consumer.h"

using namespace std;

Consumer::Consumer(const int cc, int rate, SharedQueue& sq)
    : consumer_count(cc), consumer_rate(rate),
      shared_queue(sq), producer(nullptr)

{
    threads = new thread[consumer_count];

    active_consumers_count.store(consumer_count);
}

Consumer::~Consumer()
{
    for (int i = 0; i < consumer_count; i++)
    {
        threads[i].join();
    }

    delete[] threads;
```

```
}
void Consumer::print_spaces(const int thread_id) const
{
    int k = producer->get_count() + thread_id;
    for (int i = 1; i < k; i++) cout << "                    ";
}
```

...

Member function start() spawns the consumer threads (listing 16.15)

Each consumer thread executes member function consume(). At the start of each loop, the thread sleeps for a random number of seconds. It creates queue_lock using queue_mutex. The while loop tests the condition. As long as the condition is true that the shared queue is empty, and still, there are active producer threads, the consumer thread waits on condition variable consumer_cv. Each time the condition variable is notified, the thread attempts to lock queue_lock. If the lock succeeds, the while loop can test the condition again. If the condition is still true (another consumer thread made the queue empty again and at least one producer thread is still active), the thread unlocks queue_lock and stays in the while loop.

If the condition is false, the consumer thread exits the while loop and enters its critical region, where it removes value from the queue. If the queue just became not full, the thread notifies all the producer threads waiting on the condition variable producer_cv. The thread must unlock queue_lock before leaving its critical region.

Listing 16.15   (Program 16.4 ProducerConsumer): Consumer.cpp (part 2 of 2)

...

```
void Consumer::start()
{
    for (int i = 0; i < consumer_count; i++)        Spawn consumer threads.
    {
        threads[i] = thread(&Consumer::consume, this, i + 1);
    }
}

void Consumer::consume(const int thread_id)         The producer's
{                                                    control variable.
    condition_variable& producer_cv = producer->get_cv();

    while (true)                                     Sleep for a random
    {                                                number of seconds.
        this_thread::sleep_for(
                        chrono::seconds(rand()%consumer_rate));

        {
            unique_lock<mutex> queue_lock(shared_queue.get_mutex());
            {                                        Create the unique lock
                                                     queue_lock from the queue mutex.
```

Wait on condition variable consumer_cv while the queue is still empty, and there are active producer threads.

```
while (    shared_queue.is_empty()
      && (producer->get_active_count() > 0))
{
    consumer_cv.wait(queue_lock);
}

if (shared_queue.is_empty()) break;      ◄──── All done if the
                                               queue is empty.
int value = shared_queue.remove();       ◄────
                                               Remove a
print_spaces(thread_id);                       value from
printf("%4d (%1d)    \n",                       the shared
        -value, shared_queue.size());          queue.

if (shared_queue.just_became_not_full())
{
    producer_cv.notify_all();            ◄──── If the queue just became
}                                              not full, notify producer
        }                                      threads waiting on
    }                                          producer_cv.
}       ◄──── Unlock the queue mutex
             upon exiting the block.

active_consumers_count--;                ◄──── Decrement the number of
                                               active consumer threads.
print_spaces(thread_id);
printf("    Done!\n");
}
```

The test program prints the heading and creates the `Producer` and `Consumer` objects and sets each object to point to each other. It then calls the `start()` member function of each object, which will create and start the producer and consumer threads. That will generate output like that shown at the beginning of this section.

Listing 16.16 (Program 16.4 ProducerConsumer): `tester.cpp`

```
#include <iostream>
#include <time.h>

#include "SharedQueue.h"
#include "Producer.h"
#include "Consumer.h"

using namespace std;

int main()
{
    const int QUEUE_CAPACITY = 8;

    const int PRODUCER_COUNT = 2;
    const int PRODUCER_TIMES = 5;
    const int PRODUCER_RATE  = 3;
```

```
const int CONSUMER_COUNT = 3;
const int CONSUMER_RATE  = 5;

for (int i = 1; i <= PRODUCER_COUNT; i++)
{
    cout << "Producer #" << i << "   ";
}
for (int i = 1; i <= CONSUMER_COUNT; i++)
{
    cout << "Consumer #" << i << "   ";
}
cout << endl;

srand(time(0));

SharedQueue shared_queue(QUEUE_CAPACITY);

Producer producer(PRODUCER_COUNT, PRODUCER_TIMES,
                  PRODUCER_RATE shared_queue);
Consumer consumer(CONSUMER_COUNT, CONSUMER_RATE,
                  shared_queue);

producer.set_consumer(&consumer);
consumer.set_producer(&producer);

producer.start();
consumer.start();

return 0;
}
```

The shared queue

The Producer and Consumer objects

Point the objects to each other.

Start the threads.

16.4 *A final note on multithreading*

This chapter presented only a very brief introduction to an important software design topic. Designing and developing a multithreaded application correctly is a major challenge. Because the runtime system usually determines the order that threads are created and executed, timing issues can cause random and irreproducible behaviors from one run of the application to another. Debugging then becomes a nightmare. Another debugging headache is deadlocks. A deadlock occurs when all the threads are blocked, and the entire application hangs.

Even when multithreading is designed properly, increasing the number of threads does not mean that an application's execution time approaches zero! Mutexes and condition variables have performance costs themselves. The costs of context switching can overwhelm the benefit of having more threads. Designing a multithreaded application can be a delicate balancing act if the goal is to increase performance without increasing complexity.

Summary

- Knowing how to design multithreaded programs is important with multicore computer systems. Designing, developing, and debugging multithreaded applications are major challenges.

- Multiple threads (execution paths) may attempt to access shared resources of the application simultaneously. We must protect the shared resources.

- The code in each thread that accesses the shared resource is the thread's critical region.

- Use a mutex to guard each critical region with mutual exclusion.

- A mutex that is locked uniquely does not allow any other thread to lock it. If a thread attempts to lock a mutex that is already uniquely locked, the thread is blocked until the mutex is unlocked. Then, the thread can try again to lock the mutex.

- A mutex that is locked in shared mode allows other threads to simultaneously lock that mutex also in shared mode, as long as no thread has already locked the mutex uniquely.

- A thread must unlock the mutex before it exits its critical region. Otherwise, a deadlock may occur.

- A condition variable works with a mutex to synchronize the simultaneous operation of multiple threads.

- A thread waits on a condition variable as long as the associated condition remains true. When the condition variable is notified by another thread, a thread that's waiting on the condition variable unblocks and checks whether the condition is still true. If the condition is false, the thread can enter its critical region. Otherwise, it resumes its wait.

index

Symbols

+ operator   173
<< operator   28, 139–141, 174, 175, 300, 442

A

abstract classes   86
Abstract Factory design pattern   248–256
  definition   248
  example, after using   249
  example, before using   249
  generic model   255
abstraction   14
accelerate() function   78, 86
accept() function   309–311, 320
accessors   105
A class   126
acquire_data() function   211, 215, 218, 220
active_consumers_count atomic integer object   483
active_producers_count atomic integer object   481
active_producers_count– autodecrement   479
active_producers_count member variable   479
active_technicians_count variable   473
ActivitiesReportVisitor class   307, 308, 313, 315, 318, 319
actors   66
Adaptee class   269
Adapter class   269
Adapter Design Pattern   258–272
  alternative model   270–272
  definition   258
  desired features   259
  example, after using   265

example, before using   259
  generic model   269
add_days() function   114, 115
add_days() member function   111, 112
add_days() public member function   120
add() function   21, 28, 37–40, 164, 165, 166, 393
add_hall() function   303
add() member function   50, 73
add_sport() function   303
adjust_headlights() function   78
ADVENTURE genre   25
afunc function   126
aggregation   84
aid_fundraising() function   275, 277
algorithm() function   233
AlgorithmOutline superclass   221
algorithms
  encapsulating and Strategy Design Pattern   222
  encapsulating that operate on data collection   296
  quicksort algorithm   440
Alumni class   273, 279
amount_owed() function   171–173
amount parameter   172
analyze_data() function   211, 215, 218, 220
append() function   147, 156
application design   58
  when to do   76
apply_brakes() function   78, 86
Appointments class   147, 156
appts.append(d2027) function   153
arithmetic, with loops   108
arrays

RELATED MANNING TITLES

Simple Object-Oriented Design
by Mauricio Aniche

ISBN 9781633437999
192 pages, $59.99
April 2024

Grokking Functional Programming
by Michal Plachta

ISBN 9781617291838
520 pages, $59.99
September 2022

Grokking Simplicity
by Eric Normand

ISBN 9781617296208
592 pages, $49.99
April 2021

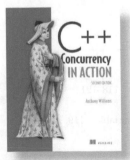

C++ Concurrency in Action, Second Edition
by Anthony Williams

ISBN 9781617294693
592 pages, $69.99
February 2019

For ordering information, go to www.manning.com